William O'Connor Morris

Ireland, 1494-1868

With two introductory chapters

William O'Connor Morris

Ireland, 1494-1868
With two introductory chapters

ISBN/EAN: 9783337323127

Printed in Europe, USA, Canada, Australia, Japan

Cover: Foto ©ninafisch / pixelio.de

More available books at **www.hansebooks.com**

Cambridge Historical Series

EDITED BY G. W. PROTHERO, Litt.D.

FELLOW OF KING'S COLLEGE, CAMBRIDGE,
AND PROFESSOR OF HISTORY IN THE UNIVERSITY OF EDINBURGH.

IRELAND.

London: C. J. CLAY AND SONS,
CAMBRIDGE UNIVERSITY PRESS WAREHOUSE,
AVE MARIA LANE.
Glasgow: 263, ARGYLE STREET.

Leipzig: F. A. BROCKHAUS.
New York: MACMILLAN AND CO.
Bombay: GEORGE BELL AND SON.

IRELAND

1494—1868

WITH

TWO INTRODUCTORY CHAPTERS

BY

WILLIAM O'CONNOR MORRIS,

COUNTY COURT JUDGE OF THE UNITED COUNTIES OF
ROSCOMMON AND SLIGO, AND
SOMETIME SCHOLAR OF ORIEL COLLEGE, OXFORD.

CAMBRIDGE:
AT THE UNIVERSITY PRESS.
1896

[*All Rights reserved.*]

EDITOR'S PREFACE.

The aim of this series is to sketch the history of Modern Europe, with that of its chief colonies and conquests, from about the end of the fifteenth century down to the present time. In one or two cases the story will commence at an earlier date, but this will only be by way of introduction. In the case of the colonies it will naturally begin later. The histories of the different countries will be described, as a general rule, in separate volumes, for it is believed that, except in epochs like that of the French Revolution and Napoleon, the connection of events will be better understood and the continuity of historical development more clearly displayed by this method, than by any other.

The series is intended for the use of all persons anxious to understand the nature of existing political conditions. "The roots of the present lie deep in the past," and the real significance of contemporary events cannot be grasped unless the historical causes which have led to them are known. The plan of the series will make it possible to treat the history of the last four centuries in considerable detail, and to embody the most important results of modern research. It is hoped therefore that the forthcoming volumes will be useful not only to beginners but to students who have already acquired some general knowledge of European History. For those who wish to carry their studies further, the bibliography appended to each volume will act as a guide to original sources of information and works more detailed and authoritative.

Considerable attention will be paid to geography, and each volume will be furnished with such maps and plans as may be requisite for the illustration of the text.

PREFACE.

IT is hardly correct to say that Irish History is deficient in dramatic passages, and in scenes that lend themselves to picturesque description. A Froissart would have given life and beauty to the exploits of many of the Anglo-Norman warriors; a native chronicler of poetic genius would have made the deeds of more than one of the Celtic Princes, especially of Shane O'Neill and of the illustrious Tyrone, shine out in brilliant significance. The story of the sieges of Londonderry and of Limerick, and of the battles of the Boyne and of Aghrim has been told by eminent writers; but these have belonged to the conquering race; and the works of writers of the conquered race on these events are dull and imperfect. Irish History contains episodes that a Walter Scott would have animated and made striking; but they have not been treated by a master hand; a "vates sacer" has not appeared to give them attractive form and colouring.

This side, however, of Irish History is not that which possesses the greatest interest. The march of Irish affairs after the Anglo-Norman conquest has been, for the most part, outside the great movements of the European World; there has been no Irish Bannockburn and no Irish Flodden; many eminent Irishmen have been more conspicuous in foreign lands than their own. Irish History is most valuable on its internal side, that is, as it unfolds the conditions and circumstances under which the Irish People has existed through many centuries, and has become what it is. The story to a superficial mind may appear "a tale of little meaning," a wearisome account of the long and hopeless struggle of a weak dependency with an infinitely more powerful nation and state. But the series of events which constitutes Irish History is of no ordinary interest to the true historical student and to thinkers and statesmen worthy of the name. The annals of few countries so clearly illustrate the evident sequence of cause and effect in the evolution of the life and the fortunes of a misruled, backward, and most ill fated community. Irish History, especially when contrasted with that of England, shows most strikingly how calamitous were the effects, in the Middle Ages, of the complete absence of a strong monarchy and a strong central government from a land abandoned to feudal oppression and to Celtic tribal disorder and discord. It shows very plainly how ill it may be when a people much superior in civilisation and wealth tries to rule a people inferior in these respects; how misconceptions and fatal mistakes may follow; how efforts to extend the domain of good government may lead to gross and far-spreading injustice. It illustrates only too vividly how terrible may be the results of conquest carried out piecemeal, through long spaces of time, and of wholesale confiscation following in its train; and it signally proves how dreadful may be the issue of conflicts in which a feeble subject race defies the power of a great ruling State, in times of fierce religious and national passion. It indicates, on the other hand, how infatuated are attempts such as these; especially when the weaker people is torn by intestine broils and divisions, and, while it beards an enemy tenfold in strength, throws its chances away in its insensate quarrels. Irish History places in the fullest light the evils of wrong done in the name of religion; of a system of government framed on the principle of the ascendency of a mere sect; of society formed, in all its parts, on the domination of a small caste, and on the denial of right to a conquered people; of the divisions of race and faith rending a community

Preface. vii

in twain, and forbidding the fusion of classes kept apart, and of commercial restrictions of extreme harshness; and it teaches a whole series of economic lessons, throughout its long course, of the greatest value. It must be added that it bears witness to the truth, that it is difficult for a Teutonic people to manage, or even to understand, a Celtic, particularly when the latter is on a plane of life, usages, and habits completely different; and that British policy for Ireland, however well-meaning, has often been mistaken, owing to sheer ignorance, and has been repeatedly and most unfortunately too late, even in its best and wisest remedial measures.

The History of Ireland, besides, if I do not err, is deeply interesting for another general reason. Philosophy attests the moral government of the Universe, and rightly asserts the freedom of the will of man. But History recognises and teaches how immense is the power of circumstance in shaping the fortunes of states and nations; and points out that these repeatedly have seemed to depend on what we in our ignorance call accidents. This has especially been the case in the course of the affairs of Ireland; and it cannot fail to attract the attention of a thoughtful mind. Over and over again it has seemed as if Irish History would have been completely changed, with happy results, but for slight incidents that appear but the freaks of Fortune. To refer to a few instances only—how different it would have been if Henry of Anjou had not turned aside from the conquest in his power; had Edward I done for Ireland what he did for Wales; had Henry VIII lived a few years longer; had William III been true to his nature in the affair of the Treaty of Limerick; had not Lord Fitzwilliam been recalled by a petty intrigue; had Pitt, on the occasion of the Union, compelled George III to bow to his will, as he had compelled him before; had Catholic Emancipation been accomplished with "the wings" in 1825! In these, and many other important passages of

Preface.

Irish History, circumstance, that seems almost fortuitous, has played a decisive and an adverse part; and a kind of dark and mournful fatality, like the song of the chorus in the Greek Drama, appears to play over a protracted and unhappy tragedy. This is given to us as an ensample, and affords matter for reflection.

I have written this work on Irish History with a reference to these leading ideas and from these points of view. I have, I hope, composed the narrative in the spirit in which every narrative of the kind should be composed. I have endeavoured to trace the causes of events, to show their connection and relations, to tell the truth fearlessly, to be strictly impartial, and yet always to make allowance for the stress of circumstance, and for the frailties, the passions, and the ignorance of humanity. I shall have gained my object if I shall have directed the attention of thoughtful minds in Great Britain and Ireland to Irish History. The subject, for various reasons, is of supreme importance to the people of both countries.

As I have been confined within rather narrow limits of space, I have been obliged to be chary of notes. I have enumerated in the Appendix the authorities, to which the reader may be referred. Those which seem to me of special value are printed in italics.

I have to thank Professor G. W. Prothero for his admirable skill and care in editing this book, and also the Treasurer and Librarian of the King's Inns, Dublin, for much valuable information.

WILLIAM O'CONNOR MORRIS.

GARTNAMONA, TULLAMORE.
December 17*th*, 1895.

TABLE OF CONTENTS.

			PAGE
Chapter	I.	IRELAND BEFORE THE ANGLO-NORMAN CONQUEST	1
,,	II.	THE ANGLO-NORMAN CONQUEST OF IRELAND. STATE OF THE COUNTRY FROM THE REIGN OF HENRY II TO THAT OF HENRY VII	24
,,	III.	IRELAND DURING THE TUDOR PERIOD TO THE END OF THE REIGN OF HENRY VIII	59
,,	IV.	IRELAND TO THE END OF THE REIGN OF ELIZABETH	83
,,	V.	FROM THE DEATH OF ELIZABETH TO THE RESTORATION	122
,,	VI.	FROM THE RESTORATION TO THE CAPITULATION OF LIMERICK	163
,,	VII.	THE PERIOD OF THE PENAL LAWS IN IRELAND. THE REVOLUTION OF 1782. .	197
,,	VIII.	GRATTAN'S PARLIAMENT. THE REBELLION OF 1798. THE UNION	249
,,	IX.	FROM THE UNION TO CATHOLIC EMANCIPATION	289
,,	X.	FROM 1829 TO 1868	316

APPENDIX.

LIST OF AUTHORITIES		355
INDEX .	. .	366
MAP OF IRELAND .	.	at end

ERRATA.

p. 25, l. 11, *for* home *read* Rome.
p. 362, l. 16, *for* Maddon *read* Madden.
p. 362, l. 27, *for* Pieces *read* Précis.

IRELAND.

CHAPTER I.

IRELAND BEFORE THE ANGLO-NORMAN CONQUEST.

Prehistoric Ireland. The Milesian conquerors. The Irish an Aryan Celtic race. Pagan Ireland. The island cut off from the Empire. First traces of Irish history. The mission of Patrick and its results. Ireland little affected by the consequences of the barbarian conquests and the fall of Rome. Splendid achievements of the Early Irish Church. State of society in Ireland before subsequent invasion and conquest. The Monarchy. The inferior kings. The chiefs and other orders. The tribes, clans and septs. The settlement of the land. The Church. The organisation and features of society. The arts of war and peace in Ireland. The Brehon laws. History. Poetry. Music. Architecture. Sculpture. The characteristics of the Irish. The Danish invasions. Brian. Decline of the Monarchy, and of civilisation. Proximity of England to Ireland. The island exposed to Anglo-Norman conquest.

THE traces are faint of the prehistoric race which spread over Ireland in remote antiquity. The island is particularly rich in stone; it contains numerous Cyclopean remains; but it has nothing like Stonehenge in extent and grandeur. Tradition indicates that it was peopled from the East; the Fomorians have been called a Turanian tribe; the Firbolgs were probably of the stem of the Belgæ: the Tuatha-ua-Danaans, "adepts in Druidical and magical rites"—not impossibly a sacerdotal caste—are said to have been of Pelasgic origin. The evidence of language, however, admirably sifted by Zeuss, proves that the main body of the Irish people, of which History takes account, was an Aryan community of the great Celtic stock, once dominant in Britain, in Gaul, in Spain, and scattered over other parts of Europe. It seems probable that it belonged to the tribes of the Gael rather than of the Cymry,—these last perhaps the Cimmerii of Greek story, the Cimbri, at one time the terror of Rome, and the fathers, almost certainly, of the Celts of Wales. A migration of warlike Celts from Spain, after long wanderings through the Scythian wastes, overran Ireland before the Christian era; the Milesian settlement seems to point to a real conquest. Heber, Heremon, and Ir, the sons of Milesius, are as mythical perhaps as Romulus and Remus, as Arthur and Modred, as Hengist and Horsa; but the families of the leading Irish chieftains, tradition affirms, sprang from their loins; and the Milesians seem to have been an aristocratic order. They are described as "bold, honourable, daring, prosperous, bountiful, and not afraid of battle or combat."

The land inhabited by the Irish race is widely separated from the rest of Europe, and is surrounded by Atlantic waves and tempests. Phœnician and Spanish traders seem to have reached its shores, as far back, perhaps, as the day of Carthage; but the Celts have never had a turn for the sea; and Ireland assuredly was, to Roman eyes, even more cut off from the world than Britain. Cæsar scarcely alludes to the island at all; Agricola thought it not worth invading, though a single legion and a few auxiliaries would, in his judgment, have made the conquest certain. The Celts of Ireland were left to themselves, and to their primitive life and usages, long after Gaul had fallen under the power of Rome, Britain had known the presence of Roman colonies, and the Celt of the Iberian Peninsula had felt Roman bondage. They, therefore, had no experience or taste of the civilisation that followed the march of the legions; and the peculiarities of the land they dwelt in, divided by forests and immense peat-mosses, swept by torrents of rain from the West, and with a climate, then and long afterwards, injurious to health, would naturally have kept them in a state of backwardness. Yet in the first centuries succeeding the birth of Christ, we perceive in Ireland, if, no doubt, faintly, the image of an Aryan people established everywhere, and possessing the characteristics of the great Aryan family. A dim shadowy monarchy was in existence; the names of Conn of the Hundred Battles, of Feredach the Just, of Felim the Lawgiver show that Ireland had her mythical Tullus, and her mythical Numa. A gradation of noble orders appears, in which probably great fighting men, Druids, and poets held a prominent place; and traces are found of a growing tribal system. Erinn was pagan, and given to idolatry, like Paul's Corinth, but its paganism seems to have been more akin to nature-worship and the cult of the Sun, than to the horrid superstitions of the Cymric race—half thralls of the Druidic priesthood—which had their chief seats in Anglesea and in parts of Gaul, and which terrified even the trained Roman soldiery. The land seems to have been not divided: there was "not a ditch, nor fence, nor a stone wall," ran an ancient legend, until long afterwards; and the population was, probably, still largely nomade. But agriculture, and all that this implies, was common; parts of the community were certainly seated on the soil, under the system of common ownership, and of patriarchal custom, which forms a distinctive mark of an Aryan race.

Ireland remained completely outside the track of the first great barbarian invasions of the Roman Empire, and of the influences which these brought with them. The decline of the

Imperial power in Britain is attested by a raid on the sea-board of Wales led by Niall of the Nine Hostages, a warrior king of the great Milesian stock, and with difficulty repelled by Stilicho, the conqueror of Alaric, and the friend of Claudian. "The ocean foamed with the oars of the Scots," the poet wrote; this was perhaps the first instance of the descents of the Pictish and Scottish races on the decaying settlements of Roman Britain. The embryo kingship of Ireland was held by the Hy-Niall— the fathers of the O'Neills of History, the most illustrious of the Irish chiefs—for a period of nearly five hundred years; and, doubtless, as nomade life disappeared, the archaic organisation of the Aryan races developed itself more thoroughly on the land, in the village community, the sept, and the clan. But, as has always been the case with Aryan peoples, in certain stages of their growth and progress, and has been especially the case with the Celt, Ireland was a land of incessant strife and war; like the Hindoos, the Hellenes, the Latins, the Teutons, the Irish Celts were in a state of perpetual tribal discord. Light breaks first on Ireland in the fifth century, when this chaos of rude and wild heathendom was gradually made a Christian body of men united in some measure by a living and common faith. Patrick is a grand historical figure, surrounded as he is by a halo of legends; the success of his mission was decisive and complete. Irish Paganism, possibly for some time in decline, yielded rapidly to the influence of the Saint; "the lights of the Druids were quenched and their spells were broken"; the pagan chiefs bowed before the man of God; not impossibly what was worst in Irish pagan usages— still conspicuous in ancient Indian law—was swept away by his amending hand. And Patrick was the founder of that noble Church, which from Ireland sent the everlasting light through a world convulsed by the death-throes of Rome, and overspread, for ages, by ever increasing gloom.

We leap over four stormy centuries, in which the mould of

modern Europe was cast, in the fusion of barbarism and the wreck of the Empire. Fierce and wild races from the deserts of the East poured over the provinces of that Imperial state, which for centuries had held the world at peace, and had been deemed eternal in its majestic structure. Rome was sacked over and over again; the new Rome on the shores of the Bosporus was threatened by conquering Semite hordes; Attila and his Huns were, with difficulty, expelled from Gaul; Charles of the Hammer just saved the West from the arms of the Saracen. Meanwhile the Teuton had founded settlements in Italy, in France, in Spain, and in England, destined to become the beginnings of mighty kingdoms; and at last the genius of Charles the Great constructed a new Empire in the midst of the Continent, extending from the Elbe to the Ebro; and this, though girt round by still untamed tribes, was to be the fruitful germ of the civilisation yet to come. To this source we may largely ascribe monarchic government, the feudal system, the medieval Church, the conception of the state, and the organisation of the land in Europe; the arrangement everywhere bearing the mark of rude and general conquest, and of the ideas of Rome, blending with those of the old Aryan communities. As had been the case before, Ireland was not affected directly by these stirrings of the world, and by the immense consequences following in their train, though indirectly she had a part in them. She continued isolated, to a great extent, so far as regards her secular life, her political existence, and her social usages. The loose supremacy of the Hy-Nialls went on; but it does not seem to have acquired strength, or to have possessed the character of a real Monarchy. The country fell under the rule of four or five houses of chiefs, lords of dominant and powerful tribes, which had more or less subdued the inferior septs and clans; and these were nearly always at feud with one another. The peculiar organisation of the land had become, doubtless, less archaic than it had been; collective ownership, the growth of the patriarchal idea, extremely strong in the Aryan races, still prevailed, but had become less general; agriculture had created separate ownership, and that to a very great extent; and the chiefs of the different tribes, septs, and clans, had gained increased power, and enlarged landed possessions, by processes curiously like those of the feudal system.

But if the History of Ireland, in those ages, does not, for causes plainly to be traced, show much political or social growth, it discloses one of the grandest and most remarkable religious movements the world has beheld. St Patrick, we have seen, made Ireland Christian; the island, enclosed by the great sea of the West, was beyond the sphere of the gigantic movements which, north, east, south, and west, overthrew the Empire. The intellect, too, of the Irish, like that of all Celts, is keen, vivid, and especially skilled in communicating its ideas wherever it extends; and the Irish and Celtic nature is strongly emotional, and vehement in its enthusiastic fervour. These facts explain the astonishing part Ireland played in the extension of the Christian faith, from the sixth until nearly the tenth century. Torn as the land was by intestine broils, the Church maintained a vigorous life of its own; it had its scores of bishops, a great array of clergy, hundreds of holy men in its religious orders; its monasteries, schools, and colleges were many and flourishing. Learning and piety spread from these centres of light happily not disturbed by the shock of falling Rome; Ireland became a seat of Christianity of a peculiar type; and she diffused the sacred influence over many lands, doing great things to uphold Christendom, and to preserve the Word in the ages of barbarian conquest. This, indeed, was the most glorious work of the Early Irish Church, a "lasting possession" for the family of man. The zeal of Columba and his successors raised the lamp of life on the shores of Iona, and sent its rays over heathen Scotland. It burned in the

Holy Isle of Lindisfarne; the Saxons of Northumbria felt its influence, soon after Augustine had landed on the plains of Kent. Irish missionaries preached in Wales, and beyond the Severn; their glory shone in many lands of the Continent. Their voices were heard along the Jura; in the Alpine ranges of wild Switzerland; beside the banks of the Maine and the Rhine; telling the tidings of great joy to savage conquerors, who still bowed down before Thor and Woden. It is a most significant fact that Charles the Great—the embodiment of civilisation in his age—had a singular esteem for holy men from Ireland; they were often guests at his Imperial table. And as Ireland sent forth her teachers of the Faith, so she received within her borders thousands of Christians flying from the savagery and turmoil of the dying Roman world. Merovingian kings found a home in Ireland; monks, bishops, and priests sought a peaceful refuge from lands watered by the Nile, the Seine, and the Danube, in the crypts of Armagh, and where the Shannon flows beside the lonely churches of Clonmacnoise.

We may now glance at the state of primitive Ireland, at her institutions, her social structure and her laws, and at the progress she had made in the arts of life, before she felt the effects of invasion and conquest, that is, after the beginning of the ninth century. The ideas that were to prevail in most parts of Europe, and that flowed largely from barbarian dominion, mingling with the influences of Imperial Rome, had not had much power over her people, because she had been little in contact with them. The conceptions of monarchy, with a strong central government, of a church modelled on the Roman type, of aristocracy strictly ordered, of assemblies which were to enact laws, of land stamped with the feudal system, of cities with municipal rights—the conceptions, in a word, that appear in the medieval state, were not in existence or were very weak, for Ireland had been nearly a stranger to them. Ireland, nevertheless, presented the image of an Aryan community, as yet backward, but progressing to a state of higher developement. A monarchy existed, and though in name elective, it had become hereditary in the Hy-Niall line, as the Empire was in the House of Austria. The monarch had little sovereign power; he was not, in any sense, the Head of a state; he had no Parliament, no Army, no Courts of Justice. But he was the acknowledged superior of every other chief; he seems to have had a right to demand their services, and the armed forces of their tribes in time of war; he had a claim to something resembling a national tribute. He had a Court, and all that pertained to it; a nobility like the feudal Companions; a retinue of Bards and Judges of high degree; and he perhaps assembled the chief men of Ireland, and possibly representatives of the different tribes, at Tara, the place of royal gatherings. He was regularly crowned with solemn rites; his coronation had much in common with the coronations of the German Cæsars. The King of Ireland received the crown, after religious ceremonies, august and striking; in the presence "of the Princes of the Land," of "the Bishops," of the "free states," and possibly of men chosen from the people[1].

Four or five lesser kings held the chief rule in Ireland, under their suzerain, the supreme Monarch. These were the heads of the most powerful tribes, which gradually had become dominant; they were akin to the great sovereign nobles of France, and to the Princes of Imperial Germany, dependent in name, but in their own "countries" rulers. Their state resembled that of their overlord; they had their Courts, their noblesse, and their bands of retainers; they exercised authority over inferior chiefs; they commanded the forces of the leading tribes, and of the communities included in them; and their influence had been for ages increasing. Their kingship, too,

[1] See a most interesting account of the coronation of a king of Connaught in the thirteenth century, in *The O'Conors of Connaught*, 83 seq.

ran in the royal lines, if subject to a kind of election; the Tanist, the successor of the dead king, was not necessarily his direct heir, though, in all instances, of his blood; he was sometimes really chosen by the tribe; and this mode of succession, which seemed so barbarous to Tudor lawyers, was in truth akin to many successions in medieval monarchies, and possibly is a source from which primogeniture arose. These lesser kings probably had the chief power in Ireland; like the great lords and princes of the Middle Ages they kept the land in a state of petty war and trouble. Beneath these kings were the minor chiefs, masters of subject tribes, clans, and the lowest units, the septs; their condition doubtless in some respects resembled that of their immediate superiors. But they were bound to them by many ties of dependence, analogous to those of the feudal system; and while their influence over the classes below them was growing, they were falling more and more under the control of the kings. The chiefs of the septs seem to have widely differed in many points from the other chiefs; the succession to their lands at least— though this is a difficult subject—was different from that of the acknowledged kings. It was more archaic, and bore the trace of the patriarchal idea of the Aryan family; but it was a mode of succession like that of the Gavelkind of Kent, though denounced as "sluttish and lewd" by the Cokes and the Spensers.

Under the chiefs, high and low, there seems to have been a local aristocracy of some kind, differing from the personal noblesse of the kings. The position of this order is, however, obscure; it may have had something in common with the Anglo-Saxon freeholder. There was a series of classes of inferior grade, but separated by well marked distinctions; they corresponded in some respects to the free tenants, the villeins, and the serfs of the feudal manor. These orders of men were dependent on the chief, his vassals, in fact, in different degrees; they owed him allegiance, and probably supplied a large part of his forces in war. But the Ceile of substance, with herds of his own, was in a far better position, and more free, than the Saer stock or the Daer stock tenants, kept in subjection, though not to the same extent, by loans of cattle from the chief, which made them his debtors, as in the case of the Plebeians and Patricians of Rome. The subjection was in proportion to the amount of the debt, but these various classes, holding land, as they did, with concurrent rights in it, as joint owners, were liable, it would appear, "to a just rent" only, though the chief's power over them had long been growing. Outside the pale of these were the Fuidhir tenants, composed largely of broken men, of captives in war, and of landless outcasts; these were also followers of the chief in battle; and they were bound to all kinds of degrading services. The chiefs multiplied this class by a variety of means, for this tended to augment their influence; they had a right to quarter retainers on them, "the coyne and livery" of another day; and they seem to have had a free hand to oppress them. The Fuidhir had no protection against "a rackrent," or indeed against any kind of exaction; his lot was, doubtless, miserable and hard. But Tudor lawyers and many writers are wholly in error, when they confound the free and other tenants of the Irish chief, with the order of the despised Fuidhirs, and describe the chief as simply a cruel lord of down-trodden serfs; the assertion is not only false, but absurd. Beside the land-holding classes, there were classes of slaves, the lowest certainly in the social scale; and as the towns were very few and small, an urban population scarcely existed.

This organisation of society—still archaic but presenting features like those of feudalism—as in the case of all Aryan races, had stamped its peculiar character on the land, on which it had been established for ages. The Monarch, the lesser kings, and perhaps all the chiefs, had appropriated large tracts of land in demesne which they certainly held as separate owners; and besides the tribute due to the supreme suzerain, the inferior rulers were entitled to different kinds of renders, within the limits of the lands of which they were the heads. Ireland as a whole was not thought of as a common country—the idea at least was very feeble—the great tribes were the main political units; and beneath these, and forming part of them, were the inferior tribes, the clans, and the septs, possessing landed usages in some respects the same, in others very different. Even the great tribes were still known by the name of Families, a sign of the force of the old patriarchal idea; their rulers were, or were believed to be, of the blood of an heroic common ancestor; the whole tribe was connected in some sense by this tie; and the land of the tribe was by tradition its common property. But these conceptions had, to a great extent, died out; the heads of the tribes may have had the descent claimed; but the tribes included, we have seen, inferior units, which certainly had not a common origin; in the tribe, and in these, the land was held for the most part, perhaps, in separate ownership; this tendency was ever on the increase; and the notion that the tribe lands were subject to collective rights, was probably, as a usage, waning away. This process was going on through the lower tribes and clans, and even down to the smallest division, the sept; separate ownership of the land was always extending; "the primitive communism" of the land was passing away. In the sept, however, the least developed unit, the family idea was still potent, and with this the notion of common property in the land. The lands of the chief of a sept, we have seen, were divided by a process akin to Gavelkind. On the death of a member of a sept, a somewhat similar mode of succession—though probably only one of several modes—was adopted, the chief, it is alleged, distributing the lands among the remaining members, the nearest in blood to the supposed common ancestor. The family idea, too, made artificial ties nearly as strong as natural in the ancient Irish household. The foster child was as much loved as the child by parentage, the godson as the son by blood, these usages, too, seeming odious to Tudor lawyers, who could not ascend to their true sources.

The primitive Church in Ireland, as in other countries, was largely moulded on the type of existing society. The Medieval Church in nine-tenths of Europe "reared its mitred front" in feudal Assemblies; it had its Sovereign Bishops in Germany; in England its Anselms, Beckets, and Huberts; its Bishops of Toulouse and Toledo in France and Spain. The ancient Irish Church was fashioned on the tribal system; the Bishops seem to have been as numerous as were the lesser tribes; they were, in some measure, perhaps, appointed by the chiefs; they were very often selected from chieftains' families. The Irish Church, too, like Ireland, was far away from Rome; in its usages and ritual, perhaps in its sacramental doctrines, it differed widely from that Imperial Church which aspired to supremacy throughout Christendom. In the observance of Easter, in the garb of its priesthood, in the arrangements about tithe, in its spiritual life, it was regarded as almost schismatic at Rome, a thing external to the true Roman communion. It was severely condemned by orthodox servants of ambitious pontiffs as rude and barbarous, as constructed upon a bad pattern, as full of enormities of many kinds; and probably its organisation was weak, its discipline somewhat lax and imperfect, its influence less than it ought to have been in a land torn by perennial discords. Its greatness is most apparent in its heroic missions; yet it had a zealous and numerous priesthood at home; and theological hatred was in excess, when St Bernard described the ancient Irish Church as "a society that had little hold on a people disorderly in worship, impious in creed, Christians in name, pagans indeed." In one respect, however, this Church

I.] *Ireland before the Anglo-Norman Conquest.* 13

seems to have been less successful in its work than might have been supposed. Sexual licence and impurity have usually been a characteristic defect in the Celtic races, they have darkened the course of French History. They appear to have been marked vices of the old Irish tribes, and the Church made very little impression on them. It has been the glory of the clergy of a later time, to have freed Ireland from this reproach to a remarkable extent.

At this period therefore, Ireland, we repeat, was an Aryan people of a somewhat archaic type, yet, unquestionably, in a state of progress, and though differing from the communities of the greater part of Europe, now beginning to grow into medieval nations, still exhibiting points of resemblance to them. Notwithstanding continual feuds and troubles, society in Ireland was kept together by a dependence of orders clearly marked, if less definite than that of the feudal system; and traditional custom and immemorial usage, we may rest assured, had immense influence. As in the case of all the Celtic races, the Irish were passionately attached to their chiefs; the devotion of the Celt, indeed, to persons as contrasted to laws, to rulers, if great, rather than to institutions, is one of his most distinctive qualities; it appears strikingly in the history of France.

We may next briefly survey the advance made by the Irish in the arts of war and of peace. The rude assemblages of the warriors of the tribes were probably even in a less sense armies, than the hosts called together by the rulers of the Franks, or even than the levies of Egbert and Alfred; and, at a later period, the weapons of the Irish soldier were very inferior to those of the Norman and Saxon. But the Celtic races have always excelled in war, if this excellence has been rendered, in some degree, fruitless, by certain defects in their brilliant qualities; and they have shown a singular aptitude, in every age, to fall in with the usages of other races in the field, to serve with distinction in foreign armies, and to achieve great things, under great leaders. Celts overthrew the Macedonian phalanx, and made their presence felt with awe in Asia; Celts, under Hannibal, crossed the Alps, and at Cannæ broke the stubborn Roman infantry. So the Irish soldiery turned the scale at Fontenoy, and at Cremona and Dettingen won the applause of their enemies; so they have earned renown, on many a battle-field, in the armies of Austria, of France, and of Spain.

The earliest Laws of Ireland seem to have been written in verse, like the Runic rhymes, or the Etrurian soothsayings. They were, we have seen, perhaps purged of evil by Patrick, who made "the Law of Nature yield to the Law of the Letter"; and they formed a huge collection of primitive customs. The oldest specimens do not go back beyond the eleventh or twelfth centuries, but they, doubtless, reproduce much of a far more ancient date. These laws have little in common with the decisions of Courts of Justice, or with Acts of Parliament, the great sources of the Law of England, for judicial tribunals, and anything like a Parliament had no existence in the Ireland of the Celt; they were the studies and reflections of generations of lawyers, known as Brehons, who, if not, in a true sense, a caste, were a corporation held in profound esteem and reverence. The Irish Brehon was an interpreter of the law and a judge; he corresponded to the Homeric Themistes, and to other legal sages of the old Aryan races. The Brehon Laws were execrated by Tudor lawyers and called the usages of a merely barbarian people; but the sentence, if not without plausible grounds, was, in the main, that of undiscerning ignorance. The worst charge made against them—that they did not recognise crimes, and that the "eric," or compensation for blood, was the highest penalty known to them—was simply due to the fact that crimes in modern law are a classification of wrongs owing their origin to conceptions that did not exist in ancient Ireland, the conceptions of Public Justice and of a Supreme State; and compensation for homicide was the common mode of redress in the primitive Aryan families. As for other parts of the Brehon Laws, which Tudor lawyers specially condemned, for example, their canons of descent and succession, these were in accord with the actual state of society, and are largely justified on an examination of it, mischievous as they may have been in a subsequent age. The Brehon Laws, so far as they have as yet been published, contain much that is just and wise; but they are deficient in breadth and comprehensive views; and they are overlaid and injured by the refined subtleties and the ingenuity characteristic of Celtic nature. They are full of conceits and extremely complex, never simple or striking in their ideas; they contrast strangely with the English Common Law, with all its faults, the expression of the mind of a masterful, and a proud, but a free people. In one respect, however, the Brehon lawyers seem to have had just and enlightened conceptions; they systematically discouraged collective rights in land, and did much to encourage separate ownership, one of the first great steps in social advancement.

The Irish have always dwelt in the long-buried past—it is a characteristic of the Celtic races; they possessed annals and chronicles even at this period. It seems vain to dismiss these records as "piles of tinted cloud" that "cannot be condensed into solid fact"; the Irish Annals, it has been acutely remarked, are singularly correct in their references to comets and eclipses, and to natural phenomena that can be ascertained; Sir James Mackintosh contends "that the Irish are enabled to boast that they possess genuine history several centuries more ancient than any European nation possesses it in its spoken language." Few of the existing Irish annals and histories are of an earlier date than the twelfth century; but they are almost certainly compiled from ancient manuscripts, some, it is believed, running up to the age of Patrick. These archaic productions are in the Irish tongue, and are for the most part hidden in national libraries; but one work of the same class, though much more modern, has been not long ago given to the world, translated carefully, and furnished with elaborate notes. The Annals of the Four Masters, collected in the seventeenth century, by learned monks of the Franciscan order, perhaps dependents of the chiefs of Tirconnell, contain an account of Ireland from the earliest times, and are, doubtless, modelled on the type of the old chronicles. They are a rude record of dry statements, without a trace of artistic skill, or a pretence to historical form or order; but we catch in the narrative the note of sorrow that seems inherent in Irish nature, and that Irish monks of that age might fitly utter. But the Irish chronicles and annals, like those of the Teutonic races, seem to have been devoid of the charm and keen intelligence which pervade the immortal work of the Greek Father of History.

The great poets of the world belong to the Semitic, the Hellenic, and the Teutonic races. The most brilliant poetry of the Celtic race is to be found in the literature of France; it has been made admirably attractive and correct by the civilisation of many ages; and French lyrical poetry justly ranks high. But who would compare the rhetoric of Corneille, the weak and lifeless creations of Racine, and the prolific but rather commonplace genius of Voltaire, with the song of David, Ezekiel's grandeur, the rush of Homer's verse, the strength of Aeschylus, the divine touch of Shakespeare, the master hand of Goethe? The poetry of ancient Ireland seems to have been abundant, but it was certainly not of a high quality. A single Irish epic exists, but a translation has not as yet been attempted. The native Irish poetry of a much later date shows grace and delicacy, even fair promise; but, as is characteristic of the Celtic intellect, at certain stages of its development, it is wanting in strength and overlaid with petty refinements and false ornaments; it continually sacrifices truth to form; it is devoid of really creative genius. Spenser wrote, with just insight, of the Irish poems of his day :—"Yea, truly I have caused divers of them to be translated unto me, that I might understand them, and surely they savoured of sweet wit and good invention, but skilled not of the goodly ornaments of poetry; yet were they sprinkled with some pretty flowers of their natural device, which gave good grace and comeliness unto them." The vein of melancholy pervading Irish nature appears very clearly in old Irish poetry, and also a kind of satiric wit; we see these qualities perhaps in the highest perfection in the pathetic ballads, and the satires of Moore. But place a ballad and a satire of Moore beside a song of Tennyson and a satire of Dryden, and the difference between the poetic power of the Celt and the Teuton will at once be perceived.

The Semite, the Hellene, and the Teuton have, also, been the great masters of song. The sweet singers of Israel have reappeared in Jewish composers of recent times, and in Jewish musical artists of extraordinary power. The legend of Orpheus attests the Greek love of melody; the Athenian drama had an orchestra worthy of it. Handel and Beethoven are the chiefs of modern harmony; the barbarous war songs of the Teutonic tribes are said to have shown a kind of rude majesty. France exhibits what is best in Celtic art; but French music, like French poetry, has never been noted for strength or grandeur. Yet music certainly held a high place among the primitive Celts, and especially so, perhaps, among the old Irish tribes. The harp was the instrument loved by the Celt; the Irish harpers were of peculiar excellence. Giraldus, a half Norman Celt of Wales, who disliked the Irish, has written "that their harpers are incomparably more skilful than any I have seen; their manner is not slow and harsh, but lively and rapid, the melody is sweet and sprightly." These ancient musicians were, perhaps, associated with, and formed part of, the Bards, held in honour by the Irish kings and chiefs, and attached to their households from the earliest times; and they had their separate calling down to the seventeenth century. The race of the harpers survived even the revolutions which overwhelmed their masters; one, Carolan, was a really great musician, renowned in the age of Swift and Berkeley; a few were to be found almost within living memory. The old Irish music was rich in melody, occasionally of a most exquisite kind; it was full too of Irish sadness and sorrow. It is to be found to this day in compositions, especially in so-called Italian airs, of which the authors have not acknowledged the origin.

In ancient Ireland, as in the rest of Europe, the noble arts of painting and sculpture had made little progress at this period. The figures in the old Irish buildings and churches, in many instances of great antiquity, are rude, unsightly, and without grace of form; they would have shocked even a primitive Hellene. But the Celtic Irish crosses show much skill of workmanship, if not remarkable beauty of design; and Irish hands have given proof of ingenious cunning, in ornaments of many kinds, in gold, and especially in illuminating sacred manuscripts. These are not specimens of artistic genius, and they disclose the Celtic tendency to oversubtlety; but they are interesting, and have a real merit of their own. Architecture, in Ireland, in this age, was certainly in a backward state, owing probably to incessant wars and feuds; few dwellings seem to have been built of stone; the petty towns were, perhaps, collections of huts, like the Gaulish oppida of the days of Cæsar; even the "forts" of the chiefs were rude and weak structures. The Celtic Irish churches were, for the most part, small, and many, it is said, were built of wood; but the remains of one or two reveal symmetry and grace, though majesty and strength are here, too, wanting. The mysterious Round Towers, it is commonly supposed, were belfries attached to the ancient churches; but the skill seen in these structures, and their

I.] *Ireland before the Anglo-Norman Conquest.* 19

shapely forms, make this supposition open to doubt, and seem to point to the work of a not Celtic race.

The essential characteristics of the ancient Irish appear even at this remote period. They were those which have marked out the families of the Celts, as these have figured on the stage of History. The Irish were brilliant rather than solid, apt to learn, skilled in diffusing ideas, but wanting in certain elements of intellectual strength belonging to other branches of the Aryan stem. In the works of the mind they were rather ingenious than great; they were subtle, not practical, not supremely gifted, not masters of the realities of things. They had fancy but not imaginative power; what they accomplished was seldom perfect; they were deficient in depth, and in the highest intelligence. In their moral tendencies they were passionately attached to persons, and had little reverence for institutions and laws; they were emotional, fickle, and easily led, more interesting than formed for high destinies. It would be unjust to describe them as a backward race, for they had been outside the influences that made for progress; but they were already being left behind by communities possessing more useful qualities. As in the case of all Celts, however, the worst characteristic of the old Irish was their never-ending intestine discord, which kept them constantly in a state of barbarous conflict. This has been seen in other Aryan races, at certain periods of their life and growth; but they have usually been able to emerge from this anarchy, and to combine into real and powerful nations. It has been otherwise with most parts of the Celtic family; and the Irish are a conspicuous instance of the fact. Nor is the history of France a proof to the contrary: however strong has been her unity for ages, no land has been torn by more relentless factions; no people has been rent by such savage feuds, especially, like the Irish, in the face of an enemy[1].

[1] Cæsar thus describes the Gallic Celts of his day. *De Bello Gallico,*

From the beginning of the ninth to the eleventh centuries, Celtic Ireland was exposed to the destructive raids of pirate hordes from the isles of the Baltic and from the shores of the Scandinavian Peninsula. The Danish invasions of Ireland ran a different course from those suffered by England at the same period. The Anglo-Saxons resisted the Danes bravely, but they never struck them down in one decisive battle. Alfred was compelled to temporise at the Peace of Wedmore; a Danish dynasty sat on the throne of England; a Danish settlement spread far inland from the Thames to the Humber; and the Danes finally became a part of the great English people, and gave it some of its very best elements. In Ireland the invaders were more than once called over by chiefs and princes ready to accept any aid against rivals and foes at home—a common and mournful result of Celtic discords; but though one Danish warrior, perhaps Lodbrog, overran and ruled a large part of the island, the Danes were ultimately subdued, and almost driven out. They appear, in fact, never to have had a permanent hold over nine-tenths of Ireland. They planted colonies along the seaboard; built probably three or four walled towns—Dublin, Waterford and Limerick are the best known of these—set up in them a rude municipal government; and created the principal fisheries of Irish salmon. But Ireland never had her Danelagh; the invaders did not blend with the native race; the Irish scarcely show a trace of Danish blood.

The Danes suffered their first great defeat at the hands of King Malachy of the Hy-Niall line—"the wearer of the collar of gold" commemorated in the verse of Moore. But the glory of crushing the pirate settlers and expelling them, for the most

---

6. 11 "In Gallia non solum in omnibus civitatibus, atque in omnibus pagis partibusque, sed paene etiam in singulis domibus factiones sunt." Of the Irish patriots of 1800–14, Napoleon says, *Corr.* 32. 328:—"Ils étaient divisés d'opinion, et se querellaient continuellement entre eux."

part, from the country, belongs to Brian—a fine historical figure—called not inaptly the Irish Alfred. Brian, one of the lesser kings of the South, was, in a certain sense, an usurper; he displaced the supreme Hy-Niall dynasty; and became Monarch in the first years of the eleventh century. His reign is still a bright spot in Irish annals; he kept a distracted land at peace; repaired much of the ravage done by the Dane; restored churches and built schools; in a word, was probably a really great sovereign. The legend that tells how a fair girl, though "rich and rare were the gems she wore," could go in safety everywhere in these golden years, is a tradition of an auspicious period unhappily almost unknown in Irish history. Yet Brian, unlike Alfred, was perhaps only a great chief, passionately revered and loved by his tribal subjects; he founded no institutions and made no laws; his good works passed away with him. His name, however, is still famous as the hero of the most decisive victory ever won over the Norse races, which, as we have said, freed Ireland largely from them. The great fight of Clontarf, in which the Celtic tribes, assembled from every part of Ireland, and aided by friendly Scots from the Lowlands, overthrew, under the aged king, the heathen host of Sitric and Sigurd, and drove it into the devouring sea, rang through Christendom as a mighty deliverance, and was long mourned as a woeful day by the Danes. It attests the valour of the Irish race in war; and Irishmen, even now, as they survey the scene, still rich with memories of a Marathon of their own, feel the pride felt by Frenchmen for Valmy and Jemappes.

Brian was slain at Clontarf, and his death became the signal for a renewal of the tribal wars of Ireland. There is reason to believe that the inferior kings and chiefs had acquired increased influence in the Danish wars, and that this became greater in the period that followed. Their dependent noblesse grew more numerous; their rude military forces were much augmented; they multiplied their degraded Fuidhir vassals, thus encroaching on the rights of the freemen; and they maintained a considerable traffic with England in slaves. The ancient organisation of the tribes, clans, and septs, and the primitive settlement of the land, appear to have been much broken up; and power largely passed into the hands of rude princely warriors, the heads of predatory levies, continually at feud. The Monarchy meanwhile, hereditary no more, was almost in abeyance, or was made only the temporary prize of contending chiefs; the Church and all that pertained to it suffered much; society in Ireland was being dissolved, and her early civilisation was disappearing, while neighbouring races were being formed into nations, and making a rapid advance in the arts of life. Towards the middle of the twelfth century, Turlogh, the head of the great tribe of the O'Conors of Connaught, became in a certain sense Monarch, after years of disastrous strife with rivals: but he was only " King with opposition," in the old chronicler's words; he never ruled over a united people. He probably was, however, an able man; fine edifices remain, the work of his hands; and he did much to improve his peculiar realm of Connaught, by bridging the great dividing stream of the Shannon, and making it a waterway for his "fleets." After a period of fresh disorder he was succeeded by his son Roderick, the last Monarch of Celtic Ireland.

The Irish meanwhile had, for more than a century, maintained an increasing commerce with England, and had come, in some measure, under English influence. Irish princes had married into great Norman houses; the Irish Church was regarded with more than the old disfavour by prelates in close communion with Rome, who surrounded the throne of the Anglo-Norman kings. England, too, after a short but decisive struggle, had fallen under the sword of William; and his strong, centralised, and, in the main, wise government had done much to make her a real and a great nation. She was ruled by a race of renowned warriors, as superior to every other race in Europe, as the Romans were to the neighbouring Latins; the Norman aristocracy were invincible in the field, and foremost in policy, and in the arts of peace. And at the head of this dominant caste, was a great sovereign and statesman, Henry of Anjou, one of the chief founders of the English Monarchy, who doubtless saw what were its natural limits. The course of events, therefore, directly tended to bring Ireland under the power of England, and to lead to the subjection of the weaker country, far below England, too, in civilised life. Yet Ireland was a land of considerable extent; she was separated from England by a stormy sea, and by the mountain ranges of Wales; her pathless, wooded, and waste tracts were not easy to overrun and occupy; and she was inhabited by a race, in many essential points differing very widely from the English people, and already not well disposed to the "Saxon." The Book of Fate had not yet been opened; but Nature herself had provided that the conquest of Ireland might prove a difficult and protracted task.

CHAPTER II.

THE ANGLO-NORMAN CONQUEST OF IRELAND. STATE OF THE COUNTRY FROM THE REIGN OF HENRY II TO THAT OF HENRY VII.

The designs of Henry II for the conquest of Ireland. The Bull of Adrian. Dermod, the dethroned king of Leinster, applies for aid to Henry. The descents of Fitzstephen and Fitzgerald followed by that of Strongbow. Easy superiority of the Norman arms, but no real invasion attempted. Henry II in Ireland. The Synod of Cashel. Policy of the king. He leaves Ireland not having effected the Conquest. Visit of John to Ireland, and his subsequent efforts to extend the power of the Crown. State of Ireland at his death. The period between the reign of John and the accession of Henry IV. Apparent progress of the power of England in Ireland, and its real decline. Many and various causes of this. Transformation of the settlers into the "degenerate Englishry," in parts of the island. The Pale. The Anglo-Irish Land. The Celtic districts. Condition of these separate divisions of Ireland. The Church of the Pale. The ancient Irish Church. Abuses in each, and evil results of their hostility. The conflict of laws in Ireland. The English and the Brehon Law. Bad results of the conflict. Prevalence of misrule and disorder, and miserable state of the humbler classes. Low state of intellectual life in Ireland. The period from the death of Richard II to the accession of Henry VII. Rapid decline of the power of England, and marked advance of the Irishry. Danger of the Pale. The real faults of government in Ireland. The Earl of Kildare supreme in Ireland when Henry VII becomes king. Henry obliged to temporise. After long hesitation the king sends Sir Edward Poynings to effect a thorough reform in Ireland.

HENRY II had hardly been seated on the throne, when John of Salisbury, a trusted priestly envoy, was sent to Rome to treat for the conquest of Ireland. The king simply followed, in this respect, the policy of his most renowned ancestor. Hildebrand had encouraged William, in his descent on England, on a plea of reforming the old Saxon Church; Henry sought the support of Nicholas Breakspeare—an Englishman, the Pope Adrian IV—to further, on a pretext of the same kind, his designs against the Ireland of the Celt. He found in the Pontiff a willing assistant, for the dislike felt at home to the primitive Irish Church had only increased with the lapse of time; and the Popes had lately made more than one attempt to reform a communion they deemed not orthodox. A legate had visited the island a short time before; and though at a synod of churchmen convened at Drogheda, the question of Easter had been settled in the Roman sense, and the Irish Church had nominally accepted the Roman discipline, still this rude branch of the Christian Tree of Life was regarded as an irregular sapling. Adrian had no difficulty in granting the king his apostolic sanction to subdue Ireland; his English and Roman sympathies probably concurred. The Pope announced in a Bull that he claimed a right to dispose of "all islands on the globe," and that subject to the suzerainty of the successors of Peter[1], "we do hold it good and acceptable, that, for extending the borders of the Church, restraining the progress of vice, for the correction of manners, the planting of virtue, and the increase of religion, you do enter this country, and execute therein whatever shall pertain to the honour of God, and welfare of the land; and that the people of this land receive you honourably, and reverence you as their Lord."

Had Henry, backed by the authority of the Pope, trodden in the steps of the great Conqueror, invaded Ireland with a real

[1] See the Bull at length in Leland's *History*, 1. 8, ed. of 1773.

military force, and placed the whole island under genuine Norman rule, he might have had to win a battle of Hastings, but he would have laid the foundations of a solid government, and Irish History would have run a different course. Unhappily, as often has been the case in Irish affairs, the king was turned away from his first purpose, by events which led him into other directions. He was engaged in a disastrous contest with the Celts of Wales, which may have made him cautious, as regards those of Ireland; had become involved in war, about his possessions in France; and he had to struggle for years with Becket and the Church. Time passed; and what might have been the occasion for a conquest of Ireland, harsh but complete, ended in a mere filibustering raid, of evil omen to England and Ireland alike. The tale of the lust of Dermod, and of the wrongs of O'Ruarc, may be as mythical as that of Lucrece and Tarquin; all that is certain is that, a long time afterwards, Dermod was deposed from the kingship of Leinster by Roderick O'Conor, the titular Monarch, and that Dermod carried his complaints to Henry, reckless of the consequences, after the Celtic fashion. A few words, dropped by the king in Aquitaine, gave the exile the encouragement he sought; and he applied to Richard de Clare, the well-known Strongbow, and to Robert Fitzstephen and Maurice Fitzgerald, Norman adventurers settled for some time in Wales, for aid to regain his forfeited kingdom. A bargain was easily struck with warriors, ready for feats of arms, and any daring enterprise that might bring glory, and plunder with it. Strongbow was promised the hand of Eva, the daughter of Dermod, and ample domains in the richest parts of Leinster; Fitzstephen and Fitzgerald were to receive large grants of land; and the invasion of Ireland was to be the consequence.

Fitzstephen was the first to make the descent; he landed at Bannow, on the coast of Wexford, in the beginning of May 1170. The number of his force has been estimated at from 1000 to 2000 men, a mere handful to attempt a conquest; but it had a company of Norman knights at its head, and a body of men at arms, and of trained archers, an array infinitely more formidable than the rude Celtic levies. Having been joined by Dermod and his auxiliaries, the Normans advanced against Wexford; and the townsmen, composed, in part, of Danes, successfully repelled a first attack. Fitzstephen, however, resolved to do or die, set his transports on fire, cutting off all retreat; and confident in himself and in the warriors in his train, he so overawed the defenders by his daring attitude, that their arms dropped from their hands, and they gave up the place. The invaders, reinforced by Fitzgerald and a few hundred men, advanced into the wilds of Ossory—on the borders of Kilkenny and the Queen's Counties;—they were entangled amidst peat mosses and defiles, where the light Celtic Kerns proved dangerous foes; but Norman craft and prowess prevailed; the Celts of Ossory, lured to offer battle in a plain, were easily overwhelmed and put to flight. By this time Roderick had assembled a great motley host, having summoned all the tribes to his standard; and though many of the chiefs held treacherously aloof, he marched to oppose the already exulting conquerors. The king, however, an Irish Louis le Debonair, lost an opportunity to strike down his enemy; priests, possibly already lending an ear to Rome, induced him to make terms with Fitzstephen; Dermod was restored to his kingship of Leinster, while the Norman adventurers were allowed to make a settlement along a strip of the seaboard of Wexford. The raid had proved the superiority of the Norman in the field, in Ireland, as in every part of Europe, and the essential weakness of the Irish Celtic Monarchy; it was to be the prelude of many woes for the island.

The Norman eagles quickly scented their prey; in the early autumn of 1171, Strongbow had landed at Waterford, with a force of the same quality as that of Fitzstephen, but probably two or three times larger, and commanded by warriors of high renown. The old Danish city along the Suir was assailed, and sacked, after a scene of carnage; Richard de Clare was given the hand of Eva, with the inheritance of the Leinster kingship; the building in which they were made man and wife, known as Reginald's Tower, is still in existence. Dermod now made claim to the supreme Irish Monarchy; and his son-in-law, bearing all resistance down, pressed forward to seize and master the capital, then also inhabited, in part, by Danes. The governor, Hasculf, evidently a Dane, abandoned the city, and with a band of followers betook himself to his shipping in the Bay; and Strongbow, throwing a garrison into the place, overran the rich plains of Meath and Kildare, carrying devastation and terror in his path. Nothing seemed able to withstand the Norman; but a sudden turn took place in the invading tide of fortune. Henry, more jealous perhaps than any of his predecessors of the aggrandizement of his powerful noblesse, resented an enterprise undertaken without the regular sanction of the Crown; he prohibited the passage of supplies to Ireland, and ordered Strongbow and his companions in arms to return. Just at this time too, Hasculf had come back to Dublin, at the head of Scottish and Norse bands, and had laid siege to the city from the sea; while Roderick, again collecting a Celtic host, sat down before it, along its western front. The garrison was only a few hundred men; but the Norman warrior never confessed defeat; and a desperate sally, which has preserved the names of Raymond Le Gros and Miles de Cogan, compelled the affrighted besiegers to disappear. The invincible adventurers retained the capital; but Fitzstephen had been hemmed in at Wexford; and Strongbow had failed in an attempt to come to his relief.

These predatory attacks had proved the ascendency of the

Norman knight and his men at arms; but they had merely planted a thorn in the side of Ireland; they had been only to a certain extent successful. Henry set foot in Ireland in October 1172, at the head of an army probably 6000 strong, under the command of 400 Norman knights; and though this was an insignificant force, compared to that which had won the day at Senlac, he perhaps hoped to complete the conquest. His conduct in Ireland reveals the statecraft, the organising genius, the administrative gifts, which have marked him out as a great ruler; yet he was ultimately made to learn that he did not possess the means to reduce the island to real subjection. He asserted his authority as "Lord of Ireland," in a series of acts of harshness and clemency; but, true to his mission as a Son of the Church, he sought to enlist her great spiritual power on his side. At a general synod, held at Cashel, under the sanction of the Pope, and attended by several English Bishops, it was solemnly proclaimed that "Ireland had received a Lord and King at the hand of Providence"; and the Irish Church was assimilated to the Anglo-Norman model, with protestations against "its abuses and vices." It is doubtful, whether any large number of the Irish Celtic clergy expressed their assent, and their Church was practically but little changed; yet for the present, at least, the king had been declared ruler of all Ireland by Right Divine. Meanwhile Henry had taken care to secure the submission of the late invaders, by granting them the territories they had seized, to be held as ordinary fiefs of the Crown; and the chain of feudalism was thrown over the whole country, by the assertion of his title as its superior lord, illusory as the pretence was. The magnificence and the power of the great Angevin king seem to have fascinated most of the Irish chiefs; they were entertained by him in royal state in Dublin; they made homage, and offered tribute, in return for his politic arts and courtesies; and though Roderick held aloof for a time, he soon consented to become a vassal king of Connaught. The supremacy of England, at least in name, over all Ireland, was thus affirmed; and, at the same time, Henry made an attempt to give it reality within the tracts of Leinster, which had been, in a certain measure, subdued. Parts of this region were made shireland, and were placed under the system of administration and law, which had grown up in England since the Norman Conquest. A governor was appointed with vice-regal functions; something like a great Council was established; Courts of Anglo-Norman law were created; and the "men of Bristol" were given a charter for Dublin.

The genius of Henry had traced the lines of conquest; it had not completed a single part of the edifice. No train of colonists followed his army to people the districts it had overrun; that army, besides, was much too weak to attempt to keep hold on the whole country. The king, too, had been forced to temporise with Strongbow and his companions in arms; he made them, indeed, his vassals in name; but he did not curtail their overgrown power, an essential condition of the existence of order and law. The authority of the Crown was feeble even in the Anglo-Norman region, known afterwards as the English Pale; and in the Celtic region beyond it was almost a nullity, for the submissions and tributes of the Irish chiefs, even if continued, made it, in no sense, sovereign. Yet had the king remained any length of time in Ireland, he possibly might have established the Monarchy, and made its influence for good felt throughout the island. Unhappily he was obliged to quit Ireland, owing to the quarrel with Rome caused by the murder of Becket; and he was engaged for years afterwards in the ill-omened contest due to his rebellious sons and his consort. "He departed from Ireland," said an acute historian[1], "without striking one blow, or

---

[1] Sir John Davies on Ireland before 1603. (The Morley Edition, p. 222.)

II.] *The Anglo-Norman Conquest of Ireland.* 31

building one castle, or planting one garrison among the Irish; neither left he behind him one true subject more than those he found there at his coming over, which were only the English adventurers spoken of before, who had gained the port towns in Leinster and Munster, and possessed some scopes of land thereunto adjoining, partly by Strongbow's alliance with the Lord of Leinster, and partly by plain invasion and conquest."

Henry II seems to have perceived the tendency of the Irish Celt to love men, not things; "the people of that land," wrote the Tudor Davies, "did always desire to be governed by great persons"; and the renowned Plantagenet flattered this sentiment. He sent his son John, while still in his teens, with a goodly array of Norman knights and nobles, to restore order, if possible, in the Anglo-Norman tracts, and especially to propitiate the rulers of the Celts, now for years in frequent revolt from the Crown. The mission, however, of John failed; the petulant youth and his gay companions insulted and terrified the Irish chiefs, and what was perhaps worse, harassed the Anglo-Norman settlers by pretensions to parts of their honours and lands, creating the division between the English and the Anglo-Irish "interests," which had evil results during successive centuries. John was chief governor of Ireland during Richard's reign; and when on the throne, in his mature years, made a real and serious effort to complete the Conquest, and to extend the dominion of the Crown and its influence for good. His policy was marked by his tyrannous nature, but also by the statesmanlike views he had inherited from his illustrious father. He visited Ireland—in itself a great thing—and throughout his reign endeavoured to bridle the proud nobles, who were tearing their feudal lordships to pieces. He enlarged four counties, already shireland, into twelve, bringing the invader's rule to the line of the barrier stream of the Shannon; he placed them, nominally at least, under the power of the Crown. He also built Royal Castles—one, at Trim, still existing—to occupy points of vantage within the territory of the king; and he enjoined the great feudatories to keep on foot the armed arrays they were bound to maintain. He laboured, too, evidently, in many ways, to improve the state of the Anglo-Norman settlement. The citizens of Dublin obtained a charter; the Courts of Justice were made more efficient, and administered law beyond their former bounds; the Great Charter was extended to the "King's Irish lieges," the name of an Archbishop of Dublin being on the document. John, however, made no attempt to subdue the great Celtic land beyond the growing Pale; he left it to its feuds, its troubles, its usages; he only sought to conciliate the Irish chiefs, under the easy conditions imposed by his father, and to gain from them allegiance and tribute.

The real condition of Ireland, at the death of John, may be collected from many instructive records. After the lapse of not far from half a century, the Conquest was little more than it had been in 1172. The Anglo-Norman settlement was very weak: a stream of colonists would not flow into it, across wide hill ranges and a tempestuous sea. There was no regular army to support the Government, for this was inconsistent with the ideas of the time; and, spite of punishments and menaces, the great Lords employed their feudal retainers not in the service of the Crown, but to aggrandize themselves, or to fight with each other. The Pale was not parcelled out among its chief possessors, with a view to military defence, or the requirements of war; the great Castles were erected where the owners chose; and this territory was dangerously open to attack. The domain even of comparative law and order had virtually been but little extended. The administration of the justice of the Crown was of no avail in the lands of the ruling nobles; these were scenes of lawless disorder and bloodshed, like the vast lordships of that arrogant noblesse which boasted "that the

The Anglo-Norman Conquest of Ireland.

waves were before the sea," and "that they were Rohans if they could not be kings." There was no effective central government, and nothing like a People, even within the circle of the so-called shires; all was tyranny, violence, feudal oppression. The true Irish land, still two-thirds of the island, was left divided among its Celtic chiefs, who submitted themselves to their distant suzerain, or took up arms against his nobles, just as it suited their fickle purpose; this region was also given up to ever-increasing anarchy. Strangely, too, though the Pale had been pushed further, the influence of the Celt was growing within its borders, owing to a most remarkable change of usage and manners, to be noticed afterwards when it becomes fully manifest. England, at this period, had little more hold on Ireland, than the Mogul Empire had on India in the days of Clive and Hastings.

A period of more than six generations of man divides the reign of John from that of Henry IV. To outward seeming the power of England over Ireland had been extended during this long space of time. Edward I and Edward III would have thought it foul scorn had their supremacy over the whole of the island been questioned in Parliament, or in a Court of Justice; it had repeatedly been acknowledged by Irish kings and chiefs. The ascendency, too, of the arms of England had been proved decisively throughout this period; the Anglo-Normans and the Englishry, as their successors were called, were irresistible in the field against the Irish Celts, who could not contend, in fair fight, with the knight, the man-at-arms, and the English longbow. Now and then indeed, the light-armed Irish soldiery struck down Norman and Saxon, as in Fitzstephen's time, in cunningly laid ambushes, or in an intricate country; Black Friday, long a day of mourning for the townsmen of Dublin, commemorates a successful Irish raid and massacre. But English conquest made steady progress, if we look at material force only; the De Burghs carried their arms through Ulster and Connaught, and the Geraldines to the extreme verge of Munster; the old kingship of Roderick was effaced at Athunree; the invasions of the Bruces were formidable for a time, but came to an end after the rout of Dundalk; the Irishry stooped their heads, like reeds, at the sight of the footmen and the bows and bills of Richard II. Nor can it be said that, in all these years, anything like a general resistance was made to the advance of the English enemy, if made in earnest. Occasionally an Irish Vercingetorix appeared; the heroic deeds of Aedh O'Conor, and of Cathel of the Red Hand, have been handed down, by tradition, to modern song[1]; Art MacMurrogh was, for a time, the terror of the Pale; Donald O'Neill—a descendant of the Hy-Niall monarchs—seems to have aimed at forming a great league under Edward Bruce, to overthrow the Englishry. But national effort there was none, for the national idea did not exist; the Irish chiefs, ever divided by tribal discord, growing only worse with the progress of time, seemed unable to unite for a patriotic purpose; they either fought singly against the enemy at hand, or wasted their strength in destroying each other, or, as often happened, called in the Englishry to come to their aid against their fellows—conduct too characteristic of all the Celtic races, but especially, as we have said, of the Irish family[2].

The dominion of England, nevertheless, had made no real advance in this period; the influences that in Ireland would have produced good government, had certainly, on the whole, declined. In addition to the causes before referred to, which had led to the feebleness of English power and to misrule and anarchy in Irish affairs—the absence of a steady influx of settlers—the want of a regular army to complete the conquest,

[1] See Campbell's poem *O'Connor's Child*.
[2] So Tacitus of the Celts of Britain, *Agricola* 12, "Dum singuli pugnant, universi vincuntur."

and to vindicate the authority of the state—the neglect and misuse of the feudal militia—the lawless ascendency of the great nobles—the disregard of precautions to defend the Pale—and the abandonment of the Celtic tracts to the native chiefs and tribes—other causes had arisen, in the thirteenth and fourteenth centuries, to prolong and even aggravate the resulting evils. Thousands of colonists, doubtless, had set foot in Ireland between the reigns of John and Henry IV; but a counter-current had checked the stream; many had returned to England, unable to endure the misgovernment and oppression existing everywhere; the settlement of the Englishry remained very weak. Three or four times, during this period, the forces of the Crown had been asembled, and had easily crushed the foes they encountered; but no army, as had been the case before, was kept together to hold feudalism down, to overawe the Irishry, to maintain English rule. While, too, the great nobles continued to neglect their duties, made no provision for the defence of their domains, wasted their feudal arrays in petty wars and broils, and, in a word, abused the large powers in their hands, a series of accidents had made their authority perceptibly less where it conduced to good. Some of the old Anglo-Norman Houses had died out; the lands of others had passed into the hands of heiresses, whose lords lived on their estates in England; the heads of not a few had quitted the country; and thus absenteeism, disastrous at all times, and especially disastrous in a feudal age, had begun to produce its manifold ills in Ireland. Another change, too, in the position of the feudal noblesse, had not only injured the power of the state, but had proved very destructive of order and law, in a considerable part of the ill-fated land. Apart from the De Burghs, the great families of the Geraldines and Butlers had become the chiefs of the descendants of the Anglo-Norman conquerors; and these had acquired by royal grant or usage, rights and powers even larger than those bestowed somewhat carelessly, at first, on the companions of Strongbow. Within the vast region extending between the verge of Kildare, by Kilkenny, and Limerick, to where the wilds of Kerry meet the Atlantic, these nobles were all but sovereigns in their palatinates, and possessed, in fact, nearly the whole power of government. They created knights, levied war at pleasure, convened feudal assemblies, and held courts of justice; they were, in a word, superior to the state and its will; it is scarcely necessary to indicate the results.

Other causes concurred still further to lessen the authority of the Crown in Ireland, and to prevent the existence of well-ordered government. The direct influence, nay, the presence of the king was essential to the welfare of the Feudal Monarchy; he was the true source of Right, and the champion of Law; he checked the excesses of an encroaching baronage; he was the vigorous protector, in his own interests, of the Church, the subject classes, and the entire community. Strong as had been the Conqueror's deeply founded government, it almost went to pieces, when Henry II was entangled in foreign quarrels and wars, when Henry III showed himself unable to rule, and during the inglorious reign of Richard II; the complete ascendency of Edward I in his realm was largely due to his devoting his genius to advancing the greatness of England on the spot, and to the extension of Royal Justice at home. Henry II and John apparently felt that their personal rule in Ireland was required; and in no part of the dominions of the English Crown was this salutary element of power so needed to keep overbearing feudalism down, to restrain English misrule and Celtic anarchy, to promote the growth of civilised life. Most unfortunately, for nearly two centuries, Ireland, as has been the case almost ever since, was left without this beneficent influence; Edward I did not care to visit the country—one of the few errors of his glorious reign —though he evidently perceived what good might have followed; Edward III thought of it only as a field for recruits, and for revenue in his protracted wars; the showy and frivolous Richard II was the one sovereign who set foot in Ireland, from 1210 to 1394. Even his apparition proved how immense would have been the advantages to a distracted land, had an English monarch directly controlled the administration of Irish affairs, and taken the government of Ireland in hand. But, as we have said, this was denied by fortune; the very keystone of the Medieval Monarchy, on which the edifice in the main depended, was left out of the arch in Ireland. What wonder then that it was weak and tottering; what wonder that, in the greatest part of the country, the central government was reduced to nothingness; that feudalism, lawless and all powerful, threw its destructive shadow over other parts; and that the rest of the island remained the domain of the Celt?

In the absence of the king, a long series of Viceroys, succeeding each other at brief intervals of time, ruled, or rather pretended to rule, Ireland. This, which constituted the only central government, did not practically extend beyond the Pale, except occasionally, and by fits and starts; but its nature was such, that it did not increase the influence or the power of the Monarchy; that it provoked injurious dissensions and feuds; that it did not promote social or political progress. The Viceroys were chosen from different orders of men; they received commands from the seat of power in England, repeatedly changing and discordant; they held different, nay opposite views, as to the direction and management of Irish affairs. Some, like Gaveston, put their trust chiefly in an imposing display of military force; others, like Lionel the Duke of Clarence, aimed at aggrandising the influence of the Crown and giving effect to the will of its ministers, regardless of the means, however unjust; many, chosen from the official class of nobles, and even of plebeians rising in the state, tried to strengthen the English settlement in the Pale, to weaken the dominant Anglo-Norman Houses, and to reduce the Irishry, as they were called, to submission, often taking severe, nay atrocious, measures, to attain what they deemed necessary ends; the majority, perhaps, drawn from the old Norman families, adopted an exactly opposite course, upheld feudalism and the abuses of its power, and lorded it over Saxon and Celt alike. For Ireland, therefore, there was nothing like a continuous and a systematic policy; the administration, and the acts of the government, often inconsistent and at odds with each other, kept the land in a state of unrest and trouble; all that was certain, if irregular, was harsh violence and tyranny exercised in high places. Now and then the power of the Crown was asserted by iniquitous and unscrupulous means; now and then sentences of forfeiture were pronounced against powerful absentee nobles; the lands of old Norman Houses were occasionally seized to make way for a colony of fresh English settlers; and, in the case of Lords of the Pale, and even of Irish chiefs, proscription and confiscation were sometimes frequent. On the other hand, Geraldines and Butlers, when enthroned at the Castle, exacted vengeance from those who had wronged their retainers and themselves; oppressed and harried the Englishry of the Pale; and were especially hostile to the subordinates sent from England to observe or to control their acts. The general result, besides misrule, confusion, disorder almost everywhere, was to make the distinction between the recent English settlers, and the old Anglo-Irish inhabitants of the land, of which traces may be found, even in the days of John, more marked and profound, with the progress of time; the "English and Anglo-Irish interests" became intensely hostile, and at continual feud; and the effects, in weakening the power of England, were evil and manifest.

The most remarkable cause, however, and certainly not the least effective, of the failure of the advance of English power, and of misgovernment in a large part of Ireland, remains to be noticed and explained. The conquerors, we have seen, had borne their arms everywhere; they had spread far beyond the Shannon in Connaught; they had reached the Atlantic line of the coast in Ulster and Munster; and they had planted settlements in these distant regions, while they were dominant throughout three-fourths of Leinster. They might have established English rule in these wide territories had they remained true to the usages of their race, and had not these been largely transformed by a most singular process, in the course of time. But in different degrees, and in a variety of ways, the descendants of the invaders and their followers adopted the customs of the children of the soil; changed from Norman lords into Celtic chiefs; preferred tribal authority to feudal power, and even tribal life to the life of their fathers, nay, in remote districts put on the Irish garb, actually lost the use of their native tongue, and trained their levies for the field after the Irish fashion. Symptoms of the metamorphosis had shown themselves within a few years from the first invasion; but, by the close of the fourteenth century, they had made whole counties of Ireland almost Celtic, though once leavened with Norman and English elements; and this revolution had had a potent effect, in narrowing the bounds of English dominion, and in producing misrule and anarchy. The causes of a phenomenon which gave rise to passionate efforts of many English governors[1] to prevent what they deemed an appalling evil, and which English writers have fiercely denounced, are worthy, perhaps, of a passing notice. The Anglo-Norman probably found it more easy to oppress vassal dependents and villeins, by throwing feudal duties aside, and playing the part of an Irish chief; he would, doubtless, largely increase his

[1] These efforts culminated in the celebrated statute of Kilkenny, 40 Ed. III, enacted during the Viceroyalty of Lionel Duke of Clarence. It was confirmed over and over again, but to no purpose.

authority, in the midst of surrounding Irish clans and septs, by conforming to Irish modes of life and habits. But the paramount cause, it appears likely, was the peculiar influence which the Celtic genius has had in affecting races in contact with it. Butler and Geraldine fell under the fascinating spell of the daughters of the land whom they had made wives[1]; the hard nature of Norseman and Teuton yielded to the charm and communicative power of Celtic ideas, as France has made Alsatian and Lorrainer her own; and the whole course of Irish history attests the fact. The "degenerate Englishry," as they were called, were in immense numbers in the South and the West of Ireland, and even in parts of Leinster, at this period.

Ireland had thus already become the misshapen and withering limb of the great English Monarchy. The island contained three distinct divisions presenting strongly marked, but very different features. Of the twelve counties which John had made shireland, eight had almost ceased to retain this character; the Anglo-Norman or English Pale had narrowed into the four original shires, Meath, including Westmeath, Louth, Dublin, and Kildare. In this fine rich tract, bounded by the Barrow, the great lakes of Westmeath, the Mourne range, and the sea, the rule of the native chiefs had been almost effaced; the land had been divided among noble houses of Anglo-Norman and English descent, lords of dependents and tenants of the same race, and little affected by contact with the Celt, but with a subject population of the Irishry in their midst. The Pale was the domain of by far the greatest part of the civilisation which had grown up in Ireland;

---

[1] So Davis, a man of genius, finely wrote:
"Those Geraldines! those Geraldines! not long our air they breathed,
Not long they fed on venison, in Irish water seethed,
Not often had their children been by Irish mothers nursed,
When from their full and genial hearts an Irish feeling burst!"
The Spirit of the Nation, p. 98, Ed. 1870.

the numerous castles of its ancient Barons, some still existing, were imposing structures; the agriculture of this region to this day seems more orderly and long settled than in the rest of the island. Dublin, the chief town of this comparatively favoured land, had become a city of some importance, possessing municipal rights, and a few fine buildings; its townsmen conducted a tolerably good trade with England, and especially with her great port of the West, Bristol. The Parliaments of Ireland, long ago established, were usually assembled in the expanding capital; here, too, was the Castle, and the Royal Courts of Justice administering English law throughout the Pale; and the authority of the Legislature, the Viceroy and the tribunals of the state, was generally recognised within its limits. Troubles and acts of oppression were but too common; the feudal arrays of the Pale were often called out in "hostings" against the "Irish enemy"; the ascendency of one great dominant House, at least, was repeatedly adverse to peace and order. But the sons of the conquerors and their successors had struck root in the Pale, and became a real and settled colony; the whole region, if not to be deemed prosperous, was an oasis in a desert compared to the other parts of Ireland.

Yet even the Pale was a distracted land, often a scene of deeds of blood, and of anarchic tyranny. The arrays of the Celts occasionally broke through the Marches, ill-defended, and without sufficient fortresses; pouring down through the defiles of Wicklow, across the great expanse of the Bog of Allen, and from the "gate of the North," as it was called, near Dundalk, they waged a predatory war with the English settlers. The burghers of Dublin were, over and over again, affrighted by the fires of the Irish foray; and more than once the weak feudal militia proved no match for the armed swarms of the active "Irish enemy." The subjugated, but untamed, Irishry of the Pale sometimes took part in these destructive raids, rising against masters, feared, but abhorred; the lot indeed of these vanquished children of the soil, in the peculiar seat of the Englishry, must have been hard in the extreme. As was often seen, at this time, in such cases, in Europe, this population, with some exceptions, was left under its native usages; it was treated as completely alien by the conquering race; it was outlawed in the relations of ordinary life; and, in the administration of justice, it had scarcely any rights. It was no felony for an Englishman to slay "a mere Irishman"; but this immunity was not reciprocal; the Irishman who killed an Englishman was held to be a murderer; and the same unfair and odious distinction was maintained in litigation of every kind. The evils resulting from this state of things have possibly been unduly magnified, and could hardly have been very great in other parts of Ireland; but they must have tended, within the narrow limits of the Pale, to promote discords and animosities of race, and to disturb and injure the frame of society. The worst feature, however, in the condition of the Pale, at this period, has yet to be noticed. The heads of the Geraldines, the great House of Kildare, were the feudal suzerains of a large part of this region, many, too, were chiefs of the state at the Castle—the well-known seat of the English Government—and their overgrown authority was too often displayed in a rule of oppression, gross wrong, and exaction. They were tyrants even of the Anglo-Norman Baronage; compelled the levies of these to follow their standards, in feuds with the Butlers, or in strife with the Celt; kept the citizens of Dublin in awe of their power; and repeatedly perverted the course of justice. The abuse of their dominion, however, was most ruinously shown in a mode of extortion adopted, in part, from Irish chieftains, who, we have already seen, had a right to quarter retainers on their degraded tenants, and, in part, from the Anglo-Norman usage of purveyance. The Kildare Geraldines and their armed followers ate up the resources of the Pale by what became known as the rapine of "coyne and livery," a kind of freebooting, of which it was said, "that if it had been practised in Hell, as it hath been in Ireland, it had long since destroyed the very kingdom of Beelzebub[1]."

Outside the Pale, spread what may be called the Anglo-Irish region, that in which the Englishry, to a great extent "degenerate," were intermixed with the Irishry only in part conquered. This great tract, comprising, with some additions, the eight shires of John, referred to before, formed the counties now known as Wexford and Waterford, Carlow, Kilkenny, Tipperary, Cork, Limerick, and a part of Kerry; and stretched from the course of the Slaney to the mouth of the Shannon, and thence to the hill ranges of the Bays of Kenmare and Dingle. In Wexford, the south-eastern nook of this land, the settlement founded by Fitzstephen had become established; the mountains of Wicklow divided it from the Pale; but it was a colony resembling that of the Pale; its inhabitants, to this day, show scarcely any Celtic blood. Along the southern coast, the counties of Cork and Waterford were still largely peopled by men of English race, ruled by the descendants of Anglo-Norman lords; but the Irishry had considerably encroached on their bounds, and filled many of the inland districts, especially where these were hill countries. Nearly all the remaining parts of the Anglo-Irish territory were comprised in the numerous lordships of the Butlers and of the Geraldine Desmonds, a far spreading branch of the great House of Kildare, and exhibiting very similar qualities. The Butlers were the feudal lords of a Baronage, largely of Norman and English origin, and of a population of settlers still, in part, English; but association with the aboriginal race had had its effects in their vast domains; the sons of many of the colonists had become "degenerate"; some of the early colonies had disappeared; and the Irishry, pressing in on the conquerors in their midst, had impregnated

[1] Davies 229, 30.

them with Celtic elements of all kinds. The change had been made more marked in the lands of the Desmonds; in these the Norman and English settlements had been, from the first, comparatively weak, and had, to a great extent, perished; the inhabitants had become for the most part Celtic. Within this domain too lay a great region, never affected by Norman or Saxon influence, wild hills and plains, closed by valleys and defiles, and spreading from the Shannon to the Atlantic, where Irish clans and septs maintained their rude freedom, and Irish chiefs defied or followed their Desmond suzerains, in war and peace, at their own will and pleasure. The Butlers, better known as the Lords of Ormond, had but slightly conformed to the Irish usages; but the Desmonds, far removed from the Pale, and surrounded by Celts on every side, had become, at least while they lived among them, "more Irish," it was said, "than the Irish themselves," and had adopted the "sluttish Irish customs and habits."

The Anglo-Norman Land was not wholly without signs of civilised life and social progress. The fertile plains of Kilkenny and Limerick were studded with castles and noble abbeys; there was a considerable trade between the ports of Munster and Spain; the Butlers and the Geraldines were even patrons of learning. These great Norman families, too, it appears certain, retained much of their feudal state, even when they became more or less Irish; the Plantagenets welcomed their heads at Court, and treated them with the highest distinction; they perhaps adopted the ways of the Celt, in order chiefly to please the Celts around them. Nor were they inveterate enemies of the Irish chiefs; they blended with them freely in marriage; and the Irish chiefs in turn learned much from them, especially in architecture and the art of war. On the whole the ruling orders in this region, whether Norman or Irish, formed a real noblesse, with differences of race between them indeed, but not given up to mere barbarism, the common reproach of many historians. But their territories were not the less a theatre of bloody strife, of misrule of all kinds, of almost incessant disorder and lawlessness. From Kerry to Kildare the land was torn by the fierce conflicts of Ormonds and Desmonds; the Englishry and the Irishry perished by tens of thousands, in feuds that made order and peace impossible; the first conditions of social well-being and prosperity could not exist or grow up. If exaction, too, in the Pale was grievous, it was infinitely worse in the Anglo-Irish Land; the coyne and livery, extorted by Geraldine and Butler, throughout their lordships, was like the ravage of locusts; the Celtic chiefs improved on an evil example; huge predatory levies were kept on foot, destroying and harrying whole counties. Nor could justice and righteous law have a place in the signiories of the great nobles; the king's writ had no force in these; their seneschals administered a kind of rude medley of English and Irish custom and usage corruptly, and at the will of their lords; the pleasure of an Ormond or a Desmond was supreme in his Court; and the prevalence of the Brehon law, in the Celtic regions, alongside quite a different system, there is reason to believe, did much mischief. The condition of all, save the dominant classes, was one of general poverty and harsh subjection; and, as we have said, the descendants of many of the first colonists had fled from a country unfit to live in.

We turn to the third division, the Celtic Land, still nearly altogether the seat of the Irishry. This great region included the whole of Ulster, and of Connaught, then comprising the County of Clare, and also a part of the Midlands of Leinster; it contained the present counties of Down, Antrim, Londonderry, Donegal, Tyrone, Fermanagh, Cavan, Armagh, Monaghan, Roscommon, Leitrim, Galway, Mayo, Sligo, with Offaly and Leix, now the King's and Queen's Counties, in addition, as we have seen, to Clare. The conquering race had invaded and held it in part; but the feeble colonies they had planted had dwindled away, and in some counties had been blotted out; they were a mere remnant in the midst of the conquered; and though swarms of Scots had descended on the coasts of Ulster, these were as yet mastered by the aboriginal people. The great Norman nobles, too, had nearly disappeared; the De Courcies, struck down by the iron arm of John, had sunk into the lords of a petty fief in Munster; and the De Burghs, rich as they were in Plantagenet blood, had become "degenerate Englishry" in an extreme sense; and with their dependent barons and vassals, in the words of the chronicler, "had been metamorphosed like Nebuchadnezzar, who, although he had the face of a man, had the heart of a beast;......insomuch as...... they had no marks or differences left amongst them of the noble race from which they were descended; they grew to be ashamed of their very English surnames, and took Irish surnames and nicknames[1]." Ulster, Connaught, and a tract of Leinster were, therefore, the seat of the Irishry; in these provinces the descendants of the Irish kings and chiefs, still numerous, and possessing more than their power of old, lived in rude independence amidst their tribes, clans, and septs, little really affected by the march of conquest, and ruling communities still following the usages and the ways of life of the Celt.

It would be a mistake to suppose that civilisation had no trace of existence in this part of the island, as it certainly had in the remaining parts. There was already a large trade between Galway and Spain, and between Ulster and the South of Scotland; the Irish chiefs, in imitation of Norman art, had constructed many fine edifices of stone, especially fortresses and religious houses; they had improved the weapons and discipline of their armed levies; they had intermarried repeatedly into great Norman Houses; their sons—a

[1] Davies 297, '8.

sure mark that they were held in honour by the most haughty of dominant races—having been often lords of daughters of the noblest Norman families. This, nevertheless, like the Anglo-Norman Land, was a centre of continual broil and discord, and of lawless disorder abounding everywhere. The chiefs made frequent descents on the Pale, especially along its northern frontier; some had crossed the Shannon and made settlements in Leinster and Munster, driving out, or keeping down, the diminishing Englishry. They were, too, as had been the case at all times, in never-ceasing tribal war with each other; their savage feuds made whole counties desolate; and "degenerate" as many of the Anglo-Normans had become, they appear to have still held them as traditional foes, or took sides with them in their incessant quarrels.

A great change, meanwhile, fraught with many evils, had been passing over the Irish community, in this, as in other parts of the island. Tribal life, usage, and law, as we have pointed out, still existed in the Pale and the Anglo-Irish tracts, here almost effaced, there still vigorous; but they were dominant forces in the Irish Land; this was still Celtic in government, customs, and manners. But, as had already begun after the Danish wars, the primitive institutions of the old Irish race had, by this time, been largely transformed; the archaic type of society had been partly broken up with consequences of a disastrous kind; the ancient Celtic civilisation was dying out. The supreme hereditary Monarchy was a thing of the past; a tie had ceased to exist which, in some measure, had kept together the community as a whole. The chiefs, who had survived Norman and English invasion, had grown in power within their dominions; they had conquered many inferior clans and septs, and had reduced these to complete subjection; they had multiplied their companions in arms, and made them a rude military noblesse; they had encroached on the rights of the free clansmen and Ceile, and had largely turned them into dependent vassals; and they had greatly increased the classes of their Fuidhirs and serfs, and more than ever laid a heavy hand on them. A kind of barbarous feudalism, in some degree, doubtless, imitated from the Anglo-Norman model, had thus replaced, in a great measure, the old tribal organisation of the land; this still existed, and was even deeply rooted; but it was gradually yielding to harsher modes of rule, and to a state of society showing a marked change for the worse. The Irish chief had become more and more a tyrant, a head of savage warriors who carried out his will; his tribe, clan, or sept had become more and more his inferiors; this was especially seen in his "bonaghts and cosherings," the Celtic counterparts of "coyne and livery"; in a word, the bonds, which had linked together the ancient Irish "Family," had been weakened and, in many parts, severed. This naturally led to ever-growing disorder and troubles; in fact the Irish chiefs seem, at this period, to have been more than ever at feud with each other.

An influence, too, of the most potent kind, which in happier lands has been, so to speak, a strong cementing force in the social structure, was a source of ill-will and disunion in Ireland. The Church in England, and, indeed, in Europe, many as were its shortcomings, nay its vices, had done wonders in promoting just government, in keeping oppressive feudalism in check, in raising the humbler orders of men to a higher estate, in extending the domain of order and peace, in a word, in furthering the good work of its Master. The results in Ireland had been the very opposite, owing to the division which had existed, from the first moment, between the two really distinct communions, which had been formed after the Norman invasion. Henry II had set up, under the Bull of Adrian, a Church on the orthodox Roman model, and this became the Church of the Pale; the primitive Irish Church of History remained practically unchanged in the Celtic regions. There were marked differences between the two; but differences of ritual and of doctrine were made deeper and worse by distinctions and hostility of race; the Church of the Pale was that of the Englishry; the Irish tribes clung to their ancient Church; and perpetual discord reigned between them. Churchmen of the Pale went on "hostings" against the clans and septs; looked on the priests of the Celts as barbarian enemies, and shut them out like pariahs from their communion. The clergy of the old Irish Church did the same, and banned and cursed their Norman and Anglo-Saxon rivals. The feud was most bitter and never-ending; religion, which, elsewhere, threw an arch of peace over waters of civil and social strife, created in Ireland two hostile camps exasperated by fierce sacerdotal passions. Nor can it be said that either Church produced many saintly champions of the faith of Christ, even many men of exalted piety. Several prelates of the Church of the Pale were charged with odious and wicked crimes[1]; its clergy are said to have been self-seeking, avaricious, cruel to the Irishry in their midst, nay the scum and refuse of the Church in England. The Celtic Church, on the other hand, had ceased to be a shining light of Christendom; its bishops and clergy, at this period, have been described generally as barbarous, ignorant, and, sometimes, vicious and lawless[2]. Ireland had nothing like the noble succession of great churchmen, who were the saving health of the English monarchy in the Middle Ages.

Unity of law has been a strong moral tie to keep society together in all ages. This, we have indicated, did not exist in Ireland; the laws of England were dominant in the Pale; they were mixed up with Celtic usage in the Anglo-Irish

---

[1] Thus Henri de Londres, an archbishop of Dublin, and a witness to Magna Carta, was accused of an atrocious fraud. Leland I. 206.

[2] Thus an Irish archbishop of Cashel is said to have committed murder. *Ibid.* 234.

counties; the Brehon Law was supreme in the Celtic Land. This, we have said, was not a peculiar wrong, in the case of Ireland; a similar state of things was to be found in most countries, where different races were subject to medieval monarchies. But the ascendency of English Law must, we have remarked, have pressed severely on the Irishry of the Pale; excluded as they were from its Courts of Justice, and from its protection, but not its penalties, it must have often had iniquitous results. The benefits of English Law were, indeed, conferred, as a privilege, on five families of the great Irish chiefs,—the "quinque sanguines" of old kingly rank—and were also given freely to the native race as denizens; but this very circumstance shows that those who were deprived of this coveted boon had real cause of complaint; and the Irishry of the Pale, it must be borne in mind, more than once entreated Plantagenet kings, in vain, that the rights of English Law might be extended to them. On the whole, there can be little doubt that this kind of outlawry and ostracism of part of the subject people was a grievance, and a cause of ill-will and disorder.

The intermixture of English and Irish law, in what we have called the Anglo-Irish region, seems to have been attended, also, with real evils. This was denounced over and over again in the Parliaments of the age, and prohibited by many severe statutes; and the principal reason assigned was not ill founded. The Brehon Law, we have said, did not recognise crimes, for it had no conception of a state or of public wrongs; and the eric or compensation was the only penalty it inflicted even for the worst deeds of blood. When, therefore, it penetrated into domains where it came in contact with English Law, it appeared an immoral and even a wicked usage that almost secured immunity for crime; it has been called "an ingenious contrivance for compounding felonies"; and as crimes and outrages of every kind were prevalent in these very districts, it was not unnaturally condemned as a "damnable custom," by minds on the side of order and civilised life, especially as these did not understand its principles. The Brehon usages, again, in the Celtic Land had bad results in the existing state of society, though they had been certainly improved by the Brehon lawyers, who had brought into them parts of the Canon, and of the Civil Law of Rome. The elective system of Tanist succession appears to have become much more common, and the hereditary principle to have been much less respected, in these centuries of increasing tribal warfare; and Tudor lawyers, strongly prejudiced as they were, were probably not in error when they maintained that—apart from opposition to English power—this led to confusion and endless discord. Very possibly, too, the mode of descent, known as Irish Gavelkind, by which the chief distributed, on the death of a member of a sept, his lands,—some, indeed, say the entire sept-land—among all the remaining members, harmless as it may have been in a primitive age, became adverse to social progress, and to good agriculture, in more modern days[1]; though, doubtless, it was mere exaggeration to assert that "it was the true cause of the barbarism and desolation of the land[2]."

As has usually been the case in misruled countries, the unhappy and backward condition of Ireland was conspicuously seen in the poverty of the state, and the miserable position of the more humble orders of men. Notwithstanding wars with Scotland and France, and peasant risings, and the Black Death, England, at this period, was, by many degrees, the

---

[1] Modern writers, notably Mr Hallam and Mr Goldwin Smith, seem to have underrated the evils resulting from the state of law and usage existing in Ireland, at this period. The evidence on this subject of many contemporary statutes, and of very able Tudor statesmen and thinkers, can hardly be questioned.

[2] Davies 291.

most wealthy of the nations of the North; her society, if cast in a feudal mould, exhibited a well compacted gradation of classes, from the noble down to the small holder of the soil, all, as we see in the pictures of Chaucer, apparently contented with their lot in life. In Ireland, it was altogether otherwise; the feeble central government had hardly any revenue; the scanty taxes were squandered in incessant strife, or could not be collected owing to feudal exaction; the tributes of the Irish chiefs were very seldom paid; the usual returns to the Exchequer were "In Thesauro Nihil." As we have seen, many of the English colonies had vanished, the settlers having left the island in thousands; elements favourable to the formation of a middle class in Ireland—already strong in English national life—had thus been dissipated or destroyed; they could not grow up and become vigorous in a land of continual war and confusion. As for the peasantry, if they could be called by the name, and the population of either race, placed at the bottom of the social scale, they were in a state of extreme wretchedness, like the serfs of France, or the predial slaves of Germany. The great nobles and their dependent barons, the leading and even the inferior Irish chiefs, lived in a kind of rude wasteful grandeur, fattening on plunder gathered in on all sides; but their villeins, their Fuidhirs, their degraded bondsmen, were thralls in hopeless distress and want. "What common folk in all this world"—so ran a state paper of a later date, but doubtless applicable to this time—"is so poor, so feeble, so evil beseen in town and field, so bestial, so greatly oppressed and trodden under foot, fares so evil, with so great misery, and with so wretched a life, as the common folk of Ireland[1]?"

In intellectual life and energy Ireland was as backward as in her material condition. Successive generations of great

[1] State Papers II. 14. Referred to in Froude's *History of England* II. 283, '4.

rulers and statesmen had made the government of England the best in the world; her Parliaments were already the rising power in the state; they were national councils in no doubtful sense; they were full of elements of increasing strength and wisdom. And there had been a corresponding movement in the mind of England; Oxford, from the first years of the thirteenth century, Cambridge at perhaps a somewhat later date, had been centres of fruitful mental activity; Wycliff had been the herald of the Reformation; a noble, nay, a popular literature had appeared, seen in the masterpieces of a great poet, Chaucer, and in the keen and even tragic satire of Langland. Ireland in every particular showed an unhappy contrast to these glories of genius in the highest places, and to these brilliant triumphs of the understanding of man. Her government, confined to the nook of the Pale, was such as has been already described, feeble, without definite policy and aim, capricious and harsh in many acts of violence, but usually impotent to do good, never enlightened, statesmanslike or, in any sense, national. Her Parliaments, little more than Conventions of the Pale, were ruled by a few great nobles and churchmen, for a free and strong House of Commons could not exist in a land of tyranny and war, and where, except Dublin, there were but a few towns above the rank of villages; their legislation was petty, local, selfish, timid,—that of a colonial caste in the midst of enemies; it had nothing resembling the noble statutes enacted at Westminster at this period, the still living sources of English law and liberty. So it was, too, with the work of the mind in Ireland; this exhibited lethargy, neglect, nay even a marked decline. The Brehon lawyers, indeed, we have said, did much to make the letter of their laws better; learned men were to be found in many religious houses; there were poets, annalists, and bards in the Celtic Land of the same type as five centuries before; a kind of literature grew up within the Pale; the Anglo-Irish lawyers could show many able "clerks," especially in scions of old Norman Houses. But an attempt to found a University in the capital had failed; there was nothing like an Irish Oxford or Cambridge, no William of Wykeham or William of Waynflete; the churchmen of both Churches had scarcely a name acknowledged by posterity as really great; the level of knowledge throughout the country was pitiably low. Darkness had settled on the ill-fated land which had irradiated Europe at an earlier age; and this while England was basking in light, and when Christendom had felt the first day-spring of a new era.

From the death of Richard II to the accession of Henry VII—that is throughout nearly all the fifteenth century—the state of Ireland became in every respect worse. The causes of the change are easily discerned. Talbot, indeed, the terror of the French name, overthrew Celtic tribes in more than one encounter; and a few able military governors of the Pale appeared. But the Lancastrian Kings completely neglected Ireland, between conquests in France and civil war at home; the reins were thrown on the necks of Viceroys, who exaggerated all that was bad in the misgovernment of the past. The feud between the "new Englishry" of the Pale, and the "old Englishry" in it, in part "degenerate," became more than ever envenomed; obscure governors sometimes struck down great nobles, or played them against each other, to keep up a show of power; but ultimately the dominant House of Kildare became more than ever the oppressors of the Pale, and held its nominal rulers in fear and subjection. Meanwhile a miniature of the Wars of the Roses was seen in the increasing strife between Ormonds and Desmonds, the first supporters of the House of Lancaster, the second devoted to the House of York; local broils were replaced by far spreading warfare, more sustained, for it had a plausible cause or a pretext. The flower of the colonists, too, perished on English battle-fields, in the contest for the throne; and the land was deprived, to a large extent, of the few remaining elements of its military power. The refluent stream of the departing Englishry became more rapid and strong than before; the depopulation of their settlements went on apace; their colonies, in whole districts, completely disappeared.

In this state of affairs, the Irish chiefs still further encroached on the conquering race, in wild incursions and predatory strife; they seized and occupied a large part of the Pale; when Bosworth was fought the four shires had been narrowed into a little strip of territory about fifty miles long by twenty broad, extending from Dundalk, on the northern verge of Louth, nearly by the course of the Boyne and the Liffey, and thence to the edge of the hills of Wicklow. The weakness of the Englishry had become so complete that, like the effete Portuguese in Africa, they paid a "Black Rent" to their once contemned enemies; and—a marked sign of humiliation— they shrank behind a ditch, built to keep out the rising tide of the Celts. Had the Irish possessed a real leader, or been capable of a vigorous and general effort, the invaders must have been driven into the sea; the settlement of the Pale would have gone like other settlements. It is unnecessary to repeat that exaction, anarchy, and misery had become worse than ever; in the picturesque words of a chronicler of the day, "Ireland is the land that the angel understood; for there is no land of so continual war within itself; ne of such great shedding of Christian blood; ne of so great robbing, spoiling, preying, and burning, ne of so great wrongful extortion continually, as Ireland[1]."

England had been dominant in Ireland for more than three hundred years, and might have reduced her to subjection, over and over again, with fortunate results to both countries, had she really put forth her power. It is an error to imagine that, during this long period, she had been a regular oppressor

[1] Ware, *Writers of Ireland*, p. 90.

of the native people, or had dark and evil designs against it. Many Viceroys, indeed, did harsh things; but they were, perhaps, more severe to the Lords of the Pale, than to the Irishry almost outside the sphere of their influence. It is untrue, besides, that the conquering settlers had been cruel, as a rule, to the native race; the Norman bore no dislike to the Celt, and treated him for the most part as a loyal vassal; this was hardly the case with the Anglo-Saxon Englishry; but the animosities of faith and blood, so terrible afterwards, were as yet not very strong. The faults in the rule of England were altogether different: they were those of negligence, ignorance, want of insight; and accidental circumstances had also their part. The first Norman descents accomplished hardly anything; the governments that succeeded only formed a weak Pale, and a feudal land beyond it; and no attempt was made thoroughly to subdue the native Irish. Feeble and irregular efforts of power had divided Ireland into a declining colony, a land of contending nobles, and the regions of the Celt; this state of things had ended in the decay of the Pale, in the general diminution of the English settlers, in the wide-spread lawlessness of the Celtic tribes, in almost universal misrule and disorder.

The worst instance of neglect, perhaps, was the absence from Ireland of her sovereign lords; the presence of the English kings might have done wonders; but a series of mischances kept them out of Ireland. The charges of persistent cruelty and wrong disappear; but the state of Ireland, at the end of the fifteenth century, was not the less disastrous for England and the lesser island. The whole country was a prey to anarchy—a thing of wounds, bruises, and putrefying sores; the germs of civilisation had been well-nigh destroyed; Ireland, Norman, Saxon, and Celtic alike, had in the course of ages distinctly gone back, and showed less signs of progress than in the reign of Henry II. The conquest made piecemeal, the complete want of anything resembling good general government, the scarcely checked domination of noble and chief, the strife between the Churches, and the conflict of law, had been some of the manifold causes which had reduced Ireland to her wretched condition, and had all but extinguished the rule of England. And beside this unhappy and distracted land, lay England, rich in national strength, and, even after a period of war, full of elements of progressive national life; and her statesmen doubtless already felt that, sooner or later, Ireland must become an English dependency. The greater and lesser countries were on a plane of civilisation and wealth completely different; should a conflict arise it was easy to perceive that if it were not made, in a short time, decisive, it might be protracted for many years, especially as the subjugation of Ireland required a real effort.

Henry VII sat on a tottering throne, long after he had been proclaimed king. His power in England was thwarted by plots and factions; in Ireland it was little more than a name. Gerald, the eighth Earl of Kildare, revered as the "Great," in the traditions of a race devoted to leaders of men, was Viceroy, and supreme at the Castle; but his authority in Ireland was very different from that of an ordinary governor of the Pale. He was connected by marriage with the chiefs of the O'Neills, and with the Butlers of Ormond, his feudal enemies; he had immense influence with the Desmonds of his blood, having saved them from an arbitrary act of attainder. Nature, too, had made him a remarkable man, abounding in wit, resource, and capacity; he could rule, with excellent results, in the interests of the Crown, if given a free hand to do as he pleased; but he was equally ready to conspire against it, if crossed in any of his ambitious purposes. Henry was compelled to negotiate with a most dangerous subject; and events soon showed what was the ascendency of Kildare, and what a shadow was English power in Ireland. The Earl, like all the Geraldines, was true to the House of York; he seems to have aspired to play the great part of a Warwick; he crowned the Pretender, Simnel, with his own hand; and he despatched from Ireland the force which was destroyed at Stoke. The threats and remonstrances of the king proved vain; and notwithstanding this act of flagrant rebellion, Kildare received a pardon, and was kept in his government. Ere long he took up the cause of Perkin Warbeck; and, meanwhile, the impotence of the state being more than ever manifest, the discords and troubles of Ireland continued to increase, and the ruin of the Pale seemed fearfully imminent. Henry was forced at last to take a decided course; he resolved to try to effect a thorough change in the system of government and administration that had so long prevailed in Ireland. Sir Edward Poynings, a member of that able official class, encouraged for centuries by the Plantagenets, and especially favoured by the Tudors, was placed at the head of affairs in Ireland, and charged to make a searching and complete reform. The subordinates who accompanied him—a significant fact—were soldiers, churchmen, and lawyers of English birth; the Anglo-Irish had been removed from the Castle.

CHAPTER III.

IRELAND, DURING THE TUDOR PERIOD, TO THE END OF THE REIGN OF HENRY VIII.

The government of Poynings an epoch in Irish History. The Parliament of Drogheda. The reforms it accomplished. "Poynings' Law," and its objects. Kildare placed again at the head of affairs in Ireland. Nature of his government. The Battle of Cnocktue. Character of the Earl. Splendour of the House of Kildare. Gerald, the ninth Earl, made Deputy. The policy of conquest and confiscation in Ireland rejected by the king. His plan for governing Ireland. Kildare, after a short interval of time, replaces Surrey as Deputy. He is imprisoned in the Tower, but made Deputy again in 1532. Danger of England in 1534. Kildare sent again to the Tower. The Rebellion of Silken Thomas. Danger of the Pale and of English power in Ireland. Siege and fall of the Castle of Maynooth. Collapse of the rebellion. Death of Earl Gerald. Execution of Silken Thomas and his uncles. Ruin of the House of Kildare. A child, Gerald, saved to restore the family. The Reformation in Ireland. State of the Church of the Pale and of the Celtic Church. Policy and measures of the king. The Parliament of 1536. The king made Head of the Church, and before long King instead of Lord of Ireland. Other reforms. Opposition. Attempts made by Anglo-Norman lords and Irish chiefs to rise. Battle of Bellahoe. Rapid decline of the insurrection. Progress of the English arms in Ireland. Henry carries out his scheme of Irish government. The Parliament of 1540-2. Success of the king's policy. Ireland at peace. Reflections.

THE Viceroys of Ireland had had the title of Lords Lieutenant, or were Deputies of these; there was scarcely any difference

between their functions; Poynings had the inferior rank of
Deputy. His government marks an era in Irish history,
though it was brief, transitory, and with few immediate effects.
A Parliament was convened at Drogheda, in the beginning of
1495; a long series of laws was passed, designed to curtail the
power of the great nobles, to provide for the defence of the
Pale against Celtic tribes, and to extend the influence of
English Law, and of the Tudor Monarchy. An opportunity
was found to attaint Kildare and some of his kinsmen; the
Earl, after a show of fruitless resistance, was made prisoner
and sent off to the Tower. At the same time, an attempt was
made to check the waste and rapine of coyne and livery, by sub-
stituting a kind of local tax, and to put an end to the excesses of
feudal lawlessness. The dominant Anglo-Norman Lords of the
Pale were forbidden to make war, or to "propose ordinances,"
without the consent of the Executive Government; they were
not to assemble their levies of armed retainers; their rude
war-cries were to be heard no more; their authority in towns
was greatly reduced; they were not to oppress the inferior
Baronage, and their vassals and dependents of English blood.
Precautions, too, were taken for the defence of the Pale; the
ditch was to be repaired and manned; the feudal militia was
to guard the marches; the practice of the long bow, beginning
to die out, was to be restored and vigorously maintained; and
the usages of the Irishry were not to exist in the Pale,
especially the eric, or the fine of blood, murder being made
subject to all the results of treason. The statute of Kilkenny,
besides, was revised and confirmed, as had often been the
case in the preceding century. This famous law was enacted in
1367, under the Viceroyalty of Lionel Duke of Clarence, and
formed a code of peculiar stringency, intended to keep the
Englishry and the Irishry completely apart. It treated the
Pale as a separate region, continually exposed to the attacks
of enemies, and always to be kept in a state of defence; it

prohibited intermarriage between the two races, the extension of the Brehon Law and of Irish customs within the precincts of the English Land, and everything that tended to fuse together the Saxon and the Celt. It had, however, been long nearly a dead letter, effaced by influences it could not resist, though probably not altogether powerless; its revival, as before, was to be of little purpose.

This legislation of Poynings, and his administrative acts, resembled the policy of one of our great Viceroys, in the early days of British rule in India, whose aim was to restrain the misconduct and greed of the Company's chief officials, yet who thought only of the purely English settlements, and regarded the native races with distrust and aversion. The remaining laws of the Deputy's Parliament had, we have said, as their object to make English Law, and the power of the Crown, of greater effect in Ireland. The principal officers of the State, including the Judges, had previously, it would appear, held their places for life, and had been appointed, perhaps, by the Viceroys; they were now to hold strictly at the king's pleasure, a provision, which, within the limits of the Pale, gave a large increase to the Royal authority, and to the Council supreme at Windsor or Greenwich. Concurrently with this enactment, the whole body of law, which successive Parliaments had passed for England, was introduced into Ireland and given full effect; this sweeping change must have likewise tended, not only to improve the course of justice, and the security of property and private rights, but also to add to the power of the Monarchy, as far as this, for the present, extended. Yet these measures, far-reaching as they seemed, were of much less importance than another reform, especially known as "Poynings' Law," which had great and permanent results in Irish affairs, though this may not have been the design of its authors. The Viceroys of Ireland had, hitherto, convened Parliaments almost as they pleased; one Parliament had voted a crown to Simnel, another had perhaps declared him a traitor; and these assemblies, often irregularly convened, had been usually mere instruments of the men in power at the Castle, or of the great and tyrannical feudal nobles. Their legislation had thus been repeatedly inconsistent, harsh, and unwise; and it had been, in many instances, marked by oppression, and iniquity to the colonists of the Pale. It was, therefore, deemed advisable to secure the control, and even the initiative of making laws, to the Crown; and it was enacted, "that no Parliament should in future be holden in Ireland, till the king's lieutenant should certify to the king, under the great seal, the causes and considerations, and all such acts as it seems to them ought to be passed thereon, and such be affirmed by the king and his council, and his licence to hold a parliament be obtained." This provision, Hallam has justly remarked, "placed a bridle in the mouth of every Irish Parliament," for it made the king and his council the sole arbiters of what it was to attempt or accomplish; and possibly we may see the profound Tudor statecraft, in this effective, but indirect, stroke of policy. But the authority given to the Crown and its ministers, which assured the subjection of the Irish Parliament, and which, in subsequent times, was fiercely denounced, was certainly regarded, for many years, as a protection against Viceregal oppression and feudal excesses, within the borders of the Pale [1].

The rule of Poynings, however, was but for a moment; and parts of his work were to disappear with it, if parts were ultimately to prove enduring. The Deputy represented the "English interest"; the Anglo-Norman "interest" of the Pale resented an ascendency it had always hated, and what it deemed an attack on its rights; and throughout Ireland the thousands of Kildare's adherents, of both races, stirred in

[1] This is proved by the repeated requests of the Englishry of the Pale, in the sixteenth century, that Poynings' Law should not be suspended. See too the remarkable speech of Flood on this subject.

threatening wrath. Desmonds and even Ormonds joined in complaints, with chiefs of Celtic tribes in the North and the West; and Poynings, besides, had been unfortunate in a skirmish beyond the verge of the Pale. The story has often been told of the Earl's conduct, when summoned before Henry VII and his Council. "I will take your Highness as my advocate against these false knaves," he is said to have exclaimed, with adroit flattery; and he brazened out a charge, that he had burned the cathedral of Armagh, by adding, with ready wit, "that he only thought of burning the bishop," perhaps a prelate of questionable fame. The king answered the protest of the indignant Council that "all Ireland cannot govern this man," by retorting "this man then shall govern all Ireland"; and within a few days Poynings was recalled, and Kildare, restored to his lands and honours, was made chief ruler of Ireland again, the attainted traitor, too, having become a kinsman of the House of Tudor, by a great English marriage. Whether true or not, the tale proves how weak and vacillating, as regards the affairs of Ireland, was English policy at this period; but probably it represents the king as more fickle and pusillanimous than he really was. He seems to have been menaced by an armed Irish rising, more formidable than had occurred for years; he was entangled in difficult disputes with Scotland; and the power of the O'Neills, kinsmen and allies of Kildare, was, perhaps, required to keep down the Scottish settlers, who had established themselves on the coast of Ulster, and who, apparently, were sometimes harrying the Pale. It deserves notice that, just at this time, Henry invoked the aid of Alexander VI to restore order and peace in Ireland, through a Commission of which the heads were the chief English bishops.

The return of Kildare to power restored the ascendency of his House, and of Anglo-Norman rule, and caused the defeat in Ireland of the "English interest." The Earl, however, upheld most of the reforms of Poynings, and proved himself to be a very able governor, and a loyal subject of the Tudor monarchy. His immense influence in Ireland continued to grow, through the authority with the great nobles, and the supremacy over the Celtic chiefs, which he owed, in part at least, to his high qualities; he exercised it with conspicuous skill and success. He repelled, with his Desmond kindred, an attempt made by Perkin Warbeck to attack Cork; carried the arms of the Crown far beyond the Pale, in "hostings" against the "Irish enemy"; and yet commanded the reverence of many an Irish chief, even besides those allied to his House, for power always has a fascination for the Celt. The most remarkable of these exploits was his victory over the Celts of Connaught, led by one of "the degenerate De Burghs"; they perished in thousands on the field of Cnocktue; this decisive triumph marked the turn in the tide which had set against the Englishry for a long space of time, and drew forth a savage exclamation from one of the nobles of the Pale, significant of their sense of the humiliations of the past. Kildare, too, seems to have been an upright ruler of the land, of which he was all but the sovereign; he received the Garter and gifts of lands from his grateful king, and a brief season of peace was seen in Ireland, during the later years of his reign as governor.

The great House of Kildare, indeed, at this time shone out with a lustre which made it prominent, even among the most noble Houses of England, and which mournfully contrasts with the darkness of its fall. Gerald was a patron of art and science; he felt the intellectual movement of his age; the learned student, the canvas fresh from Italian hands, the library filled with goodly volumes, were seen in his stately castles amidst the throng of his men-at-arms and Celtic kerne, and among the minstrels and bards of chiefs of the Irishry. At Maynooth, at Glyn, at Dingle, at Youghal, from the verge of the Pale to the far plains of Kerry, the glory of the

Renaissance was not wanting in his halls, and in those of his Desmond cousins; it blended with the pomp and circumstance of feudal grandeur and war, and with whatever remained of the poetry and art of the native Irish race. Ariosto recorded, in graceful verse, what the Geraldines were in this day of their renown[1]; and the Ghirardini, beside the Arno, rejoiced to learn, from the Great Earl himself, how mighty was their name, in a far island of the West[2].

The Great Earl was slain in 1513, in a skirmish with one of the chiefs of Offaley. The chronicles of both the races in Ireland agree in describing him as a most remarkable man; he had ruled the country, too, for nearly the third of a century. He was succeeded as Deputy by his son Gerald, called also the "Great" in Celtic annals; but, if a gallant warrior, and not devoid of parts, apparently without his father's resource, not skilled in reading the signs of the times, and destined to a most unhappy fate. The Earl trode, for some years, in his predecessor's footsteps; crushed Irish risings beyond the Pale; extended the now advancing power of the Englishry; and, save that he was often at feud with his Ormond kindred, maintained the ascendency of his House unchallenged. By this time Henry VII had died, and his son Henry VIII had ascended the throne; but England was still being dragged in the wake of Spain; the young King was involved in wars with France; and, as had happened over and over again, the affairs of Ireland attracted little attention. The fortune of the House of

---

[1] See the *Orlando Furioso*, Canto X. Stanzas 87–8:
   "Sono due squadre, e il conte di Childera
   Mena la prima; e il conte di Desmonda
   Da fieri monti ha tratta la seconda.
   Nello stendardo, il primo ha un pino ardente;
   L' altro nel bianco una vermiglia banda."

[2] See the letter of the Earl in *The Earls of Kildare*, by the Duke of Leinster, p. 64.

Kildare seemed at its topmost height, when the Earl attended Henry to the Field of the Cloth of Gold, and, like his father, wedded a near relation of the King.

The change, meanwhile, which, for some years, had been passing over the English Monarchy, was beginning to produce its effects in Ireland. The dynasty of the Tudors had, by degrees, acquired stability, and was growing in strength; the power of feudalism was passing away, with the decline of the great nobles, in a new era; and Wolsey, the Richelieu of his day, was extending the influence of the Crown in every direction, and turning the government into a scarcely veiled despotism. It was impossible that these tendencies should not affect Ireland; and the condition of the island, where a still struggling colony with difficulty maintained the English name, and where feudal and Celtic chaos prevailed in the great tracts beyond the still narrow Pale, seemed to invite the presence of Royal authority, to subjugate, to civilise, and to enlarge the domain of order. The state papers of the time had begun to teem with accounts of the misrule of the Anglo-Norman lords, of the barbarism of the Celtic chiefs, and of the wretchedness of a community the prey of lawlessness and incessant wars; and numerous schemes had been proposed, especially by English observers on the spot, for reducing the country to complete subjection, and putting an end to disorder and anarchy, by making the power of the Crown absolute, and by colonisation following a thorough conquest. Under the influence, probably, of views of this kind, another turn occurred in the affairs of Ireland; Kildare, though apparently still in power, was removed from his government in 1520; and Lord Surrey, the son of the victor of Flodden, one of the most trusted of Henry's soldiers and statesmen, was placed in his stead, as Viceroy, with the fullest powers. The counsels of Surrey were in accord with the new policy just referred to; and stern and harsh as they certainly were, it is to be regretted,

Ireland during the Tudor period.

perhaps, that they were not followed, as we watch the subsequent course of Irish History. Surrey, full of the absolutist ideas of the time, was all for making the king supreme in Ireland, the uncontrolled master, in fact, of everything; and he advised that the country should be subdued once for all, and should be effectively colonised by English settlers, introduced in such numbers as to secure their ascendency. But he warned the king that the task would be long and difficult, owing to the extent of Ireland, and the many obstacles the island presents to an invading enemy; to people it, too, with Englishmen, sent from a distance, across the sea, would be far from easy; and a considerable military force would be required. "This land," he wrote with just insight, "is five times as large as Wales, and when King Edward I set on hand to conquer the same, it cost him ten years ere he won it all, although for the most part he was present in his own person; and there is no sea between England and Wales. I fear therefore it cannot be so soon won as Wales was......6000 men is the least number you must occupy[1]."

This policy, however, singularly like the "Thorough" of Strafford in another age, much as it may have been approved by Wolsey, ran counter to the inclinations of the king, and was rejected by him through all the troubles of his reign. Henry VIII was a tyrant, in many of his acts; History sternly condemns his savage temper, and his selfishness almost without a parallel; but a Celt himself, to a certain extent, he had genuine sympathy with a Celtic race; and he had formed views on Ireland and Irish government, remarkable for their enlightened wisdom, the best, perhaps, considering the circumstances of the time, that were ever conceived by an English statesman. He turned a deaf ear to the argument of force, and refused to listen to plans for conquering Ireland with the

[1] State Papers. Carew I. 18. Surrey to Henry VIII. June 30, 1521.

sword, and for "planting" the whole country with English colonies. He wished, indeed, to be a real king in Ireland, and to make his kingship a good influence; to remove or to lessen the ills that afflicted the people; to promote order and the authority of law; in his own words, "to heal the great decay of that fertile land for lack of politic governance and good justice"; and he had a scheme of his own to attain these objects. His idea was to make the power of the Crown felt everywhere, alike by the Anglo-Norman nobles, and by the all but independent chiefs of the Irishry, but to accomplish this by kindness, not by the strong hand; and, with this end in view, he desired to confer honours on them, to bind them to the Crown by the tie of gratitude, and through them to rule the whole Irish community. The Monarchy would thus be supreme in Ireland; it would gradually bring good government and peace with it; but it would rest on an aristocracy of Irish origin; and without violent or dangerous change, it would make its benefits felt through all ranks of the people. It is remarkable, too, that Henry perceived that the law of the Anglo-Saxon was ill fitted to win the sympathy of a Celtic race; and he sought to respect the Celtic usages in his project for governing Ireland as a whole. "Show unto the Irish lords," he wrote to Surrey, "that it is requisite that every reasonable creature be governed by a law.......But if they allege that our laws be too extreme and rigorous......ye may ensearch of them, under what manners, and by what laws, they will be ordered and governed, to the intent that if their laws be good and reasonable, they may be approved[1]."

Henry, we shall see, did not renounce this policy, though events told strongly against it afterwards. Surrey was recalled from Ireland to conduct a campaign in France; and Kildare, after a brief interval of time—he had become an object of suspicion to the king—was restored to his estate as Deputy.

[1] State Papers II. 52, 53. Froude's *History* II. 263.

Years passed, in which Wolsey and his master were engaged in vast designs of conquest abroad, in trying to hold the balance between France and the Empire, in keeping down the power of the House of Commons; Ireland once more almost passed out of sight. Kildare continued to rule as before; but he was jealously watched by his Ormond enemies—his sister, the "Great Countess," was the chief of these—and complaints were repeatedly made of his conduct. Long impunity, however, made him incautious; he wrecked the Pale with the old exactions of his House, levying "coyne and livery" in defiance of the law; he married two of his daughters to Irish chiefs, O'Connor and O'Carroll, whose tribes had been for ages a thorn in the side of the Englishry, for their territories lay on the verge of the Pale; and he was looked up to as their suzerain by the Celtic clans and septs, from the ranges of Ulster to the far hills of Kerry. He was accused, too, of dabbling in treason, and of treating with Francis I and Charles V, when at war with England, through his Desmond kindred; and in 1527 he was imprisoned in the Tower. Wolsey scornfully denounced him, "as King Kildare, who reigned rather than ruled in Ireland"; but he was ere long set free, and allowed to return to Ireland, his connexion with the Tudors standing him, perhaps, in stead. He had soon thrust aside a Deputy, Skeffington, who had been set as a kind of watch on his acts; and in 1532 he was again at the head of affairs in Ireland, as Deputy of the king's natural son, the young Duke of Richmond.

The triumph of the Earl, it appears, impelled him into most dangerous and unwise courses. He dismissed the Archbishop of Dublin from his place as Chancellor; kept the Council at the Castle in a state of terror; interfered with the judges in the administration of the law; ruled, in a word, as his fathers had ruled in a different age. He also carried fire and sword through the lands of the Butlers, at this moment powerful at

Court, from their relationship with the rising star, Anne Boleyn[1]; and he was charged with encouraging chiefs of the Irishry to make inroads upon the borders of the Pale. All this, however, might have gone for nothing, had he not at a most critical juncture been suspected, at least, of fresh acts of treason. By this time the divorce of Catherine had caused the sudden disgrace of Wolsey; the Church in England was being severed from Rome; and Henry, backed by the mass of the nation, but opposed by many of the nobility, and nine-tenths of the clergy, was threatened by Charles V and Clement VII. The air in England was thick with sinister rumours; it seemed not improbable that risings at home might find support from enemies abroad. Kildare corresponded, perhaps, with the Emperor, through the Desmonds, as may have been the case before; the time for trifling and hesitation had passed; in 1534 he was once more a prisoner in the Tower. He seems to have had a foreboding that evil days were at hand; he appointed Thomas, his eldest son, to act as his Vice-deputy; he certainly removed the artillery of Dublin Castle to Maynooth and other fortresses of his own; and possibly he hoped that rebellion would come to his aid[2].

Lord Thomas Fitzgerald was a mere youth, not without parts, but hot-headed and rash; a report that "his father had been cut shorter, as his issue should bee," sent him on the path that led to the ruin of his House. Despising the warnings of the chief Geraldines, he lent an ear to the counsels of his leading Celtic kinsmen; and "assurying himselfe that the

---

[1] Margaret, the daughter of Thomas, seventh Earl of Ormond, married Sir William Boleyn, and was the grandmother of the future Queen Anne. Her son Sir Thomas Boleyn became Earl of Ormond; the head of the Butlers, Pierce, accepting the lesser title of Earl of Ossory.

[2] The act of attainder of Kildare is the principal, almost the only, evidence of his conduct; a judicious enquirer will not rely too confidently on a Tudor act of attainder.

knot of all Ireland was twisted under his girdle," he rushed madly into a war with England. He rode through Dublin at the head of a band of retainers; flung the sword of state on the table of the amazed Council, and having denounced the King in impassioned language, declared that "he would meet him in the field, not serve him in office." Celtic harpers greeted him as "Silken Thomas"—a badge of silk was on the helmets of his men—and bade him "not to tarry any more"; he strode wildly forth to assemble his forces. He was soon the leader of a motley array, chiefly of Celtic Kerne from the borders of the Pale; and he urged the heads of the Butlers to take up arms, "offering to divide the realme of Ireland with them." He had ere long sent envoys to the Pope and to Charles V; the hour had come "to punish Henry for his heresy, lechery, and tyranny."

Foreign aid, however, as was seen afterwards, proved a light of false hope to Irish rebellion; no armament from abroad was sent to Fitzgerald. The Butlers, too, scorned the offers of their foe; the Geraldines of Munster kept aloof; the rising, in the main, was a Celtic raid sustained by the retainers of Kildare in the Pale. Yet the dominion of England was for some months in peril, so precarious even now was her hold upon Ireland. Dublin had been wasted by a destructive plague; the citizens, weakened and disheartened, agreed to open their gates to Silken Thomas; and though afterwards they plucked up courage to resist, the Castle was besieged by a large rebel force, and, being without ordnance, was in grave danger. Meanwhile the Archbishop, who had been deprived of the seals, was murdered in an attempt to escape; Fitzgerald closed the capital by his sails in the Bay; and the habitations of the loyal settlers of the Pale were ravaged by plundering swarms of banditti. An armed force was despatched from England; but its march across the Welsh mountains was slow; it was retarded by contrary winds for weeks; and its commander, Skeffington, the late Deputy, hesitated, for some time, to try to retake Dublin. Soon after its landing Fitzgerald attacked and cut off one of its detachments; the troops were unable to prevent the destruction of Trim, the chief town of Meath, and of the large village of Dunboyne. Skeffington, too, fell ill, and, during a whole winter, the English army simply did nothing. But for the energy of the Butlers, the Pale might have been lost, and a new conquest of Ireland have been made necessary. These feudal enemies of Kildare, however, invaded his lands, and wrecked his castles; they compelled Lord Thomas to raise the siege of Dublin; in a word they held him in check by a predatory war.

Skeffington was, at last, on foot, in the spring of 1535. The object of his attack was the Castle of Maynooth, a great stronghold from which the Geraldines had often issued with their feudal arrays to overrun the Pale, and the Land of the Celt. The fortress had always been deemed impregnable; but the Tudors had made their artillery a formidable arm; and a breach was made ere long in the external defences. It is uncertain whether the place yielded to treachery, at last, or to fair fighting; but the garrison was, to a man, butchered; and the Irish Annals have bitterly denounced the "Pardon of Maynooth." The victors exacted a savage vengeance from Geraldine retainers who fell into their hands; the territories of the Kildares became the spoil of their swords; and in a few weeks the rebellion collapsed. Lord Thomas, who had retreated beyond the Shannon, in the hope of stirring up the Celts of Connaught, found himself deserted by his late allies; the chiefs, who had thronged to his standards, forsook him and fled, carried away by panic or the fickleness of the Celt; characteristically they betrayed and turned against each other, when the Englishry had made their power felt. The unfortunate youth surrendered to Lord Leonard Grey—the brother-in-law of his father—who had replaced Skeffington, at least in the command of the army; and "the words of comfort" he confessedly "spoke" were, perhaps, a promise that his prisoner's life was to be spared. Earl Gerald had ended his days, a few months before, in the Tower.

The conduct of Henry, at this juncture, was singularly characteristic of the man. The weakness of the Irishry had been made manifest; the king, in a sudden fit of wrath, took counsel whether the whole of Ireland could not be confiscated and made the prize of the Crown. He gave up, however, this extreme purpose, and had soon returned to the wise policy, which really he had never abandoned. But he laid a heavy hand on rebellion; he was embarrassed by Lord Leonard Grey's language, but Silken Thomas was sent before long to the block; five of his uncles perished by the same sentence, two, apparently, without any proof of guilt; and the House of Kildare was struck down by a sweeping attainder. A child, afterwards Gerald, the eleventh Earl, was the only scion left of the ancient family which had overshadowed Ireland with its power; his safety was due to a mere accident. His kinswoman Mary[1], wife of Brian O'Connor, chief of the greatest tribe on the edge of the Pale, carried him into the difficult wilds of Offaley; the act of pious care still lives in Celtic tradition.

An invasion made by Grey—he had become Deputy—into the territories of the Desmonds, and beyond the Shannon, marked the final close of the great rising of 1534. Meanwhile events in England had widened the breach between the Tudor Monarchy and Rome; the Reformation had begun in a complete change in the ecclesiastical order which had prevailed for centuries. Henry VIII had declared himself supreme Head of the Church; the Episcopate had been made

---

[1] Daughter of Gerald the ninth Earl, aunt of the eleventh, and half-sister of Surrey's fair Geraldine. *The Earls of Kildare*, pp. 121, 125.

an instrument of the Crown; the Religious Houses were being swept away; and Thomas Cromwell, with a ruthless but steady hand, was effectually crushing resistance down. That a corresponding revolution should take place in Ireland was accepted as a matter of course; the example of the greater country should be followed by the less; Henry turned his attention to the twofold Irish Church. This institution had been, in some respects, modified during the course of the preceding century and a half. The Church of the Pale had extended its bounds so far as regards the heads of the clergy; more sees than of old were filled by Englishmen, for the Lancastrian kings and Henry VII had courted the Popes; and this was the case, too, with the best benefices. On the other hand, the Irish chiefs seem to have altogether lost their authority over the ancient Celtic Church; the Popes nominated some of the Bishops; it was crowded by a priesthood dependent on Rome, in defiance of celebrated English statutes; it was putting off its native complexion, and gradually becoming more and more Papal. The long standing feud between the two Churches remained, however, as bitter as before; the Church of the Englishry was to the Church of the Irishry, what the Jew was to the despised Samaritan; each embodied the discord of separate races.

Meanwhile the corruption of the fifteenth century had deeply affected both Churches; low as had been the state of their spiritual life, this seems to have become even lower than before. Religious houses and buildings, indeed, multiplied; the land was strown with edifices, in too many instances emblems of superstition subdued by priestcraft. But if contemporaneous evidence speaks truth, crime, profligacy, indolence, neglect of duty prevailed, far and near, in the two communions; the light within them had become darkness. Several dignitaries of the Church of the Pale were at least charged with atrocious deeds; an archdeacon was hanged for murder in 1525[1]; and Bishops of the Celtic Church were described as men of blood and violence. Simony and waste ran riot in many sees; hundreds of churches, it was asserted, lay in ruins; whole dioceses were left without a due supply of ministers. Some monasteries, as in England, did good work in teaching; the great majority, it has been written, abounded in sloth, incontinence, and all kinds of vices. The worst abuses were, perhaps, found where the influence of the distant Pontiffs was strongest; the "Bishops of Rome"— exaggerated as may have been the language—were denounced, "for having preferred to the administration and governance of many parishes, vile and vicious persons, unlearned, being murderers, thieves, and of detestable dispositions[2]." As of old, however, intellectual torpor was perhaps the most striking feature of either Church. England had had a crowd of distinguished churchmen, even during the evil days of the fifteenth century. Wolsey, the foremost statesman of his time, made the diffusion of education his special care; Warham, Fisher, and others were eminent Prelates. But in the age of Erasmus, of Colet, of More, the Church of the Pale and the Celtic Church remained in Ireland in outer darkness; the movement of the Renaissance had scarcely any influence on an ill-informed and superstitious priesthood, not a single ecclesiastic made a conspicuous mark in Theology, Science, or the New Learning. The laity, for the most part, were in the same state of ignorance; "Lollardry" had been scarcely heard of, even in the Pale; it was wholly unknown in the land of the Celt. The community had hardly felt the rays of the day-spring already high in the heavens.

The attempt to reform the Irish Churches followed the precedents that had been set in England, and was conducted upon the English model. The chief instrument employed by

[1] *The Earls of Kildare*, p. 97.
[2] Carew Papers, 31 May, 1534.

Henry and Cromwell was an Englishman, Browne, Archbishop of Dublin, who simply endeavoured to obey his masters. A Parliament was assembled in 1536; and, imitating what had been done at Westminster, it declared the King the Head of the Church in Ireland; cut off that Church from dependence on Rome; made the Irish Bishops satellites of the Crown; and began the dissolution of religious houses. A subsequent Parliament made this spoliation complete: monasteries and nunneries were blotted out by scores, and deprived of their broad lands and possessions; and a change was effected besides, that must have appeared significant. The Kings of England had been Lords of Ireland only, holding the land, under the old bull of Adrian, as vassals, in theory, of the Holy See; this fiction was, once for all, abolished; and Henry assumed the title of King of the island. Reforms in doctrine and ritual were not made; but, exactly as had been the case in England, "idols" were thrown down, "shrines" of peculiar sanctity, and "Holy Roods," especially hallowed by Rome. The jurisdiction of the bishops was somewhat enlarged, no doubt to increase the Royal authority; and a singular effort was made to extend English influence, by securing to "Englishmen" the best preferments, and by the establishment of "English" schools apparently within the limits of the Pale.

Reforms like these, mere experiments of foreign power thrust upon a community that could hardly heed them, must obviously have had but little effect. They were probably carried out in the Church of the Pale only, and were scarcely heard of in the Church of the Celt, still beyond the bounds of the Land of the Englishry. They caused, however, some disorder and trouble in the Pale; Browne was denounced by Cromer, the Primate of Armagh; and there were bickerings between Anglo-Norman Lords, for the most part blindly devoted to Rome, and the administration of the Castle on the spot. But there was no Pilgrimage of Grace in Ireland, no deaths of Catholic or Protestant martyrs, no scenes like the murder of the Carthusian monks, no mighty upheaval of social forces, such as marked the Reformation in its course in England. Religion, ultimately to be the occasion of appalling woes, did not as yet really disturb the Irish community; even the suppression of the religious houses seems not to have called out a word of protest. The agitation, however, such as it was, in the Pale, quickened a movement of a more formidable kind, which for some time had been on foot in Ireland, and came, to a certain extent, to its aid. The severity shown by Henry to the House of Kildare, the conviction, as it was said, "that the King would never rest, until he had had the blood of the Geraldine race," had exasperated and alarmed the still powerful kinsmen of a family, but yesterday almost supreme in Ireland; and these began to contemplate another rising. Conn, chief of the warlike tribe of the O'Neills, a descendant of the royal Hy-Niall line, and nearly allied in blood to the Earls of Kildare, was the master spirit of this new league; but Desmond and the Geraldines of Munster concurred; and they were joined by other chiefs of the Celts of the South, and by Brian the head, as we have said, of the Celts of Offaley, all connected with the great fallen House. Preparations were made to attack the Englishry; arms were collected, and clans mustered; and the late reforms in the Church, and what had followed from them, were employed to give the movement a religious aspect, and to invoke foreign assistance for it. Paul III and Charles V were adjured to support a Holy War in Ireland, with a heretic king; and the Pope certainly seemed to lend an ear to these prayers.

The rising, however, menacing as it appeared, though it broke out in places, quickly came to nothing. The preservation of the young heir of the Kildares was, probably, a main object of the league; after hair-breadth escapes, and long wanderings from Offaley, into the Desmond lands, the child, like the Charles Edward of another day, was loyally passed on from clan to clan, as devoted to the Geraldine name, as to the chiefs of their own race; and he made at last his way into France, still pursued by Henry's vindictive hate. Charles V, too, held in check by Francis I, and even inclining to an alliance with England, had no thought of giving aid to Irish rebels; Paul III was powerless without the emperor. The intended insurrection never came to a head; O'Neill, indeed, made a bold attempt to march southward, and join Desmond; but he was defeated at Bellahoe, on the edge of the Pale; and the Holy War ended in a few petty raids. Grey advanced, for the second time, into the depths of the country; the march of his troops was more impeded by the difficulties of almost impenetrable tracts, of woods, morasses, and wild hill ranges, than by enemies worthy of the name; and though the subduing of those obstacles took many months, his progress met scarcely any other resistance. Desmond and his Anglo-Norman and Celtic dependents sent in their submissions throughout Munster; and their example was followed by the Irish chiefs who had taken part in the late conspiracy. The Deputy treated all with praiseworthy clemency, and Henry appears to have approved of this conduct. But Grey was a near kinsman of the House of Kildare; its boyish head had contrived to escape; this, and a quarrel with the men in power at the Castle, was probably the cause of his ill-explained fall. He was denounced by the Butlers, as a friend of the Geraldines, and met the doom of a traitor a few weeks afterwards, one of the darkest acts of a sanguinary reign.

Ireland was, for the moment, almost in repose; Henry seized the occasion to give effect to the policy he had thought out for the country. Heads of the great Anglo-Norman families, and leading chiefs of the Celtic tribes, were invited to Court, to meet the king; and a real effort was made to bind them to the state, by the ties of self-interest, and of the sense of gratitude, and to govern Ireland by an aristocracy of this kind. Earldoms were conferred on O'Neill, the late rebel warrior, on O'Brien, chief of the Celts of Thomond, and on the head of the "degenerate De Burghs"; inferior peerages were created also; Desmond and other lords renewed their allegiance; and heralds proclaimed, in the style of their craft, that these "high and mighty persons had made due obeisance at Greenwich." Other means were adopted, besides, to make the leading men of the Anglo-Irish and Irish races attached to the Crown, and even loyal subjects. In many instances, nobles and chiefs had agreed with Grey, and even with previous deputies, to surrender their lands, and to take grants of them, to be held by the English feudal tenure; these arrangements were now generally carried out; and if they ran counter to Irish usage and law, and especially to the ancient mode of Tanist succession, they conferred advantages on the grantees, for they increased the power over their dependent vassals, which had been their object, perhaps for centuries. In addition Henry bestowed lands, of the lately abolished religious houses, on the new nobility he had created; and these men, good Catholics as they may have been, accepted eagerly spoils that seem to have been lavished wholesale. This policy, according to the fashion of the time, received legislative sanction, with due solemnity. A Parliament sat in Dublin, from 1540 to 1542; it was attended, for the first time in history, by prominent chiefs of the Irish race, as well as by Anglo-Norman lords, who had very seldom attended before; and apart from other enactments, dealing with reforms in the Church, all that had lately been done by the King was approved. A very important change, in harmony with Henry's Irish policy, and no doubt in compliance with his will, was, also, made in the administration of affairs in Ireland. By this time order had been restored within the Pale, owing probably to the fall of the House of Kildare; and the domain of English law, and the course of English justice, seem to have extended nearly as far as the shires made by John. Commissioners were now appointed to hold Courts in other and more distant parts of the island; and in exact accord with the ideas of the King, they were to take account of native Irish usages, and to deal with the Irishry, as with a people "not so perfectly acquainted with the laws, that they could at once live and be governed by them[1]."

The effects of this enlightened system of government were remarkable, and deserve attention. Sir Anthony St Leger, one of the best of deputies, carried out skilfully the King's policy; the success he achieved was great and decisive. The long distracted land was at rest for some years; signs of prosperity appeared, not only within the Pale, but in the half barbarous regions beyond. There was not a semblance of Irish disorder, even in the last troubled years of the reign of Henry; an Irish contingent appeared in the ranks of the English army that invaded France, in 1543-4, and captured Boulogne. There were elements certainly of future evil in the changes that had been made in the Church; but these were not as yet active; there was as yet little religious strife in Ireland. Law had more influence than it had had ever before; the newly appointed Commissioners had done excellent work; above all the Anglo-Norman lords and the Celtic chiefs, through whom Henry sought to make his government felt, were obedient, and seemed in a state of content. A state paper of the time describes Ireland in these remarkable words: "The winning of the Earl of Desmond was the winning of the rest of Munster with small charges. The making O'Brien an Earl made all that country obedient. The making of McWilliam Earl of Clanricarde, made all that country during his time, quiet, and obedient as it is now. The making of McGilpatrick Baron of

[1] Leland II. 180, 184 has described Henry's Irish policy better than any other modern historian.

Upper Ossory hath made his country obedient.......And the gentleness that my Lord Deputy doth devise among the people, with wisdom and indifference, doth profit and make sure the former civility, so as presidents in Munster, Connaught, and Ulster, by God's grace, make all Ireland, without great force, to be obedient[1]."

Not a few of the inveterate ills of Ireland appear in the period we have just surveyed. The weakness of English rule is seen in the vacillating conduct of Henry VII, and until after the end of the Kildare rebellion. The English and Irish "interests" were at feud, and prevented anything like a systematic policy up to the time of Lord Leonard Grey; this was to be visible again at subsequent periods. The enemies of England, as in the days of Bruce, saw that Ireland was her weakest point; this was to be recognised in succeeding centuries. The state of the Irish Churches had perhaps become worse; it had not been improved by Henry's reforms; the greatest part of the country was still almost half barbarous. But civilisation and all that it implies, owing in some degree to the measures of Poynings, but much more to recent events, had successfully laid hold of the Pale; we hear no more of coyne and livery, and feudal rapine; the settlement had been firmly established. The Ditch, and all that this meant, were things of the past; the power of the Crown, with good results, had extended far beyond the old borders. Much impression had not been yet made on the rude disorder of the Anglo-Norman land, and of the still far-spreading land of the Celt; these were still under a bad feudalism, and the domination of chiefs, who had destroyed much that was best in primitive Irish society. Something had been done, however, even in this respect; the judicious policy of Henry VIII was being attended with promising results. The aristocracy he had formed looked

---

[1] Carew Papers II. 246, 8 May, 1553.

up to the Crown; to a certain extent governed in its behalf; it was not impossible that it might become akin to the great nobles of England in the course of time. The Monarchy, in a word, had spread its arms far and wide; its influence had been distinctly beneficent; it had enlarged the limits of order and peace. Had this state of things been allowed to continue, Ireland might gradually have become a prosperous land; her history might not have been what it is, one of the most woeful in the annals of mankind.

CHAPTER IV.

IRELAND TO THE END OF THE REIGN OF ELIZABETH.

The Protestant Reformation of Edward VI in Ireland. Its effects superficial. Bellingham Deputy. Invasion of Leix and Offaley. The reign of Mary Tudor. Catholicism restored. Leix and Offaley conquered and colonised, and made the Queen's and King's Counties. Failure of the settlement. Elizabeth Queen. Her Irish policy at first like that of Henry VIII. The Parliament of 1560. The Anglican Reformation in Ireland. Its effects and prospective dangers. Beginning of troubles. Shane O'Neill. He is elected chief of his tribe. He defeats Sussex. He repairs to the Court of Elizabeth, and returns to Ireland. Treacherous policy pursued towards him. He assumes the title of the O'Neill and tries to subjugate Ulster. He is attacked by Sir Henry Sidney, and a league of Irish chiefs. His death and character. The Parliament of 1567-9. Attainder of Shane O'Neill. Act to make all Ireland shireland. Connaught divided into six counties. Disputes between the English and Irish interests. Opposition to interference with Poynings' Law. "Killings" of the Irishry in Leix and Offaley, and in Wicklow. Projects of colonisation in Ulster. Smith and Lord Essex. Sir Peter Carew. The rebellion of James Fitzmaurice of Desmond. Its causes. Attempt to stir up a Holy War in Ireland. The Desmond rebellion and how it began. Gregory XIII and Philip of Spain. Frightful guerilla war in Munster. The rising of Lord Baltinglass. Defeat of Lord Grey in Wicklow. Massacre of Spaniards and Italians at the fort near Smerwick. End of the Desmond rebellion. Death of the Earl. Confiscation of his possessions. The attempt to colonise them of little effect. Sir John Perrott Deputy. His character and beneficent government. Parliament of 1585-6. The settlement of Connaught. Sir William Fitzwilliam Deputy. His evil conduct. Hugh O'Neill, Earl of Tyrone. Causes that led to his rebellion. He becomes the O'Neill. His ability as a soldier. Battle of the Yellow Ford. Defeat of the English. O'Neill tries to form a great Irish league. He outwits Essex. Mountjoy Deputy. He overruns Ulster. Skilful resistance of O'Neill. Gradual advance of Mountjoy. Landing of a Spanish force at Kinsale. Defeat of O'Neill. He retains his lands and honours. State of Ireland at the death of Elizabeth. Reflections.

THERE were few signs in Ireland of the many troubles which convulsed England after the death of Henry VIII. There was no conflict between an old nobility and new men gorged with the spoil of Religious Houses; no strife of factions, like that which raged around the throne of a boyish king; no risings of injured peasants repressed, in whole counties, by a foreign soldiery; no fierce struggle between contending faiths, as Protestantism, by degrees, made its influence felt. But Somerset and Northumberland, backed by Edward VI, had tried to put Catholicism down in England; Catholic ritual and doctrine were abolished; the service of the Mass was replaced by a new Liturgy; the Breviary was turned into the Book of Common Prayer, published in the vulgar tongue, and open to all readers; the administration of the Eucharist was completely changed; and—most significant, perhaps, of all to the mass of the people—the churches were stripped of their costly ornaments. As in the preceding reign, it was deemed in the nature of things that this revolution should extend to Ireland, a mere dependency of the Crown of the Tudors. It was in vain that a wise man at the Castle declared that "things should be letten alone, as king Henry had ordered, otherwise hurly burlys would happen"; the new religious system was to be transferred to Ireland. Sir Anthony St Leger, it deserves notice—the ungracious duty had been devolved on him—did not attempt to assemble a Parliament, to carry out the will of the English Council of State; he simply issued a proclamation announcing the change. The Liturgy was read in English, in a few churches of the Pale; a certain number of Prelates concurred; one Bishop at least, a Protestant zealot, became a missionary of the reformed doctrines, renounced the solemn rite of the altar, and condemned his clergy as superstitious Papists; and, as had happened in England, relics, pictures, and images,—symbols of a faith that had been held for centuries—were removed, apparently, from many places of worship. Their removal aroused the passionate wrath of the congregations in more than one instance; it was occasionally accompanied by wrong and outrage. Attempts were made to retain the sacred emblems, when several churches were sacked and pillaged by English troops.

These changes, however, had little effect throughout the mass of the Irish community. There were disturbances, indeed, in the Catholic Pale; Dowdal, the successor of Cromer in the see of Armagh, and other bishops made angry protests; the brethren of suppressed monasteries stirred feebly, in different parts of the country, and began to form elements of troubles yet to come. But the Reformation had scarcely reached the land of the Irishry; apart from a few wild mob gatherings, the body of the people remained quiescent; the Anglo-Norman lords and the Celtic chiefs, contented with Henry's late policy, made no call on their vassals and clansmen. In truth, Ireland was too inert, too sunk in ignorance, too backward, too distant from the great movement of the age, to be violently agitated by the new doctrines, or by the innovations made by Somerset's Council. In other lands the revolution in faith and thought had shaken society to its innermost depths; the seamless garment had been rent asunder, and Christendom was tearing the shreds into pieces. There were wars and rumours of wars in five-sixths of the

Continent, a League of Smalkalde, a Battle of Mühlberg; Luther had aroused Germany, Calvin awakened France, Rome summoned, in self-defence, the Council of Trent; the armed advance of Protestantism was being confronted by the Catholic revival, and its quickly growing forces. In Ireland, ultimately doomed to a hideous strife of creeds, the mighty religious movement of the sixteenth century as yet exhibited itself mainly in insignificant wranglings and petty broils.

The reign of Edward VI in Ireland, however, was disturbed owing to a change in secular policy. The Irish tribes of O'Moore and O'Connor held the great region of Leix and Offaley, extending to the borders of the Pale, and stretching thence, westwards, to the course of the Shannon. From this region, bounded on one side by broad hill ranges and on the other by the lakes of Westmeath, and fronted by woods, thickets, and the morass of Allen, armed clans had often invaded the seats of the Englishry, and had harried them up to the walls of Dublin. The chiefs had exacted the Black Rent for a long series of years; and Brian O'Connor, as we have seen, was not only a near kinsman of the House of Kildare, but had taken part in the late risings. He had, however, submitted, like the other lords and chiefs, and had perhaps been promised a peerage by Henry; and O'Moore certainly seems to have become completely reconciled to the king's policy. But Leix and Offaley formed a tempting spoil; this hostile Celtic land was a menace to the Pale; and the English Council resolved to abandon the system of Irish government, which had had such good results, and to extend its power, by arms, into this coveted tract. Sir Edward Bellingham, an able soldier, became Deputy in St Leger's stead; and little difficulty was found in charging the two chiefs with conspiring with France, then at war with England, and with meditating renewed "treasons." The English soldiery were soon hewing a path through the wilderness, which, at that time, spread from the banks of the

Barrow to the verge of Connaught; Bellingham, carefully selecting points of vantage, carried his arms as far as Athlone, on the Shannon; and forts were built in the midst of Leix and Offaley. O'Moore and O'Connor, it is said, were invited to England, and then treacherously thrown into prison.

"The rough handling of the Deputy makes all men despair," was the bitter exclamation of the great Earl of Desmond, loyal as yet to the faith he had pledged to the Crown; the invasion of Leix and Offaley certainly marked a new era in Irish history, the beginning of many disasters and woes. The accession, however, of Mary Tudor to the throne, for a moment arrested the march of conquest; Bellingham died, and was replaced by St Leger; the new Deputy was again directed to effect another great religious change. The transformation was what it had been twice before; Catholicism was set up, in Ireland, exactly as it was set up in England; the Mass was restored, and the old ritual; the churches were decked out with the old ornaments, so far as these had been saved from heretics; the people were absolved from the guilt of schism; and the supremacy of Rome in spiritual affairs was unanimously voted by a complaisant Parliament, amidst public and solemn thanksgivings. In Ireland, however, as in England, the lands of the Religious Houses were not given back; the Crown, too, retained considerable ecclesiastical power. It was with Catholicism, also, as it had been with Protestantism; the revolution in faith was not followed by any striking or memorable results. The zealous Protestant Bishop, indeed, disappeared; one or two of his brethren, perhaps, were deprived of their sees; but there was no violent religious conflict, no great stirring or shock of warring opinions. Ireland had still no martyrs of either of the contending faiths; the community remained undisturbed and passive. While persecution was raging in England, while

Huguenots were sent to the stake in France, while the marriage of Philip and Mary seemed to portend the speedy triumph of Rome, while Paul IV was preaching a Crusade, throughout Europe, on behalf of the Church, the shock of the great struggle hardly moved Ireland.

The restoration of the old faith and ritual scarcely retarded the advance of the power of the Englishry. The young Earl of Kildare had been allowed to visit England; through the influence of Reginald Pole he regained his lands and his honours. It was otherwise with the chiefs O'Moore and O'Connor; their territories had been marked down by the spoiler. O'Moore had died in his foreign prison; Brian O'Connor was sent back to his tribe; for his daughter, the Irish annals record, "had crossed the sea to fall at the feet of the Queen"; and "there were rejoicings in Leath Mogha[1], for it was thought, by all, that the O'Connors' Fally would never behold Erin again." But Thomas Radcliff, Lord Sussex, had been made Lord Lieutenant; the Irish Council were men of the "English interest"; and Surrey's schemes of conquest and colonisation were vigorously taken up. On pretexts of "rebellion," either flimsy or untrue[2], an English force was marched into Leix and Offaley; the lands of the chiefs and their tribes were declared forfeited; and Maryborough and Philipstown, the chief towns of the Queen's and King's counties, —two new shires created by these means—still commemorate one of the worst acts of this reign. Scores of colonists were poured into the conquered region; but, like other settlements, before and afterwards, this settlement proved a complete failure. The colonists were far too few in number; no arrangements were made to allot a reasonable share of the lands that had been seized to the despoiled Irishry;

---

[1] Leinster.
[2] See Leland, II. 221 and Carew State Papers, I. 262, February 25, 1557.

and the ultimate result was only to form a weak class of new possessors of the soil, hemmed in by the descendants of the injured chiefs, and of their devoted septs and clans, brooding on hopes of vengeance, and even yet to prove by no means contemptible foes.

The first years of Elizabeth's reign were peaceful in England and Ireland alike, a striking contrast with those she lived to witness. Her throne, indeed, seemed for a time in peril, owing to the league between France and Scotland, and to Catholic intrigues at home and abroad; but Philip steadily took her side; her authority was established after a few months. The policy of the queen was judicious and cautious; she put an end to a disastrous war with France; she withdrew from continental affairs; she thought of England, and its interests, as her main object. In Ireland something of the same kind was seen; Elizabeth retained the men in office; but she sought to return to the mode of government of which Henry VIII had set an example. She would not listen to the complaints of Sussex against Anglo-Norman lords and chiefs of the Irishry; she rejected his schemes of colonisation and conquest. She, indeed, sanctioned what had been done in Leix and Offaley; and she turned an eye towards Ulster, where the power of England was weaker than in other parts of the island, and where whole districts were ravaged by continual feuds between the O'Neills and other chiefs and the Scottish settlers. But it is remarkable that she wished to give back the O'Moores and O'Connors parts of their lands; even as regards Ulster, her chief thought was peace. This policy, doubtless, was in part due to the charges of recent Irish wars and conquests—she was thrifty in this as in all matters—but she seems at first to have had a real wish to try to rule Ireland, as her father had tried, through an aristocracy of Norman and Irish blood, formed by the Crown.

In England, meanwhile, another great change in ecclesiastical and religious affairs had been made. Elizabeth had wished to reestablish her father's system, that is, to secure the supremacy of the Crown in the Church, to do away with the jurisdiction of Rome, and yet to maintain, for the most part, the ancient faith; but the growing Protestantism of the nation proved too strong for her. The English Church was finally detached from the Holy See; its polity and doctrines were so arranged as to combine much of the work of Henry VIII with some of the reforms of Edward VI. As the pendulum had swung round in England, it was taken for granted that it was to swing round in Ireland; the new system was to be adopted in the lesser island. At a Parliament assembled in Dublin in 1560, the Catholicism which Mary Tudor had restored was declared unlawful, and a thing of the past, and Elizabethan Anglicanism was set in its stead. The supremacy of the Crown, in the Church, in Ireland, was asserted, as in the time of Henry VIII, if not in such offensive language; the jurisdiction of the Pope was no longer to exist; and the Mass and the old ritual were condemned by law, with the ornaments and other symbols of the old faith. The Protestantism of the Council of Somerset was to be accepted, also, as the national faith; the new Liturgy, the new Prayer Book, the new sacramental system, were introduced once more, with modifications of no great importance; and the services of the Church were to be performed in the English tongue, assumed to be the "vulgar" tongue by a monstrous fiction. The provisions for the extension of "English schools" were reenacted along with those that made "Englishmen" the possessors of the richest and best benefices; and a religious test was imposed, perhaps for the first time. The clergy were made to take an oath of supremacy; this was an obligation too on laymen in the service of the state, and even in the profession of the law; and attendance at the churches where the new faith was taught was enjoined, nominally at least, under different kinds of penalties.

The immediate effects of these fresh changes were, however, as before, not very great in Ireland. The Catholic Pale, indeed, seems to have been aroused; the Parliament was, for this reason, suddenly dissolved; and two of the Irish Prelates, at least, resigned their sees and refused to conform to what they considered unlawful heresy. But, as had happened already, and from the same causes, the revolution in the Church was not acutely or generally felt; it did not provoke any kind of rising; it probably did not extend far beyond the Pale; and the Irish community was not in the state in which it would move deeply the hearts of men. Yet it led to more discontent than had been the case before; and signs were not wanting that it might become a source, in the future, of many evils. The power of the Englishry was advancing rapidly, and was associated with the rule of the sword, and conquest; and the new Anglican system was that of the foreign invaders, and of the always detested Church of the Pale. The Irishry, on the other hand, were being gradually subdued; the old Celtic Church was turning towards Rome; its clergy, driven from their altars, in parts of the country, were becoming bitterly hostile to every English influence; and their authority was increasing, as that of the chiefs diminished. In circumstances such as these, should a strange religion, with its observances embodied in a strange tongue, follow the march of conquest, and be imposed on a subjugated and reluctant people, especially in a struggle of contending faiths, it is not difficult to foresee the results.

The comparative tranquillity of Ireland was now disturbed by a difficult and protracted contest, which placed strikingly on the stage of events one of the most remarkable figures in Irish history. Conn O'Neill, we have seen, had been ennobled by Henry VIII; he had been made Earl of Tyrone, with remainder to a son, of the name of Matthew, who had received the title of Baron of Dungannon, as his lawful heir. The

Earl, however, had another son, Shane, a conspicuous specimen of the genius of the Celt; and Shane had made a great name for himself, in raids against the Scots of the Ulster seaboard, and in feuds with the tribe of the O'Donnells of the North, the hereditary foes of the once royal O'Neills. He was a bitter enemy, too, of his brother Matthew, an ally, it appears, of the Englishry of the Pale; in one of many skirmishes Matthew was slain (1558); and, as we have said, these troubles had engaged the attention of the Queen and of her Irish Government. On the death of the Earl (1559), Shane was solemnly chosen by his clansmen chief of the great race of the O'Neills; the dignity recalling the ancient glories of the monarchs of the Hy-Niall line, and giving a suzerainty over all the clans of Ulster. This was a scornful rejection of the English earldom, and of the arrangement effected by Henry VIII; it was practically a defiance of English power; and, in the eyes of the men at the Castle, it was an act of rebellion, as marked and heinous as the expulsion of an English Resident, by a vassal Prince in India, would appear at Calcutta at the present day. Sir Henry Sidney, Deputy, for the time, for Sussex, remonstrated with the lately elected chief; but Shane, as the state papers acknowledge, had, by many degrees, the best of the argument. His brother Matthew was probably not legitimate; and his tribe had never renounced their right to proclaim a chief according to old Celtic usage.

A series of negotiations followed: Elizabeth, clinging to her father's policy, convinced, perhaps, that her Irish Council were in the wrong, attempted to patch matters up with Shane, who, in turn, adroitly maintained his position. The Queen, however, yielding at last to Sussex, the unscrupulous advocate of extreme measures, consented (1560) to make war on "the Irish rebel"; Shane was attacked by Sussex advancing from the Pale, and by the Scots, and the O'Donnells lying on his rear. But the chief had the inspiration of a true soldier; he turned against the foes nearest at hand, contrived to separate the O'Donnells from the Scots, and then completely defeated Sussex, apparently an incapable man in the field. The infuriated Lord Lieutenant had recourse to the deceptions and crimes, which have left a deep stain on English policy in its dealings with Shane; he did not hesitate to plot his enemy's murder. Shane, however, who seems to have thought the Queen his friend, virtually offered to make her arbiter of his cause; he repaired (1562), in Celtic state, to the Court of Elizabeth, as an Eastern Prince does to that of Victoria. His Irish accent, his strange attire, the aspect of his rude noblesse and kerne, provoked merriment and contempt at first; but the chief was more than a match for the scoffers. Elizabeth, and even Cecil, thought the occasion a fitting one to lay a trap for Shane; he was to be detained in England, perhaps not to depart with his life. But Shane, with the peculiar skill of the Celt, flattered the Virgin Tudor to the top of her bent, and seems to have really changed her purpose; the death of the son of the late Baron Matthew had given a new complexion to affairs; and Shane was permitted to return to Ireland. He had agreed to an arrangement, which would have made him a mere vassal of the English Government, and have combined the Irishry of the North against him. He went back to his country with a fixed resolve to disregard a compact imposed by force.

When his foot was once more on his native heath, the chief boldly threw off the mask. He had kept his eyes and ears open at the Court of the Queen; he had learned that Mary Stuart was already at the head of a conspiracy to win the throne of England, supported by English Catholic nobles, and by her kinsmen of the House of Guise; he had been in correspondence with the ambassador of Spain; he knew that the forces of Sussex had been lately reduced. He attacked (1563) the O'Donnells and other chiefs, his foes; swept Ulster with his kerne, from Lough Neagh to Lough Foyle; fell on an English garrison at

Armagh; and even threatened a descent on the Pale. The Lord Lieutenant marched against him in vain; the English troops were unpaid and mutinous; Shane's Geraldine cousin, the Earl of Kildare, held back from an enterprise he disliked; and Sussex retreated, ashamed and discomfited. Treachery was attempted again when force had failed; a device was tried to lure the Irish chief to Dublin; Sussex wrote that his sister would perhaps give him her hand; before long poison was laid for him, a crime tacitly approved by the Irish Government. Shane, however, saw through, or baffled these wicked expedients; parleys and negotiations were again set on foot; and Elizabeth, at last, had recourse to the policy, which, in the case of the great Earl of Kildare, had been adopted by Henry VII. An amnesty for the past was promised; and Shane, with reservations little more than nominal, was allowed to retain his title as chief of the O'Neills, involving the suzerainty of Ulster at least, and perhaps the ancient claims of the Hy-Niall monarchs (Nov. 1563). The dangers, which had begun to surround her at home and abroad, doubtless, forced the Queen to make this immense concession.

The conduct of Shane, up to this time, had shown intelligence and powers of a very high order. The chief, however, had ere long given proof of the fancifulness, and the inability of Celtic nature to see things as they really are, vividly portrayed in Shakspeare's Owen Glendower. Shane openly defied the power of England; erected a fortress near the verge of the Pale, significantly called "the Englishman's hate"; held up the Council at the Castle to scorn and ridicule; laughed at English titles conferred by Elizabeth; and ravaged more than one outlying English settlement. At the same time (1565) he made a determined effort to subjugate Ulster, and even a part of Connaught—almost an act of madness as affairs stood; he tried to crush the O'Donnells, and all the chiefs of the North; his rude forces were seen in the lands of the De Burghs; he lorded it over the Irishry from the Bann to the Shannon. Yet, to do him justice, he ruled his own tribe with wisdom and talents admired even by his enemies; he was not only, they admitted, the "one strong man in Ireland," but a "Prince" who knew how to make himself "loved and obeyed." At last Shane was heard to boast that "Ulster was his own"; that "he was the O'Neill and would hold what he had won"; and the dream seems to have crossed his mind that he would yet revive the Hy-Niall kingship, the sovereign of an Ireland freed from the stranger. A conflict had become inevitable with the power he had provoked; but Sidney had been set in the place of Sussex; he was an adversary of a very different quality. The Deputy assembled a considerable force; sent a detachment to fall on Shane's rear from Derry; and easily persuaded the chiefs of the North and the West to form a league against their dreaded tyrant. Shane, however, was not unequal to himself; he sent messengers to the rulers of France, and to Scottish nobles hostile to England; he made an appeal to his Geraldine kinsmen; he mustered the warriors of his devoted tribe; and nerved himself for a desperate effort. But no friendly succours came from abroad; the Desmonds of Munster were afraid to stir; Sidney advanced steadily, like Bellingham taking possession of important points of vantage; and the territories of the chief were savagely harried. Meanwhile the English had marched from Derry; and the Irish auxiliaries gathered in from all parts of Ulster. Shane and his faithful clansmen stood bravely at bay; but he was struck down in a decisive battle, in which the O'Donnells and other Celtic chiefs joined the Englishry against the son of their ancient kings, as Indian Princes fought against Hyder and Tippoo. The chief took refuge in the camp of the Scots of Ulster; he was ignominiously slain in a drunken brawl; the deed was perhaps instigated by one of Sidney's officers (1567).

Shane O'Neill stands forth, in striking relief, through the

dismal tragedy of Irish history. We know nothing of him save from his enemies; these, indeed, have acknowledged his great parts; but they have covered him with the most foul obloquy. An impartial judgment on the singular career of this remarkable personage will be very different. He was a man of lust, but his was the century of Henry VIII, and of Henry of Navarre; he was a man of blood, but more free from its stain than scores of the foremost men of his age; if he broke faith, his was not the infamous guile of soldiers and statesmen who planned his murder. He possessed, in the very highest degree, the excellences and defects of the genuine Celt; his veins were full of Geraldine blood, but he was a great Irishman in his essential character. He certainly was a distinguished leader in war; he ably governed clansmen who died for him; he was adroit and skilful in trying crises; he outwitted and baffled Elizabethan councils; like others of his line he wished to unite the Irishry against the foreign invader. But he was a Celt, who lived in the past, and whose imagination could not confront realities; it was insanity to think of the days of his fathers; to challenge England to deadly strife; above all to try to destroy the very men, in whom he might, otherwise, have found auxiliaries. Yet the most remarkable feature in this passage of history is the attitude and conduct of nearly all the chiefs of Ulster. They had been cruelly wronged by Shane; some had been for years his inveterate foes. But they must have perceived the advance of the English conquerors; they might have foreseen that the ruin of Shane would in the long run probably be followed by their own. Yet they joined Sidney to destroy a great man of their race; for the idea of nationality did not exist in them; they could not look beyond their septs and their clans; they were still slaves of mere tribal discord.

The attainder of Shane O'Neill quickly followed his defeat; the "rebel's head, bodied with a stake, stood on the top of Her Majesty's Castle." Tirlogh Lenagh, a kinsman of the defeated chief, was placed in possession of parts of his lands, as Mir Jaffir succeeded to Surajah Dowlah; he was to be a mere puppet of the Irish Government. A Parliament was convened in 1567—8; some of its enactments were significant in the extreme of the growing expansion of English power in Ireland. The whole country was to be made shire-land; Connaught was divided into six counties, including Clare and part of Munster; the assumption of the title or the authority of a chief, in any tract made shire-land, was declared criminal. A considerable administrative change, meanwhile, had taken place in the remoter parts of the island. Commissioners, we have said, had been chosen by Henry VIII to do justice in regions beyond the Pale, in some measure in accordance with Irish usage; and the experiment had had considerable success. This system was not formally altered; but, as the march of conquest progressed, the Commissioners were invested with military power, were always attended by a large armed force, and became known by the name of Presidents. There were now two, one for Munster, and one for Connaught; they went circuit and administered justice; but their chief mission was to keep the Irishry down. In Roman phrase, they had become Proconsuls, rather than Prætors; they were men of the sword, much more than of law. It deserves notice that this Parliament was less submissive than its predecessors had been, perhaps because it was stronger and more numerous. Sidney tried to suspend the celebrated Law of Poynings, which gave the initiative in legislation to the Crown, and to impose measures of his own on the Parliament; but a steady resistance ended in a compromise; and there was another conflict between "the English interest," long supreme, and the Anglo-Irish of the Pale.

Parts of Ireland ere long became scenes of barbarities to be deplored by History. The military force in Dublin was small; the Englishry were on the path of conquest, with spoliation following in its train; the power of the Irishry, and even of the Anglo-Irish nobles, had been, to a considerable extent, broken. Chiefs of the scattered tribes of Leix and Offaley were, it is said, decoyed, with hundreds of clansmen, by Sidney to death, and massacred through an act of the blackest treachery[1]. The clans of O'Byrne and O'Toole, which had often made raids on the capital from the wild hills of Wicklow, were hunted down and slaughtered by little bands of soldiers with citizens of Dublin in their wake; "the general killings of the Irishry" became a phrase at the Castle. Ulster, however, was the theatre, perhaps, of the worst of these deeds, for the greed and cruelty of private adventure ran riot without control on the part of the state. The discovery of the New World, as of a great Land of Promise, had filled the mind of England with vast colonizing schemes; Ireland was nearer at hand than the Far West; the vultures, it was said, flocked to make her their prey; the nobler eagles flew across the ocean. One body of Englishmen made an attempt to found a settlement on the coasts of Down; another, under Walter Devereux, Earl of Essex—Elizabeth gave him her special blessing—made a similar attempt on the coast of Antrim. Both enterprises came to a miserable end; but the atrocities, of which Essex and his men were guilty, stand out hideously, even after the lapse of centuries. Fraud and chicane, too, fitly succeeded violence, to effect odious and unjust conquests. Obsolete claims to lands possessed by the Englishry in bygone ages, before the Pale had been narrowed, were set up and audaciously pressed; Sir Peter Carew, a knight of Devonshire, distinguished himself by demands of this kind, which received countenance from the Queen and her ministers. The alarm in the Pale, and far beyond its borders, became so great, that

[1] The Massacre of Mullaghmast, as it was called, stands out in the Irish annals as a most atrocious deed of blood. If the story be even partly true, Glencoe was a trifle compared to it.

even the loyal Butlers declared that this wrong could not be endured; two of the name actually appeared in arms.

Meantime troubles had arisen in the south of Ireland, leading ultimately to a protracted conflict, the most horrible and revolting that had as yet been witnessed. The honours and the lands of the Desmonds had been inherited by Gerald, the thirteenth and last Earl; they carried with them the suzerainty of nearly a third of Munster, and the allegiance of clans and septs of the Irishry, from the plains of Cork and Limerick to the Kerry ranges. Gerald was a feeble and half-hearted man; but the feuds of his house with the Butlers had never ceased; and the Butlers had long been fast friends of the Crown and the Englishry. Elizabeth warmly took their side; the Earl of Ormond, in a sense her kinsman, had been a playmate of Edward VI—that "young Solomon," as she described the King; and though she had turned a deaf ear to the counsels of Sussex, who demanded "the extirpation of the Geraldine rebels," she peremptorily ordered Sidney to "do Ormond justice" (1567). The Deputy had soon brought Desmond to his knees; but he made the Earl's brother, Sir John of Desmond, the temporary guardian of the Desmond lands; and Desmond was arrested and sent to England. Sir John of Desmond met the same fate; and this, Sidney himself asserts, was the occasion of the long and bloody strife that followed[1]. Sir James Fitzmaurice, a cousin of Desmond, an able and even a brilliant man of action, took up arms to defend his House; the Geraldine baronage, and their Celtic dependents, were hastily summoned into the field; another attempt was made to stir up "a Holy War[2]." The time seemed not without promise; Elizabeth had been excommunicated by Pius V; another Pilgrimage of Grace appeared at hand in England; and the yoke of Anglicanism, as it was extended, had begun to weigh

[1] Carew MS. March 1, 1583.
[2] See the proclamation, Carew MS. I. 397, 1569.

heavily. The rising, however, came to nothing; Fitzmaurice, indeed, made wild raids through different parts of Munster and Leinster; but he was not upheld by the great Desmond following; the Earl, not improbably, disapproved of his conduct. Sidney, ably seconded by Sir John Perrott, the President of Munster, a remarkable man, put the petty insurrection easily down. Fitzmaurice was only too glad to make his escape from Ireland.

This outbreak, however, was but the prelude to a movement of an infinitely more formidable kind. The late Catholic plots in England had failed; Mary Stuart was made to feel she was a close prisoner; she had been the cause of the doom of Norfolk (1572); the great northern Earls had appeared in the field in vain. But Rome had found fresh weapons to renew the contest with the heretic Queen she had banned and proscribed; England swarmed with seminary priests and Jesuits stirring up rebellion in the name of the faith; and if Philip still held cautiously aloof, the duel between England and Spain had begun, in the exploits of Drake and of English volunteers in arms against Alva in the Low Countries. Things in Ireland seemed to portend trouble; the Englishry of the Pale had deeply resented an attempt made by Sidney to levy a tax by the prerogative, without the consent of Parliament, and the efforts made to impose the Anglican doctrines on them; and there were disturbances in Ulster, and in parts of Connaught. Gregory XIII, vindictive and sanguine, seems to have persuaded himself that, in England and Ireland, there would be a general rising in the quarrel of the Church; and he lent a ready ear to plans for the Crusade. These were soon forthcoming, obscure as his advisers were; Fitzmaurice, who had gone from Court to Court in Europe, to seek assistance in the cause of Ireland, was eager to call the Geraldines to arms again, and to make another desperate appeal to fortune; the Pope was convinced that a Holy War would, this time, infallibly succeed. A descent on Ireland was arranged at the Vatican; the enterprise was placed under the auspices of Nicholas Sanders and Father Allen, two celebrated emissaries of the Holy See; a Papal banner was solemnly blessed; Fitzmaurice was seconded by Thomas Stukely, an English adventurer, driven from his country, but for many years in the pay of Spain; nor can it be doubted that Philip assented, nay promised to send Stukely with an expeditionary force. The King, however, did not fulfil his pledge; Stukely put to sea, indeed, with some eight hundred Spaniards; but he received orders ere long that made him land in Portugal. Fitzmaurice nevertheless, with Sanders and Allen, reached the coasts of Kerry in the autumn of 1579; the sign in which they were to conquer was unfurled; and the Irishry of Munster were adjured to rise in the cause of the Pope and the head of the Geraldine name.

The Earl of Desmond had been permitted, long before this time, to go back to Ireland. But he had been subjected to the severest conditions; he had actually made a surrender of his lands to the Crown; he was watched with suspicion by the heads of the Government. Whether, at this conjuncture, he had been plotting treason; or whether he was goaded into a rebellion he deplored; or whether, like a weak creature, he rushed madly to his fate, he suddenly threw in his lot with Fitzmaurice, and began a contest, which he ought to have known was hopeless. A great and general rising, however, took place; the name of the Desmond, if not of the Pope, was a talisman; and from the hills of Tipperary to the Atlantic, the Munster Geraldines and their Celtic vassals sprang to arms. A grave disaster befell the rebels at the outset; Fitzmaurice, a man of parts and resource—he had never put faith in the weapons of the Church, but irreverently trusted those of the flesh—was slain in a skirmish with one of the chiefs of Connaught, who characteristically refused to take part with him, and was only too willing to join the Englishry. The rebellion, nevertheless, assumed vast proportions, and gradually became of a most frightful character. Its theatre was the wide expanse of hill, valley, and plain, stretching from the range of the Galties, to the distant sea of Kerry; and this was an almost impenetrable region at the time. Immense masses of forest covered whole counties; the roads were few and bad, the defiles intricate; and the open lands—oases in an unexplored wilderness—crowned with the castles of Geraldine and Celtic chiefs, and dotted with the habitations of their vassals and serfs, were scarcely accessible through morasses, thickets, and all kinds of obstacles. This great tract was entered by a few hundred English troops, supported by irregular bands of the Butlers; but the progress of the invaders was slow in the extreme, and scarcely anything was accomplished for many months. The struggle, as always happens, in instances of the kind, acquired from the first a terrible aspect; two or three fortresses of the Desmonds were sacked, their garrisons ruthlessly flung from the battlements; fires rose from leagues of woodland, and devoured hundreds of wretched victims; the infuriated soldiery, often caught in ambushes, without discipline, and forced to live on pillage, committed atrocities fearful to record. The Geraldines and their Irish allies resisted savagely; issuing from fastnesses and labyrinths of the great forest wastes, they swooped down on outlying towns, cut off hostile parties, and, in a word, stung fiercely, like venomous insects driven from their nests. The horrors of the worst kind of guerilla warfare raged, unchecked, over the fairest parts of Munster.

The far-spreading rising had ere long received unexpected support from two quarters. The Englishry of the Pale, we have seen, had had grounds of complaint; Lord Baltinglass and other Anglo-Irish nobles—the Earl of Kildare perhaps shared their counsels—broke out into rebellion at this conjuncture. The name of the Holy Father was again employed; and Sanders, perfectly aware by this time,—his colleague Allen had been slain in a skirmish—that the Geraldine war in Munster was not a war maintained by real allies of Rome, sought to become a champion of the Pope in Leinster. An accident gave Baltinglass temporary success; Lord Grey de Wilton, who had been made Deputy, carelessly attacked the rebels in one of the defiles of Wicklow, and was defeated with not inconsiderable loss; the Celtic clans of this mountainous region, as had often happened before, made the overthrow complete. The rebellion, however, speedily collapsed, no doubt because the central Government was at hand; and Baltinglass and several of his companions were sent to the block. The second enterprise was of more importance, and seems to have caused much alarm in England. Philip made a secret attempt to send aid to Desmond; a body of Spaniards and Italians effected a landing near Smerwick, on the seaboard of Kerry, a principal seat of the Geraldine rising. Money and munitions were in abundance, and a fort was built; but the invaders were surrounded by an English squadron; Grey, hastening from Dublin, attacked them from the coast; they surrendered, it would appear, at discretion. They were deliberately butchered, in cold blood, on the plea that they had no commission from the King of Spain.

A determined effort was now made to bring the Geraldine war to an end. Pelham, a stern soldier, was placed at the head of three or four thousand English troops; the Earl of Ormond marched with his feudal levies; both leaders sought to destroy the remaining Desmond castles, and to force the rebels to fight a decisive battle. These attempts, however, were almost fruitless; more than one stronghold was razed to the ground, but the enemy refused to be brought to bay; and the swarms of the Irishry still proved dangerous, amidst wilds where pursuit was hopeless. Another method of warfare was then adopted; the country was turned into a desert by the invading force; the growing crops were rooted up, the harvests burned; the population was ruthlessly hunted down; no mercy was shown to sex or old age. This horrible work went on for nearly two years; the retainers of the Butlers made themselves conspicuous for the barbarities they inflicted on their foes of centuries. Devastation and slaughter told at last; nobles and chiefs fell off from a lost cause; clans broke up, and melted away, to escape famine and misery worse than death; and many were forced to take up arms against former comrades to save their own lives. The terms the traitors were compelled to accept show how frightful the struggle had become; no Irish soldier was promised quarter until he had brought with him an Irishman's head. Meanwhile the unhappy Earl of Desmond was driven from place to place, with a price set on his head, and vainly endeavoured to avoid the certain coming doom. He had feebly let things drift, and shown no skill or courage; he had made offers to Pelham that did him no honour. Yet he was still attended by hundreds of devoted followers—so great was even now the power of the Geraldine name. He was at last surprised and killed in a nook of Kerry; the war had lasted nearly four years; its appalling traditions still live in Munster.

The Crusade of Gregory had proved a failure; the Desmond war and the rising of the Pale were not, at bottom, religious movements. Religion, however, had part in them; its influence in the troubles of Ireland was on the increase. The Anglican Church, growing out of the Church of the Pale, was not loved even in the Pale itself; it had become more full of abuses than ever—a mere whited sepulchre it was scornfully called; its heads shared in the misdeeds of the Irish Government; it was associated with oppression, and had begun to persecute; its doctrines and ritual, foreign and Protestant, were being forced on the Irishry, as English rule made progress; it carried with it not peace and goodwill, but the pitiless sword of the alien conqueror. The ancient Celtic Church, on the other hand, had become a spiritual outpost of Rome; the Pope appointed the Bishops even more than of old; the priesthood hated the Englishry with quickened hatred. The Church was still filled with survivors of the clergy of the Religious Houses; it was crowded with emissaries of the Holy See denouncing Elizabeth the arch-heretic; its influence, powerful among its superstitious flocks, was being concentrated against the power of England. The aspect and character of the two Churches had thus changed in the course of time: the Church of the Pale, no longer Roman, but Protestant, was an enemy of Rome; the Celtic Church, condemned as heterodox of old, had become a faithful satellite of the Pope; and while the ancient discords were more fierce than ever, the Anglican Church had been made a support and a sign of conquest, a moral influence of the worst kind, while the Celtic Church had become a rallying point for the Irishry, its priesthood foes of England, and champions of the race being conquered. The growing strife between Anglo-Saxon and Celt was thus being embittered by a growing strife of religion; this added fuel to a rapidly extending flame; and yet, we repeat, it was not yet intense, nothing resembling what it was to be in the future.

The most remarkable event at this time in Ireland was the disposition made of the great Desmond possessions. The Earl, we have seen, had surrendered these to the Queen; and even long before he drew the sword, a body of adventurers had proposed to take over his lands from the Crown, and to plant in them a great English colony. Cecil, to do him justice, rejected this scheme; yet, not improbably, it reached Desmond's ear, and this may have been one cause of his ill-fated rising. The project, however, was eagerly favoured, when his vast territory had become forfeited; though it deserves notice that a confiscation on this scale had voices against it in the Irish Parliament[1]. The immense domains of the famous Geraldine House—some half-million of acres held in complete ownership—were parcelled out among "undertakers," as they were called—English gentlemen, for the most part, from Devon and Somerset; and the English Council made a serious effort to secure the success of the new settlement. In the attempts at colonisation made hitherto, especially in that of Leix and Offaley, the colonists, it was recognised, were much too few; they could not establish themselves in the country; they either disappeared or became a feeble remnant unable to make English influence felt. Precautions were taken against results like these; the undertakers were to live on the lands allotted to them; the grants were not of large extent; forts and houses and dwellings were to be built; and the lands were to be largely peopled with occupiers of the soil of English origin. The experiment, however, was not successful; a considerable number of undertakers obtained grants; some of the descendants of these are owners of lands to this day in the counties of Limerick, of Cork, and of Kerry. But many of the undertakers eluded the terms imposed on them; never visited their possessions and became absentees; and never established English tenants in them. In other, and perhaps frequent instances, the phenomenon of the past was repeated; the English farmers and labourers sank into the mass of the Irishry around, and were soon "degenerate."

A brief period of repose followed, one of the few seasons of promise in Irish history. Sir John Perrott—we have met him before—was at the head of affairs at the Castle; he was the best governor of Ireland in this disturbed century. One act of wrong may be laid to his charge; evil statecraft was

[1] The lands held only in mere suzerainty were not comprised in the forfeiture.

a characteristic of his age; he kidnapped the heir of the O'Donnells of the North; and the deed was to have untoward results. But this is the only blot on his good name; his rule was marked signally by wisdom and justice. Sir John was probably a bastard of Henry VIII; his ideas of government in Ireland were those of his father. He had been deeply impressed by the horrors of the Desmond war, largely due to the weakness of the English forces; and—in accordance with the experience of ages—he entreated the Queen to keep up a real army in Ireland. He also extended the limits of English power, for he created seven new counties in Ulster: if this creation was, to a great extent, nominal, in other respects he almost exactly followed the best parts of the Irish policy of Henry VIII. He assembled a Parliament in 1585: like that of 1540, it was attended by Irish chiefs; he seems to have really won their hearts. The most striking feature of his conduct, however, and that which makes him most nearly resemble the King, was the settlement he effected of a large part of Connaught. Many of the chiefs of the province surrendered their lands, and took them back to be held on English tenure; the process, indeed, had been going on, throughout Ireland, for a series of years. The new mode of ownership had, for some time—if this was a narrow and strained construction—been interpreted as interfering with, perhaps subverting, the ancient Celtic organisation of the land, as annulling, at least greatly lessening, the rights of the free Ceile and of tenants of the superior classes; there is too much reason to believe that, in many instances, the chiefs accepted these grants for this very purpose; they had been encroaching for ages on their less dependent vassals. Perrott provided against this abuse of power; in most of the grants made to the chiefs of Connaught, their inferiors were made tenants holding of the Crown—rents being substituted for the old Celtic renders—and the chiefs were indemnified by various means. It has been truly remarked that, in this way, "a large peasant proprietary" was created; and though a President of Connaught was, ere long, guilty of many acts of odious oppression, "the creation was probably the cause of the comparative tranquillity of Ireland for many years[1]." Indeed not a few of the chiefs of Connaught took up arms for England, at a great subsequent crisis; and this settlement of the land may have been a reason. Perrott left Ireland, it should be added, regretted by all sorts and conditions of men.

The events that followed the departure of Perrott strikingly illustrate the fluctuations in Irish policy, which so often marked the course of the Government in power. Sir William Fitzwilliam became Deputy; he was of an arbitrary and tyrannical nature; a Verres, too, in unscrupulous greed; his rule, and that of his next two or three successors, was the very opposite to that of Perrott. Ulster had not yet been nearly subdued; the authority of England in that province was extended by acts of all kinds of oppression. More than one chief was treacherously done to death; large ransoms were extorted from others; the advance of the law and the faith of England was accompanied by a series of wrongs; a chain of forts was constructed to bridle the country. These severities were certainly the main cause of the last great rising of Elizabeth's reign, which seriously threatened her rule, for a time, in Ireland, and brought prominently out the remarkable parts of a most distinguished specimen of the Irish race. Hugh O'Neill was the second son of Matthew, Lord of Dungannon, who, we have seen, had perished in a quarrel with Shane. Matthew had always adhered to the "English interest"; and, after his death, Hugh had been sent to England, and carefully educated at the Court of the Queen. His early associations, therefore, were wholly English; unlike his uncle Shane, he had ample means to become conversant with English affairs, and

[1] Lecky, *History of England in the Eighteenth Century*, II. 105.

to form a just estimate of the power of England; and unlike him, too, he had much more of the Anglo-Norman than of the Celt in him—the O'Neills and the Kildares were nearly allied in blood—for he could grasp realities, and had no vain fancies; he possessed not only, in a high degree, ability in the field and wisdom in council, but also prudence, real insight and judgment. And the first acts in the life of O'Neill prove that he sought to stand well with the English Government. He had made a name for himself in the Desmond war, he had received the thanks of the high Council of State. The Earldom of Tyrone, too, was at his express request revived by Elizabeth in his favour, though with a strictness that made him her mere vassal; the object of this policy, he must have seen, was to make him a check upon Tirlogh Lenagh, the nominal successor of Shane O'Neill; and yet he executed his trust faithfully. He made himself an instrument of English rule even in the territories of the O'Neills, and treated several of his prisoners with stern severity.

The evil deeds of the men at the Castle, however, gradually turned O'Neill against the English Government; he felt, he wrote himself, that his "destruction was planned." He had, also, peculiar grievances of his own, beside the wrongs that had been done in Ulster; the heir of the O'Donnells, who had been entrapped by Perrott, had effected his escape, and wedded his sister; and he had a deadly feud with Sir Henry Bagenal, an English officer of rank, who held lands of the O'Neills. He had thus private injuries to avenge; and, on the death of Tirlogh Lenagh Tyrone, as he should be called, was elected their chief by the voice of his tribesmen, and assumed the old hereditary title of The O'Neill. It is probable, however, that he took this step rather from necessity than of his own desire: he was already suspected by the Irish Government; he might have been driven from his lands, perhaps murdered, had he rejected the offer of his clan; he consented to follow a course he perhaps regretted. But that Tyrone should be declared the O'Neill, that he should place himself in a position, in which he might lay claim to the suzerainty of Ulster, perhaps of Ireland, was, as in the case of Shane, thirty years before, rank treason in the eyes of the Queen and her Council; it was resolved to make war against this "second arch rebel." Yet negotiations went on for many months, for Elizabeth evidently did not wish to strike; and Tyrone made an impression on her mind by able expositions of the numberless wrongs that had been done to the chiefs of the Northern Province.

The sword was not drawn until 1596; the contest was desultory and intermittent for a considerable time. The English forces in Ireland were, as usual, weak; the nobles of the Pale were slow to appear in arms; the Irish Council ere long discovered that it had to deal with a far-sighted and most able enemy. Tyrone sent envoys to Madrid and Rome, adjuring Philip to avenge the Armada, and Clement VIII to support a persecuted Church; more important certainly, he worked hard to stir up the ashes of conflagrations of the past, and to arouse the Irishry, throughout the island, to unite in something like a national war. But the most remarkable feature of his conduct was this: in complete contrast to Shane O'Neill, he made friendly overtures to the chiefs of Ulster, and won them, almost to a man, to his side; his kinsman, now head of the great O'Donnell clan, threw himself passionately into his cause; the two principal tribes of the North, divided for ages by angry feuds, were thus combined against English rule for the first time. The war went on fitfully for nearly two years, in the wide region of forest and plain, broken by innumerable water lines, which extends from Lough Neagh to the heads of the Shannon; the Irishry were, on the whole, victorious. Many chiefs of Connaught took part with the English, grateful for the wise and just policy of Sir John Perrott, notwithstanding recent acts of wrong done by Bingham, a President of the Province; but they were defeated by O'Donnell, among the hills of Roscommon. Tyrone himself was nearly always successful; he turned his light-armed kerne to the best advantage; defended position after position, with admirable skill, baffling, harassing, and often beating his exasperated foes; and more than one English commander, who had won his spurs in the Low Countries, succumbed to his strokes.

A signal disaster of the main English force sent ere long a passionate thrill, far and wide, through Ireland. Tyrone, fully alive to the essential difference between the Celtic kerne and the English soldiery, had armed and disciplined parts of his levies, for some years, on the English model; the Irish footman, for the first time in history, was enabled to encounter the English on equal terms. The Irish leader had been laying siege to a fort called Portmore, on the verge of Armagh; his bitter enemy, Bagenal, marched to its relief, with an army perhaps 5000 strong; on the 14th of August, 1598, he found Tyrone with his troops, probably in equal numbers, entrenched in a formidable position at Yellow Ford behind a small feeder of the Blackwater. Bagenal pushed forward, through well-laid obstacles; Tyrone had placed a body of picked men in ambush; and when the English were entangled in the difficult ground, they were charged in front and flank with irresistible effect. The swords of the Irishry were soon cleaving their way through a multitude of panic-stricken fugitives; the rout was complete, and for some time the English soldier would not face his long-despised enemy[1].

Tyrone instantly turned his success to account. He sent emissaries again to Spain and the Pope; called on the clans of

[1] In the picture of the battle, in the Library of Trinity College, Dublin, the English and Irish soldiers are armed in the same manner and are in the same formations. Leland, II. 336, says that the English, man to man, were inferior to their adversaries.

Wicklow to rise, and on the remnants of those of Leix and Offaley; and hastened in person southwards, in the hope of arousing another rebellion, in the great name of the Desmond, still deep in the hearts of thousands of devoted men. The Government in England was gravely alarmed; Elizabeth despatched Essex, the hero of Cadiz, with an army of fully 20,000 men, to crush "her Irish rebel" with overwhelming force. But Essex proved a most incapable leader, brilliant as he certainly was in fight; he marched towards Munster in the first instance, and he was defeated, with heavy loss, on the edge of the Pale, by chiefs of the O'Moores and the O'Connors burning to avenge their wrongs. His subsequent conduct is most difficult to understand; it gave colour to the charges soon made against him. The English commander consented to meet Tyrone; in a parley that followed, the artful Irish chief perhaps unfolded schemes that could only lead to treason, and certainly sent his adversary away outwitted, and pledged to an ignominious truce. The army of Essex, already shattered, was spread over different parts of the country; had Tyrone received the assistance he had some right to expect, the power of England in Ireland might have been shaken to its base.

Once more, however, foreign aid to Ireland failed: the friendly sails from Spain were delayed; the gift of the Pope, a crown of feathers—a phœnix rising from its ashes—must have seemed a mockery; the "Earl of Straw," the heir of the Desmonds—he was so called in ridicule by Celtic wit, which seldom spares a jest at misfortune—could not gather together the Munster Geraldines; the opportunity, at the decisive moment, was lost. Essex was recalled by his indignant sovereign; the English army, largely increased, was placed in the hands of Charles Blount, Lord Mountjoy, a soldier of parts and of long experience. Tyrone and the Northern chiefs were left almost isolated, though the Irish tribes on the borders of the Pale kept detachments of the invaders in check, sallying from the glens of Wicklow, and across the waste of Allen. Mountjoy advanced steadily, adopting the system of warfare proved to be successful before; his army, carefully supplied from the rear, established itself by degrees in the enemy's country, growing in strength, as it moved slowly forward; and points of vantage were occupied and firmly held. Tyrone, nevertheless, and his brother-in-law O'Donnell, made a stubborn and protracted resistance: the scene of the contest—the strip of country between Lough Neagh and the long course of the Erne, and covered by the Blackwater in front—was not dense with forests like the Desmond land, but a labyrinth of rivers, lakes, and woods; the Irish chiefs long held Mountjoy at bay, making good use of their water lines, often striking outlying posts with effect. The English commander, having made his base secure, ere long pursued the atrocious but efficacious methods, which had at last prevailed in the great Desmond rising. His forces were pushed forward in separate bodies, carrying devastation and death in their track; their march was seen in the flames of hamlet and cottage, and in the destruction of everything that could yield food; and the Irishry, armed and unarmed, were slaughtered wholesale. The barrier of Ulster was at last forced; the torrent of invasion rolled forward, sweeping obstacles away in its lava-like course, until it reached the interior of the Northern Province. Still, however, Tyrone and O'Donnell fought sternly on; few dependent chiefs and tribes fell away; the horrible struggle was maintained for a long succession of months.

The arrival at last of help from Spain gave a new turn to the still doubtful contest. Don Juan D'Aquila landed at Kinsale, in the south of Munster, in September 1601; he was at the head of 3000 or 4000 men, followed by another little expeditionary force. The enterprise, however, had been ill directed; the descent was to have been effected on the coast of Sligo, where Tyrone could easily have joined his allies, and made the war in Ulster formidable in the extreme. But phantoms rose before the Spanish seamen; the wreck of the Armada had reached that coast, and ten or twelve large warships had perished; the invaders had chosen to follow the old path of commerce between Spain and the southern parts of Ireland. Tyrone and O'Donnell found themselves compelled to move across Ireland from North to South; their famishing levies dwindled away rapidly, in a march of nearly two hundred miles, through intricate obstacles of many kinds; they were but an armed mob when they reached the hill ranges overlooking Kinsale. By this time an English fleet blockaded the port. Mountjoy, loyally seconded by the nobles of the Pale—true as steel like their English Catholic brethren in the face of the detested Spaniard—had laid siege to the place inland; the foreigners were hemmed in and shut up. Tyrone proposed to give his troops rest; to form an entrenched camp and to hold a position, from which he could fall on his enemy's rear; O'Donnell urged an immediate attack; the counsels of Celtic rashness prevailed. Mountjoy drew a detachment from his lines; the rebel army, weakened and harassed, was easily routed; the divisions of its chiefs contributed, perhaps, to the result. The Spaniards were, ere long, permitted to depart, Don Juan cursing his allies with true Castilian pride; and, after a few struggles, marked by the heroic defence of Dunboy, a great Celtic stronghold, the long protracted rebellion finally collapsed. Ireland lay prostrate at the feet of Mountjoy; but the resistance of Tyrone had been so formidable that his fate was very different from that of Shane O'Neill. Clearheaded, and able to see things as they were, he accepted the terms offered by Mountjoy; he renounced the princely title of the O'Neill, but was allowed to retain his lands and his earldom. It is said that he shed tears when he heard of Elizabeth's death; he was a great man who felt sympathy with a great woman.

Ireland to the end of the reign of Elizabeth.

The state of Ireland, after the contest with Tyrone, was one of appalling desolation and woe. Even within the Pale, but little ravaged by war, a seat of trade and comparative order, the price of the necessaries of life had risen fourfold; beyond, from the hills of Antrim to the shores of Cork, the land was a waste of ruin and despair. The commerce with Spain had almost disappeared; the town of Galway has never recovered this loss. Whole counties were strown with the wrecks of abbeys and castles, fine monuments of mediæval genius; they were not to be replaced, as has been the case in England, by modern structures of beauty and grandeur; other storms of destruction were to break on Ireland; but that of the sixteenth century was the most fatal to art. The most terrible feature of the time, however, was the fate that had overtaken the great mass of the people. A third part of the community, it is believed, had perished, victims of the sword, of famine, of fell miseries, to which few parallels can be found in history. Great tracts were deserts of more hideous aspect than even the battle-fields of the Thirty Years War, and the Palatinate and its cities, when given to the flames. Flocks of wolves howled over thousands of corpses, left unburied amidst broken heaps of villages; the air was thick with flights of birds of prey far and near feasting on human carrion; Elizabeth had been told, before the war had ended, that "she reigned in Ireland over ashes and dead carcasses." As for the survivors of the tragedy, "out of every corner of the woods and glens they came creeping forth upon their hands, for their legs could not bear them: they looked like anatomies of death; they spoke like ghosts crying out of their graves." In the agony of desperation and want many a mother devoured the babe she had slain: troops of gibbering idiots gave awful proof how the minds of men had given way under the stress of horror and fear.

The spiritual and religious state of Ireland had much in common with this material ruin, but presented ominous features especially its own. We have already seen how the Anglican Church, an offset of the old Church of the Pale, but Protestant and opposed to Rome, was following in Ireland the march of conquest, and was being forced on a reluctant people, and how the old Celtic Church, become intensely Papal, was being made more hostile than ever to English rule; we have also noticed the numerous resulting evils. We may shortly glance at the condition of thought and feeling, and of piety and morality, that was being developed out of this inauspicious order of things. The dignitaries of the Anglican Church remained true to the worst hatreds of the Church of the Pale, and regarded the Irishry as a detested race; and as their Church was being extended by the sword, their influence for evil was widely diffused. They had become tools of the men at the Castle; their animosities were quickened by the zeal of creed; they persecuted harshly far and wide; an Anglican Archbishop had watched with delight the torture of a Prelate appointed by the Pope. Their spiritual authority, however, was next to nothing; heads of a Church that had no hold on the people, their clergy might spread over many districts, and engross most of the good things of the world, but they preached, for the most part, in empty churches, though attendance at these was prescribed by law; they were regarded as mere creatures of the English enemy, talking blasphemy in a foreign tongue; their voices were raised, in vain, in a wilderness. As always happens, too, in the case of a communion like this, religious indifference, sloth, inertness, were the characteristics of its scanty flocks; the spirit of Protestantism had as yet scarcely entered the country, if that of intolerance was abroad; and, for the rest, the old abuses of the Church of the Pale, simony, profligacy, waste, the decay of churches, and wickedness raised to high places, abounded in its successor, with little change. As for the Church of the Irishry—apart from its devotion to Rome—superstition was its most marked feature; and its priesthood as yet had made no impression on the ignorance, the licentiousness, and the odious vices apparently general among all orders of men. It was, of course, a bitter enemy of the Anglican Church; but Ireland, we repeat, had not yet had experience of religious hatreds at their worst.

The intellectual life of Ireland continued to be, as was indeed natural, deplorably weak throughout this period. Trinity College was founded in 1591; it was to become a mother of eminent men, but it was as yet only in its first infancy. A few books were published in Dublin, but they were mostly produced by English pens; the best commentaries on Ireland, at this time, were, with hardly an exception, the works of Englishmen. Two or three of the Irish Chancellors of the day were learned and even distinguished men; the influence of the Irish Bar was growing, as English law spread beyond the Pale; the Irish House of Commons, largely increased in numbers, more than once resisted Tudor stretches of power with the spirit of the volunteers of 1781-2, and had, doubtless, members of parts and capacity. But in the age of Shakespeare, of Spenser, of Bacon, when the intellect of England flashed out in a glory of Dramatic Art, of Song, of Philosophy, certainly more splendid than has since been seen, no great writer or thinker appeared in Ireland; her literature in the sixteenth century is the dross of antiquity, useful only as a witness to her unhappy fortunes. The learned researches of the Brehon lawyers, the poetry of the native bards and minstrels, were probably less abundant in these troubled years than they had been in preceding ages; the destruction of the Religious Houses, the wrongs occasionally done to the Celtic priesthood, nay, their increased activity in the cause of Rome, contributed probably to this decline. The annalists and chroniclers, however, seemed to have toiled on; and a native literature was growing up of an historical kind, of a significant character, which it has ever since retained. It was marked by a note of unceasing sorrow; by fear rather than hatred of the conquering race; by a concentrated, but intensely narrow love of country; above all, by an inability to see that the many woes of Ireland had their counterparts, as a rule, in the history of the time.

Signs of the old and long-standing ills of Ireland are still manifest in this period. English policy fluctuates, if usually harsh; the Government at the Castle varies in its conduct and aims; the "English and Anglo-Irish interests" repeatedly clash; ruthless conquest is carried out piecemeal; colonisation fails as in the Plantagenet age. The peculiar and striking features, however, of this time are of a different kind. The march of conquest in Ireland is slow and uncertain; it is usually sustained by inadequate force; but it has a character of atrocity and systematic cruelty, which it did not possess in preceding centuries. Not to speak of the contest with Shane O'Neill, the Desmond rebellion and the war with Tyrone were, we have said, attended by events of horror, of barbarity, of inhuman destruction, conspicuous, even in an age of violence; Ireland was to endure perhaps even more severe trials, but hardly again such a protracted agony. It was a special characteristic of this period, too, that attempts were made over and over again to assimilate Ireland to a Tudor ideal, to force on the Irishry modes of life and thought, alien to them, and disliked or abhorred. The old policy of keeping Saxon and Celt apart, of preventing the fusion of the two races, was abandoned, as English rule advanced; the statesmanlike policy of Henry VIII—to make England supreme in Ireland, but to give the Irish a share in government, and to respect their ancient customs and usages—was in turn replaced by an opposite policy; Ireland was to accept, in all things, whatever Englishmen should impose. This was most evident in the efforts made to extend the domain of the Anglican

IV.] *Ireland to the end of the reign of Elizabeth.* 119

Church; but it was apparent in all the relations of life; projects to extirpate Brehons, bards, "poets," and to coerce the Irishry to conform to Anglo-Saxon ways, were in high favour at the seats of power in those days. The hatred, the loathing, the pitiless contempt felt by the conquering towards the conquered race is, also, an unhappy feature of the time; the Englishry regarded the Irishry as the worst kind of savages[1].

We may glance at the causes of this evil state of things; for it left unfortunate results behind. Something was due to the nature of Irish conquest—a prolonged strife exasperating the fiercest passions—and something to faults in the English national character, stern, and devoid of sympathy with other races. But England, throughout this period, was either engaged in watching secret but most dangerous foes, or was in a death struggle with Rome and Spain; Ireland, in the crisis of the sixteenth century, was the scene of conspiracies against her power, recurring over and over again; and though the Irishry received little aid from Philip and the Popes in their frequent risings, we cannot feel surprise that England struck hard, and crushed rebellion with an unsparing hand. This was the main cause of the frightful atrocity, which marked the Irish wars of those days; and if we recollect that England fought for existence, the result becomes a subject more of regret than of wonder. As for the efforts of later Tudor statesmen to compel Ireland to accept an alien faith, and to conform to usages prescribed for her, this was in accord with the spirit of the age, as we see it in many parts of Europe; indeed something of the same kind was seen in the system of legislation and the mode of government adopted in England in the Tudor period. The sentiments unhappily felt by

---

[1] Shakespeare, the embodiment of English genius in that age, and it must be added of English prejudice, places but one Irishman on the stage, and he is a contemptible fool.

Englishmen towards Irishmen are, in part, explained by the passions aroused in a protracted conflict; but they flowed, also, from another source. England and Ireland were lands as far asunder as the poles, in wealth, civilisation, and social progress; the one was the first nation in Europe, the other the most backward community; this largely accounts for the scornful aversion of the conquering to the conquered race.

Impartial history properly condemns much that was done in Ireland in this period. Man, however, is the creature of his age; and all that is worst in Irish affairs had its parallel in contemporary events. If rebellion in Ireland was mercilessly crushed, and the island was strewn with ashes and blood, Alva did the very same things in the Netherlands, and was more pitiless than Sussex and Mountjoy. If we blame the perfidy with which Shane O'Neill was treated, it was the age of the odious "serpent of Florence," of the massacre of St Bartholomew, of the murder of Coligny. We regret attempts to force the Anglican Church on the Irishry; but these were as nothing to what was done to stamp out heresy in Spain and in Italy, and to place whole orders of men under the yoke of Rome. The slaughter at the fort of Smerwick was a crime; but it was a trifle compared to many a deed of blood, of which France was the scene in the civil wars of the time. The sixteenth century, in fact, was an age of violence, when Christendom was torn in pieces in a deadly strife; and Ireland had but a share in the conflict. Let it be said, too, that Elizabeth and English statesmen were often ignorant of what was being done in their name in Ireland; it should be added that the weakness, the want of concert, the divisions of Irish nobles and chiefs, and the still backward state of almost the whole community, contributed to the unhappy fate of their country.

The prospect for Ireland was not wholly dark at the close of the sixteenth century. Civilisation had established itself in the Pale; this region, indeed, had almost lost the name, as the limits of English power advanced; nearly the whole island had been made shireland. There was a semblance at least of constitutional government, as the Irish Parliament advanced in influence; the domain of order and law had been largely increased. The land had been cruelly wasted by the sword; but the sword had hewn its way through the dense jungle of half-barbarous feudal and Celtic rule, which had been a barrier for ages to every kind of progress; it might yet inaugurate a better order of things. The conflict, which had been so prolonged and grievous, was not yet wholly one of race and religion, although tending in both directions; the wounds it had inflicted might perhaps have been healed. Ireland, if we except a part of Ulster, was completely in the hands of the conquerors; the dark course of her fortunes might even now have been turned. The policy of Henry VIII had become impossible; but if Ireland, at this juncture, had been placed under an enlightened despotism, like that of India, that respected native usage and law while it maintained the rule of civilised power, her future history might have been very different. She was in a state not unlike that of France after the peace of Vervins, exhausted by war, torn by angry passions. But she was to find no Henry IV and Sully; she was to proceed along a path thickly strown with disasters and sorrows.

CHAPTER V.

FROM THE DEATH OF ELIZABETH TO THE RESTORATION.

An amnesty proclaimed at the accession of James I. Tyrone is received at Court, with his kinsman O'Donnell, made Earl of Tyrconnell. Religious troubles easily put down by Mountjoy. Abolition of the Brehon Law and Celtic usages, in all parts of Ireland. Substitution of English law and the English system of land tenure. Consequences of this revolution. The flight of Tyrone and Tyrconnell, and of other Irish chiefs. Confiscation of their territories. Six counties of Ulster at the disposition of the Crown. The Plantation of Ulster. Peculiarities and characteristics of the scheme. The effects of this colonisation perhaps exaggerated. The prosperity of Ulster, however, begins from this time. Resentment of the Irishry of Ulster. Progress of confiscation in time of peace. The beginning of the era of Protestant ascendency in Ireland, and of Catholic subjection. Decline of the independence of the Irish Parliament, and the causes of this. Deceptive tranquillity and prosperity of Ireland after the death of James. The state of the island really dangerous. The reign of Charles I. The Viceroyalty of Strafford. His tyranny; the evils it produced, and the good it accomplished. The great Ulster rising of 1641. There was no general premeditated massacre. Spread of the insurrection. Defection of the old Catholic Englishry. Civil war in Ireland. The Catholic confederation of Kilkenny. Extreme significance of this assembly. Division of parties in it, and the results. The Cessation of 1643. Tortuous policy of the King. Prolonged negotiations. The Glamorgan Treaty. The Peace of 1646. It concedes hardly anything to the Confederates, and especially to the Celtic Irishry. Indignation of the extreme parties. Rinuccini and

CH. V.] *From the death of Elizabeth to the Restoration.* 123

Owen Roe O'Neill. The Battle of Benburb. Results of O'Neill's victory. Danger of Dublin. Ormond resigns his office to representatives of the Long Parliament, and leaves Ireland. Jones defeats Preston. Inchiquin defeats Taaffe. The Confederates treat again for peace. The Peace of 1648. Ormond returns to Ireland. The Royalists and Confederates unite after the death of the King. Departure of Rinuccini from Ireland. O'Neill stands aloof. Battle near Dublin and defeat of Ormond. Death of O'Neill. He had turned to Ormond when it was too late. Cromwell lands in Ireland. Drogheda and Wexford. The Cromwellian conquest of Ireland. The settlement of the land. Government of Cromwell. The beginnings of the Irish Union. The Restoration. Reflections.

THE reign of James I, if not an eventful, is a very important period in Irish history. It was inaugurated by measures, intended, no doubt, to bind up, in some degree, the deep wounds of the people. An amnesty was proclaimed for all that had been done in the war; a veil of oblivion was thrown over the past; the brother of O'Donnell, the chief lately in arms, was made a peer, as Earl of Tyrconnell; and Tyrone and the new Earl were received in state at Court. Parts of the country were stirred, ere long, by religious troubles; but these were of no present interest; they were significant, at most, of dangers yet to come. The Catholic world seems to have believed that James would reverse the policy of his predecessor; and when this expectation had proved almost vain, the priesthood of the Irish Catholic Church, long devoted followers of the Holy See, succeeded in provoking a few angry risings. The clergy of the Anglican Church were driven from their homes, in two or three of the principal towns of Munster; the Mass, nominally at least proscribed by law, was celebrated with great pomp in many places, and mutterings of rebellion were even heard. Mountjoy, however—he had been made Lord Lieutenant—easily put down a petty sacerdotal movement which had scarcely any general support; Ireland, in fact, had been so exhausted by war that the community, as a whole, was quiescent. There was no Irish Gunpowder Plot; and when, as the result of that unhappy crime, many Catholic priests were expelled from Ireland, there was no murmur of open discontent.

By this time the whole island had been made shireland; the king's writ was supposed to run everywhere; the king's judges went regular circuits; the machinery at least of English law had been set up in the four Irish provinces. But that law was largely encountered and checked by the medley of feudal and Celtic law and usage, which still prevailed in great parts of the country; it was still, to a considerable extent, a dead letter. Within the limits of the old Pale it probably was completely supreme; it determined the rights of all classes of men; its odious distinctions between the Englishry and the Irishry had become obsolete, if not yet abolished by any act of the state. Beyond, in the Anglo-Norman lands, its influence had been immensely extended; it had effaced the jurisdiction of the great feudal nobles, as these had yielded to the advance of conquest; it had replaced the will of Butler and Geraldine in their vast palatinates. But even in this region it was crossed and thwarted by Anglo-Norman and Celtic customs; the Brehon lawyers had still power; the laws they administered had wide influence; and the English system of tenure was in direct conflict with the ancient Celtic organisation of the land, which, in many districts, had not disappeared. In the Celtic Land, as we may still call it, subdued and ravaged as it had been, English law was opposed by these and other hostile elements; the primitive modes of Tanist succession and of Gavelkind were in common use; indeed the claim of a tribe to elect its chiefs had, as we have seen, led to two bloody wars. But in this, and in other large parts of Ireland, what was most in antagonism to English law, was the archaic land-system of the Irish Celts, still deeply and widely rooted in the soil. This system, as we have said, had been encroached on, and weakened by the Irish chiefs for ages; and the practice, which had become frequent, of surrendering lands to a great extent, to be regranted and held by English tenure, had blotted it out in many counties. But the old relations springing from the land, and powerfully affecting whole orders of men, remained in full force, in an immense territory; and millions of acres were still parcelled out between owners possessing the rights of chiefs, and their free tenants and vassal dependents, each class holding by immemorial custom.

The opportunity was now taken to extend English law to every part of Ireland, to annihilate the old Celtic laws and usages, and consequently to destroy the Celtic land-system, the mould of society in many and great districts. This was part of the policy of forcing the conquered to adopt the institutions of the conquering race, which had been in progress for a series of years; but Tudor lawyers, we have seen, had a peculiar aversion to almost everything savouring of Irish law, the result partly, at least, of their ignorance, if not without foundation in reason. English law was pronounced the sole law of the land; the Brehon Laws were condemned as evil customs; Tanistry and Gavelkind were declared illegal; English modes of succession were made to prevail everywhere; the English methods of holding land were substituted universally for the ancient Irish methods; and surrenders and regrants of land were very generally made. This revolution, searching and immense, was doubtless attended with some good results; Tanistry and Gavelkind had caused real evils, and were hardly compatible with social progress; the law of the Eric-fine had done mischief; the primitive system of Irish land tenure seemed as far behind the age as the feudal system, to which, loose and ill-defined as it was, it bore, we have said, a kind of resemblance. But a sudden change affecting the relations of life, especially as it was thrust on a reluctant people, provoked, far and wide, discontent and alarm. The

Brehon judges were regretted as martyrs; the effort to destroy their cherished customs was resented by the Irishry as a cruel injury; the new law of the alien shocked their deepest sympathies. This was especially the case in all that was connected with the land; the conversion of Irish into English tenures unquestionably annihilated rights wholesale; over large areas, and in many thousand instances, the free Ceile, the Saer stock and the Daer stock tenants, in different degrees joint owners of the soil, sank into the position of mere tenants at will, in fact, nearly that of the degraded Fuidhirs. It is true that the privileges of these classes seem to have been considered in some cases, where lands were surrendered and granted again; but this was not of common occurrence. As a rule, the claims of the members of the tribes, clans, and septs, to the lands which they had held for ages were trampled under foot; and this in considerable parts of Ireland. The consequences were not difficult to perceive; it was as if the Village Community and the Joint Family were effaced by a freak of mere power in India.

The abolition of Celtic usage and law was followed by a confiscation of immense proportions. Tyrone and his kinsman Tyrconnell suddenly fled from Ireland; they were accompanied by several inferior chiefs; the fugitives were proscribed and attainted; and the vast territories, which they still ruled, were forfeited. It is useless to enquire whether they had plotted treason—the charge usually made on occasions of the kind—or whether they knew they were doomed beforehand; but Tyrone assuredly was not a man precipitately and unwisely to rush into danger. The suzerainty of the exiles extended over the six Ulster counties of Armagh, Cavan, Monaghan, Fermanagh, Tyrone, and Donegal; and it appears certain that this large tract, comprising more than three millions of acres, was declared to be at the disposition of the Crown. An effort was now made to pour into this region a great stream of English and Scotch colonists, and to make it the seat of a strong settlement attached by blood and faith to the British name. The genius of Bacon and the experience of Davies presided over this new "Plantation"; precautions were taken to avoid the failures of previous attempts at colonisation of the kind. The lands chosen for the settlement seem to have been not more than half-a-million or six hundred thousand acres[1]; but these we know comprised the best lands; the residue, then a tract of moor, woodland, and waste, was probably abandoned to the native race. In the arrangement and distribution of the lands to be colonised the example of the Desmond forfeitures was, in part, followed, but large deviations also were made from it. Parts of the lands were granted to "undertakers" of English and Scottish origin, and parts to officers who had served in the late war; and care was taken, as before, that the grants should be small, in fact much smaller than had been the case in Munster. But very stringent conditions were imposed to prevent the evils which had occurred previously; points of vantage were to be strongly occupied; the settlers were to build fortified dwellings, and, as a rule, to be always resident; their lands were to be thickly peopled by men of their own blood; a colony, really of a military type, was thus to be established in the midst of the Irishry, and to be kept if possible free from contact with them. In other, and very important respects, the Desmond precedent was completely set at nought. A considerable part of the lands to be planted was allotted to the Irishry to be held, as owners and tenants, by English tenure; they were thus to be indemnified for what they had lost, and to be isolated as a separate people. The Anglican Church, too, obtained large grants; and a great tract in the county of

---

[1] For the very difficult question of the extent of the original forfeitures, and of the lands actually settled, see, and compare, Hill, *Plantation of Ulster*, Introduction, 4, and Pynnar's *Survey*, Ibid. 445, 589. Leland, II. 429 seqq. Reid's *Presbyterian Church*, I. 86. Hallam, III. 504.

Derry was handed over to London merchants free from the conditions before referred to.

The prosperity which a part of Ulster has enjoyed has been ascribed by a series of writers to this "Plantation"; but there is much exaggeration in the assertion. Many families, indeed, of English and Scottish descent—especially of Scottish —established themselves in the tracts which had been assigned to them; and the colony was from the first more thriving than any preceding colonies of the kind. But, as had happened in Munster before, the conditions of the settlement were ill observed; non-residence was common, lands were not occupied by a sufficient number of the immigrating race; the Irishry largely intermingled with it, spite of every effort to keep them apart. Derry, too, became especially a land of absentees; of the six counties in which the Plantation was made, the children of the soil remained the mass of the population in three. Down and Antrim had been colonised before, without interference on the part of the state, by successive inroads of Scottish settlers; these counties are, by many degrees, the most prosperous and the richest in Ulster, and those that show the greatest preponderance of Teutonic blood. It seems probable that the progress of Ulster, which certainly dates from the seventeenth century, was rather due to the colonising genius of the Scotch and to a continual influx of men of their race than to the Plantation, considered by itself; this, in many respects, was hardly successful. Still the advance which Ulster has made in the course of time coincided with that of the settlement of the reign of James; and this was, doubtless, a potent element in it. On the other hand the Plantation was, beyond dispute, a cause of many and dangerous evils. In the allotment of the forfeited lands, the rights of the native race were destroyed or neglected; chiefs of families held in reverence for ages were rudely despoiled; the tribal system of tenure was broken up; whole classes of occupiers of the soil were injured. To the feelings engendered by this violent change we must mainly attribute another great rising, attended with most unhappy results, and fraught, for a time, with grave peril to the state.

Ireland was now completely in the conqueror's hands; as far as the sword and law could effect it, the type of Celtic society had been nearly effaced. There was still an opportunity to make order and prosperity grow up under a good government, like that, as we have said, of India at this day; but the course of events was unhappily different. The country, as had been the case for years, was an object for the English adventurer; the men at the Castle had, for a long time, been eager to gorge themselves in forfeitures; the necessities of the king were great. Under the operation of these causes, confiscation went on at a prodigious rate; whole tracts were wrested from their possessors by atrocious wrong. In five or six of the central counties thousands of acres were seized and transferred; a large part of Wicklow was torn from the mountaineers, for generations the enemies of the Pale; the same process took place in other counties. The means adopted to produce these results were an odious combination of tyranny and fraud. Obsolete claims to lands were set up by descendants of colonists of Plantagenet times, as had been done by Sir Peter Carew; hundreds of ancient Royal grants were pronounced invalid; the right of the Crown to large domains was asserted with success; legal ingenuity and chicane were taxed to pick out flaws in titles. The work of rapine was assisted by a brood of harpies, known by the evil name of "discoverers," by servile judges, by terrified juries; under these influences it made rapid progress. At last an attempt was made, on a mere technical plea, to confiscate the great district of Connaught, which had been the subject of Sir John Perrott's settlement; but this claim was bought off for the present; James probably was afraid to maintain it. But "the ravage of war," in the words of Burke, was carried on "in peace," over a large part of Ireland;

thousands of the Irishry and some of the old Englishry felt that their lands were marked down as a prey; insecurity and alarm prevailed far and wide.

Events, meanwhile, had been tending to increase and widen the division of faith in the Irish community, and to make the resulting evils more general and intense. The Anglican Church had, by this time, been established in every part of the island; it had taken possession of all that belonged to the Church of the Pale and the ancient Celtic Church; it was, in fact, the only ecclesiastical body recognised by the law. Its characteristics had not changed, or had changed only, perhaps, for the worse; it remained an instrument of the rule of the Castle; it persecuted in the midst of a conquered people. If it had begun to produce a few eminent men, it was as full as before of the old and bad abuses; as a spiritual agency it had made no progress; and it was more hostile than ever to Rome and to the great mass of Irishmen —more Catholic than they had been at any time—for it had been affected by the religious movement of England, and many of its clergy were extreme Puritans. At the same time, the power of the Anglican Church had, in another way, been immensely extended. It had been the Church only of a feeble colony; it was now the Church of a great dominant class, spreading as conquerors over many parts of the country; and this class, settled amidst the Irishry, was strongly and aggressively Protestant, upheld Protestantism as a sign of supremacy, and regarded with peculiar aversion and contempt Catholicism and the subjugated Catholic Celts, nay even the old Englishry, nearly all Catholics. The era of Protestant ascendency, and all that the word implies, had, in fact, already begun in Ireland; a dominant Church was supported by a dominant caste, and both laid a yoke on the neck of five-sixths of the people. The inevitable result was to quicken religious discords, and to make them far more bitter than they had ever been.

The same consequences had been produced by another and different series of causes. The Catholic Church of Ireland had become every year more a satellite of Rome; its clergy—hundreds of whom were emissaries of the Papal Court—were probably the most Roman in Europe; and, persecuted as it had been and despoiled, it hated the Anglican Church, the Irish Protestant name, nay Protestant England, with unceasing hatred. The influence of its priesthood too had greatly increased, for, as we have said, this had rapidly grown, as the power of the Irish chiefs had declined; and if its moral authority, as a Christian order of men, was not yet what it was to become, it was the spiritual leader, we must not forget, of the Catholic Englishry, and of the Irish Celts, that is of the immense majority of the Irish people. It had thus become a representative, in a certain sense, of the Irish Catholic community as a whole; it naturally inspired this with its own sentiments; it exasperated the feelings of anger and fear already quickened by conquest and other wrongs. Simultaneously with this, the Irish Catholics had been subjected to different kinds of grievances, on the ground of their religion only. The sectarian tests of the reign of Elizabeth had been almost idle and empty menaces; the oath of supremacy had been scarcely ever tendered; attendance at Protestant worship had not been enforced. All this had, by degrees, been changed, as the march of conquest had advanced in Ireland and Irish Protestantism had acquired more strength; Catholic "recusants," as they were now called, were, in many instances, kept out of the service of the state, debarred from holding offices and from the practice of the law, nay fined and made liable to other penalties, because they would not accept the tests now often imposed on them. This system of persecution, doubtless, was rather teasing than cruel; but the era of Catholic subjection had, also, opened for Ireland; and from this and the other causes referred to, religious animosities had been greatly augmented.

The Government at the Castle had undergone, at the same time, a well marked change. It had long been composed wholly of the "English interest"; but soldiers were now replaced, for the most part, by Anglican Churchmen and men of English law; a Government of this type was naturally harsh to the subject races over which it ruled. It was not a general or equal despotism, but rather a bureaucracy, exclusive and severe; it weighed heavily on the Catholic Celt, and even on the Englishry of the old faith; its principal work was to look out for forfeitures, which it often enforced by the very worst means. Another institution of Ireland, too, which had given signs of promise, had been transformed. The Irish Parliament, we have seen, had grown out of the Conventions of the Pale, had gradually acquired no little influence, and had shown, more than once, in the sixteenth century, a sentiment of independence, even a love of liberty. These hopeful germs had been destroyed: in spite of a protest made by the Baronage of the Pale, the class most worthy of honour, perhaps, in the country, James, with a stroke of the pen, created forty boroughs out of "beggarly hamlets," of "no account"; and the Irish House of Commons was unfairly packed by nominees of the Crown and members of the ruling English colonies, who had been established in power in the land. The single Irish Parliament of this reign enacted some good and useful laws, especially an act for effacing old distinctions of race, so far as legislation could effect this object. But it was chiefly remarkable for a fierce quarrel between the English and Protestant party, and the Catholic "recusants" of either race; these were overborne, but still formed a minority which could make itself felt. The Irish Parliament had thus become essentially an instrument of English power and of the dominant Anglo-Protestant interest, which always had a majority in it; it did not, in any true sense, represent the country; it lost its old independent spirit; it was, as a rule, submissive and servile, though occasionally affected by gusts of passion. Without the support of a strong community, of anything even resembling a section of public opinion, it had little in common with the great Houses of Westminster.

Ireland, however, at the death of James I, was apparently tranquil, nay in a state of progress. Peace had repaired some of the ravages of war; the introduction of a vigorous race of settlers had improved husbandry and the face of the country; signs of material prosperity began to be seen. The mass of the people, too, seemed quiescent; and English statesmen, with the optimistic fancies which have often deluded them in the case of Ireland, announced that "the strings of the Irish harp were in tune," and that the Irish were orderly, even contented. Yet elements of ill-will, of passion, of strife were gathering beneath the surface of things, more dangerous perhaps than at any previous time. The Irishry fiercely resented the fall of their chiefs, the extinction of their customs, the annihilation of their rights, and especially the destruction of the tribal land-system; the Continent had received despoiled Irish exiles, trained to war, and thirsting for revenge for wrong; the reiterated process of confiscation had aroused anger and terror. The domination, too, of the Anglican Church, the vexatious persecution which it promoted, above all, the extension over great parts of the country of numbers of settlers, seated on the land, as a caste alien in race and faith from the children of the soil, had provoked deepseated and bitter discontent; their feelings were quickened by the Catholic priesthood, more powerful than it had ever been, and were shared by many of the old Englishry. The Government, besides, was a bad Government, harsh, sectarian, narrow, often iniquitous; it was trying to wrest everything to submission to the rule of the Castle, repeatedly abused for the very worst purposes. As the general result, the divisions of race and faith, unhappily the cardinal fact of Irish History, were never before so profound and menacing. The separation between the Englishry in the Middle Age, and the aboriginal Celts, in every part of Ireland, was as nothing compared to the deep distinction between the English and Scotch settlers and the Irishry of the existing time; the feud between the Norman Church of the Pale and the ancient Church of the Celts was a trifle compared to the hostility, in Ireland, of Anglicanism and Rome; and all the evils of disunion had thus increased and multiplied. It should be observed, too, that the lines between races and faiths, except in the case of the old Englishry, nearly all Catholics, were coincident; the Colonists were Protestants, the Celtic-Irish Catholic; and the fact would necessarily aggravate any dangers at hand. And it might well be, in the actual state of Europe, when the great Catholic reaction seemed certain of success, in the first triumphs of the Thirty Years War, and when Protestantism was being forced back in Germany and in England, that, in Ireland, the division of creed would be attended with the most fatal results.

The first years of the reign of Charles I are remarkable only, as respects Ireland, for vacillation in the rule of the Castle, for the continuance of its bad modes of government, and for the utter disregard which seems to have been shown to the stand made against the King in the English Parliament. The duplicity however, which was the most marked feature of the conduct of Charles in Irish affairs, was soon exhibited by a striking example. The King made a solemn promise in reply to a remonstrance from Ireland addressed to him, that the confiscations in Connaught should not proceed, on the technical pretence which had been made for them; he added that a prescription of sixty years should prevail against a claim of the Crown in order to check the continual forfeitures of land; he pledged himself to mitigate the tests imposed on "recusants"; and he received £120,000—a great sum for the Ireland of that age—as the consideration for what were called his "Graces." But he availed himself of an infringement of the celebrated Law of Poynings, to prevent these concessions from being ratified by a statute made by the Irish Parliament; and he soon showed that he would not fulfil his word. In 1633 Strafford was sent to Ireland; the Viceroyalty of that most remarkable man forms a memorable passage in Irish History. The Irish policy of the great despotic statesman had, as we have said, much in common with that which Surrey had proposed a century before to Henry VIII. Strafford wished to make the King absolutely uncontrolled in Ireland, and practically to subjugate the island by another conquest. For this purpose he largely increased the Irish army; and if this force was to be employed against English liberty it was also to uphold in Ireland the rule of the sword. Strafford, too, spurned "the Graces" aside; he pressed on the work of spoliation in Connaught, with a determination and constancy that bore resistance down; and there can be little doubt that many other parts of Ireland were marked out "for his majestic rapine." At the same time he laid a weighty and levelling hand on all orders of ruling men in the island; the Council at the Castle, Nobles, Prelates, Judges, and leaders of the colonial caste, bowed submissively to his imperious will; "the King," he boasted with reason, "could do what he pleased in Ireland." And Strafford, like Thomas Cromwell in England, saw how a Parliament could be made to carry out his work; thrusting aside the fears of his weak master he often assembled the Irish Parliament; and if he induced it to pass some salutary laws, he played its discordant factions against each other, and compelled it to be his accomplice in promoting arbitrary power. The Viceroy even went so far as to attempt to enforce religious conformity throughout the country, and to prop up Anglicanism by fresh penalties, the least statesmanlike of all his acts. Ireland was kept for years under a stern despotism, maintained by the strong arm, and by a master mind.

The tyranny of Strafford, severe as it was, brought, nevertheless, good fruits with it. He enforced order with a steady will; he made law obeyed and respected, to a degree never seen in Ireland before. The great despot, too, kept the petty despots under; from the prelate and the peer to the last settler, the classes, which had domineered in Ireland, found their occupation of wrong gone; the jackals shrunk from the lordly lion. If he confiscated, on an immense scale, this was done without distinction of blood and creed; the lands of Protestant and Catholic, of Saxon and Celt, were equally grist to his mill; Irishmen had alike to submit to the rights of conquest. If the Church policy of Strafford, too, was bad, especially in irritating the Scotch colonists, devoted adherents of John Knox, he was the first and one of the few Viceroys who made a real effort to reform the flagrant abuses of the Irish Anglican Church; and many as were his faults, it may be said of him, that he stood supreme above Irish factions, and gave Ireland at least a strong and firm government. Nor can it be doubted that this eminent ruler greatly improved the material state of the island; he opened sources of commerce, lessened taxation, encouraged agriculture in many ways; and Ireland owes her linen manufacture to him. The good results were seen in a very short space of time; the prosperity of Ireland, such as it was, made a marked and even a rapid advance. An historian, by no means partial to Strafford, has thus described what was best in his rule: "Peace, order, obedience and industry distinguished the present period from that of any former administration; the value of land was increased; commerce extended; the customs amounted to almost four times their former sum; the commodities exported from Ireland were twice as much in value as the foreign merchandise imported; and shipping was found to have increased even an hundredfold[1]."

---

[1] Leland, III. 41.

The great Viceroy fell: and the Irish Parliament, which had meekly obeyed his imperious commands, turned suddenly against him in the hour of peril. It impeached several of Strafford's creatures; agents were despatched to England to remonstrate, and to set forth its grievances. This committee seems to have been in close relation with the popular leaders in the Long Parliament; it played on the necessities and the fears of the King; Charles consented, at last, to concede "the Graces" unjustly withheld by a Royal breach of faith. The time for compromise, however, had passed; a frightful explosion in Ireland was about to burst. At the Castle the reins had fallen into the hands of William Parsons and John Borlase; the Lords Justices—as their title was—were utterly unfit to rule the country, in the season of trouble which now had opened. By this time Scotland had risen against the Crown; a Scottish army had entered England; the Long Parliament was in conflict with the King; in England and in Ireland alike the power of the state appeared greatly weakened. The opportunity was not missed by a knot of men—nearly all descendants of chiefs of different degrees, who had lost their lands through the Plantation of Ulster and other confiscations of the two last reigns—to strike a blow to regain their possessions, and to stir up a great Irish rising. The soul of the League was Roger O'Moore—a scion of the old race which had ruled in Leix; he had the sympathy at heart of the heir of Tyrone, an exile held in honour at the Court of Spain, in the armies of which he had served with distinction; and he found associates in O'Neills, Maguires, Macmahons, O'Reillys, Byrnes, representatives of ruined tribes, clans, and septs. The plan of the conspirators was to seize the Castle of Dublin, and to paralyse the Government on the spot; and then to arouse the Irishry throughout Ulster, to summon them to arms to avenge their wrongs, and to take hold again of their lost lands. The design was favoured by some of the Irish priesthood, and perhaps by two obscure men of the Englishry of the Pale; it received countenance from Spanish statesmen; and Richelieu, at this moment no friend of England, appears at least to have connived at it.

The meditated attack on the Castle failed; it had been disclosed by a mere accident; and two of the rebel chiefs were arrested. But a general rising took place in Ulster; on the night of the 22nd of October 1641, the Irishry sprang up and swept over the province, from the borders of Armagh to the hills of Donegal. The forts, which had been constructed as centres of defence, were suddenly seized in different places; some of the few towns that were rising were captured; the colonists and their families were driven from their homes in many of the districts which had been lately settled. It has been alleged by a series of writers that a great and preconcerted massacre occurred of men, women and children of the British name; the number has varied from 300,000 to 50,000 victims. But this is a myth devised by passion and self-interest; unquestionably much that was atrocious was done, as has always happened in crises of the kind: there were cruel scenes of revenge and blood; but the deaths of the settlers caused by violence seem not to have been more than a few thousand, though doubtless numbers perished from other causes, cold, exposure, and the hardships of winter. It should be added that, whatever the reason, all of Scottish blood were spared at first by the rebels; Sir Phelim O'Neill, one of their chief leaders, announced that they were in arms in the name of the King; these two facts alone tell strongly against the theory that there was anything that can be called a general massacre[1]. On the other hand the colonists, stricken down at first, had ere long

[1] It is impossible, in a sketch like this, to examine the question of the alleged massacre of 1641. The subject has been exhaustively and very ably treated by Mr Lecky, *History of England in the Eighteenth Century*, II. 128, 156.

stood savagely at bay; and, after the fashion of a dominant race, they were guilty of barbarities of all kinds, probably worse than any inflicted on them. And when armed troops at last appeared in the field, the conduct of their leaders seems to have been such as it was in other Irish rebellions; the country was harried far and wide; the insurgents were slaughtered without mercy, or regard to infancy, sex, and age: the Irishry were treated as mere beasts of prey. The rebellion followed the course of recent confiscations; it extended into Wicklow, Longford, and one or two other counties, which had been scenes of recent "plantations."

The rising of the Celts of Ulster soon received the support of another but very different movement. The old Englishry of the Pale and in other parts of Ireland were, we have seen, nearly all Catholics; they had suffered from the religious persecution of late years; they were exasperated by the severe measures taken against the Catholics of England by the Long Parliament. An Act of that Assembly, wholly unlawful, and trampling on the rights of the Irish Parliament, which offered lands in Ireland to such "adventurers" as would advance money to put down the Ulster rebellion, had alarmed and provoked some of their leading men; the Lords Justices had grossly affronted several Lords of the Pale by hinting that they were in the plot of O'Moore; they had refused to convene the Irish Parliament, which would have at least listened to complaints of grievances; and a widespread feeling of panic was abroad, exhibited in stories of hideous portents, that Catholicism in Ireland and the Catholic name were to be extirpated by a Puritan crusade. Many Catholics of the Pale at last rose in arms, and many of the Catholic Englishry in other counties; but they professed, and doubtless felt, they were loyal to the Crown, and they rose only to defend their religion, threatened, as they not unjustly believed, with destruction. A considerable irregular force was arrayed and placed under the command of Preston, a scion of one of the Houses of the Pale, who had seen much service; and the insurrection spread over parts of Leinster and Munster. Meanwhile the rebels of Ulster had passed under the control of Owen Roe O'Neill, a kinsman of the illustrious Tyrone, and a distinguished soldier in the army of Spain ; and O'Moore—evidently a very able man—had the address to bring together the leaders of both risings, and to persuade them to act in concert in the war. The "armies" of the Irishry and the Englishry thus nominally coalesced, though they had scarcely a single object in common ; and their chiefs were completely separated in their aspirations and views.

The insurrectionary forces, though mainly composed of peasants hardly armed, and the rudest levies, had soon swarmed over large tracts of the country, keeping, as a rule, divided from each other in the field. The resistance they encountered was fitful and weak, for events had well-nigh paralysed the power of the state. The Lords Justices made scarcely a sign, and have been charged with letting the rebellion go on in order to reap a crop of forfeitures; the Royal army, commanded by Ormond, a most noble-minded servant of Charles, was deplorably small, and full of discontent; the Long Parliament, if burning to strike down the "accursed Irish Papists," whatever their race, was engaged in a bitter quarrel with the King, and was unable to act with effect in Ireland. Civil war raged in three of the Irish provinces, in a desultory fashion, for many months; Connaught alone was kept in comparative peace by Clanricarde, the head of the ancient De Burghs, and one of the best and truest of the Cavaliers. The struggle was still often marked by atrocious deeds, when Protestant and Catholic, Saxon and Celt, encountered each other in irregular strife : these scenes formed a hideous war of race and religion. But when anything like real war was conducted, Preston and O'Neill kept their troops

v.] *From the death of Elizabeth to the Restoration.* 141

under, upheld discipline, always gave quarter; Ormond, too, acted as became a soldier; Lord Inchiquin alone, in command for the Crown in Munster, gave a free hand to the excesses of his men, nearly all of the colonial Englishry, and allowed their evil passions to run riot. The conflict disclosed no events of interest; there were two or three sieges of walled towns; but nothing worthy of the name of a battle was fought; the scene was one of petty skirmishes, general confusion, and bloodshed. Numbers, however, and enthusiasm told by degrees: the Royal army, and the scanty levies sent in driblets, from time to time, by the Long Parliament, gradually lost their hold over five-sixths of the island, though they retained possession of many of the towns and forts. By the summer of 1643, the rebel forces were masters of by far the greatest part of Ireland.

A remarkable effort had, meanwhile, been made to give the two-fold rising coherence, and even a constitutional aspect. The rebellion in Ulster, we have seen, had had the support of some of the Irish priesthood; and the Catholic Primate of Armagh had described it as just. This was a significant prelude to what followed; a synod of the great body of the Catholic clergy met in Kilkenny in May 1642; and an Assembly, professing to represent the Catholics of both races, in all parts of Ireland, met also, in the same place, in October. It deserves notice that this Convention, which spoke for the first time in the name of an immense majority of the Irish people, was brought together by sacerdotal influence; nothing could prove more the power of the priesthood, and how even the germs of Irish national life, which in no age had a chance of being developed, had long before this been wholly extinguished. The Assembly—it strongly resembled in form the General Assembly of the Kirk in Scotland—was composed of clerical and lay members; it called itself the "Confederation of the Irish Catholics"; it assumed most of the authority of a real Parliament, and of the executive government of the state.

It was ruled by a Supreme Council, with subordinate provincial and lesser Councils; the Supreme Council took into its hands the general direction and control of the war, and nearly the whole administration of civil affairs. The Confederates repudiated with indignant emphasis the charge that they were, in any sense, rebels; "Irishmen, unanimous for God, for King, for Country,"—such was the device on their common seal—they declared that they were in arms only to defend the rights of the Church, of the Crown, of Ireland; and while they announced themselves loyal subjects of Charles, they avowed their hostility to the Long Parliament—and especially to its Puritan zealots—flinging back on these the charge of rebellion. They prepared lists of grievances and demands to be laid before the King; and at the same time the Council divided Ireland into four districts to be held by its troops, and sent envoys to Foreign Powers—France and Austria were the chief of these—to seek assistance, or, at least, sympathy.

Had the Confederates, at this juncture, been swayed by a single commanding and able ruler, and been firmly united in mind, they possibly might have obtained terms for Ireland, which would have made a change in her subsequent history. The civil war in England had gone against the Parliament; its authority in Ireland was very weak; and if Charles cared little about any of his Irish subjects, he probably preferred the Catholic Irish at heart, to English Puritan and Scotch Presbyterian settlers, even if these formed a new "English interest." Ormond too, inclined strongly towards the old Englishry; he had, in fact, kinsmen in the Confederate ranks; Clanricarde, a Catholic himself, held the same sentiments; and both nobles, foremost among the servants of the Crown, detested the men in power at the Castle, and had no liking for the dominant colonial caste in Ireland. A settlement, therefore, might have been effected, which would have undone some, at least, of the

v.] *From the death of Elizabeth to the Restoration.* 143

wrongs of the past; the Long Parliament might have accepted a compromise, for its power was, at present, in the greatest danger. But there was no Tyrone in the Supreme Council, no one deserving the name of a true statesman; and once more the divisions, which so often have wrecked Irish hopes, deprived the Confederates of weight and strength, though in this instance Celtic want of insight was not chiefly to blame. The sacerdotal party thought only of the claims of the Church; wished to establish it in complete ascendency; aimed at making Ireland a satellite of Rome, a Catholic outpost against Protestant England. The old Englishry sought merely to obtain a mitigation of the religious tests, to secure freedom of worship and just government: they had a traditional aversion to the Celtic Irishry; and they condemned to a man the rising of Ulster, and the deeds of blood which had been the consequence. The Irish Celts and their leaders, on the other hand, had their eyes fixed on their tribal possessions; they loved their ruined altars, but their hearts were set on being masters again of their lost lands; and they had bitterly resented a resolution made by the Supreme Council, which dashed these hopes. The Confederacy, formidable as its appearance was, was thus really little better than a rope of sand, which an accident, or even a slight strain, might dissolve, or at least render of not much practical use.

A truce or cessation, as it was called, was made between the Confederates and the King, in the autumn of 1643, to the intense indignation of the men in power at Westminster. Negotiations went on for many months, interrupted by occasional skirmishes in the field and by the conflict of race and creed continuing to rage in many parts of Ireland. Extravagant demands were made on Charles by agents of the Catholic Irish League and of the Protestant settlers, significant of the passions burning in their hearts; but these were dismissed and came to nothing. The position of the King had become difficult in the extreme; to yield to demands of Irish Catholics would increase the anger of Puritan England, nay irritate his most devoted friends; every allowance certainly is to be made for him. But nothing can excuse the perfidious selfishness of his conduct, at this crisis of Irish affairs; it was a principal cause of his unhappy fate. His object was to induce the Confederacy to give him armed support, and yet to concede as little as possible to them, and he employed Ormond, now Lord Lieutenant, to make what he called "the best bargain" for him, and to treat openly on this basis. But, seeking as it were to have two strings to his bow, he empowered a favourite, Glamorgan, to deal in secret with the Catholic Irish, and to offer large terms, in the hope of gaining their assistance, in any event. This Kingcraft seemed, for a moment, successful; the Confederates trusting to Royal promises sent a contingent of troops that landed in England, and made preparations to send more; and though these auxiliaries were destroyed by Fairfax, Protestant England and the Parliament were long kept in dread of an invasion of Papist Irishry, more abhorred than savages, and stained, as it was noised abroad, with the blood of a hideous massacre. Meanwhile, Ormond, loyal and honest, proposed a settlement which went no further than to secure a kind of toleration for the Irish Catholics, and a limited freedom of Catholic worship; Glamorgan held out brilliant but indistinct hopes, and made offers more ample than those of Ormond; but neither the one nor the other fell in with the demands of the extreme Confederate parties, or agreed to an Irish Catholic ascendency, or to a revolution in the ownership of the land. Ere long Glamorgan's dealings were found out; Charles instantly disowned them in fear and trembling at the anger of the incensed Parliament; and as Naseby had by this time been lost, and the cause of the King was on the verge of ruin, a majority of the Confederates thought that all that was to be done was to accept the terms

v.] *From the death of Elizabeth to the Restoration.* 145

of Ormond, almost illusory as they were. They had gained scarcely anything, and had provoked the indignation of the great mass of Englishmen; there can be no stronger proof of the weakness and absence of wisdom, and of the divisions, which prevailed in their councils.

The "Peace of 1646," as it was called, however, did not bring the civil war in Ireland to an end. Charles, now a captive in the hands of the Scots, let Ormond know that he would not be bound by it—he feared Presbyterian and Puritan wrath—the men of violence in the Confederacy protested against it. The priestly party had, for some time, been backed by Rinuccini, a nuncio from Rome, and a representative of ultramontane policy, and of the Catholic revival, its passions, its hopes; and Rinuccini had no notion of consenting to the terms of Ormond for Catholic Ireland. He cared nothing for the cause of a heretic king; he had regarded Glamorgan as an empty boaster; he was determined to secure Ireland for the Church and the Catholic Powers of Europe. Drawing the priests and their followers in his wake, he flung himself into the arms of Owen Roe O'Neill and of the insurrectionary Celts of Ulster, indignant to a man that their claims to the land had been disregarded in the negotiations of late years. A sudden turn in the war had just given O'Neill extraordinary influence in the Confederate councils. Monroe, an officer in command of the Parliamentary forces in Ulster, had sought an opportunity to attack O'Neill; on the 5th of June 1646, he crossed the Blackwater, not far from the scene of Tyrone's victory at Yellow Ford, and fell on the Irish leader near the village of Benburb. He was at the head of some 7000 men; O'Neill was, it seems, inferior in numbers; but he contrived to keep his enemy all day in check, until he had called in an outlying detachment; and he skilfully assailed Monroe with decisive effect, as that commander was about to retreat. The army of Monroe, nearly all Scots, fighting hopelessly, with a river at its back, appears to have been almost destroyed; its remains fled in utter rout, far beyond Armagh, leaving the Irishry masters of the greatest part of Ulster.

This victory raised Irish hopes to the highest pitch of daring; Rinuccini and his adherents beheld a vision of Ireland saved by a Catholic Holy War; O'Neill and his Celts thought the time had come when the land would be set free from the stranger. The moderate party in the Confederacy was swept away; amidst Te Deums in Catholic places of worship, execrations of heresy and its votaries, and wild gatherings of the Irishry in arms, the war broke out fiercer than ever, and spread far and wide. Preston and O'Neill continued in command; they approached Dublin with a motley force of probably 20,000 men, much larger than any which could be opposed to it. The capital was for a time in real danger: but Preston and O'Neill disliked each other; their troops were men of different races and thoughts; Irish divisions and jealousies fought once more on the side of the enemies of the Irish cause, and paralysed the arms that sought to uphold it. The menacing demonstration came to nothing: a long series of negotiations followed, in which Ormond endeavoured in vain to induce the Confederates to accept the Peace. His resolution was ere long taken: it was worthy of his noble and high-minded character. The Parliament and the Army were now supreme in England; reinforcements were being sent by degrees to uphold the Protestant name in Ireland, and to make English authority felt; the King was a discrowned prisoner, weaving the web of guile, in which he was to be fatally meshed. Ormond had no thought of leaving Ireland a prey to Rinuccini and rebellious Celts in arms; of blotting out the English and Scotch settlements; of making the island a scene of turbulent anarchy; and as he could rule no longer himself, he handed his trust over to the

v.] *From the death of Elizabeth to the Restoration.* 147

rulers in power. He resigned his Lieutenancy to Commissioners named by the Parliament, and left Ireland still a loyal servant of the Crown.

At this critical juncture the tide turned quickly and strongly against the Confederates in the field. Dublin had been placed in the hands of Michael Jones, a stout and able Puritan soldier; he succeeded in mustering a respectable force, and he completely defeated Preston near the borders of Meath. Meanwhile Inchiquin, a scion of the great race of O'Brien, who had gone over to the side of the Parliament, had stormed the holy city of Cashel; in a short time he routed the Confederate Taaffe, in a combat amidst the Tipperary wilds. These defeats, and the growing power of the Houses at Westminster, placed the Moderate party in the Confederacy in the ascendant again; Rinuccini and O'Neill resisted in vain; negotiations were opened once more with Ormond and with Henrietta Maria, the Queen of Charles, both at this time in France. A treaty was made towards the close of 1648[1] containing somewhat larger concessions than that which had proved abortive two years before; and Commissioners of Trust, as they were called, were appointed to see its provisions executed. This compact was accepted by the great body of the Confederates as all they could reasonably expect; Ormond returned to Ireland, and a large part of the Confederate forces united with a few thousand Royalists, still willing to follow their old leader; the whole being placed under Ormond's command. The execution of the King ere long followed; and this tragic event gave a great increase to the power of Ormond thus strangely restored. The old Englishry, who had never lost their attachment to the Crown, took up arms again in its cause, and shook off all contact with rebel Celts; Inchiquin returned to his former allegiance, and appeared in the field with his Munster

[1] It was not actually signed until 14 January, 1649, but it had been arranged some time before.

levies; and Ormond soon found himself at the head of forces formidable in numbers at least. A thrill of loyalty had passed over Ireland, and had produced great and unexpected results.

Rinuccini had left Ireland by this time; he had failed to annex the island to the Holy See. Owen Roe O'Neill, however, remained; it ought to have been his first step to join Ormond and the Confederates in the war. The English Parliament had marked down his Celts for vengeance, and had disposed beforehand of Irish lands; he should have made common cause against the common foe. But he bitterly resented the late peace and the attitude of the old Englishry; no provision had been made for the forfeited lands; he kept aloof from his former allies, nay negotiated with Parliamentary men in England—a passage of history that remains obscure. Meanwhile Ormond and his forces overran the country; even the Scots of Ulster had declared for the King, for the tragedy at Whitehall had stirred all Scotsmen; Derry and Dublin were the only towns of any size that held out for the Regicide Commonwealth; the prospects of Charles II seemed so promising that his arrival in Ireland was daily expected. Ormond laid siege to Dublin in the summer of 1649; and his success was, at Westminster, deemed to be certain. In an attempt, however, to cut off supplies from the Bay, he extended his army, and was struck down by Jones; his retreat from the capital was the first signal of the discomfiture of the Confederate cause. It was now known that Cromwell was on his way to Ireland; Owen Roe O'Neill turned at last to Ormond, and offered to unite with him against the dreaded invasion. But the divisions of Irishmen had done their work; the opportunity, as had happened so often, was lost; a terrible hour for Ireland was at hand. O'Neill died a few weeks afterwards; he was certainly a brave and accomplished warrior; he is still a hero of the traditions of the Irish Celt; but he was evidently devoid of statesmanlike

v.] *From the death of Elizabeth to the Restoration.* 149

wisdom. He is largely to blame for the disunion that did so much to wreck the cause of his countrymen in the long civil war; he seems, like so many Celts, to have been carried away by fancies, and to have been unable to understand hard facts[1].

Cromwell landed in Dublin in August 1649, at the head of 10,000 men of the New Model, the invincible soldiers of Naseby and Preston. In justice to a great ruler of men it is necessary to remember from what point of view he regarded Ireland and Irish affairs. A Puritan of the sternest type, he hated Irish Catholics, whether Celts or Saxons; he had witnessed a combination to make Ireland a place of arms for the Catholic Powers, a centre of the detested influence of Rome. But, in addition, he believed that Ulster had been the scene of a general massacre of the British settlers; the Protestant caste in Ireland, in his eyes, was the only order of men that could be true to England, nay capable of being a civilised race; he knew that England had been threatened by an invasion of the abhorred Irishry, during many years; the great majority of Irishmen were resisting England to the last[2]. He had resolved, therefore, to lay a heavy hand on Ireland; to exact a terrible vengeance, righteous in his belief; to be the chosen instrument of the wrath of God, in punishing an accursed and rebellious people. His feelings, in a word, were those of the Englishmen of his day who had devoted their lives and swords to the Puritan cause, indeed of the great body of Englishmen, whose hatred and contempt of the Irish had

---

[1] The confused and complicated events of the civil war in Ireland from 1641 to 1649, are better described by Mr Gardiner than by any other historian. Leland's narrative is also good. For the feelings of the Irish Celts, see two remarkable ballads by Thomas Davis and Sir Gavan Duffy in *The Spirit of the Nation*, 11 and 28.

[2] For Cromwell's views on Ireland, at this conjuncture, see Mr Gardiner's *History of the Commonwealth and Protectorate*, I. pp. 139-40, 147-8, and a remarkable letter of Cromwell, pp. 163-4.

only increased; they were shared by his army of fierce zealots; and the fanaticism of his men was, no doubt, quickened by the prospect of a rich spoil of Irish land.

The Puritan army had reached Drogheda in the first week of September. The place, a walled town, of some strength, was held by Sir Arthur Aston, a Royalist officer, with about 3000 men, in a great measure English. Cromwell's batteries ere long effected a breach: the besieged, however, held stubbornly out; a fierce assault was made on a shattered rampart; and Cromwell passed the word round, that there was to be no quarter. A horrible scene of bloodshed followed; Aston and many of his troops were slaughtered; little mercy was shown to the Irishry in the town; Catholic friars were seized and killed in cold blood. Having struck a blow meant to deal terror, Cromwell marched southwards along the coast; he had the command of the sea, and knew its value; he was aware of the obstacles to an advance inland, and of the dangers of the Irish climate to English soldiers,—proved by the experience of many wars; and he had determined, with true military insight, not to penetrate into the interior until he had made his power felt. He was before Wexford in the early days of October; the townsmen, it is said, had done much injury to English shipping by acts of piracy; at all events they were nearly all "Irish Papists." The place fell mainly through an act of treason, but the atrocities of Drogheda occurred again; the butchery that went on seems to have been deliberate. Friars were also, in this instance, marked down for vengeance; the crucifixes they held out, in hopes of mercy, were signs of idolatry in Puritan eyes; they were pitilessly slain as the most hateful of men. "God," wrote Cromwell to Speaker Lenthall, "in His righteous justice brought a just judgment upon them."

The deeds done at Drogheda and Wexford were of the most ruthless kind; Puritan wrath was certainly one of Crom-

v.] *From the death of Elizabeth to the Restoration.* 151

well's motives. But they were not without example in the wars of that age; it was necessary to strike a terrible blow, in the existing state of affairs in Ireland; and as the English troops of Aston were the first to suffer, military ends were perhaps the principal object. Be this as it may, the cruel fate of Drogheda caused the surrender of many fortified towns; that of Wexford opened the south of Leinster to Cromwell. The victorious army now marched inland; the campaign that followed was not without changes of fortune. Cromwell was forced to draw off from the walls of Waterford; and though Kilkenny fell to his arms, a stern resistance was offered by Clonmel, where Hugh O'Neill, worthy of his illustrious race, kept the conqueror at bay for more than two months. Whether these checks are to be ascribed to the courage of despair, aroused by a struggle of life and death, exasperated by ferocious passions, or more probably to the great difficulty of conducting war in an intricate country—from the days of Strongbow to that of Mountjoy the chief obstacle to invasion from England— the ultimate result was scarcely retarded. The task of Cromwell in Ireland was ere long completed; the ever recurring divisions and feuds of Irishmen contributed to the event, as had so often happened. The impulse which had united Ormond and the Confederates, for a time, soon lost its force and gave way under the stress of defeat; the Royalists, for the most part Protestants, had little in common with Catholics in arms, opposed to them in the field but yesterday; and this was notably the case with the levies of Inchiquin, composed, as we have seen, of English settlers, and hated by the Catholics since the storm of Cashel. A great defection took place in Munster; thousands of the troops of Inchiquin and Ormond went over to the Puritan camp; the hopes of Charles II in Ireland were suddenly quenched; the Confederacy once more was almost broken up. Cromwell took his departure from Ireland in May 1650; he had, as always, shown himself to be a great soldier, if humanity shudders at Wexford and Drogheda.

A large part of Ireland had now been subdued, but Ormond had still an army in the field; it was not impossible still to defend the line of the Shannon and the wilds of Connaught. But Ormond was a Protestant and a servant of the young King; the war in Ireland had aroused the worst religious passions, especially since the advent of Cromwell; the conduct of Charles in Scotland, where he had declared himself the instrument of the Presbyterians in power, had filled the Irish Catholics with terror and despair; and a new schism divided their councils. The sacerdotal party came once more to the front; a Catholic Bishop appeared in the field and fell, preaching a Holy War with his dying lips; Catholic priests assembled their flocks in thousands, denouncing Ormond and the "Dagon of loyalty"; Catholic Ireland was told to stand aloof from a false king, from heretics in the guise of Royalists, from Protestants whatever side they took in the war; and in these circumstances it was but too evident that the contest could not be long maintained. Ormond was driven from Limerick, where he had hoped to make a stand, by a rabble maddened by these wild appeals; and after parleying with the Confederates for some time, he returned to France feeling all was lost. His office was conferred by Charles on Clanricarde: an Irish Catholic, it was hoped, could yet do something with Irish Catholics; and Clanricarde made strenuous efforts to win over the Moderates of the League to the side of the King. The priestly leaders, however, prevailed; they actually offered Ireland, as a kind of prize, to the Duke of Lorraine, and were indignant that the offer was refused. Meanwhile Ireton, who had taken command of Cromwell's army, had advanced to the Shannon; Athlone was captured, and Limerick fell after another noble effort of Hugh O'Neill; and Galway was before long surrendered, the military operations of the Irish having

v.] *From the death of Elizabeth to the Restoration.* 153

been almost paralysed. The civil war in Ireland had come to an end; the catastrophe had been accelerated by one of the worst instances of Irish dissension that history records.

Ireland lay prostrate at the feet of Cromwell; the doom of the great Puritan was sternly enforced. Some of the leaders of the rebellion of 1641 had perished; some remained to fall into the hands of the hangman. The religion of the great body of the Irish people was proscribed, as idolatry to be purged out of the land; the celebration of the Mass was made a crime; not a few priests who tried to live among their flocks, and to do their sacred office in secret, were carried off to the West Indies and sold as slaves. This was the fate, too, of many of the Irishry who had appeared in arms; merchants from Bristol contracted for the odious traffic of shipping them to Barbadoes for the planters; hundreds were doubtless thrown to the sharks on the voyage; but the descendants of the exiles are still known as what are called "the low whites" of the island. The lot, however, of the great body of the Confederate forces was less wretched; it was shared by numbers of Irish Catholics who could no longer live in the land of their birth. Ever since the days of Tyrone and Desmond Irish soldiers had made their way to the Continent; it was deemed good policy by the English Council of State, to encourage an emigration of this kind and to drain away elements that might become perilous. From 30,000 to 40,000 men, who had served, for the most part, in the late contest, were thus allowed to depart from Ireland; they flocked to the camps of foreign Powers; and they formed the first contingent of the host of Irish exiles, bitter enemies of the British name for more than a century and a half.

The subjugation of Ireland inspired Cromwell with a project of colonisation and of settling the land, more general and complete than had been ever thought of. The Long Parliament, we have seen, had offered forfeited lands to "adventurers" who had advanced moneys in the Irish war; the Puritan army was formidable and large; and unhappily nearly the whole of the Irish people had been in arms against the newborn Commonwealth. Protestant Royalists had fought for Charles with Ormond; even the Irish Presbyterians had resisted Cromwell; the old Englishry and the Irishry, all Catholics, with few exceptions, had been in the field against Puritan England, for long years; the Irishry of the Celtic race in Ulster were stained with the blood of 1641. Enormous confiscations had been already made; Cromwell resolved to "plant" the "adventurers" and his victorious soldiery in these tracts in Leinster, Munster, and Ulster; and to compel the "rebel" owners of land to take refuge in Connaught. The forfeited lands in four counties were set apart for the use of the Commonwealth; those in eighteen were to be bestowed on the "adventurers" and the Puritan host; those in seven were to be given to the English army at home, and to the levies of Munster which had deserted the King. The lands were to be allotted at nominal prices, to pay the "adventurers" and the arrears of the army; the portion of those who had lost their possessions was to be "Hell or Connaught," a phrase that has come down to this time. Spoliation, on this gigantic scale, was veiled under a semblance of law; "Courts of Claims" were set up, in which those who could prove "constant affection" to England since 1641 were not to be ejected from their lands—the judges, be it observed, were Puritans;— but a test of this kind was well-nigh mockery. About 40,000 new owners of land were thus to be scattered over three-fourths of Ireland, and even, to a certain extent, in Connaught; for that province at last was not exempted from large forfeitures. But it should be observed, as had so often occurred before, the owners of land were alone to be disturbed; the cultivators of the soil were to remain on it, hewers of wood and drawers of water for Puritan masters.

The Confiscation was carried out by degrees from 1652 to 1654. The Royalist Protestant owners were largely spared; but numbers of the old Catholic Englishry and of the Irish Celts were deprived of their estates, and were, as it was called, "transplanted" to Connaught. Millions of acres were transferred by these means; descendants of barons of the Pale and of Irish chiefs were proscribed and ruined by equal wrong; the distinction of blood between the two races was thus lessened, and that of religion was made more marked; all had been condemned as "Papists" and "rebels." Thousands of "adventurers" and soldiers were poured into these districts, all Protestants, probably for the most part Puritans, and animated by hatred and scorn of the Irishry in their midst. The method by which the settlement was at last completed curiously illustrates the ideas and sentiments of the time. The "adventurers" and the soldiers were "planted" together for the sake probably of common defence; and the lands were to be distributed to the soldiers by lot, for they had announced that they "would rather take a lott upon a barren mountain from the Lord, than a portion in the most fruitful valley of their own choice." Unfortunately, however, when the trial came the military saints rose up in wrath; the lands to be divided were of most unequal value; those whose lot fell on a bad heritage quarrelled with those whose lot fell upon a good; they had ceased to approve of the ways of Providence. After long disputes and troubles, a very able man, Dr Petty, was selected by Henry Cromwell—he had been made Deputy by the Protector—to carry out the scheme of colonisation in a rational way. Petty made an excellent survey of Ireland,— a remarkable performance for the seventeenth century—and distributed most of the forfeited lands among the new colonists in tolerably just proportions, and with a due regard to value.

The results of Cromwell's settlement of the land of Ireland must be noticed when, a few years afterwards, it was modified to a considerable extent. Enough here to say that in large parts of Ireland it placed a ruling caste, in the main Puritan, and almost wholly of English descent, on the neck of the Catholic Irish people; and—apart from special causes of decline—such a scheme of landed relations could not really flourish. Yet there is much evidence that Ireland made material progress in the years that followed; though probably this, in a great degree, was another illusion of English statesmen. It is true that, except during the shock of the Cromwellian storm, the country was less ruined and harried than in the wars of Elizabeth's reign; yet civilisation was generally effaced where it had begun to make its influence felt; a number of towns and villages were destroyed; a third part of the population, it has been said, disappeared again. In circumstances like these the establishment of a strong Government—for Cromwell ruled in Ireland with a high hand—the introduction of a new breed of colonists, and the advance of agriculture in their train, above all the enforcement of order and law, seem to have produced beneficent results, as regards the resources and the wealth of the country; these certainly increased, as in the time of Strafford. The peace, indeed, was the peace of oppression and despair; signs were soon seen that it could not be lasting; the ashes were burning beneath the surface. Nevertheless Clarendon, an unwilling witness, thus described some effects of Cromwell's rule in Ireland; "there were many buildings raised for beauty, as well as use, orderly and regular plantations of trees, and fences and enclosures raised throughout the kingdom, purchases made by one from another, at very valuable rates, and all other conveyances and settlements executed, as in a kingdom at peace with itself[1]."

Cromwell effected one great Constitutional change in the Government of Ireland deserving special notice. The Long

[1] See Macaulay's essay on Sir William Temple, II. 12, ed. 1854.

Parliament, we have seen, had violated the rights of the Irish Parliament; the Irish Parliament had had, for years, a strong Catholic minority in it. This state of things was not to be endured by the great Puritan despot of England; besides, Cromwell doubtless perceived that the parliamentary unity of the Three Kingdoms was necessary to secure for England a leading place in Europe. He did away with the Irish Parliament, but summoned a certain number of members, of course of the dominant race and faith, to represent Ireland in his reformed House of Commons; he was thus the precursor of the Union of another age. His rule in Ireland continued to be the stern tyranny it was from the first, but not a murmur of discontent was heard; the land, we have said, was at peace under the Puritan sword. Henry Cromwell, who remained at the head of Irish affairs, was a right-minded and humane man; he restrained the fanaticism of his Council to a certain extent; but the great mass of the Irish people was kept in a state of abject submission. The revolution, which after the death of Cromwell led to the Restoration of Charles II, ran a course, in Ireland, somewhat like that in England. There was no Rump like that of the Long Parliament, but the army and its leading chiefs were divided; Ludlow, who had been appointed to command in Dublin, aspired to play the part of Lambert; but a junta of the old Royalist officers seized the reins of power, and soon came into communication with Monk. A slight attempt at opposition was made by Cromwellian soldiers, who had settled on their lands; but Ireland like England declared for a "free Parliament," and Charles was ere long seated on his Irish throne.

During the period we have been just surveying some of the characteristics of the Ireland of the past disappear or become less prominent. We pass from the Ireland of the Pale extended by conquest, but still largely affected by Celtic usage, to an Ireland subjugated and under English law; we reach a time of something like Constitutional Government supreme in every part of the country; we see at the Castle the rule of the soldier replaced by that of the prelate and lawyer, and of the commanding mind of Strafford. An era of horrible civil war follows; the hostile races and faiths of Ireland encounter each other in deadly conflict; an immense majority of the Irish people, at a time when religious passions had peculiar force, engage in a struggle with Puritan England; and Cromwell closes the strife, crushing Ireland down, and ruling the country with an iron hand after effecting an immense change in its social condition. The period, as a whole, contains two phases; each presents dark and sinister features, and reveals much that History deplores, if all is not disastrous and evil.

In the first phase peace is not broken by the sword, but an archaic type of society is effaced by the introduction of English law and land-tenures, by force; and vast tracts of Ulster are torn from their old possessors, and made the seat of a colony foreign in faith and blood. Large confiscations follow that are mere acts of wrong; and the extension of the sphere of the Anglican Church, the continuous immigration of Protestant settlers, the fierce resistance of the Irish Catholic Church, and the religious persecution which is the result, enormously increase animosities of creed and enlarge the old and deep divisions of race in Ireland. The Irish Parliament, also, is packed, in the interest of the Crown and of the English and Scotch colonies; and an era of despotic rule is marked by the perfidy of Charles I, by Strafford's tyranny, by the attempt to confiscate wholesale, by mere arbitrary power. Yet civilisation did, to some extent, make real progress in those days, especially in Ulster; and the organising genius of Strafford and his firm and equal government unquestionably caused material prosperity to advance.

In the second phase the seeds of evil bear their natural fruit:

the rising of the Celts of Ulster in 1641, to be distinctly traced to the spoliation of their lands, and the defection of the old Catholic Englishry, mainly due to the wrongs done to their faith, lead to a murderous civil war. In this the power of England is shaken for a time; Catholic Ireland, divided against herself, defies Protestant England and keeps her in dread of invasion at a most critical time; but after a struggle protracted for years, she succumbs, largely owing to her own disunion. Cromwell then subdues Ireland as she was never subdued before; he confiscates millions of acres of Irish land; he makes a conquering army of Puritan soldiers lords of a Catholic people vanquished and abhorred; he establishes Protestant Ascendency, and its correlative, Catholic subjection, in Ireland, in the very worst form. Nevertheless Cromwell's Irish policy had a good side; it secured order and a kind of social progress: above all it prefigured the Union.

Three great facts appear with peculiar clearness through the troubled confusion of this whole period; they should be steadily kept in mind. Firstly, the annihilation of old Celtic usage, especially of the tribal land system, the substitution of English law, the confiscations of the reigns of the two first Stuarts and of the rule of Cromwell, the establishment of the dominant Anglican Church, and the ascendency secured for English and Scotch settlers—all this was a continuation of the Tudor scheme of forcing foreign institutions on the Irish people. Part of this policy was, in a sense, successful; part was unquestionably well meant, but much of it was due to sheer cupidity, to bad statecraft, to the passions of conquest; but its results in the main were to make the great mass of Irishmen more hostile to England than they had ever been, and to aggravate the divisions and strife of races in Ireland. Secondly, the interference of the Crown with the Irish Parliament, and the arbitrary conduct of the Long Parliament in imposing on Ireland measures of its own, did infinite mischief of many kinds; the growth of constitutional government was stopped; undue favour was shown to a ruling caste, which felt that it was given a free hand to oppress; the foundations of many evils in the future were laid. The third and most striking feature of the period was this—the religious discords of Ireland became suddenly more intense than they had ever been; and in the struggle, which was the result, they seem to make other divisions less, nay to efface them to some extent. In the Civil War, from 1641 to 1650, the name of Protestant and Catholic separated the hostile camps more thoroughly than that of Saxon and Celt; but the distinction of religion, it must be borne in mind, largely coincided with that of race, and had only lately acquired a special prominence of its own. Cromwell made this distinction extraordinarily wide; the Protestant Irish, in his eyes, were the sheep to be protected in the fold; the Catholic Irish were the goats to be hunted away and destroyed, and difference of race was of little moment. Religion appears from this time forward to be the determining force in Irish History, which seems to revolve, as it were, around the destinies of an Ireland of opposite faiths; and yet perhaps if not so plainly manifest the distinction of race had after all the most potent influence.

The progress of English power in Ireland, in this period, bears the character it bore in the age of Elizabeth; it was often marked with guile and most atrocious deeds; and the wrongs of Ireland were many and cruel. Yet parallels to them may be found in contemporaneous, even in more recent history; this must be taken into account in a fair review of the subject. Most of the confiscations which took place in Ireland, from the days of Mountjoy to those of Cromwell, were iniquitous in the extreme; but it was the time of the Edicts of Restitution, and of the rapine carried out in Germany with even less pretence to justice. The perfidy of James I and of Charles I, and Strafford's tyranny in Irish affairs, resemble

v.] *From the death of Elizabeth to the Restoration.* 161

parts of the stern policy of Richelieu in France; all were alike instances of the abuse of the rights claimed by kings in the seventeenth century. What was done at Drogheda and Wexford was less horrible than what was done at the sack of Magdeburg; Cromwell may have thought of what had been charged against Tilly. The Cromwellian conquest of Ireland had much in common with the Republican conquest of La Vendée; in both cases a community relatively small rushed to arms against a great nation, which claimed its allegiance, at a grave crisis; in both cases the vengeance inflicted was frightful. The peace given to Ireland by Cromwell, indeed, was very different from the peace given by Bonaparte to La Vendée; but, in a matter like this, the standard of opinion in the seventeenth century completely differed from that of the nineteenth, especially in a religious contest. For the rest, the aversion and contempt, due to causes before referred to, with which Ireland inspired Englishmen, were naturally increased in this period; and her divisions, her weakness, her wretched state, contributed, as before, to bring on her much that she suffered. "A people," it has been truly said, "divided internally, and without the element of political organisation, invites the sword of the conqueror[1]."

The Irish community was being now cast into a mould of usage, of life, of relations, which, though modified to a very great extent, has never yet been completely effaced. In everything, but especially in the land, and in by far the greatest part of the country, a ruling and foreign Protestant caste were made masters of a conquered Catholic people; each was divided from the other by the most unhappy memories. Protestant Ascendency and Catholic Subjection were giving the social structure, so to speak, its form; the distinction of religion, we repeat, seemed to have replaced the old distinction

[1] Gardiner's *History of the Commonwealth and Protectorate*, I. 176.

of race, though perhaps this was in appearance only. The condition of things thus evolved was pregnant with evils, and has been attended with calamitous results; and though it had had its origin in the past, it was in a great degree brought about by the Cromwellian Conquest. The despotism of Cromwell was a bad government; but it produced, in Ireland, some good fruits; and had it been gradually made to conform to justice, to wisdom, to reason, to right, it might have established an order of things which would have been its vindication in the sight of history. This, however, was not to be the course of events in Ireland; light was not yet to shine on her dark destiny.

CHAPTER VI.

FROM THE RESTORATION TO THE CAPITULATION OF LIMERICK.

Contrast between England and Ireland at the Restoration. Confusion and disorder in Ireland. Multiplicity of claims arising from the land. The policy of the King dictated by Clarendon. The Church restored. Presbyterian ministers expelled. Lavish grants of land. The declaration of the King as to the land. The Acts of Settlement and Explanation. Wrong done to many Catholic owners. Injustice of the arrangement as a whole. The Cromwellian Conquest and settlement in the main confirmed. The results. Protestant ascendency and Catholic subjection made permanent. The Viceroyalty of Ormond. Restrictions on the commerce of Ireland. The Viceroyalties of Lord Berkeley and Lord Essex. Ireland comparatively prosperous and free from trouble at the death of Charles II. Accession of James II. What his Irish policy ought to have been. His views on Irish affairs. Clarendon made Lord Lieutenant. Tyrconnell possesses real power. He transforms the army in Ireland. He is made Deputy. The military and civil power handed over to the Catholics. Rising of the Irishry. The Revolution of 1688. Attitude of Catholic Ireland. The Irish spring to arms. The colonists driven into Ulster. Enniskillen and Londonderry. The siege of Londonderry. Heroism of the defence. The siege raised. The Battle of Newton Butler. The Irish Parliament of 1689. Character of its measures. These have been much misrepresented. Invasion of Ireland by Schomberg. He is compelled to retreat into winter quarters. William III takes the field. The Battle of the Boyne. Fine conduct of the Irish horse. Defeat of the Irish army and flight of James. The first siege of Limerick. Fine exploit of Sarsfield. William raises the siege. Marlborough takes Cork and Kinsale. Great results of this success. Ginkle takes Athlone. Battle of Aghrim. Defeat of the Irish army. The second siege and the capitulation of Limerick. The Articles. Departure to France of a large part of the Irish army. Reflections.

THE contrast, continually on the increase, which England and Ireland always presented, was more conspicuous at the Restoration than at any previous time. In England the Monarchy and the Church had fallen; but the civil war was not a death struggle; the supremacy of the law had been maintained; the type of civilised life had not been broken up; the land had not been torn from its owners wholesale. The condition of Ireland was altogether different; a horrible conflict of races and faiths had been prolonged for nearly ten years; the structure of society had been overthrown; and a huge confiscation, greater than any other of the kind, had seated a Puritan army on the soil, the rulers of a conquered Catholic people. On the return of Charles II to the throne the peace enforced by Cromwell in Ireland ceased; everything became confusion, disorder and trouble; and, at the prospect of a change in the existing order of things, there were wild stirrings of fear, of hope and of passion. This movement was chiefly associated with the land—thrown, it was said, "like a stag to a ravening pack of hounds"; and the new Government was beset by many kinds of claimants, eager to retain what they had already won, or to recover possessions taken from them in the Revolutionary period now come to an end. The Cromwellian soldiery laid their hands on their swords and vowed they would keep what the Lord had bestowed; the "adventurers" were equally bold and tenacious. But Royalist Protestants, who had served with Ormond, and Catholic Confederates, who had been in arms for the King, insisted on being restored to the lands of which they had been deprived by Cromwell; leaders of the Celtic Irishry made the same demand; and Royalist officers sought to obtain compensation, in land, for arrears of pay. The Anglican Church, too, had lost its estates; its episcopate seems to have almost disappeared, though its ritual and worship had not been proscribed; and the Presbyterian clergy of the Scotch colonists had, in Ulster, and even in the other provinces, encroached on its benefices, to a certain extent.

The task before Charles in Ireland was difficult in the extreme; to do justice was perhaps impossible. The conduct of the King, however, reflected the passions of the hour, and was marked by the favouritism and the want of good faith characteristic of his House. A considerable part of the Cromwellian forfeitures had not yet passed out of the hands of the state; the Anglican Church regained its possessions, including its large revenue of tithes; and its hierarchy was replaced in its old splendour. The Presbyterian ministers were expelled from the glebes and houses they had obtained; a test was ere long imposed on them, resembling that which had been imposed on Catholics—(Nonconformist persecution prevailed in England)—this compelled a certain number to leave Ireland; and though not the cause of much present mischief, was ultimately to lead to grave evils. At the same time large grants of land were made to the Duke of York, to Ormond, and to other friends of the King; and several of the great nobles of the old Catholic Englishry recovered the estates of which they had been despoiled. Many thousands of acres were thus bestowed, without regard to equity or sound policy; but Charles had been persuaded, or had persuaded himself, that, with dexterous management, a sufficient fund of land would remain to satisfy the great crowd of claimants. In this, as in all other matters, Clarendon was, for the present, his chief adviser; like nine-tenths of his countrymen, Clarendon hated the Catholic Irish with intense hatred, and wished to uphold the Protestant and colonial caste in Ireland; and the King probably shared this feeling, at least had no desire to be a Don Quixote, and to show Irish sympathies that would offend Englishmen. It was announced that the "English interest" was to be maintained in Ireland; and the Government issued a Declaration, arranging the claims to the Irish land upon this basis. The "adventurers" and the Cromwellian soldiers were, with some exceptions, to retain their possessions; certain classes of Protestant owners were to regain their estates; and some lands were allotted to Royalist officers, in discharge of their pay. These demands would obviously absorb the great bulk of the land; but there remained the large body of the Irish Catholic owners, perhaps 4000 or 5000 persons, and what was this order of men to receive? An expedient was devised, which was not the least base of the many devised by Stuart statecraft. The Catholic owners were to be restored; but their restoration was not to take place until they had satisfied a test of "innocence," severe as that of Cromwell's "constant affection," and so framed that few, it was thought, could get through its meshes. It was nothing to Charles that he had made solemn pledges to them on many occasions; they were a weak and inconvenient class of "Irish Papists," to be disposed of by one means or another.

The Irish Parliament had by this time been restored as part of the old Constitution of the land; it was to give the Declaration the sanction of law. But it was full of Protestant, even of Puritan zealots; scarcely a Catholic, in fact, had a seat in it; and an outcry arose against the proposed arrangement, denounced as too favourable to the subject race and faith. The discussion was transferred to the Council at Whitehall, which kept a strict hold, under Poynings' Law, on the assembly in Dublin, in this matter; but though angry clamour was frequent and loud, little change was made in the original terms, and an Act, known as the Act of Settlement, was passed, confirming the distribution of the Irish land, of which we have seen the main outlines. Meanwhile, however, an incident had occurred which threw everything into confusion again. A Commission had been appointed to decide who "were innocent Papists"; and, strange to say, many more Catholic owners contrived to satisfy the iniquitous test of "innocence" than Charles and his advisers had deemed possible. The "English interest" in Ireland broke out into wrath; an insurrection was threatened by the Cromwellian soldiers; the Castle was for some time in danger. After months of delay and bickerings of all kinds a compromise was at last effected; an Act of "Explanation" was added to the Act of Settlement. The adventurers and the soldiers were forced or induced to surrender a third part of their lands; the Catholic owners adjudged "innocent" were reinstated; and a few were restored by the special favour of the King. But the great body of the Catholic owners, from 3000 to 4000 in number, were not allowed to try to make proof of "innocence"; they were shut out from all hope of relief; they were deprived of their ancestral estates for ever, an act of the grossest and most cruel injustice. Many of the injured class carried their swords to the Continent, and became another contingent of exiles eager to avenge their wrongs on the English name.

The settlement of the Irish land thus effected was alike unwise and unjustifiable. The dominant Church of a caste regained all that it had lost; courtiers and favourites obtained possessions to which they had no claim; the Cromwellian forfeitures, immense and unjust, were to a considerable extent ratified; thousands of despoiled owners were deprived of their rights; the seeds were thickly sown of a harvest of evil. The most striking feature certainly of the scheme, and that attended by the most lasting results, was the confirmation, in a very great degree, of the huge confiscation due to the sword of Cromwell. The two Acts of Settlement, as they may be called, permanently transferred to Protestant English owners, for the most part of the Puritan faith, at least a fourth part of the land of Ireland; and these were surrounded by a Catholic people reduced to serfdom, but retaining the Celtic memory of the past. This state of things was to prove enduring; but Cromwell's project of colonising the Irish land, effectually and on an enormous scale, failed, as projects of the kind had failed before. The number of the settlers was, from the first, too small; the Cromwellian soldiers sold their allotments wholesale; most of the "adventurers" were absentees, adding thus to a list already too large; the colonists who remained sank, in thousands of instances, into the mass of the Irishry in their midst, a transformation which had been seen through centuries. The ultimate effect of the Cromwellian Conquest was to plant in the land of Ireland three or four thousand owners, alien in race and faith from the occupiers of the soil, and separated from them by the worst traditions[1].

The confirmation, however, of the Cromwellian forfeitures gave to the Protestant Ascendency, which, we have said, had before this time been established in power, a great addition of strength and influence. The Protestant English and Scotch colonists were now the possessors of perhaps three-fourths of the soil; a fourth only was left to the old owners, the Catholic Englishry and the Catholic Celts; and beneath these were the conquered Catholic Irishry, five-sixths of the population of the country. In by far the greatest part of Ireland, therefore, a dominant caste, distinct in blood and religion, and hostile to the mass of the people, had been made owners of nearly all the land; the subject race had sunk into mere occupiers. The

---

[1] Mr Lecky's *History of England in the Eighteenth Century*, vol. II. chap. 6, contains an admirable sketch of the Cromwellian confiscations and their results. See also Mr Prendergast's *Cromwellian Settlement of Ireland*, and Lord Edmond Fitzmaurice's *Life of Sir William Petty*.

VI.] *From the Restoration to the Limerick Capitulation.* 169

only exception to this state of things was found in the colonised parts of Ulster, where the settlers were numerous, and of all classes. The social relations, connected with the land, which would grow out of this state of affairs would necessarily bear the marks of their origin; from this time forward, agrarian discontent, occasionally associated with rebellious movements, becomes a marked feature of Irish History. But if Protestant Ascendency, as we have said, was most distinctly apparent in the land, it had become established in every part of the political and social life of Ireland, almost as completely as under the rule of Cromwell. The Irish Catholic Church, indeed, and its priesthood were not persecuted as they had lately been; and after the Restoration, the Catholic faith was usually tolerated, even protected. But the Irish Parliament was composed of Protestants; Protestants, as a rule, filled every office of trust; Catholics, except at rare intervals of time, were excluded from the administration of the state, and even from municipal offices. Ireland was thus finally separated into the two divisions, to which we have so often referred; Protestant Ascendency was embodied in the English and Scotch Protestants, a caste possessing almost supreme power; Catholic Subjection was seen in a vanquished Catholic people. The distinction, too, between the old Englishry and the Irish Celts had become much less marked; both races had been involved in a common wreck of fortune.

The order of things which the Restoration left standing in Ireland was unnatural, and was certain to lead to ills in the future. For the present, however, the land was at peace; the strong hand of Cromwell was still felt; after a brief interval of passing trouble Protestant Ireland saw its domination secured; Catholic Ireland acquiesced, brooding only on its wrongs. This period of repose, broken by faint stirrings of unrest, disorder, and smothered discontent, signs of passions smouldering beneath the surface, continued for nearly twenty-five years, and was perhaps the longest of its kind that had yet been seen. The government, during the greater part of this time, was placed in the well-tried hands of Ormond, created a duke by Charles II, and perhaps the foremost subject of the Crown; his Viceroyalty was one of no little interest. Ormond was not a statesman of a high order, but he was an administrator of considerable powers; and if feeling and interest made him incline to the side of Protestant Ascendency somewhat too much, he had none of the English contempt for Irishmen; he was a true and noble-minded Irishman at heart, he had a genuine and a patriotic love for his country. His conduct in peace had some points in common with his conduct during the protracted Civil War. A Protestant himself, and a loyal subject, he upheld the "Protestant interest," now supreme in Ireland; and he refused to listen to complaints against the Acts of Settlement—they were, in his view, necessary to maintain the present order of things—a resolve not surprising in his case, for they had made him the master of large estates. He had little sympathy, too, with leaders of the Irish Celts; he had not forgotten their attitude in the war; they had repudiated his advice on the Acts of Settlement; and, not improbably, he felt towards them as the great nobles of the old Englishry had felt for ages. Nor did he do much to mitigate the state of Catholic subjection he found established; he did not use his immense influence to introduce Catholics into the Irish Parliament; he left Protestant Ascendency to rule, throughout Ireland, in the Municipal Bodies, which especially controlled the petty boroughs of James; he did not admit Catholics to offices of trust; he did not dispense, as had been often done before, with the religious tests to which they were exposed. Nevertheless Ormond was a good governor,—wise, moderate, upright, strictly just—within the limits of the system made to his hand; he maintained order and law with success; like Strafford he kept petty tyrants under; he won the esteem even of the oppressed Catholics. Above all, while he upheld the Anglican Church, he gave its Catholic rival real freedom; its clergy, rescued from the proscription of the Cromwellian era, and allowed to do their offices among their flocks, acknowledged him as their benefactor and friend.

This policy was not profound or far-sighted, but it was wise, prudent, and perhaps suited to the time. In other respects Ormond was more free to act; his administrative capacity was conspicuously shown. True to the example of all the best Viceroys, who felt that Ireland required a strong central government, he greatly increased and improved the army; and he set on foot a militia in the Irish counties which performed the functions of a good local police. By these means he was enabled to put down every attempt to disturb the public peace, to make his government respected by all orders of men, to secure obedience in a country ever distracted by savage animosities and feuds, even if it seemed for the moment at rest. But the most striking feature of Ormond's rule was his unremitting and successful zeal in promoting everything that could advance the prosperity and material wealth of the country; "he trode here," he said, "in the steps of Strafford"; and he was worthy of the great man, in this respect, his model. He encouraged the trade of Ireland in many ways; he paid much attention to her agriculture; he stimulated the manufacture of linen, nearly abandoned during the late civil war; he gave a remarkable impulse to the manufacture of wool, already a promising Irish industry; he introduced machinery of many kinds from England. Ormond, too, was almost the first projector of what may be called Public Works in Ireland; and he was an excellent patron of arts and learning. He founded a great Hospital for soldiers, like that at Greenwich; the University of Dublin owed much to him; he re-established a school[1], near his an-

[1] Kilkenny College, originally a foundation of the Cathedral of St Canice.

cestral town, Kilkenny, which was soon to form the young minds of Swift and of Berkeley.

Under the government of Ormond, and, indeed, through the whole of the reign of Charles II, Ireland made decided material progress. The existing order of things seemed firmly established; the dominant caste made civilisation spread; the wealth of the country largely increased; something like prosperity appeared again. Dublin grew into a city of 50,000 souls; a few of the seaport towns revived; Belfast began to show signs of thriving; there was a real advance in husbandry and trade. Macaulay has described in picturesque language Petty's settlement in the wilds of Kerry; and doubtless there were other settlements of the kind, oases in rude and half-peopled deserts. This progress, however, met a sudden check, the first of many checks of the kind, attended ultimately with evil results. In conformity with the selfish legislation of the day, Ireland was excluded from the Navigation Acts of England; she was thus almost shut out from trade with the colonies; and her ship-building industry, in some degree, suffered. These restrictions probably were as yet not much felt, in the case of a poor and backward country; but another restriction did real injury. A period of agricultural distress in England was followed by a rapid decline in rents; and the English Parliament, in consequence, forbade the import of animals of most kinds, and even of meat, from Ireland, the principal sources of her still scanty wealth. This prohibition aroused the anger of Petty, a keen and able economic thinker, who had feathered his nest through the Cromwellian forfeitures; he compared it to the colonial tyranny of Spain[1]. Ireland, nevertheless, continued to advance, in spite of the loss of a most important market; her woollen manufacture especially throve. The time had not yet come when she was to learn how mischievous commercial restrictions could prove.

[1] *Life of Sir William Petty*, p. 143.

VI.] *From the Restoration to the Limerick Capitulation.* 173

There were two interludes to Ormond's government; they were significant, in some degree, of the future. Lord Berkeley of Stratton was made Lord Lieutenant in 1670; the appointment was part and parcel of the French policy inaugurated by the Treaty of Dover, which involved concessions to all Catholic subjects of Charles. Catholics were admitted, in Ireland, to different offices; the Mass was celebrated in Dublin with extraordinary pomp; an attempt was made to introduce Catholics into Corporate Bodies; an outcry was raised against the Acts of Settlement. This policy aroused the indignation and fear of the Protestant caste in all parts of the country; but it was reversed when Danby became Minister, and the French alliance was denounced at Westminster. Lord Berkeley was replaced by Lord Essex; Protestant Ascendency was completely restored in Ireland; and the reports that had been spread about "a second 1641," and an "Irish St Bartholomew," proved wholly groundless. Ormond was before long in office again; he steadily followed the course of conduct of which we have given a brief description. He kept the hostile races and faiths of Ireland at peace; maintained order with a firm but kind hand; and continued to make earnest and successful efforts to improve the material state of the island. It is remarkable that during the last agitated years of the chequered reign of Charles II Ireland was apparently in deep repose, illusory as the appearance was. The furious passions engendered by the Popish plot led, indeed, to one most unhappy event: Oliver Plunkett, the Catholic Archbishop of Armagh, was charged—a barbarous falsehood—with a treasonable design to stir up a rebellion in Ireland, and was executed at Tyburn after a mock trial; but this was the only Irish victim of Oates and his crew, while noble blood flowed freely on English scaffolds. While Shaftesbury was shaking the state to its basis, while England was being convulsed by maddened factions, Ireland remained quiescent under Ormond's rule, though Shaftesbury had tried to make her a pawn in his game.

The calm prevailing in Ireland was but little disturbed when James II ascended the throne. Faint murmurs were heard from the Catholic priesthood; petitions against the Acts of Settlement were preferred; there was some agitation in the ranks of the dominant race. But nothing like the disorder of the Restoration was seen; the active leaders of the Irishry had disappeared; and the Irishry remained passive in the silent endurance, often characteristic of the Celtic nature, before it breaks out into a burst of passion. Had James been a statesman of real parts, had a Richelieu or a Wolsey been in his councils, an occasion had now perhaps presented itself to do much to settle the affairs of Ireland, possibly even to give a new turn to her history. The power of the King in England was great, owing to the strong reaction of the last few years; his authority in Ireland was very large; in every part of his dominions he had no common influence. In these circumstances a wise and able ruler might conceivably have wrought an effectual change in the dangerous and false state of things in Ireland; have made Protestant Ascendency less harsh, and Catholic Subjection less painful; have in some measure smoothed away the lines that separated hostile races and faiths; above all have tried to conciliate by doing justice. There was very little in the mere letter of the law[1], to exclude Catholics in Ireland from offices in the state, from the legislature, from municipal rights; and the tests in their way had been seldom enforced until after the beginning of the

---

[1] Macaulay, *History of England*, II. 383, ed. 1858, note, seems to think that the only religious test imposed on Irish Catholics at this time was that created by the old Act of Supremacy of Elizabeth. A more stringent test was, however, imposed by the 17–18 Car. 2, chap. 6, though it seems not to have been often enforced. Irish Catholics at this period were not so much proscribed by law as by the force of Protestant ascendency.

seventeenth century. If James had cautiously ignored these obstacles; if he had gradually admitted Irish Catholics into the service of the Government and the administration of affairs, if he had given them something akin to civil equality, the Protestant Irish would doubtless have made angry complaints, but he would hardly have set Englishmen strongly against him, great as was their dislike of "Irish Papists," or have provoked dangerous opposition at Westminster. The King, however, might well have gone further; it was essential to place landed relations in Ireland on a reasonably sound and natural basis. Ancient confiscations should not have been touched; but the Cromwellian confiscations were not of old date; they were, in numberless instances, grossly unjust; and the Acts of Settlement were tainted throughout with wrong. The Catholic owners, despoiled without getting a hearing, ought certainly to have been permitted to assert their rights; and those who had been pronounced "innocent," under a legitimate test, might have been indemnified by grants of Crown lands in England—Petty actually proposed a scheme of the kind[1]—or by grants in the American colonies. As for other Catholic owners wrongfully dispossessed, their estates had been obtained at a nominal price; and their present possessors might have been rightly asked to pay the state a larger part of their real value, and thus to create a fund which would have afforded the old owners a measure of relief. By these means the most glaring evils in the land system of Ireland would have been partly removed, and animosities of race and faith would have been probably lessened.

James, however, was in no sense a statesman; and except Ormond, whom he removed from his post, he had no able counsellor on Irish affairs. His views respecting Ireland were for a time uncertain; he hesitated before he committed himself to a policy fatal to himself and his House. Like all the

[1] *Life of Sir William Petty*, p. 273.

Stuarts, he cared little about his Irish subjects; he had much of the English aversion to the race; as a King of England he felt he was bound to support the Protestant "English interest." But he was a bigoted Catholic, on the other hand; and, unlike his illustrious grandfather, Henry IV, he was ultimately to show that he thought a Mass was worth a great deal more than a Crown. His first measures for Ireland appeared moderate; he appointed Clarendon Lord Lieutenant, with directions to uphold the Acts of Settlement, but to admit Catholics to office in the state; and Clarendon, though an obsequious courtier, had all his father's contempt for Irishmen, and was decidedly a friend of the ruling Protestant caste. Two or three Catholics were admitted to the Council in Dublin; had things gone no further, an act of justice would, in the eyes of History, if not of partisans, have excused a technical breach of the law. But Clarendon was soon made to feel that he was not a real governor. The command of the army in Ireland had been placed in the hands of Richard Talbot, the well-known Tyrconnell; and if Talbot's faults have perhaps been magnified, he was certainly a rash and intemperate man, a Catholic of the most extreme type and bitterly hostile to the Protestant name in Ireland. Talbot practically thrust the Lord Lieutenant aside, and began to do acts of high-handed power, alike reckless and of evil omen to the state. He disbanded the militia formed by Ormond because it was composed, in the main, of Protestants; he dismissed Protestant officers from the army wholesale; he placed Catholic officers in their stead; and he filled the ranks with the Catholic Irishry. It was his boast, and it soon became evident, that the power of the sword was being transferred from the dominant to the subject race in Ireland.

Tyrconnell's conduct naturally provoked the resentment of the classes that ruled in Ireland—an alien caste hemmed in on all sides by enemies. But anger changed into consternation and dismay when the news arrived, in the spring of 1687, that Clarendon had ceased to be Lord Lieutenant, and that Tyrconnell had been made Deputy. James had now embarked on the disastrous course which was soon to lead to the ruin of his throne; and there can be no doubt that, like his ill-fated father, he had resolved to make use of Catholic Ireland in the attack he had begun on Protestant England. He had in Tyrconnell a tool to his hand; the Deputy instantly effected a violent change in the whole order of affairs in Ireland, which literally set everything upside down. The Irish army was increased and filled with Catholics; the dominant Protestants were replaced by men of the despised race and faith, in all departments of the state. The Bench was packed with Catholic Judges; the municipal bodies were remodelled, and made Catholic; Catholic magistrates and sheriffs were appointed by scores; in civil administration Catholics were made supreme. The result was such as has often been seen, when a down-trodden order of men suddenly acquire power; a Catholic ascendency vehemently avenged the wrongs a Protestant ascendency had done; the Protestants, dominant but yesterday, suffered gross injuries, in every relation and walk of life. Tyrconnell ere long had denounced the Acts of Settlement, which, indeed, had ceased to protect titles, owing to decisions of the lately made Judges; he certainly contemplated a great transfer of the Irish Land. This became the signal of a wide-spread agrarian rising; old dispossessed owners claimed their lands again; the new landlords were unable to assert their rights; floods of the infuriated Irishry swept away Petty's settlement and other centres of industry; anarchy ran riot over whole counties. Ireland wore the aspect of France, in 1789, when the flames of many a château expressed the hatred the peasant bore to his seigneur; and a great emigration of the Protestants of all classes followed.

The Revolution by this time had taken place in England;

William and Mary had been made King and Queen; James was a discrowned and fugitive exile. Catholic Ireland, however, declared for him to a man; and Catholic Ireland, but a few months before apparently in a state of torpid submission, sprang to arms with the passionate impetuosity of the Celt. The Irish Catholic, indeed, had no love for the House of Stuart, but he felt that its rights were bound up with his own; and the time had come, he believed, to take vengeance for the past, from the days of Elizabeth to those of Cromwell. Once more, therefore, the great body of the Irish people threw itself violently across the path of England, at a critical and Revolutionary time; and the traditional hatred of the Irishry felt by Englishmen, was quickened to fury by the recent conduct of James, in bringing over regiments from Ireland, to menace his English subjects. Prudence and reflection were cast to the winds; few countries have ever beheld such an armed rising as that of Ireland at this conjuncture. The army was suddenly increased sixfold in numbers; out of a population of perhaps a million and a half of souls, 100,000 were made ready for the field, an effort greater than that of France in 1793-4. The movement comprised all Irishmen of the Catholic name, for the extinction of the old tribal system had effaced tribal discords and jealousies; the old Englishry and the Celtic Irishry had been brought together by common suffering; and potent incitements added their impulse. Tyrconnell declared that now or never was the time; priests, as in former days, preached a Holy War; France, it was noised abroad, would soon aid Ireland; hundreds of exiles, disciplined in foreign armies, flocked to the Irish shores to train the masses of levies. In a few months the bodies in arms were great; and if the infantry were ill equipped and of little worth, the cavalry, largely composed of men of birth, with good officers, as a rule, at their head, was a force that was in no sense to be despised. The leaders belonged, for the most part, to the old Englishry, but some were of genuine Celtic blood.

The levies of the Irishry were soon in motion, overrunning the three southern provinces like a horde. The Englishry in Munster and Connaught made an attempt at resistance, but Lords Inchiquin and Kingston were beaten in the field; the force of overwhelming numbers swept away all before it. The colonists and their families, who were driven from their homes, turned towards the powerful settlements in the north, largely peopled by men of their own race and faith; Ulster was their City of Refuge in the hour of trial. Some betook themselves to the lesser towns, which had been rising in parts of the province; many gathered behind the line of the Erne, and were welcomed at Enniskillen, a fortified place, the centre of a strong Protestant colony; but the great majority, it is said 30,000 souls, made their way to the extreme verge of the north, to Derry. This city, we have seen, had a name in the days of Shane O'Neill; it had been afterwards destroyed by a Celtic raid; but it rose from its ashes when the great Plantation was made, and it had become the seat of the government of the London merchants, who had obtained the tracts of confiscated land in the neighbourhood. The burghers had given the place the name of their great capital; and Londonderry had been for some time a thriving and growing seaport of Ulster. The town was protected by a rude wall and a ditch; a few guns—they may still be seen, preserved, through two centuries, with pious care—crowned a rampart that seemed incapable of defence. The population, however, were sturdy Protestants of Anglo-Saxon and Scottish blood; they had lately given a proof of their quality. At the approach of one of Tyrconnell's Catholic regiments, thirteen apprentices had shut the gates; they were made heroes by the rest of the townsmen. Londonderry, however, had consented to receive a small Protestant garrison within its walls; this was in the hands of an officer, of the name of Lundy, believed to be true to the Protestant name.

England and France were, before long, at war; the great rivals, William III and Louis XIV, representatives, in a certain sense, of Protestantism and Catholicism still in conflict, were contending for the prize of dominion in Europe. James had resolved to go to Ireland to support his own cause; he landed at Kinsale in the spring of 1689. He had received some funds from France and a few hundred officers, but Louis had refused to send an army; France did not possess the command of the sea; she required all her forces to maintain a struggle which was soon to rage from the Theiss to the Scheldt. James had entered Dublin by the end of March; he was welcomed with all the pomp the capital could display; a flag streaming from the Castle and bearing the device "now or never, now and for ever[1]," expressed the passionate hopes of Catholic Ireland. By this time a large Irish army, from 25,000 to 30,000 strong, had entered Ulster and drawn near Londonderry; the command had been bestowed on Rosen, a French general of some distinction; French officers were forming the Celtic levies; the principal, almost the last bulwark of Protestant Ireland seemed about to fall. James set off from Dublin, confident of success; an incident he thought decisive increased his hopes just as he arrived in Rosen's camp. Lundy, who controlled the military force within Londonderry, had betrayed his trust; he had actually sent away two regiments despatched from England to defend the place; he entered into secret parleys with the enemy; he deserted at a moment he deemed opportune. Londonderry was thus abandoned to herself; but she had no thought of yielding to "Irish Papists"; she nerved herself for a struggle of life and death. Some seven thousand men were

---

[1] This device reappeared, in several places, at the General Election of 1892. The Celts have long memories.

found able to bear arms; these gathered around the little garrison; in an incredibly short time all had been made ready for a desperate and protracted defence. A cry of "no surrender" burst from the walls when James approached relying on Lundy's treachery; and on the 19th of April a formal summons to give up the town was rejected with contempt.

A siege followed, not the least memorable of the great sieges of which History tells. Fire opened on defences which the French officers believed could not be held for two days; reiterated assaults were courageously made. But the men of Londonderry clung to their walls; the strictest discipline was admirably maintained; select bodies of volunteers were placed, each in its own station, to guard the ramparts; in a short time fierce and determined sallies discomfited and amazed the host of the enemy. And, while military order was sternly upheld, nothing was left undone to keep enthusiasm at its height; Baker, a soldier, won the hearts of the townsmen; a clergyman, Walker, stirred the whole town by his impassioned appeals to the God of battles; hours were devoted to fasting and solemn prayer; the fervour of religion, the pride of race, the scorn of the enemy, the hatred of ages, kept up the defenders, when it was said, "they were as the Israelites in the Red Sea." The besiegers, maddened by a resistance they had treated, at first, as a jest, ere long made ready for a decisive effort; in the first week of June a resolute assault was made against the weakest point in the ramparts. The Irishry fell on, in overwhelming numbers, and with valour acknowledged by their foes; but the stubborn endurance of the defence prevailed; the women of Londonderry rushed into the fight when the issue was for a time doubtful; the assailants at last were driven away in defeat.

The siege was now turned into a blockade, an agony ever increasing during many weeks. The Irish army closed the approaches to the town; lined on either side the banks of the Foyle, the river that brought the port its wealth, and ere long drew a great boom across, to prevent the arrival of relief from the sea. But Londonderry remained defiant, though the crowds of fugitives within the walls were consuming fast the store of provisions which had been laid in before the contest began. The ramparts were manned, heavy as was the hand of death; arms were found to grasp weapons which other arms had dropped; stern voices mingled the watchword of "no surrender" with appeals to the Most High to save his children from the "idolatry of Rome" and the "cruelties" of the Celt. A prospect of relief appeared at last; the sails of an expeditionary force were descried in the Bay; but they drew off, for their leader, Kirke, thought it had become impossible to effect a landing; and the beleaguered town was left to its fast-failing resources. The sufferings of the besieged soon became intense; the refuse of the sewer, the vermin of the street, were welcome additions to the wretched supplies of food; and Rosen—he had only just taken the command in person—tried barbarous expedients to compel the garrison to yield. But nothing could subdue those undaunted spirits; the dread approach of famine was despised; the dole of bread was carefully preserved for the haggard spectres that guarded the walls; death was dreaded as little as the detested enemy. The city was on the brink of starvation, when, on the twenty-eighth of July, three vessels were seen bearing down on the obstacle thrown across the Foyle. Kirke had received positive orders to relieve the place; the boom was broken, after a first effort had failed—the horror of the suspense was long remembered—and Londonderry was set free from her pain. The siege had lasted a hundred and five days; soon all that was seen of the Irish army was the cloud of dust that marked its retreat.

The raising of the siege of Londonderry gave a new turn to the war; the men of Enniskillen defeated the Irishry at

vi.] *From the Restoration to the Limerick Capitulation.* 183

Newton Butler. in a fierce encounter[1], chiefly remarkable for the bloody revenge taken by the colonial caste on the enemy. Meanwhile James had gone back to Dublin, and had been engaged in setting up his government; he had become a mere puppet in the hands of French officials and soldiers, and of the Irish leaders. One act of his administration deserves severe censure; he issued a base coinage, remembered for years as a wicked fraud by the Dublin citizens; and he gave a free scope to the ascendency of the men of his faith, which had been the chief work of the reckless Tyrconnell. In the existing condition of Ireland, however, measures like these cannot cause surprise: his treasury was empty and his army was in the field; the wrongs of Catholic Ireland were cruel and many; religious passions had been stirred up to frenzy; and, in this, as in all other instances, allowance must be made for a Revolutionary time.

The King convened the Irish Parliament in May 1689; the conduct of that assembly has been the subject of the misrepresentation of partisan writers; but if some of its acts were indisputably bad, few are without precedent or partial excuse; others are fairly entitled to praise; and the crisis, we repeat, must be taken into account. The Parliament was for the most part composed of Catholics; but there were more Protestants in it than there had been Catholics in any Irish Parliament for many years; this partial transformation was an inevitable event. Nor was it composed in the main of Irish Celts; it contained many members, indeed, of great Milesian Houses; but the large majority was formed of the old Englishry, men of birth and honour, in many instances; and there was a considerable admixture of very distinguished lawyers. Two measures of the Parliament have been denounced as unparalleled in their reckless barbarity; the Acts of Settlement

[1] Colonel Wolseley, an ancestor, we believe, of Lord Wolseley, distinguished himself greatly on this occasion.

were summarily repealed; an Act of Attainder was passed against about 2,500 persons, supposed to be adherents of William III, if they did not return to Ireland on a given day. The Acts of Settlement, however, were utterly unjust; they were of recent date and had been the subject of protests over and over again: as for the Act of Attainder, it was levelled against presumed enemies of James, who had left the country; and in this respect it bears a strong resemblance to the decrees of the Convention of 1793, against the French emigrés, which History has, on the whole, justified. It deserves notice, moreover, that innocent purchasers, after the Acts of Settlement, were to be indemnified; the Act of Attainder, too, was conditional only, and, as a matter of fact, a Bill of the same kind was actually passed by the English House of Commons; and if we recollect how little respect had been given to titles to Irish land for ages, what injury confiscation had wrought in Ireland, and especially what were the animosities of the hour, this legislation is not to be blamed without reserve. Another Act of the Parliament of 1689 has also been described as of the very worst kind; it declared the independence of the Irish Parliament, and that Ireland was not bound by laws passed at Westminster. This, however, had always been the doctrine of the best Irish lawyers; it had been asserted in more than one Irish Parliament; the encroachments, in this respect, of the English Parliament had been of comparatively modern origin; the worst, perhaps, was that of the Long Parliament, in the matter we have seen of the "Adventurers'" lands[1]. On the other hand some measures of this Parliament of James were not without marks of good sense and wisdom. Its Declaration in favour of religious liberty savoured of the Declaration of

---

[1] For the question of the independence of the Irish Parliament see the excellent work of the Rt Hon. J. T. Ball, *Irish Legislative Systems*, Chapters 4, 5, 6. Macaulay, *History of England* IV. 216, begs the whole question.

VI.] *From the Restoration to the Limerick Capitulation.* 185

Indulgence made by the King; but it made a really just partition of the property of the Church between the rival faiths; and it can hardly be blamed for taxing absentees, an order of men disliked in Ireland since the feudal age. It should be added that this Parliament did not insist on repealing the Law of Poynings, which, we have said, had been a cause of discontent, and which had been denounced by the Catholic Confederates of 1642-8[1].*

While James was thus playing the king in Dublin, an English army had landed on the coast of Antrim, in order to effect the re-conquest of Ireland. Its commander was an aged veteran, Schomberg; and though it was largely composed of ill-trained levies, it contained some regiments of excellent soldiers. In numbers it was about equal to the Cromwellian army, which had subjugated Ireland in a few months; but it had a very different chief at its head, and its operations seem to have been badly directed. It is not easy to understand why an attempt was not made to descend on Dublin, and strike a decisive blow; Schomberg, like Cromwell, had the command of the sea; and the Irish army, after its late defeats, was disheartened and in a pitiable plight. Schomberg, however, advanced cautiously from Carrickfergus, inland; his marches, through a difficult country, were slow; the Irish climate made havoc of his men; and his army was half destroyed before it reached Dundalk, more than fifty miles from the Irish capital. He was compelled to retreat into winter quarters; this gave James time to restore his army, and to make preparations to renew the contest. The Irishry seconded his efforts with

---

[1] Mr Lecky's account of the proceedings of the Irish Parliament of 1689 is just and impartial. *History of England in the Eighteenth Century*, II. Chap. 6. pp. 182, 190. Macaulay's is inaccurate, and conveys a false impression. See also the *Patriotic Parliament* by Thomas Davis, a one-sided but very able and learned narrative.

* See note at end of Chapter.

enthusiastic ardour; their wasted ranks were filled with thousands of recruits; and in a few months they were formidable in numbers at least, the infantry still raw and bad, but the horse good. An important reinforcement, too, had arrived: Louis had sent 6000 or 7000 French troops to Ireland to the assistance of the fugitive king of England.

The contest in Ireland had become so doubtful, that William had resolved to conduct it in person. He landed at Carrickfergus in June 1690; it is still difficult to explain why he did not aim at Dublin. He was at the head of an army of about 36,000 men, composed of many races and tongues, English, Danes, Brandenburgers, Dutch, Germans, but well disciplined and prepared for the field; two bodies were conspicuous in the motley array, the Enniskilleners thirsting for another Newton Butler, and Huguenot exiles eager to avenge the great wrong of the Revocation of the Edict of Nantes. William tacitly condemned the late campaign of Schomberg; though usually methodical and slow in war, he made his advance as rapid as possible; on the evening of the 30th June his army had reached the northern bank of the Boyne, the stream that here divides the counties of Louth and Meath. James had been advised by the French officers to fall back behind the line of the Shannon, the enemy being greatly superior in strength; but the Irish leaders had insisted on defending Dublin; and the Irish soldiery burned to strike a blow at the "Saxon." The King's forces were perhaps 30,000 strong, all, except the French, and the Irish cavalry, of very inferior quality; they occupied the southern bank of the Boyne and had been made ready to fight a pitched battle. The veteran Schomberg was the chief of William's lieutenants; the youthful Berwick, a bastard of James, the warrior of Almanza on another day, was in the ranks of the French auxiliaries. But the hero of the Irishry was Patrick Sarsfield, a scion of a House of the old Englishry, who had done good service with Churchill at

Sedgemoor, and had given proof of valour and resource in the present war in Ireland.

The battle that followed, known as the Battle of the Boyne, fought on the 1st of July 1690, was not a remarkable passage of war, but is remembered with feelings of pride and shame by the still divided races and faiths of Ireland. The position of James was strong against a direct attack; a broad and deep river ran before his front; his reserves were thrown back out of the sight of the enemy. But a narrow defile at Duleek near his rear was almost his only avenue of retreat; and this had a disastrous effect on the issue of the day. A son of Schomberg was ordered to threaten the Irish left; this movement might cause the loss of the pass; the French contingent and Sarsfield were accordingly detached to guard a point of supreme importance. Meanwhile the main body of William's forces crossed the Boyne at fords near the village of Oldbridge; the result was what almost always happens when real soldiers encounter mere rude levies. The Irish infantry, deprived of their French allies, gave way as their foemen approached the southern bank; the plain was soon crowded with flying masses hurrying towards the reserves gathered around Donore. But it was otherwise with the Irish cavalry; they made a desperate and heroic stand; Danes, Huguenots, and Englishmen were more than once driven back. Schomberg met a soldier's death in the struggle; in fact the Irish horsemen maintained their ground until William had turned, from near Drogheda, the position from his left; even then they fell back fighting on Donore. A last effort was made to resist at that place; but the battle had by this time been won; the defeated army was soon in full retreat on Dublin. The French, however, had occupied the defile at Duleek; their absence from the field was an irreparable loss; but it certainly averted a complete rout[1].

[1] A spirited account of the Battle of the Boyne will be found in the Memoirs of Dumont de Bostaquet, a Huguenot seigneur in the service of

James was soon again an exile on his way to France; his conduct at the Boyne had been unworthy of him; he had expressed his distrust of his Irish soldiers, and had abandoned them in the hour of disaster. William had before long been received in Dublin, to the enthusiastic delight of the Protestant townsmen; the government of his adversary at once disappeared. The King delayed for a time in the capital, and did not press his defeated enemy; he was perhaps kept back by the news of the reverse at Beachy Head; but, hero as he was, he was not a great captain; he never excelled in the direction of war. His hesitation enabled the Irish army, still probably 20,000 strong, to reach in safety the line of the Shannon; it had assembled around Limerick by the close of July. The city, like Londonderry, was rudely fortified; but Lauzun, the chief of the French contingent, and his officers pronounced it unable to resist an attack made by even a small force; they were, in truth, sick of the war in Ireland; they had no faith in the Irish levies; their only thought was to see France again. But the Irish leaders were of a different mind, and they found a response in the hearts of their men; Limerick was the rallying point of their race in peril; Limerick was to be defended at any risk, to the last. After angry discussions Lauzun and his regiments fell back on Galway; the Irishry were left to make a stand at Limerick. Their nominal commander was a French officer, but the real leader was their beloved Sarsfield.

Preparations for resistance were now made; the place gradually acquired increasing strength. Limerick, then the second of Irish cities, rose from an island, surrounded by the Shannon; this was approached by bridges, protected by forts,

William. He especially praises the conduct of the Irish horsemen. We have only space for a single passage, p. 272: "Nous nous mêlâmes parmi les ennemis et les rompîmes; mais le Sieur de Belcastré, commandant notre escadron, ayant été fort blessé, Varenques culbuté, le vent et la poussière nous étant contraires, notre escadron se retira en désordre."

commanding most of the space outside the walls. Unguarded points were fortified by works hastily raised; the adjoining plain was broken up by fences, and obstacles were accumulated to repel an attack. Stores of provisions, too, were brought in; the threatened garrison spared no efforts; the citizens joined heartily in the labours of the defence. William was before Limerick in the second week of August; one of the forts was captured by a sudden assault; he began to draw his lines round the beleaguered city. He had, however, only light guns with him; a siege train was still on the way; over-confidence alone can explain the mistake of challenging an enemy when still unprepared. The opportunity was seized by Sarsfield; he was informed by a deserter that the heavy guns were approaching William's camp by the roads from Cashel; and sallying from the place, he crossed the Shannon, fell on the artillery park near the hills of Silvermines, and destroyed it with a loss of scarcely a man. The stroke was brilliant and well directed; the Irish chief was soon in Limerick again.

William, a tenacious, if not a great commander, continued the attack in spite of this reverse. He contrived to repair two of the heavy guns, and kept up a desultory fire on the place; in truth, like all the officers in his camp, he was confident that it must soon fall. Limerick, however, held out with unflinching constancy; the waters of the Shannon had begun to rise; the rainy season would soon make the surrounding plain a pestilential swamp; the King resolved to try the effect of an assault before the Irish climate had decimated his men. On the 27th of August a column of picked English troops endeavoured to storm a breach still imperfect; it was followed by a considerable part of the army[1]. But the assailants encountered

[1] Macaulay, *History of England*, v. 309, seems rather to underrate the force of the assailants. The account of Dumont de Bostaquet is more full and clear. He says, pp. 287-8: "Les ennemis chargèrent nos troupes dans leur retraite, et nous tuèrent ou blessèrent plus de quinze cents

foemen worthy of their steel; the Irishry fought with desperate courage; the women as at Londonderry took part in the fight; and the attack was repulsed with heavy loss. The King, alarmed at the prospect of danger before him, raised the siege, and drew off his discomfited army; he was, in a few days, on his way back to England. The heroism of Limerick and the skill of Sarsfield kept the scales of fortune still in suspense.

Justice has not been done to the defence of Limerick by historians of the conquering race; but it may stand by the side of that of Londonderry; in both instances the courage of despair baffled the calculations of experienced soldiers, and plucked victory out of the extreme of danger. Before long Marlborough had taken Cork and Kinsale; this was the most brilliant exploit of the war; the blow was aimed at the communications of the French by sea; and it had great, perhaps decisive effects[1]. Lauzun and most of his troops took their departure for France; the defence of Ireland was left almost altogether to the Irish army. France in truth had given the Irishry but little help; like Spain, in the preceding century, she had treated them as mere pawns in her game; this was almost inevitable in the case of a power which did not possess the command of the sea, and had to send troops to a distant island, surrounded by the Atlantic, but near England and her fleets. The contending armies went into winter quarters, the English occupying the greater part of the country to the east of the Shannon, the Irish for the most part west of the river; it is unnecessary to say how unequal they were in all that makes troops fitted to take the field. Ginkle, a

hommes. Cette entreprise ne servit qu'à nous faire perdre beaucoup de monde; le regiment des gardes flamandes perdit beaucoup d'officiers, mais, plus que tous, les regiments français."

[1] Lord Wolseley, *History of Marlborough*, II. 157, 220, has given us an admirable and discriminating account of the capture of Cork and Kinsale and of the results.

Dutchman, commanded William's forces; the Irish were in the hands of Saint Ruth, a French general sent from Versailles; but they remained devoted as ever to Sarsfield, and unhappily Saint Ruth and Sarsfield disliked each other. Athlone was attacked by Ginkle in June 1691; he was soon master of the part of the town along the Leinster shore of the Shannon; but he encountered a stubborn resistance on the Connaught shore, where part of the Irish army held a fort on the passage. The assailants were more than once beaten off from the bridge which spanned the stream near the centre of the place; but they crossed on the 30th by a ford lower down and drove the enemy out of the fort, which they seized. Saint Ruth had remained inactive in his camp hard by; he had had angry disputes with Sarsfield; the fatal divisions of Ireland had appeared once more.

The French commander, stung to the quick by a defeat due to his own neglect, now determined to fight a pitched battle. Sarsfield, a much abler soldier, protested in vain; Saint Ruth would not listen to the advice of his colleague. He drew together all the forces at hand, and placed them in a position of formidable strength, their front covered by a bog near the valley of the Suck, their flanks protected on either side by obstacles, and on the left by the hamlet and the old castle of Aghrim. No effort was spared to arouse the hearts of his men; he harangued regiments in person and bade them do or die; priests with crucifixes passed along the ranks and adjured them to fight for their homes and their faith. Ginkle had reached the enemy by the 12th of July, at the head of about 20,000 men; the Irish were not more than 25,000, but they held a position of such vantage that Ginkle hesitated for a time to attack. The battle began at about five in the afternoon; an attempt against the right of the Irish failed; and Ginkle's army endeavoured in vain to make its way through the yielding morass, and to fall in force on the enemy's centre. The Irish, protected by a hastily formed breastwork, repelled successfully every attack; and Saint Ruth shouted victory as he beheld the best troops of England recoiling in defeat. An effort was next made to turn the Irish left; at this critical moment Saint Ruth was slain; and Sarsfield, on whom the command devolved, was not only ignorant of the plans of his chief, but had received positive orders not to employ the reserve. The attack on Aghrim proved at last successful, very probably owing to this untoward accident; the whole Irish army gave way by degrees, but it fought heroically while a chance was left. The hatred of the victors was seen in a hideous butchery; thousands of corpses marked the line of the rout.

The broken wreck of the Irish army drifted in part to Galway, and in part to Limerick. Galway opened its gates in a few days; most of the towns in Munster and Connaught, which held out for James, were soon given up to his rival's troops; Limerick alone continued to defy the enemy. After the defeat of William, the year before, the city had been the scene of bickerings between Berwick, the nominal governor, Tyrconnell, and the officers of the Irish garrison; the defences appear to have not been improved. Ginkle advanced cautiously against the place, and invested it with methodical care; he had evidently not forgotten the lesson taught by the assault. He kept within his lines for nearly a month, before he ventured to risk an attack; the chief bridge leading into Limerick was then all but captured, and a fort outside it was successfully stormed. By this time Tyrconnell had died; the heads of the extinct government of James were within the town, and sighed for relief; the Irish soldiery, cowed by the horrors of Aghrim, seemed unwilling to prolong a now hopeless contest. Sarsfield, with true judgment, resolved to make terms, while arms still remained in his hands; and he entered into parleys with Ginkle. The capitulation was agreed to on the 3rd of October

VI.] *From the Restoration to the Limerick Capitulation.* 193

1691; the Culloden of the Irishry had been fought; the "red eye of battle" had closed in despair on the struggles and the hopes of Catholic Ireland.

The Treaty of Limerick forms a melancholy passage in Irish History[1]. It consisted of two parts. The military articles were signed by generals of both armies—the name of Sarsfield curiously does not appear;—unquestionably they were faithfully observed. The chief of these provisions was that soldiers of the Irish forces should have a right to "enlist in the service of France." Advantage was generally taken of this condition; the great majority of the men who had made a stand at Aghrim and defended Limerick went into exile. The gallant Sarsfield was at their head; he was to die the most enviable of deaths on the field of Landen, in the face of the enemy, but in the hour of triumph. His followers were to increase the list of the Irish foes of England, and to form the nucleus of the celebrated body of men, "ever and everywhere" true to the Bourbon lilies, who were to win renown for the Irish name in war, on many a hard fought day from Cremona to Minden.

The civil articles of the capitulation bore the names of Ginkle, of the functionaries who had been made Lords Justices by William when he had left Ireland, and of Sarsfield and other superior Irish officers. Unlike the military articles, they were not respected, and the violated "Treaty of Limerick" is still properly a word of reproach. By one of the articles it was declared that Irish Catholics should have "such privileges in the exercise of their religion, as were consistent with the laws of Ireland, or as they did enjoy in the reign of Charles II"; this secured them toleration at least for their faith, if it did not make them eligible to hold offices in the State. An amnesty, too, was extended to the townsmen of Limerick, and to all

[1] The capitulation of Limerick is set out at length in Leland, III. appendix, 619, 634. It should be carefully studied. The accounts of most historians are superficial and inaccurate.

officers and soldiers of the Irish army, under conditions that must be pronounced fair; and there were other provisions of the same character. The most important, however, of the civil articles—a subject of passionate disputes afterwards—was this, "the inhabitants or residents of Limerick, or any garrison in the possession of the Irish; all officers and soldiers" of the Jacobite army in five specified counties, and all "*persons under their protection* in the said counties"; and all "commissioned officers" in counties occupied by William's troops, were to be restored to their estates, should they make submission to the new government: this provision, it was calculated, would save their lands for more than three thousand owners. Unhappily a mistake was committed here; the comprehensive words "under their protection in the said counties" were omitted in one draft; but William expressly declared that this was an oversight, and the words, therefore, must be held to have been part of the Treaty. The Lords Justices undertook to "use their utmost endeavours," that the articles "should be ratified and confirmed" by the Irish Parliament; if this confirmation was, perhaps, necessary, it was taken for granted that no difficulty could arise.

Irish History presents some points of resemblance, and others of difference, in the two periods, between the death of Elizabeth and the Restoration, and between the accession of Charles II and the Treaty of Limerick. In both instances a season of deceptive rest was followed by a rising of the subject community and by a fierce conflict of races and faiths. In both cruel wrongs were done to Ireland; the spoliation of the times of James I and of Charles I, and the frightful proscription effected by Cromwell, found their counterparts in the Acts of Settlement, and in the evil policy which led up to them. In both material prosperity faintly appears, only to end in material ruin; in both England was guilty of unjust oppression, and of forcing her institutions on a reluctant people; in both

VI.] *From the Restoration to the Limerick Capitulation.* 195

Protestant Ascendency makes progress, and with Catholic Subjection becomes more and more the characteristic type of society. The differences, however, are strongly marked; in the first period the old Englishry stood widely apart from the Irish Celts, at least until the Cromwellian Conquest; in the second they are made almost one with them, under the influence of misgovernment from which both suffer. The line between the races is thus still more lessened until it appears well nigh to vanish; but if it may yet be traced, and is real, the line between religions becomes more and more deep, and separates Ireland, more and more, into a Protestant body of settlers and a mass of Catholics. In the second period, too, civil war assumes a nobler aspect than in the first; it ceases to be on the part of the Irishry a merely tribal resistance to a conquering Power; it is notable for heroic deeds on both sides, though fatal Irish disunion is not absent. The Irish Parliament, besides, of 1689 contrasts favourably with the Confederacy of 1642-8; and, on the whole, in the second period religious passion is hardly as fierce as in the first, although it remains a dominant force. The two periods have one feature, of the very highest importance, in common: in both Ireland strikes hard at England in a time of peril and revolution; and in both Ireland has to pay the penalty.

Catholic Ireland was now at the feet of William, almost as completely as she had been at the feet of Cromwell. The men, indeed, were of different natures: but would Protestant Ireland thirsting for revenge, would the men at the Castle looking out for forfeitures, as in the day of Borlase and Parsons, would the English Parliament supreme in the State, long accustomed to meddle in Irish affairs, and eager to make an example of "Irish Papists," permit the King to carry out the principles of religious toleration and of natural justice in the case of Ireland, which he had made his own? Would the Treaty of Limerick suffice to restrain savage animosities of race and faith, cupidity, and the anger and pride of a conquering people, or would it prove worse than an empty delusion? On that issue much might yet depend, though it is difficult to suppose that, in any event, the existing state of things in Ireland could endure, or produce permanent peace and good government. But the result was to be seen ere long; Ireland was about to enter on perhaps the most sad and disastrous period of her whole history, bearing in mind the contemporaneous state of the world.

Note, p. 185. Mr Lecky, *History of England in the Eighteenth Century*, II. 183, and Mr Froude, *The English in Ireland*, I. 191, state that Poynings' Law was repealed by the Irish Parliament in 1689. This seems to be an error. No such repeal is to be found in the Acts of that Parliament set forth in Davis's work. Leland, III. 540, Edition 1773, expressly says that Poynings' Law was not repealed owing to the interposition of James. Macaulay, *History of England*, IV. 213, Edition 1858, does not refer to this subject.

CHAPTER VII.

THE PERIOD OF THE PENAL LAWS IN IRELAND.
THE REVOLUTION OF 1782.

Retrospect of Irish History, since the Anglo-Norman Conquest. The influence of circumstance on events. The Treaty of Limerick violated. Ruin of Catholic owners. The Penal Code enacted by degrees. Its threefold object, to exclude the Catholics from the land and from all power in the State, to degrade them, and to keep their Church in subjection. Its disastrous effects. Emigration of Catholics from Ireland. Distinguished Irish Catholic exiles. The "wild geese." The Irish Brigade. How the Code affected the land, commerce, and social relations. Demoralisation caused by it. Subjection of Protestant Ireland to England. Commercial restrictions. Destruction of the Irish woollen manufacture. Measures against the Irish Presbyterians. The evil results. The Irish Parliament. Its composition and weakness. Restrictions on it. Declaratory statute that the English Parliament could bind Ireland by its laws. Modification of Poynings' Law. Heads of Bills. The Irish Parliament inferior and subject. The Irish-Anglican or Established Church. Its characteristics. The Irish Catholic Church. The Irish Bench and Bar. Appearance of the country. Molyneux, Swift, and Berkeley. Their writings on Ireland. Gradual improvement before the middle of the eighteenth century. Social and political progress. An "Irish interest" formed in the Irish Parliament. Opposition to the Government. The "Undertakers." Anthony Malone. Condition of Ireland about 1760. The Whiteboy and other movements. Agrarian crime in Ireland. The first years of the reign of George III quiet in Ireland. Henry Flood. The Viceroyalty of Lord Townshend. Quarrel with the "Undertakers" and the

Irish Parliament. The Viceroyalty of Lord Harcourt. Influence on Ireland of the revolt of the American colonies. Profuse corruption. Attitude of the Irish Parliament. Extreme distress and fear of invasion. The Volunteer movement. Henry Grattan. Concession of a partial Free Trade to Ireland. Demands for Legislative Independence. The Volunteers at Dungannon. Grattan moves the Legislative Independence of Ireland. The Revolution of 1782. Relaxation of the Penal Code. Irish Literature, Art, and Science. Reflections.

A PERIOD of five centuries had now passed away, since England had begun to establish her rule in Ireland. During the first three of these she had only succeeded in making her influence felt within a narrow Pale, diminishing too in the course of time; the rest of the island had been abandoned to half barbarous feudalism, and to chiefs of the Celts. The first Tudor Sovereigns had, in different ways, made real attempts to extend the power of the Monarchy over the whole of Ireland, and to enlarge the domain of order and law; the policy of Henry VIII in this respect was, for the most part, marked by enlightened wisdom. But the King's system of government ceased with his life; and a series of unhappy circumstances destroyed the promise of the auspicious era that seemed about to open. The Reformation separated England and Ireland by degrees, if this, for a long time, was not a main cause of disunion; the advance of the dominion of England was characterised by spoliation, often unjust, and by irregular risings of nobles and chiefs; and, at the great crisis of the sixteenth century, Ireland threw in her lot with the foes of England, and was gradually subjugated by evil and atrocious methods. The struggle of race and religion, which had long been growing, now became more internecine and fierce; confiscation proceeded on a gigantic scale; the usages of the Irish Celts were blotted out; and masses of settlers, alien from the children of the soil, were made possessors of vast tracts of territory, torn from their ancient owners and occupants by all

VII.]   *The Period of the Penal Laws in Ireland.*   199

kinds of wrong. After the era of Protestant Ascendency had thus begun, the subject Catholic people rose once more; Ireland crossed England again at a most critical time; a period of savage civil war followed; and Cromwell placed the whole island under the Puritan yoke, trying to crush out all distinctions, save that of faith, enormously increasing the Protestant settlements, and governing by an absolute despotism of the sword. The Restoration, in the main, confirmed his policy; after a brief period of treacherous repose, Catholic Ireland, for the second time in the seventeenth century, took up arms against Protestant England, and engaged in a desperate strife with her far stronger neighbour at a moment of revolution and national danger. The result was what might have been foreseen: Catholic Ireland went down in an unequal conflict, having provoked the indignation and wrath of England; and she had now to abide the results of another conquest.

These considerations must be borne in mind as we review the dark and calamitous period of Irish History we are about to traverse. It should be added that if the lot of Ireland had been, for five hundred years, that of a neglected and a misruled dependency, this was less due to positive faults of her own, or to positive faults of the dominant country, than to what, in our ignorance, we must call the evil play of fortune. A series of accidents had checked the growth and development of the English power, throughout the island, in the Middle Ages; instead of a strong and well-ordered Monarchy, only a feeble settlement had been made, by the side of feudal and Celtic anarchy. Consequently, at the momentous epoch of the sixteenth century, when the world was passing into a new existence, Ireland was centuries behind England, in civilisation and social progress; this single circumstance largely explains the train of unhappy events that followed. It makes us understand, to a considerable extent, why Ireland parted from England at the Reformation; why English statesmen tried to impose their institutions on a people they deemed barbarous, and to obliterate Irish laws and customs; why the colonisation of Ireland by foreign settlers seemed necessary to the wellbeing of Ireland herself, and a policy of the first importance to the State; why, from the days of Mary Tudor to those of Cromwell, the confiscation of the Irish land was carried out as part of a system of government; why Protestant Ascendency was established by degrees, and Catholic subjection was made more and more complete. The atrocities, the crimes, the follies, the wickedness, which took place during this long agony, are not, indeed, excused by reflections like these. It is impossible to justify much that was done in the Desmond and Tyrone wars, in the conflict of 1641-9, in the Cromwellian Conquest and the settlement of the land, in the struggle of 1689-91; and not to speak of numberless things of the kind, the rapacity, the guilt, and the systematic cruelty of many Tudor and Stuart Viceroys, the greed and tyranny of successive swarms of colonists, the perfidy of Charles I and of Charles II, and the conduct of the warring races and faiths of Ireland, in instances unhappily too frequent, deserve to be severely condemned. Still circumstance, superior to the will of man, does account for much that is most deplorable in the melancholy drama of Irish History, and that almost from the beginning to the end. Not the least remarkable fact, in the course of events, was that England was, in the main, Teutonic, and Ireland, in the main, Celtic; few races present more striking features of contrast, or have found it more difficult to agree, when one is dominant and the other subject.

The Irish Parliament was convened a few months after the fall of Limerick. Every Catholic had been shut out from it by an Act recently passed by the English Parliament; in the existing condition of Ireland, indeed, the precaution probably was superfluous. The men at the Castle, we have seen, were on the look-out for forfeitures; the dominant Protestant caste was smarting from the effects of wrongs done in the late years of trouble; the short-lived ascendency of the Irish Catholics had been followed by their defeat and ruin; and Catholic Ireland was in the grasp of her conquerors. A furious outcry arose in the Irish Parliament against the article, in what was now known by the pacific name of the Treaty of Limerick, which assured Catholic owners their estates, in the counties "under the protection of the Irish army"; this, we have seen, was ratified by William III, under peculiar circumstances, by his positive order; but the concession was denounced as an act of treason to the State. The king, indeed, had, for some time, as was to be expected from his well-known character and tendency to toleration in religious matters, been trying to do justice to the Irish Catholics; he had already caused the lands of some to be restored; he had, in fact, offered them terms, before Aghrim, much more favourable than those agreed to at Limerick. Nothing, however, could stop the Assembly in Dublin; it quarrelled with Lord Sidney, who had been made Lord Lieutenant, and repudiated every part of his master's policy; and Sidney was compelled at last to prorogue and dissolve it, for it had assumed an attitude, on a grave question, the subject, in after years, of angry disputes, in which it asserted a right denied to it at Westminster. A short interval of comparative peace followed; during this time William continued to give back parts of their lands to some Catholic owners; but unfortunately he lavished enormous grants of land, forfeited in the late war, on favourites, courtiers, and Dutch soldiers, after the bad fashion of Charles II. The English Parliament took the matter in hand; condemned the conduct of the king in no measured terms; and ultimately insisted that the forfeited lands should be resumed, and disposed of anew. The Irish Parliament, meanwhile, had assembled again; William, from what motive is not known, consented that a Bill, confirming the Treaty of Limerick, should not contain the important words, on which he had himself insisted; and Catholic owners, whose rights had been saved, as being "under the protection of the Irish army," were left naked and defenceless before their foes. It was a grave breach of faith on the part of the king, even if he was not, perhaps, wholly a free agent; but William, if a great, was not a scrupulous statesman; and it is to the honour of the Irish House of Lords, that it passed the Bill by a majority of one vote only. But hundreds of Catholic owners were nevertheless despoiled; the iniquities of the "Graces," and of the Acts of Settlement, were unhappily repeated, with the attendant evils.

The Treaty of Limerick had thus been broken; it was violated afterwards in a much worse fashion. By another article—and respecting this no doubt can exist as to the words that were used—it was provided, we have said, that the Irish Catholics should possess the same rights "in the exercise of their religion," as the law allowed, and as they "enjoyed in the reign of Charles II." Though they had been subjected to many galling tests, they had been practically little molested in their faith,—passing over the persecution of Cromwell—especially in the reign of Charles referred to. But England was incensed with Catholic Ireland; the Parliament at Westminster was enacting most cruel laws against the English Catholics; and the colonists in Ireland had but one thought, that of trampling down their abhorred enemies. With the approbation of the English Parliament, and of a long succession of British statesmen, the Irish Parliament, from this time forward, and during a period of many years, extending far into the eighteenth century, passed laws levelled at the Irish Catholics, which not only cast the Treaty of Limerick to the winds and placed their faith under an odious ban, but directly aimed at depriving them of almost all rights, political, civil, nay of a social kind, and at degrading them into a mere race of Helots. We cannot dwell in detail on the execrable Penal Code[1], we can only glance at its most salient features. After the forfeitures of the reign of William III, on a final adjustment made by the English Parliament, about 300,000 acres of the Irish land had been given back to their old possessors; about 800,000 had been bestowed on new men, largely English absentees; and probably not more than one-eighth of the Irish soil, after the confiscations of a century and a half, remained in the hands of Irish Catholic owners, whether of the old Englishry, or of the Celtic race. It was the first object, however, of the Penal Code, and of its authors the ruling Protestant caste, to divorce the Catholics as completely as possible from the land, the source of wealth and political power, and to deprive them even of the remnant they still retained, after the wrongs they had endured for ages. To effect this purpose the Irish Catholic was disabled from acquiring the ownership of land, or even from having an incumbrance on it; the only tenure of land he could obtain, was a short leasehold at a rack rent, a tenure obviously designed for humble peasants; and, at the same time, the few Catholics who had preserved their estates, were compelled to allow them to be split in fragments, and to "gavel" among their children at death, the idea being that, by this provision, their "properties would soon crumble away and disappear." Other laws, all with the same fell purpose, but some inspired by evil malice and hate, were passed to complete this exclusion from the land. A Catholic estate was not to "gavel," should the eldest son conform to the dominant faith;

---

[1] Vincent Scully on the Penal Code is a book of some research. Howard's *Popery Cases* will be read with profit. Burke's *Tracts on the Popery Laws*, though mere incomplete sketches, bear the marks of his philosophic and masterly hand. The *Irelande politique, sociale, et religieuse* of De Beaumont is worth careful study. An excellent dissertation on the Irish Penal Code will be found in Mr Lecky's *England in the Eighteenth Century*, vol. I. chap. 2; vol. II. chap. 7.

a Protestant man or woman, who married a Catholic, was subject, if an owner of land, to the Code; the eldest son of a Catholic owner, who became a Protestant, was given a right to reduce his father's fee simple to a life interest, and to possess himself of the expectant estate; a wife or child, tempted to the same apostasy, was entitled to an immediate provision from the land, and was removed from the control of the head of the family.

The second great object of the Penal Code was to shut out the Irish Catholic from any place of trust in the State, nay from the pale of civilised life. He had been forbidden, we have seen, to have a seat in his country's Parliament; he was ere long deprived of the elective suffrage; he was excluded "from the corporations, from the magistracy, from the Bar, from the Bench, from the County Grand Juries, even from the Parish Vestries"; he could not "be a sheriff, a solicitor, a gamekeeper, a constable." The proscription went even lower down; the Irish Catholic could not serve in the Army or on the Fleet; he could not possess any arms or weapons; he was, in a word, "only recognised by law for repression and punishment," and disentitled to nearly all the rights of a freeman. And while this people of Pariahs, who, be it observed, formed the overwhelming majority of the community as a whole, "was excluded, in its own country, from almost every profession and from every Government office, from the highest to the lowest," the Code went out of its way, so to speak, to humiliate the whole body of the Irish Catholics, to degrade them, in a word, to the position of outcasts. It is unnecessary to point out how the laws as to the land could make the life of a Catholic owner wretched; a rebellious son, an adulterous wife could defy his authority and simply rob him; and it should be added that, even in his dying hour, he could not commit his children to the care of a guardian of his own faith; he was compelled to devolve this trust on a Protestant. Other provisions of the

VII.] *The Period of the Penal Laws in Ireland.* 207

Code ∨in: more than one chief of the O'Neills and the and P⁊ells found distinguished places in the Spanish army; barbarcⁿinent Spanish soldiers were Irish. The Austrian and Celt; tᵉ Russian armies had, also, great Irishmen among their Catholiᵤ Browne, who would have triumphed at Prague, had shut heɿ in command; Lacy, who discomfited Frederick the possess ɿn the theatre of the operations of 1866; a second made liᵼ and Lacy honoured by the Czars; Maguire and other imᵢllustrious in a subsequent age. But France was the well as iɿne of the exiles; her armies were filled with Irish "Commoonspicuous on many a field of fame; O'Brien, Lord of Viceroyided the result at Fontenoy; Lally at Wandewash laid downɿ heroic valour. Nor should history pass over the Ireland wɇs of the generations of Irish soldiers, who, low as The lasɿ was, made their country renowned in the records organisatio⳰an one Continental service. Here again France their religiᴄ principal part: the "wild geese," as they were bishops, biᵴlled, flew in thousands from Ireland, to join her exile; if tɿess than a century, it has been said, a quarter of a treason, aɿrish recruits found a place in her celebrated Irish crime. ꞇₐnd they amply justified the noble words, "Semper et ubique fideles" inscribed on their banners. They turned the scale at Almanza and Fontenoy; at Dettingen extorted from George II the bitter words, "curse on the laws that deprive me of such men"; won the admiration of Villars, of Berwick, of Vendôme, of Saxe, in many a well-contested campaign; and, whether in good or in evil fortune, were always among the best troops of France.

The history, in fact, of Catholic Ireland is largely that of those courageous exiles, during this dismal part of the eighteenth century. As for the Catholic Irish who remained at home, the consequences of the Penal Code were, in the main, such as its authors had hoped for. The few Catholic owners of land who survived, whether of Anglo-Norman or Celtic descent, sank gradually into poverty and despair; their existence was one of continual alarm and wretchedness. Involved as they were in a common ruin, old distinctions of race had almost disappeared; the sons of the Barons of the Pale and of Celtic Princes were equally despised and degraded Pariahs; they vegetated listlessly on the ancestral estates, which the law was filching from them by degrees, excluded from power and place in the State, defeated and broken down in the battle of life, insulted and oppressed even by the refuse of the dominant caste which had been made their masters. Their lives, too, were a round of anxiety and pain; they were beset by detestable harpies of the law, picking flaws in their titles, like the old "discoverers," and informing against them in the Courts of Justice, if such a name could be given to these; their foes were often those of their own households; their feelings were tortured, their families rent in twain, in the most ordinary relations of domestic life. Passing from this order of men, the Irish Catholic was not actually forbidden to trade; but he was shut out from the municipal bodies, which had great advantages in this respect, and even from many corporate towns; he was subjected to all kinds of unfair restrictions; and though many of the class did engage in commerce, and even acquired wealth in time, they were not numerous enough to make their influence felt, during the first half of the eighteenth century. As for the Catholic masses seated on the soil, they were the villeins and serfs of conquering settlers, alien in blood and creed, and for the most part hostile; and prohibited as they were from holding land, except by a tenure of the worst kind, they were reduced to a multitude of petty occupiers, discouraged in their industry, kept down through life, unable to improve their lands and themselves, and sinking into appalling poverty. Oppression and exaction on the part of the ruling class, the degradation and misery of the subject race were the necessary results of this state of things. Ireland,

Swift tells us, was, even in his time, a land of desolation and widespread ruin; and it was a land of ever-recurring famines, in which the peasantry perished in thousands. As regards Catholic Ireland as a whole, the law and everything pertaining to it had been made its most deadly enemy; and a just Nemesis brought the inevitable results. To the train of feelings produced by the Penal Code we must largely attribute the hatred of law, the dislike of the existing order of things, the dread of the Government, the jealous suspicion of the administration of justice, in all its parts, the undefined, but not the less real discontent which prevailed in Catholic Ireland even in recent times, and has by no means altogether disappeared.

The Penal Code drew an impassable gulf between the Protestant and the Catholic Irish; but, if Lazarus had the evil things of this world, many of the good things were lost to Dives. A system of legislation which placed society, already distorted by long misgovernment, upon a false and unnatural basis, which forbade kindly relations to grow up between the divided orders of a whole community, and which checked the development of industry and wealth, could not fail to react with evil effects on the classes themselves which it seemed to favour. Protestant Ireland did not thrive under the scheme of injustice which made it the tyrant of Catholic slaves; and special causes worked in the same direction. The Protestant owners of land being unable to sell to Catholics, or to borrow money from them, their estates were kept in a kind of mortmain, out of commerce, and not supplied by capital; and for this and other reasons they were usually not wealthy. Hundreds of the order, too, were mere absentees, and absenteeism enormously increased, owing to circumstances we shall briefly glance at. Numbers of landlords let their lands on long leases to persons of their own faith, who had a monopoly of the market, and paid but nominal rents. This body of men, the notorious middlemen, neither landlords nor tenants in a true sense, generally sublet their holdings three or four deep; they were the worst oppressors of the Catholic peasant: and a gradation of tenures was thus created, which meshed the land, so to speak, in destructive shackles, prohibiting improvement and secure possession. Added to the degradation of the Catholic occupant, these facts, and others to be referred to, were the principal causes that Ireland made little or no progress for a long series of years; that barrenness and misery seemed stamped on her soil; that the whole dominant caste was not prosperous. The same things were observed in the sphere of commerce, though here restriction, we shall see, had far-reaching effects; the privileges enjoyed by the Protestant trader were injurious to him in the highest degree, starved the very trade he considered his own, made him slothful, careless, and neglectful of his business. So it was in agriculture, in which the Protestant had advantages denied to the Catholic tenant; this had a tendency to encourage neglect and idleness, the natural result of unfair monopoly. The Penal Code, however, was most pernicious to Protestant Ireland in its moral effects. It cut off the upper classes from those beneath them, made them domineering, harsh, exacting, like the French seigneurs of the old *régime*; it created habits of extravagance, of lawlessness, of licentious recklessness, attended with the most unhappy results. Its influence was even worse in the lower ranks of Protestants; it marked them off as an overbearing class, encouraged to oppress and vex the Catholics in their midst, it made them insolent, conceited, and more deserving of dislike than their betters. Demoralisation, profound but subtle, and pervading the social structure from top to bottom, was, in a word, the effect of the Penal Code, as regards the whole people of Protestant Ireland.

England, too, made the Protestant colony feel that it was a subject settlement to be treated with contempt; the injurious consequences soon became manifest. We have referred to the commercial restrictions of the reign of Charles II; these were greatly aggravated in the reigns that followed. Ireland continued to be excluded from the Navigation Acts, and was still prohibited to send live animals and even meat to England, —checks on her industry which did increasing mischief as the land became, by degrees, more settled. Her woollen manufacture, however, remained; and as Irish wool was of the very best quality, a large capital was attracted to this branch of trade, and numbers of artisans found employment in it. English jealousy destroyed this promising growth; the Irish woollen manufacture was suppressed; Ireland was forbidden to export the raw material to any country, except England; even her linen manufacture was discouraged and starved. The results were, in the highest degree, unfortunate; the land was smitten, as it were, with a blight; the development of its resources was stopped; and thousands of Protestant settlers left the island, like the Englishry of mediæval times, flying from a land where they could not exist. In many other respects the dominant caste was injured and oppressed by the mother country. The Parliament of Westminster, we have seen, had, long ago, asserted a right to enact laws that affected Ireland; it "declared" that right by a positive statute, and exercised it over and over again; and it reduced the Irish Parliament to a mere vestry by methods we shall soon briefly mention. Meanwhile "the English interest" was supreme at the Castle; nearly every high place in the Government, the Anglican Church, and the Law, was filled by Englishmen, with watchful care; the Protestants of Ireland were practically shut out by a narrow, domineering, and harsh bureaucracy composed mainly of English functionaries. At the same time the scanty resources of Ireland were charged with an ever-augmented list of pensions, often of the most scandalous kind; if Parliamentary corruption did not as yet flourish, it was because the necessity had not arrived; and the men in office gave a free rein to favouritism, to jobbing, to maladministration, to waste, in every department of the public service. A cause of disunion had arisen, also, which seriously weakened the Protestant colony. So far back, we have seen, as the time of Strafford, and still more after the Restoration, Presbyterianism in Ireland had been discouraged; it was gradually subjected to a kind of proscription, for, strange to say, Irish Anglican Churchmen, almost the only members of the Irish Parliament, appear to have regarded it with peculiar dislike. The Irish Presbyterians, who formed the best element of the Protestant population of Ulster, were excluded from office in the State by strict tests; even their creed received toleration only. The injury done to them was as nothing compared to the iniquities of the Penal Code; but it divided the Protestant name in Ireland; it caused many Presbyterians to quit the island, in an emigration prolonged for years; and it drew a line, in landed relations in Ulster, between the Anglican owner of the soil and the Presbyterian occupant, which caused many evils, and is still distinctly marked.

"Protestant Ireland," it was finely said by Grattan, thus "knelt to England on the necks of her countrymen." The condition of affairs we have shortly described appeared in the institutions of the land, and throughout the frame of Irish society. The Irish Parliament had, by this time, reached the fullest proportions it ever attained; its House of Commons was composed of 300 members, a number of small boroughs having been created, in addition to the forty of James I. As a representative Body this House of Commons existed, so to speak, only in name; it had nothing to do with Catholic Ireland, save to oppress it and do it wrong; it was elected by small bodies of the Protestant caste; and it was filled by nominees of the Crown which, as yet, had a large majority of votes, and by dependents of the colonial aristocratic Houses which possessed the chief part of the land of the country. Though still fettered by Poynings' Law, the Irish Parliament had, by degrees, acquired an initiative in legislation, in a qualified sense; the Viceroy had ceased to command what it was to enact beforehand; and it had been permitted for a long time to present what were called "Heads of Bills" to him, and thus to discuss future laws within its precincts. But these Heads of Bills had to pass through the ordeal of the criticism of the Irish and the English Privy Councils; they could be amended or changed by these; the English Privy Council could throw out any propositions of the kind; and any "Heads of Bills" it returned to the Irish Parliament could be only passed or rejected by that Assembly, however they might have been transformed or altered. As a Legislature the Irish Parliament was thus a mere shadow; and in most other respects it had little power or influence. It was overborne by the English Parliament, which bound Ireland by laws passed at Westminster; its House of Lords was not even a Court of ultimate appeal. It had little control over the finances of Ireland, for the hereditary revenues of the Crown, which it could not touch or regulate, were nearly sufficient to supply the wants of the Government, at least for a considerable time; and though the Irish House of Commons claimed a right to propose and to enact Money Bills, and to be the only body that could lawfully tax Ireland, the first claim was subject to the Law of Poynings, and the second was regarded with dislike in England. The Irish Parliament, besides, had no power over the military force within Ireland; this was under the Mutiny Acts of England; and it should be added that as the Triennial and the Septennial Acts did not extend to Ireland, the Irish Parliament continued to exist during the whole reign of the Sovereign on the throne, and could be dissolved only on a demise of the Crown. An Assembly so devoid of every popular element, standing on so narrow and false a basis, so exposed to sinister and evil influence, so cabined and confined at every point, so maimed and limited in authority, was obviously a bad organ of Government, and was little respected even by Protestant Ireland. The Irish Parliament was held up by Swift[1] to execration and contemptuous scorn.

From the Parliament we pass to the Anglican Church in Ireland, which we have left out of sight for a considerable time. This Establishment, as it was now sometimes called, had undergone some changes in the course of a century, but its essential characteristics remained nearly the same. It had been adorned by a few eminent Prelates; Ussher and Bedell in the seventeenth century, King, Browne, and Synge in the next age were in different ways distinguished men; and Berkeley, illustrious in many spheres of letters, was, as a thinker, hardly inferior to Butler in his admirable writings on the Christian faith. But Swift's description of the Irish Bishops of his time—English highwaymen who had stolen the Episcopal robes—if a caricature, is not wholly false; not a few of the heads of the Irish Establishment were self-seeking, hard, worldly-minded men, such as an institution would naturally produce which was not a living Christian reality, and not strong with true spiritual strength. At this period the Irish Anglican Church had become more than ever an instrument of the State; two of its Archbishops, Boulter and Stone, were rulers at the Castle for many years, and, in fact, directed Irish affairs; but, as we have seen, it had shared the fortunes of Protestant Ireland, in some respects, and all its best preferments were held by Englishmen. For the rest it still was what it had always been, a secular rather than a spiritual arm, a Protestant outpost, so to speak, planted in the midst of Catholic Ireland, without the slightest moral influence on it, a mere source of irritation, and a badge of conquest; and it had little

---

[1] Swift, however, was not just to the Irish Parliament or the Irish landlords of his day. He was a high Churchman, and they treated the Irish Anglican Church with no favour.

VII.] *The Period of the Penal Laws in Ireland.* 215

hold even on Protestant Ireland, for like other institutions that do not fulfil their purpose, it still abounded in abuses widespread and flagrant. It was, in Macaulay's picturesque phrase, a Church that filled the rich with good things, and sent the hungry empty away. Its bishops wore purple and fine linen; its higher dignitaries formed a prosperous gentry; but its minor clergy were few and half starved, and its services were neglected in most parts of the country. Cathedrals in ruins, churches in decay, whole parishes without a priest or a curate, scandals of many kinds in clerical life, disregard of duty in high and low places—these were still the visible signs of the Irish Anglican Church; Swift, infinitely the keenest observer of his day, believed that its fall was already certain. The Church, too, it deserves notice, was betrayed and injured by its natural friends; the Irish Parliament and the owners of the Irish land not only treated it with marked contempt, but despoiled it of a large part of its property. In one respect the Irish Anglican Church harshly oppressed the down-trodden Catholic peasant, and laid a heavy and mischievous burden on him. It possessed the greater part of the tithe of the country; its ministers levied this impost in the very worst way, from the Helots of an alien communion. This was the more iniquitous, because pastoral lands had been practically discharged of tithe by a series of votes of the Irish Parliament; the charge was laid on the petty crop, which had been raised by the Catholic husbandmen. This was simply shameful and grotesque wrong; as Grattan said, the crook of the so-called shepherd was only known to the flock when it was thrust into the sheep.

The Irish Catholic Church presented a striking contrast to its pampered rival. It lay, so to speak, in the valley of the shadow of death; its priesthood were the despised and rejected of men; yet proscription and persecution could not destroy the spiritual life which was strong in it, even the organisation which upheld its structure. It no longer wore the arrogant aspect it had often worn in the seventeenth century, especially in Catholic Confederate days; but it retained its hold on the heart of Catholic Ireland; it represented in a real sense her people; it was their support in their long night of affliction. Its clergy were ignorant, nay, superstitious, as a class; but they were pious, virtuous, zealous of good works; in this period of trial and unceasing sorrows they were gradually working a moral transformation in their flocks, and weaning them from vices common to Celts, an achievement deserving the highest praise.

We turn to an institution of a very different kind, at this time confined to Protestant Ireland, and exhibiting the effects of the peculiar position made by England for her Protestant colony. The Irish Bench and Bar had played a conspicuous part in the sixteenth and the seventeenth centuries; both were virtually open to all Irishmen without regard to distinctions of creed, at least as almost a general rule; both could show a noble succession of lawyers by no means inferior to their English brethren. In the first part of the eighteenth century the profession had markedly changed for the worse, owing to the operation of the Penal Code and to the slights from which Protestant Ireland suffered. The Irish Catholic was excluded from the Bench and the Bar, which were strictly reserved for the Protestant caste; and this monopoly had its natural results in checking industry and casting a blight on talent. The chief places too on the Bench, we have seen, were in all cases bestowed on Englishmen; the Castle practically ruled the Judges and the Bar; and it should be added that the Irish Judges continued to hold their offices at the will of the Crown and had not the protection secured for their fellows in England, while the Habeas Corpus Act did not extend to Ireland. All this made the Bench and Bar of Ireland comparatively subservient, degraded, weak; the administration too of the inhuman Penal Code, which consecrated wrong in the name of justice, had a tendency in the same direction; Swift and even Berkeley had no respect or liking for the leading men of the gown in their day. Noble exceptions nevertheless existed; the Irish Bench and Bar had some eminent names even in this season of dreary eclipse. The most remarkable of these was Anthony Malone, a scion of the old race of Offaley, already conspicuous for his fine parts, and soon to appear brilliantly on the political scene.

The condition of Ireland at this period was also seen on the face of the country. Swift has informed us that the ravage done by the war of 1689-91 exceeded that done from 1641 to 1649; if this is an exaggeration we may believe his statement that, as we have said, the land was half a desert during the first quarter at least of the eighteenth century. Very few country houses or demesnes were seen; for absenteeism, we have remarked, had produced the middleman, and severed the landlord from the land; absenteeism had been greatly augmented by the exclusion of the Protestant gentry from office in the state; and, in consequence, numbers of the Irish landlords lived abroad or in England, and spent little on their estates. The commercial restrictions had the same effects; the habitations even of the largest occupiers of the soil were squalid and mean amidst the prevailing poverty; and the traveller roamed through great wastes of pasturage where agriculture scarcely existed, unfenced and half-grazed by scanty flocks and herds. As for the mass of the population, the broken remains of the tribes, clans, and septs of another age, it was huddled into miserable Celtic hamlets, or scattered in hovels in the rural districts, especially where it had been driven to the hills; its wretched appearance, its rags, its dirt, its sloth, its beggary, expressed a condition which Swift compared to that of the swine of the field, and from which even Berkeley turned away with disgust. The country too was hardly opened by roads; the forests and woods which had covered the land had, to a considerable extent, disappeared; but the means of communication were few and bad, and the tract west of the Shannon, part of the old Celtic land, was in a state of barbarism, probably worse than that which ever existed under its native rulers. Dublin, the seat of the Government, had continued to increase; and Cork, Belfast, and some of the seaport towns, presented a comparatively prosperous aspect. But the great majority of the inland towns remained petty and even decaying villages, without commerce, and showing scarcely a sign of progress. Ireland, in a word, was as a whole in a pitiable state; one special feature of the social structure was significant and deserves close attention. Her history, we have pointed out, had in the mediæval age made the developement of a middle class impossible; the events of the sixteenth and seventeenth centuries had inevitably produced the same result. Ireland at this period had scarcely a middle class at all; and this at the time when the great middle class of England was covering the seas with its merchant fleets, was beginning its reign of manufacturing greatness, and was rapidly advancing to power in the state.

The degradation of Ireland in all its classes naturally engendered feelings of arrogance and contempt on the part of its alien English masters. They looked down on the Catholic Irish as a people of serfs, and on the Protestant colony as a subject settlement, to be dealt with at the pleasure of the mother country. The Irish Catholics did not utter a murmur; but the Protestants resented the selfish policy which sacrificed them to narrow English interests and the domineering temper and self sufficient attitude of the officials from England enthroned at the Castle. The first notable symptom of this angry discontent appeared in a book called the *Case of Ireland*, written by William Molyneux, a friend of Locke, a member for the University of Dublin in the Irish Parliament, and a very able and fearless man; he was indignant at the annihilation of

Irish commerce, especially of the rising woollen manufacture; he wrote to prove that the English Parliament had no right to bind Ireland by Acts passed at Westminster; and he maintained a position which had been a subject of angry controversy for more than a hundred years with real learning and much force of argument. The English House of Commons which, we have seen, had asserted the right on many occasions, ordered the work to be burned by the common hangman; but, as Grattan said, it was more easily burned than answered; and the conclusions of the author, which probably had a preponderance of legal authority on his side, were triumphantly vindicated in another age.

During the period however we are now reviewing, the great champion of the Protestant Irish was Swift, certainly, in his peculiar style, the foremost political writer in the English tongue. Swift despised and hated Catholic Ireland; he was an enemy of the Presbyterian Irish; he is not to be relied on in his savage diatribes on the Irish Parliament and the Irish landlords, who, we have said, had injured the Established Church. But he threw a flood of light on the state of Ireland in the first thirty years of the eighteenth century; and he set forth admirably and with inimitable skill the grievances and the wrongs of the Protestant settlers. The best known exhibition of his powers was seen in the affair of Wood's patent, a job arranged by the English Government for the benefit of the Duchess of Kendal, one of the most greedy of royal favourites, which would have imposed on Ireland a base copper coinage, and probably would have disturbed her currency. In a series of letters written in homely language, but rich in sarcasm and in telling invective, Swift, in the part he assumed of a Dublin "Drapier," denounced the patent as a destructive fraud, and Wood as a wicked and rapacious trickster; and though his statements were overcharged and unscrupulous, he successfully exposed a scandalous abuse.

The fourth letter rose to the height of an argument for the liberty of the Irish legislature, and for the right of Irishmen to govern themselves; the effect it produced was widespread and magical. Protestant Ireland rallied around the exponent of the injuries done to its constitutional rights; every attempt to put Swift down ignominiously failed; the patent was cancelled and Wood disowned; and Pope recorded the triumph in the well-known line, "The rights a Court attacked, a Poet saved." Yet other political writings of Swift on Ireland are perhaps not of inferior value. His ghastly cannibal scheme to lessen Irish poverty is a piece of hideous and revolting irony; but it bears the stamp of the genius of Gulliver. His *Short View of Ireland* sums up in a few pregnant sentences the innumerable ills from which the colony suffered; it is a mine of information in a short compass. His *History of an Injured Lady* admirably shows up the Pharisaical cant in which English opinion indulged with reference to Irish affairs at the time; the lesson is even now appropriate; and the keen remark "we are in the condition of patients who have physic sent to them by doctors at a distance, strangers to their constitution and the nature of the disease," deserves the attention of English politicians at this hour. In all these compositions the "sæva indignatio" appears; but they overflow also with the many gifts which characterised the author's extraordinary mind.

Swift stirred Protestant Ireland to its depths, and aroused feelings which, having slept for a time, acquired ultimately formidable strength. Berkeley also wrote much on the state of Ireland; he was a notable contrast in this respect to Swift. We must pass over the speculations of this profound thinker on the nature of things and the understanding of men, and the admirable pages in which he unfolds, in more perspicuous and succinct language, the principal doctrines of the *Wealth of Nations*. If bitterness and anger are the essential features of Swift's writings on Irish affairs, wisdom and charity are the characteristics of those of Berkeley. He is not blind to the wrongs done to the Protestant colony by English selfishness; but he tries to reconcile the English in England and the English in Ireland by appeals to their common origin and common interests; and he labours earnestly to allay the feelings of discontent entertained by the settlers towards the mother country. The best of the Irish essays of Berkeley is no doubt the *Querist*, a masterly review of the ills of Ireland and of the remedies proposed by the philosophic author. It sets forth clearly the mischievous effects of the extravagance and the recklessness of the upper classes, of absenteeism in landed relations, of the idleness which was the besetting sin of the peasantry; it dwells on the folly of neglecting the domestic trade of Ireland because the foreign trade was checked and kept down; and it shows how unwise it is to complain of a Government, whatever may be the faults of its policy, while the community does not turn its industry to account. Berkeley's Platonism does not shrink from sumptuary laws; like a faithful disciple of the great master, he would have imposed on the state the task of moulding the social life of Ireland by law; the remarks he makes on the necessity of directing fashion, of organising labour, of discouraging waste, and on the accumulation of excessive wealth are not in accord with modern thought. But his observations on education in its various branches, especially on that of the landed gentry, in the developement of agriculture, planting and building, on the value of technical modes of instruction, and on the amelioration of the lot of the peasantry are enlightened in the highest degree; and he is never better than when he adjures Irishmen to be self-reliant, and to make the most of the order of things they find around them. Berkeley was admirable and far beyond his age in all that related to the Irish politics of the day. He distinctly perceived the evils that flowed from the separation of the Catholics from the land, in the interest of Protestant ascendency itself. He saw how the Established Church was doomed to sterility, if it stood haughtily aloof from Catholic Ireland; he urged that its services should be performed in the Irish tongue in the remote and Celtic parts of the country. With admirable liberality too he advised that the University should be opened to the Irish Catholics, an idea probably odious to most of his brethren on the Bench; and he anticipated the policy of a better age, when he asked, in the very spirit of Grattan, "whether a scheme for the welfare of this nation should not take in the whole inhabitants, and whether it be not a vain attempt to project the flourishing of our Protestant gentry, exclusive of the bulk of the natives?"

A change, gradual but making steady progress, began to pass over the state of Ireland after the first thirty years of the eighteenth century. The generation that had witnessed the Boyne and Aghrim was gone; the worst animosities of civil war had died out; Time was slowly throwing its kindly growths over a settlement of confiscation and conquest. The human conscience revolted against the barbarous laws which had been passed to degrade the Irish Catholics, and to humiliate them in the relations of life; the Penal Code, in these respects, was largely evaded. The Courts of Justice, too, felt the effects of this sentiment; the vile trade of the informer was not encouraged; by the ingenuity of legal fictions, the provisions of the Code were made means to keep Catholic estates in the hands of their owners. At the same time not a few of the Protestant gentry—Anthony Malone was a notable instance— held the lands of Catholics on secret trusts, for the benefit of the true possessors; and these trusts, though contrary to law, were hardly ever broken. The class of Catholic landlords was thus left to live in peace; and something like friendly intercourse, on equal terms, grew up between them and their Protestant fellows. No change, however, was made in the laws which forbade the Catholic from acquiring land, or even a partial interest in it; and he remained wholly excluded from office in the state, and completely deprived of political power. A Catholic class of traders was springing up, some rising in the social scale; but it was still kept in an inferior position; and as to the great body of the Catholic peasantry, they continued in a state of want and serfdom. An evil attempt, indeed, had been made, and was still being tried, to outrage their faith by a shameful expedient. They were forbidden by the law to educate their children; and Charter Schools, as they were called, were set up, in which "the young of the Papists," as they were contemptuously called, were given instruction and were fitted out in life, if they would abandon their parents and become Protestants. The Charter Schools were largely endowed and established in many parts of the country; but a system of making proselytes by unnatural means, proved, as might have been expected, a most sorry failure.

Meanwhile the material condition of Ireland was making a slow but steady advance. Despite of misgovernment of many kinds, the country was in profound peace; social order was for the most part upheld. The natural results became apparent; the wealth of Ireland increased by degrees; the restraints on her trade were, in different ways, lessened. Ireland was occasionally allowed to export live and dead stock to England; she maintained a great traffic of this kind with the Continent; she sent wool to France by smuggling in immense quantities. Her resources were thus more and more developed; while, at the same time, roads and even canals opened the rural districts and caused numerous markets to grow up under a system of local and municipal government, which, though confined to the Protestant caste, was not without real merits of its own. All this reacted with happy effects on the land; the country gentry became much more rich; they gradually ceased to be mere alien colonists, acquired local and even Irish sympathies, were "more racy of the soil," as it was said, than their fathers.

Absenteeism diminished in a perceptible way; more of the Protestant landlords became resident; the good consequences were in time manifest. The middleman tenures, indeed, remained common, with their evil effects on landed relations; the habits of the gentry hardly improved; the humbler toilers of the soil were still steeped in poverty. But kindlier feelings certainly grew up between the owners of land of the higher orders and the Catholic tenants in occupation of the soil; these turned towards their masters with something like the old sentiment of the clansmen to their chiefs, a sentiment deeply rooted in the nature of the Celt; and this feeling grew stronger in the course of time. It was at this period, and during the next half century, that most of the great country seats and demesnes that exist in Ireland were laid out and formed; and Arthur Young, who wrote in 1776-8, gives on the whole rather a pleasing account of the relations between the chief resident gentry and their dependents, if farmers of the better class. A marked improvement also took place in the towns within the reach of commerce and its benign influence. Dublin grew into a really fine capital, adorned with many noble public buildings and with institutions that told of progress. Cork too and Belfast became seats of trade; even some of the inland towns showed signs of active life. And with this material, there was social and moral progress; the influences of the eighteenth century effected something, if not much, in mitigating Protestant ascendency in its worst aspects and in making Catholic subjection less grievous; and there was a development of letters, of art and of science, on which we shall say a few words afterwards.

This change, as had been the case before, affected the institutions and the social life of Ireland. The government of the country remained much as it had been; it abounded in many, perhaps increasing abuses; it was still for the most part carried on by Englishmen. But the Irish Parliament grew in authority by degrees, for the hereditary revenue of the Crown had become insufficient to supply the demands of the State and the public service; a National Debt was being formed, and it was now necessary to convene the Irish Houses, every second year at least, in a regular manner. A party in it, slowly acquiring influence, denounced the Pension List and other acts of the Castle; as early as 1731 it began to claim a right to deal with the national funds, and the patriotism of "Tottenham in his boots," whose vote proved decisive, was long remembered as that of a champion of freedom. The power, however, of the Irish Parliament was much more augmented by the increase of the wealth and the development of a new spirit in the landed gentry. As the Protestant aristocracy grew richer and thus gained more influence in the state, as it formed more and more a resident class, as its sentiments gradually became more Irish, it began to dislike the rule of the men at the Castle and to seek to assert an authority of its own; it employed its crowd of nominees in the Irish House of Commons to resist a government to which it had been long subservient; and thus an opposition to the Crown and its measures, slowly gathering in strength, was created by degrees. The "English interest" in a word, as in bygone times, was confronted by a new "Irish interest." This body of men which was a mere oligarchy, took no thought of the mass of the people, especially of the downtrodden Catholics; it was often grasping, corrupt, selfish, more than once, borrowing an ominous name, it became an "undertaker" to do the work of the Castle, in return for a lavish bribe of patronage and place. Nevertheless the appearance of this Junta was a change for the better in the affairs of Ireland, even, in a certain sense, marked a turn in her history. The men of the "Irish interest" understood Ireland in a way beyond the reach of officials from England; they were experienced in local Irish business; many as were their faults they loved their country, after their own fashion; and, from the nature of the case, they were compelled to advocate liberal measures and to denounce abuses. A quarrel between Archbishop Stone, still the real head of the Irish Government, and several chiefs of leading Irish families ultimately led in 1753 to an angry rupture; the "Irish interest" insisted that it had a right to appropriate a surplus of national money, and came into conflict with the men in power. The Government triumphed, but with much difficulty; from this time forward the Opposition became a real force in the Irish Parliament. In this struggle it had the support of the head of the great House of Fitzgerald and of many of the principal Irish nobles; but its real leader was Anthony Malone, who, according to Grattan, gave proof of most remarkable powers as a statesman and orator.

The Established Church was but little affected by the influences of the new era. Its highest places, however, were by degrees less filled by Englishmen than they had been; some of its Prelates even took up the ideas of Berkeley as to the Irish Catholics. The position of the Irish Catholic Church was greatly improved; its worship, indeed, was still celebrated in miserable "chapels," as they were called; its stately ritual was still proscribed; as of old, it was barely tolerated by the law. But many of the restraints on it had become obsolete; its priesthood were not hunted down and banned; its organisation was rooted in the land; the Government had even entered into relations with it. Its hold on its flocks had only strengthened, as it had won its way through a sea of troubles; it embodied even more fully than half a century before, the feelings and the hopes of Catholic Ireland. Meanwhile it had wrought a marked change in the moral condition of the Irish peasantry. Its clergy had all but eradicated the sexual licence, which, we have seen, had been the reproach of the Ireland of the Celtic tribes; and though the degradation of the humblest classes was such, that a rude harem was not seldom an appendage to a great country mansion, this was looked upon as an accursed spot. The people brought up under this guidance, were servile, priest-ridden, and superstitious; but they were remarkable for their domestic virtues, and this remains to this day their character. As for the Irish Bench and Bar, a very potent influence in a country governed as Ireland was, it had undergone a change in all respects for the better. The rising generation of the Irish Judges disliked and discountenanced the Penal Code; the highest posts in the Law were sometimes held by Irishmen; the whole profession became more Irish, less subservient, more attached to their country. This change had been partly due to the fact, that though Catholics remained excluded from the Bar, many had nominally conformed to satisfy the law, like the "nouveaux convertis" of the French Huguenots, and some of these were distinguished men.

Ireland, after the middle of the eighteenth century, thus became different, in many respects, from what it had been from the reign of William III to that of George III. This progress, however, was only partial and superficial to a considerable extent; it was probably exaggerated by observers of the day. The profound divisions of race and faith, which kept society asunder, continued to exist; this ulcer had been only filmed and skinned over; Catholics and Protestants were separated by the widest barriers through life. The few Catholic gentry who remained were still a feeble and timid order of men; they were still all but outside the pale of the law; they could not lift Catholic Ireland out of subjection. The Protestants were as yet a dominant caste that held a Catholic people down; if in the most important of social relations, that between the owners and occupiers of the soil, a distinct improvement was manifest, the evils of the past were still but too prevalent. Enormous tracts of land were still held by absentees, and mismanaged in many instances; middleman tenures, if diminishing, were very common, preventing improvement and causing much mischief; numbers of the lesser gentry were oppressive landlords. Complaints of harsh extortion and wrong are to be found in several publications of the day, and even in speeches in the Irish Parliament; and though the great resident landlords did much good, as a class they were comparatively few. The condition of the great mass of the peasantry remained that of serfs; their submissiveness, even the affection they showed to superiors who happened to be kindly masters, were closely allied to the feelings of slaves. We do not hear of appalling famines again; and Arthur Young said that in the better parts of Ulster and in most of the Counties of Leinster, the humbler tillers of the soil fared as well as their fellows in England. But it was otherwise in whole tracts of Munster and in three-fourths of Connaught; the population in these was still in a state of wretchedness.

As always happens in a distempered society, a general spirit of lawlessness was still common; the upper classes, not restrained by opinion, had still, in a very great degree, the habits of extravagance and licentiousness seen in their fathers; they were given to excesses of all kinds and were most reckless duellists. As for the classes beneath them, these expressed the sense of suffering and wrong seething beneath the surface, in the agrarian risings, which, we have said, may be traced back to the immense confiscations of the past. In the first part of the century Connaught was disturbed by armed bands known by the name of "Houghers"; these destroyed the flocks and herds of men of substance in whole counties. Many years afterwards the "Oakboys" and "Steelboys" arose in parts of Ulster and caused grave troubles; unjust taxes, tithes and harsh acts of landlords seem to have been the provocation of these movements; and they were remarkable as leading to a great increase of the emigration of Presbyterian families from Ireland. The most formidable, however, of these risings—one that nearly makes a period in Irish history—was that of the "Whiteboys," as they were called; this convulsed large districts of Munster and even of Leinster; it created for a time almost a Reign of Terror; and it formed the peculiar type of agrarian disorder, which has agitated Ireland ever since, at different intervals of time. The "Whiteboys," like the "Camisards" of the Cevennes, appeared at night, in white shirts, in multitudes; the grievances they denounced were the enclosure of common lands, extravagant rents, and the impost of tithe; and they combined into an organisation of such strength that, to a great extent, they effected their objects. The law and the power of the state were confronted by the law and the power of secret societies, drawing the peasantry together into a huge League; and the mandates of this were steadily carried out by outrages of all kinds, and by deeds of blood and violence. The "Whiteboys" were only slowly put down; a Draconic Code, still in force, was required to crush them; and, as we have said, combinations of this sort, connected with and springing from the land, have never since ceased to exist in Ireland. The "Whiteboy" movement does not appear to have been in a true sense rebellious, or to have had a political object; but this, we have remarked, has sometimes been an end of Irish agrarian outbreaks; it is enough to refer to the history of Ireland within the last few years.

We may follow the course of Irish History, after the accession of George III to the throne, more closely than we have followed it of late. An incident had just occurred before, which proved the change that Protestant Ireland was going through, since the colonial caste had become Irishmen. The commercial restrictions imposed on Ireland had caused a movement to arise in the reign of Anne, in favour of a Union with England, which, like the Scottish Union, might secure a free trade; but this failed owing to English commercial jealousy. The project was revived in 1759, perhaps with the approbation of the first Pitt; but it provoked such indignation that it was quickly dropped. Another incident in the following year, showed how the "Irish interest" strong at this time at the Castle, could venture to cross the men in power at Westminster. The death of George II had brought to an end the Parliament which had sat in Dublin, without a fresh election, for thirty-three years; and it had become necessary to assemble a new Parliament. To effect this, it had been long the practice, under Poynings' Law, which we must bear in mind secured the initiative in legislation to the Irish Viceroy, to send over two or three Bills to England, to be returned by the Privy Council there; one of them was by recognised custom a Money Bill. But the Irish House of Commons had, we have seen, claimed for a long time an exclusive right to deal with Money Bills within its own sphere; and the Irish Privy Council, led by Anthony Malone, advised the English Council, on this occasion, that a Money Bill should not be transmitted to England, considering the state of Irish opinion. The English Council insisted on a settled precedent—against, be it observed, the wishes of Pitt—and Anthony Malone was dismissed from his post as Chancellor of the Irish Exchequer; but the dispute not only proved that the "Irish interest" could be independent, and took the right course, but led to irritation that soon began to fester. It should be added, as a further sign how Protestant Ireland was becoming awake, that there had been a movement for some years to extend the English Septennial Act to Ireland, and to make the duration of the Irish Parliament not coextensive with the reign of the Sovereign, in order to bring it more under electoral control. This demand had been urged by Charles Lucas, an apothecary of Dublin, who, with inferior parts, was true to the political creed of the "Drapier," especially as to the right of Ireland to self-government; and Lucas became so popular that he was chosen to represent the City in 1760-1. The Irish Protestants, in fact, had for some time resented the subjection in which they were held, and had begun to agitate for a change in the treatment they received. Swift and Berkeley had left no successors of equal power; but a popular Protestant Press had grown up; and a series of writers, some able men, had condemned the restraints placed on Irish commerce, and had dwelt on the economic ills which checked Irish progress.

Notwithstanding, however, these symptoms of trouble, the Irish Parliament and the British Government continued in harmony for some years. The "Irish interest" was in the ascendant in Dublin; combining its own influence and that of the Crown, it was completely supreme in the Irish Lords and Commons. The conduct of that Parliament, and of those who ruled it, reflected the sentiments of the aristocratic order which now virtually directed Irish affairs. The upper classes of Ireland, and indeed most of the Protestants, did not forget what their descent was, and how closely associated they were with the mother country; they were usually loyal to the Crown and to British Imperial interests, however they might wrangle with English officials on the spot. The Irish Parliament, accordingly, upheld the war policy of Pitt—it showed real sympathy with the Great Commoner—in the closing years of the Seven Years' War, and cheerfully voted large supplies; and a succession of Lords Lieutenant, who held office in the first years of the reign of George III, reported, in its favour, in language of high praise. In return for a support, by no means forced or feigned, the "Irish interest," or the "Undertakers," as they were called, were virtually made the Governors of the country; its administration, with the incidental patronage, passed into their hands. It is unquestionably true that, in executing this trust, much jobbing and even corruption may be laid to their charge; but this was inevitable in a state of things in which a strong public opinion could not exist; whatever may be said, their rule was less faulty, nay purer than that of the "English interest"; and they set on foot a system of Public Works in Ireland, which proved of real and permanent use.

The "Undertakers" besides, as we have said, were necessarily inclined to take the popular side; they endeavoured to cut down the scandalous list of pensions; and they induced the Parliament to pass Bills for making the tenure of the Irish judges secure and for extending the Habeas Corpus Act to Ireland, which, however, were rejected by the English Council. In this liberal policy they found a champion in Henry Flood, a young man of remarkable powers, and possessing solid gifts as a public speaker, who was destined to play a conspicuous, if a somewhat questionable part, on the stage of Irish History, in after years.

In 1767, George Lord Townshend, a brother of the better known Charles, assumed the reins of power at the Castle; his Viceroyalty gave a new turn to affairs in Ireland. Townshend was sent over by the English Ministry to carry out, in Ireland, a policy dear to the heart of the king; he was to break down the authority of the "Undertakers," as Bute and Henry Fox had tried to break down the authority of the great Whigs of England; but he proved a vexatious and unsuccessful bungler. After much opposition, and with great difficulty, he contrived to obtain from the Irish Parliament a vote for the "Augmentation," as it was called, of the Irish Army; and he promoted the enactment of an Octennial Bill, corresponding to the Septennial Act in England, for limiting the existence of the Irish Parliament. This probably was a Machiavellian policy; for the "Undertakers" and, indeed, the Irish House of Commons were, at heart, strongly opposed to the measure; but Townshend turned Protestant Irish opinion against them; he had persuaded himself that the change would increase his chances of destroying the "Irish interest," which he had begun for some time to hate. He was checked, however, in his career, by a sudden quarrel with the Irish House of Commons upon the subject, on which, eighty years before, it had come into conflict with Lord Sidney, and with regard to which it had been always jealous. It rejected a Money Bill, transmitted from England, on the ground "that it did not take its rise in the House of Commons"; angry debates and recriminations followed; and Townshend prorogued the Irish Parliament, not venturing, as Sidney had done, to dissolve it. The Lord Lieutenant now addressed himself, for many months, to his appointed task of striking down the obnoxious "Irish interest," and of securing a majority in the Commons for the Crown; the policy of Bute and Henry Fox was copied; several noble "Undertakers" were dismissed from office, and pensions and places were lavished wholesale to purchase votes in the Irish Parliament. English writers, in this, as in other instances, have denounced Irish politicians for accepting these bribes; but the corruption practised by Townshend was not worse than the corruption practised by Bute and Fox; it was less scandalous than that which "the English interest" had made a method of government for many years; and Englishmen at least have no right to make such a charge. Townshend succeeded in packing the Irish Parliament, when it assembled again in 1772; but he encountered such an opposition that he was ere long recalled.

The successor of Townshend was Lord Harcourt, a great peer and a skilled diplomatist; his Chief Secretary, too, was an adroit Parliamentary hand. The "Undertakers" were won over again; Flood, now preeminent in the House of Commons, was conciliated by a high and lucrative place; the same influence gained Hely Hutchinson, a lawyer of considerable repute, and an economic writer of real merit, who had condemned the impediments to Irish trade. Things went on smoothly in Ireland for a time; indeed the only important domestic measure which engaged the attention of the Irish Parliament was a proposal to tax absentee owners of land, which ultimately did not become law, owing to the opposition of Whig English Peers, and to the persuasive, but perhaps sophistical arguments of Burke, already a man of mark in the British Parliament. Foreign affairs, however, began ere long to create a great stirring of Irish opinion, which gradually produced momentous results. The quarrel with America, followed by civil war, had broken out; and, for many reasons, the American cause found support and sympathy in Protestant Ireland. England had claimed a right to legislate for America, even to tax her; the very same right, as respects their own country, had been persistently and ably denied by a long series of well known Irishmen, and even, to a great extent, in the Irish Parliament. The Presbyterians, too, who had left Ireland during a succession of years, were numerous in the army of the revolted colonists; Presbyterian Ulster was, almost to a man, enthusiastic for the success of Washington. The Irish Parliament, true to its instincts, and filled with nominees of the Crown and the great Nobles, resisted this movement for a considerable time; it passed a resolution against the American revolt; it voted large sums to maintain the war; it even sent part of the Irish army, which, it had been arranged, was to remain at home, to serve with the force under Howe, in the American contest. By degrees, however, it began to waver; the majority for the Government fell off; it oscillated with the uncertainty often seen in it, and natural to an ill-constituted assembly of the kind. Harcourt now followed in the track of Townshend, with a recklessness from which even Townshend would have shrunk; eighteen Peerages were created in a single day; extravagant patronage was scandalously abused; and corruption ran riot in the public service.

The majority of the Government in the Irish Houses was kept together by these means; but it was under the influence also of higher motives. The Protestant aristocracy, so powerful in it, was decidedly on the side of the Crown and of England, up to the last moment of the American war; the Irish Parliament continued to vote supplies for it, as late as

Saratoga and York Town; it even passed a perpetual Irish Mutiny Act, which gave the Executive absolute control over the Irish army. The course of events nevertheless compelled it, at last, to follow in the wake of Protestant Ireland, and to take part in a Revolution, in which, in its later stages, it joined enthusiastically. The condition of Ireland, when France and Spain had declared against England and become allies of America, was such as to cause profound irritation and alarm; to arouse feelings against the mother country, which might, otherwise, have been inactive for years; and at last to provoke a general demand for a thorough change in the Constitution and the administrative system established, in their present forms, for nearly a century. Ireland was all but bankrupt in 1776-9; taxation had reached its utmost limits and weighed heavily upon the country; and the Government was forced to borrow from the English Treasury, and even from a private Irish bank, to meet the requirements of the public service. The causes of this collapse were but too evident; an embargo had been laid on exports to England, on pretexts that could not bear the light; and the war with France had deprived Ireland, to a considerable extent, of the large trade, in part lawful, in part contraband, which she had been carrying on for a long time with France and which, it was said, had made Munster and Connaught French provinces. The evils of the commercial restrictions, which had kept Ireland back for generations, were thus made more ruinous; and at the same time the Pension List had enormously increased, and the corruption and waste of the Government were far worse than ever. The country, too, was left almost without defence; a great part of the Irish army was in America; an attempt to form a militia had failed; a French descent on the coasts was deemed imminent; and French privateers swarmed around the Irish ports, and preyed on an already expiring commerce.

The distress of the country caused a widespread demand for the removal of the impediments on Irish commerce, and for Free Trade on a liberal basis. Opinion had long been setting in this direction; the evils wrought by the fettering of the trade of Ireland, had, we have said, been proved by able Irish writers, from the days of Petty onward; and Hume and, above all, Adam Smith had exposed the fallacies of the colonial and the mercantile system, to which Irish interests had long been sacrificed. The Government of Lord North was willing to make large concessions; Burke pressed the claims of his countrymen, with admirable skill,—his reward was the loss of his seat for Bristol—but selfish British jealousy once more prevailed; a slight relaxation of the Irish commercial Code, made in 1778, only provoked resentment. But, in the meantime, a formidable power had grown up in Ireland, which soon told with effect on England, at this juncture pressed on all sides by her enemies. The forlorn and defenceless state of the land caused Protestant Ireland to spring to arms, in order to protect its hearths and its homes; volunteers suddenly enrolled themselves in multitudes; and before many months had passed, 40,000 men were arrayed, a powerful patriotic force, self-governed, and beyond the control of the Castle. The movement was spontaneous and universal; the Protestant aristocracy stood at its head; the Duke of Leinster, the chief of the Fitzgerald name, and Lord Charlemont were among its leaders; and though it drew its strength from the Protestant caste, Catholic Ireland gradually took part in it. There is no reason to doubt that the first object of the Volunteers was the defence of Ireland; but the development of their power and the evident fact that they were a force practically irresistible at the time, soon caused them to urge the demand for Free Trade, with an efficacy and a significance that the Government was compelled to recognise. The cannon of the volunteers of the Capital bore the ominous device—" Free trade or this"; and

Hussey Burgh, a brilliant speaker in the Irish House of Commons exclaimed,—"Talk not to me of peace; it is not peace, but smothered war. England has sown her laws in dragon's teeth, and they have sprung up in armed men."

Lord Buckinghamshire, by no means an able man, had been Lord Lieutenant for some time; he looked on, with impotent dismay, at a movement which he could not check or direct. The Volunteers, concentrating and giving effect to the passions and the will of Protestant Ireland, soon made their power felt in the Irish Parliament, which rapidly fell in with a popular rising, in which the great nobles, too, had taken part. Flood had long chafed at a silence imposed on him; he was in a short time afterwards dismissed from office; and he eagerly took up the cause of Free Trade, which he advocated with characteristic skill. He was supported by many very able men; especially by Henry Grattan, a young orator who had given proof of most remarkable gifts, and was soon to become the foremost of Irish statesmen. The united influences in favour of Free Trade had ere long irresistible effect; they were powerfully aided by combinations not to import or make use of British manufactures—an idea as old as the day of Swift, and lately adopted by the American Colonists; and the Volunteers terrified the English ministry. The British Parliament practically gave up the contest; in 1779 and the following year, a series of measures was passed, which brought the whole system of Irish commercial restrictions, so to speak, to the ground, and secured for Ireland a largely extended trade. Ireland was no longer excluded from the Navigation Acts; the traffic with the colonies was thrown open to her; she could, with large limitations, export to England; above all she acquired the right to export wool and woollen manufactures to all foreign countries, a prohibition which had done infinite mischief being thus removed.

The surrender of the British Parliament on this important

subject led to further and larger demands from Ireland. England had treated Protestant Ireland as a subject colony; she had asserted and enforced claims to bind Ireland by her laws; she kept the Irish Parliament in bondage by Poynings' Law; she had deprived the Irish House of Lords of its jurisdiction in appeals; she had denied to Irishmen valuable rights she had secured for herself in 1688. This whole course of policy had been denounced, from time to time, by distinguished Irishmen; it was now assailed by a rising flood tide of opinion. The impending triumph of the American cause gave new strength to a general impulse; America had been a contemned dependency; her example was not to be lost on Protestant Ireland. A cry for legislative independence, and for a radical change in the system of English rule in Ireland, went forth, and spread all over the country; it found expression in the different Public Bodies, from Corporate Towns to the County Grand Juries. But, as may be supposed, its great exponent was the formidable and invincible Volunteer force, which had continued rapidly to grow in numbers, and had become a disciplined, even a well equipped army, under officers, many of whom had experience in the field. The attitude of the Volunteers remained unchanged; they proclaimed their loyalty to the Crown and to England, but insisted that Ireland should obtain liberty; their weight in the scale of events was decisive, for the Government had no means to withstand their purpose, and they gathered to their side the moral forces, which otherwise might have been arrayed against them, by remaining steady supporters of order and law. The movement became so powerful, that the Ministry in England learned with alarm, that magistrates and even judges were not inclined to give effect in Ireland to an English statute, and sheriffs to execute an English judgment. "The independence of Irish legislation," wrote the successor of Buckinghamshire, Lord Carlisle, "has become the creed of the kingdom."

The Irish Parliament resisted for a time a movement which practically sought to subvert the Constitution of the country and its relations with England. Recourse was once more had to the methods employed to secure votes by corrupt agencies; a majority was obtained to uphold the Government; and it should be added that some of the leading Irish nobles feared a violent Revolution which they deemed at hand. But a strong opposition maintained the popular demand; Flood, who had long made the subject his own, condemned Poynings' Law with great force of reasoning; and other prominent men took the same side. Grattan, however, was by far the foremost champion of the claim to Legislative Independence and Self-Government; he had adopted the views of Molyneux and Swift from early youth; in April, 1780, he brought the question forward in a speech long remembered as one of his finest efforts. His address was premature and was withdrawn; and the Irish Parliament kept up for some months an attitude apparently hostile to a great organic reform. Meanwhile, however, the voice of Protestant Ireland rose higher and higher; it was felt even by the ministers in power that it had become impossible to oppose it with effect. In the spring of 1782, a great body of Delegates from the Volunteers of Ulster assembled in the Church of Dongannon; it insisted, in language of stern earnestness, on the repeal of the Act that declared the English Parliament entitled to pass laws that affected Ireland, on a thorough modification of Poynings' Law, and on other measures enlarging Irish liberty; the result was immense even in the two Irish Houses. Ere long the defeat of England in the American War caused the fall of the Tory Administration of North; the Rockingham Government came into office; and its attention was at once directed to Irish affairs. Burke had genuine sympathy with the Irish cause; this was shared, in some degree, by Fox; their influence probably swayed the great Whig magnates. The Duke of Portland was appointed Lord

Lieutenant; and a Royal Message was sent to the Houses at Westminster, to consider how Ireland was to be pacified.

The Irish Parliament had shown, by this time, that it would no longer offer a vain resistance; it was affected, too, by the change in the Councils of England; it threw in its lot with Protestant Ireland. The movement, carrying everything before it, was thus described by Portland:—"all sorts and descriptions of men unanimously and most audibly call upon Great Britain for a full and unequivocal satisfaction"; and the statement was in no sense overcharged. At this crisis the men in power in England sought to gain time to effect a compromise; they believed a violent Revolution near; Fox and even Burke had become alarmed. But Grattan refused to concede even a day's delay; on the 16th of April, 1782, he moved an address in the House of Commons, setting forth the wrongs of which his countrymen complained, and demanding the legislative independence of Ireland in their name. It was a stirring and dramatic historical scene; troops of Volunteers lined the approaches to the stately building in which the Parliament held its Session; the House of Commons overflowed with members; its galleries were crowded with all that was most conspicuous and beautiful in the aristocratic life of Ireland. The orator entranced the audience that hung on his lips; his speech, if perhaps not one of his very best, was remarkable alike for its brilliancy and its wisdom; for the eloquence in which it asserted the claims of Ireland; for the patriotic hope it expressed that England and Ireland would become fast friends, indissolubly united, when right had been done; for the sentiment apparent in many passages, that the Volunteers must not overawe the state, that wild ideas must be eschewed, that the Parliament must be supreme in Ireland—marked principles in Grattan's political creed. His specific demands were that the Act declaring that Ireland could be bound by English laws should be repealed; that Poynings' Law should be so reformed that the Irish Parliament should possess freedom; that the appellate jurisdiction of the Irish House of Lords should be restored to it and be final; and that the recent Mutiny Act, which placed the Irish army under the permanent control of England, should be completely changed.

Grattan's address was carried without a dissentient vote, amidst a tumult of enthusiastic applause. The Ministry in England had but one course to take; they yielded with good grace, and with words of sympathy. Resolutions in the English Houses were ere long followed by statutes conceding Grattan's demands, which broke the shackles which had held down Ireland, and changed her from a mere dependency into a nearly Sovereign state. English Acts of Parliament thereafter were not to affect Ireland; the Irish House of Lords regained its rights over appeals; the perpetual Irish Mutiny Act was limited. As for Poynings' Law, an Act of the Irish Parliament took away the initiative in legislation from the Viceroy; and it deprived the Irish and the English Privy Councils of the power of altering, suppressing or rejecting Bills or their Heads. The Irish Parliament was left free to discuss and to make laws in the same way as the British Parliament; but it was provided that any Bills it might pass should be returned under the Great Seal of England; it was thus subjected to a kind of Ministerial veto, in addition to the Constitutional veto of the Crown, but virtually, with almost as little effect. The security of the Habeas Corpus Act had been obtained for Ireland before this time; the tenure of the Irish Judges was ere long placed on the same footing as that of their English brethren. The vexatious tests and other disabilities which, we have seen, had been imposed on Presbyterian Ireland were also removed; for Presbyterian Ireland had flung itself into the Volunteer movement. The evil consequences of these wrongs, however, survived; they are not wholly things of the past at this day.

The political crisis, of which we have traced the course, has been rightly called the Revolution of 1782. The triumph was that of the Irish Protestant Colony; its Legislative Assembly, the Irish Parliament, had been made nearly coordinate with that of Great Britain; Protestant Ireland was all but an independent state, and in theory was united to England only by the link of the Crown. Catholic Ireland still remained a distinct people, oppressed and degraded in the relations of life; but she had in some measure shared in the benefits of increased liberty, and been raised out of bondage. Many causes had conspired still further to soften the feelings of the Irish Protestant to the Catholic, and to lead to a relaxation of the Penal Code. The Catholics had been submissive and peaceful for years; they had joined, we have said, in the Volunteer movement; they had lately been permitted to serve in the British army. Rome, too, had ceased to be an aggressive Power; the liberal and sceptical tendencies of the eighteenth century had produced a general tone of religious indifference in politics and in social opinion. The interests, too, of the Protestant Irish induced them to modify the Penal laws; the prohibition to sell or to mortgage their lands to Catholics was felt to be a grievance as time rolled on; and higher motives concurred to make them willing to lighten the chains of Catholic slavery. The movement in favour of Protestant rights had awakened sympathy with Catholic wrongs; the Volunteers at Dungannon had emphatically declared they "rejoiced" at the mitigation of the Anti-Catholic laws. Effect was given to these opinions in the Irish Parliament; a series of Acts were passed, from 1771 to 1782, which gradually extended relief to the Irish Catholics. They were first enabled to take leases of unprofitable waste; next to take leases of land for 999 years; finally to purchase land in fee simple and to lend money on land; these concessions being in Protestant interests. They were also relieved by law from wrongs which custom, however, had made largely obsolete; their estates were not to "gavel" upon a descent;

the iniquities which encouraged a son to plunder his father, and brought misery into Catholic households, were put an end to, almost without exception; measures of degradation, such as that which forbade a Catholic to have a horse worth more than £5, were repealed; and the organisation of the Catholic Church received legal sanction. The Irish Catholics, nevertheless, were still excluded from all share of political power, and were still wholly without direct influence in the state. Flood, Charlemont, and the immense majority of even the most enlightened men of Protestant Ireland, insisted that their disabilities must be maintained; and Grattan himself, who had the genius to see that "the Protestant could not be free as long as the Catholic was a slave," declared that Protestant Ascendency must prevail in Ireland.

We pass from one of the few bright passages of Irish History to glance at the achievements of Irish intellect, which we have left unnoticed for a considerable time. There was little opportunity for the development of the works of the mind during the long period of trouble and civil war, between the Desmond rising and the Boyne and Aghrim, when Ireland it may be said was finally subdued. Some excellent writers, however, appeared, especially Divines of the Irish Anglican Church: Anglican Theology was in its golden age, and the Bench and Bar of Ireland had many distinguished ornaments. The literature, too, of the native race was not without specimens of real merit; the great work of the *Annals of the Four Masters* was compiled, we have said, in the seventeenth century, and some Irish Histories showed research and learning. That literature, however, retained the character to which we have before adverted; it was a tale of Celtic sorrow dwelling on the past. In the first three quarters of the eighteenth century Ireland possessed illustrious names in many departments of letters. We have already alluded to Swift and Berkeley, the first incomparable in the field of satire, the second great as a metaphysician and a deep thinker; and to these should be added Edmund Burke, the philosophic statesman of a troubled era, and, but far less in eminence, Oliver Goldsmith, whose *Vicar of Wakefield*—that charming picture of simple life and manners—is probably of its kind unrivalled. We may refer, besides, to a list of distinguished men: Francis Hutcheson, a very able writer on moral philosophy and the Deism of the age; Leland, breathing the ideas of the most enlightened Protestants of 1771–82, whose *History of Ireland* is still of value; Warner, who first exploded the falsehoods of the alleged massacre of 1691; and a number of others we cannot dwell on. The political and economic wrongs of Protestant Ireland attracted the attention of other powerful minds; Lord Molesworth, Sir James Caldwell, and, above all, Hely Hutchinson have left works on the subject of real merit. Nor are writers of Catholic Ireland wanting, though still nearly all in the same vein of thought—Curry, whose *History of the Civil Wars of Ireland* should be studied by every candid enquirer; MacGeoghegan, who wrote well on the same theme; De Burg, whose work on the Irish Dominicans is a model of erudition and research; Charles O'Conor, a descendant of the last of the Irish Kings, and the most learned antiquary of his time. Ireland had few painters and sculptors, but her actors and musical artists were of peculiar excellence. Her architecture was hardly of high quality; some of the public buildings indeed of Dublin, constructed in this period, are remarkably fine; but the great country seats are in the bad Georgian style, and contrast painfully with the ruins of the abbeys and castles effaced in the barbarous wars of the sixteenth century.

But if the intellect of Ireland was brilliant at this time, the standard of her education and mental culture was far lower than that of England or Scotland. The books published in Dublin were comparatively few; they were often mere copies of English and Scotch publications. The aristocracy usually sent their sons to Eton and Harrow, to Oxford and Cambridge; these were assimilated by degrees to English gentlemen, though they still retained peculiarities of their own resembling those, as we have said, of the seigneurs of old France. The University of Dublin educated well the sons of the lesser gentry and professional men; but it was not supported by great public schools, as the English Universities were and are, a deficiency from which it still suffers; and it was long known by the name of the "Silent Sister." Middle-class education was wretchedly bad, for a middle class hardly existed, as we have said; and if the children of the Irish Catholic gentry, as the Penal Code was relaxed by degrees, were often trained in their first years in France, the mass of the Irish Catholics were left in gross ignorance, the Charter Schools, we have seen, having happily failed. Two characteristics of the Irish literature of this part of the century deserve attention. The works written by the conquering and the conquered race were wholly dissimilar in thought and tendency; they reflected the distinction in blood and faith rooted in the frame of Irish society; and nothing appeared to lessen this wide division, to make its lines, as it were, to run into each other. Swift and Berkeley addressed the Protestant caste; Curry and Charles O'Conor wrote for the Catholic Irishry; and, though it has been in some measure softened, this difference has continued down to the present day. A great change, however, passed over the style and language of Irish authors and public speakers in the course of the eighteenth century. Swift wrote as an Englishman in all his works; he is simplicity itself, without a trace of rhetoric; Berkeley imitated Plato, but is, nevertheless, English; the same may be said of all the best writers of Ireland until the reign of George III. But after this time elements of the Celtic mind appear strikingly in compositions even of Irish Protestants; they give life, splendour, and epigram to Grattan's speeches;

they animate the delightful pages of Goldsmith; they are seen in the gorgeous rhetoric, the exaggerated phrases, and the vehemence often found in the orations of Burke. The phenomenon is curious and not easily explained.

England must for the most part bear the blame for the misgovernment of Ireland during the long period of which we have tried to describe the character. The Penal Code, indeed, was enacted by the Irish Parliament; the oppression and exaction seen in landed relations may be laid to the charge of the Irish Protestant caste. But England and her statesmen had absolute control over Irish affairs throughout this whole time; they looked on the evil that was being done, nay encouraged its perpetration in many instances; English selfishness and arrogance are wholly responsible for the commercial restrictions imposed on Ireland and for the bad rule of the "English interest." Some excuses, however, may be rightly made for the system of iniquitous law and tyranny which prevailed in Ireland before 1782. England was incensed with Catholic Ireland in 1691; she felt her Protestant colony to be a burden. The Irish Penal Code was almost a counterpart of measures taken against the Huguenots of France; it was only forgotten —an immense distinction—that the one affected a people, the other a sect. So too, the trade legislation that impoverished Ireland was that of the colonial and the mercantile system; it was merely left out of sight that it injured Ireland infinitely more than it could injure remote colonies. Every reasonable plea must be allowed by History; but the fact remains that English rule in Ireland was nearly as bad as it could be in this period; and the lamentable consequences survive to this day. It is true that Ireland was in a wretched condition and had been misgoverned for centuries before 1691; but it is equally certain that all her ills increased, and were, so to speak, made permanent in the state of things that existed in the following age. The Revolution of 1782 was wholly the work of the

Irish Protestants; and English writers who condemn them are mere partisans. Protestant Ireland had suffered from wrongs done by England far more than America; Protestant Ireland rightly insisted on obtaining justice. The attitude, too, of the Irish Protestants has not received the commendation it deserves. They remained loyal to the mother country; they fought for her, and filled her armies; they only demanded rights long enjoyed by Englishmen. And it should be added that, in some degree at least, the spirit of liberty which animated themselves produced sympathy with down-trodden Catholic Ireland.

The Revolution of 1782, we have seen, made Ireland almost a Sovereign state, with a legislature nearly coordinate with that of England; made Ireland, in theory at least, all but an independent people. What probabilities were there that a settlement of this kind would take root, flourish, and become enduring? England had made the concession in generous words; but every English statesman of mark disliked it, and saw that it might be fraught with evil. The English and Irish Parliaments, from the nature of things, would differ in opinion, perhaps come in conflict, on questions of the gravest importance; this would inevitably strain, nay, might break up the Empire. Besides, the arrangement effected in 1782 was against the genius and the tendencies of the age; these were in the direction of the consolidation of states, not of their division into separate parts. Cromwell had accomplished an Irish Union; Petty, Montesquieu, Adam Smith, and other distinguished men had declared that a Union was the first need of Ireland. Looking, too, at Ireland and her existing condition, would the settlement of 1782 have happy results? Would the Irish Parliament, confined to the Protestant caste, and from its composition exposed to corruption, grow into a patriotic and pure assembly, govern Ireland for the general good, be proof against evil influences from without? Would "the Protestant

Settlement," as Grattan fondly hoped, "expand into the Irish nation"; would anything efface the profound distinctions which had kept Ireland a distracted land for ages, and make her a really united people, capable of self-government and fit for liberty? Could Parliamentary government really prosper in a community constituted as Ireland was, in which, it was said, "a living head was at the top of a paralytic body"; in which the middle class was still deplorably feeble, in which the mass of the peasantry remained degraded serfs? Might not occasions arise in which the old feuds and animosities of the past would break out, and tear to pieces the superficial veil thrown over the present? History was before long to answer questions which had already flitted across reflecting minds.

CHAPTER VIII.

GRATTAN'S PARLIAMENT. THE REBELLION OF 1798. THE UNION.

Ireland almost an independent state, in theory, under the Constitution of 1782. Influences that made the Irish Parliament and Ireland, in a great degree, dependent. Simple Repeal, and the Act of Renunciation. The Commercial Propositions of 1785. The Regency Question in 1789. Flood, supported by the Volunteers, endeavours to reform the Irish Parliament in 1783. Characteristics of that Assembly. Flood's reform rejected. Material prosperity of Ireland from 1782 to 1789. Necessary reforms neglected. Pitt. Grattan. Fitzgibbon. Influence of the French Revolution on Ireland. Movement in Presbyterian Ulster. Theobald Wolfe Tone. He founds the Society of the United Irishmen. His objects and policy. The Society seeks to gain over Catholic Ireland. How it is affected by the French Revolution. Agrarian disturbance. Extension of the United Irish Society. Policy of Pitt. Influence of Burke. The Catholic Relief Act of 1793. Other measures of the year. Lull in Ireland in 1794. The appointment of Lord Fitzwilliam as Viceroy. His recall. The results. Lord Camden made Viceroy. Policy of Protestant Ascendency restored. Fitzgibbon made Earl of Clare. Extension of the United Irish movement. It becomes rebellious. It makes its way into Catholic Ireland. The Orange Society and its adherents. The Defenders. Orange outrages throw many Irish Catholics into the arms of the United Irishmen. The French descent on Bantry in 1796. Apparent quiescence of Catholic Ireland. State of Ulster and of Ireland in 1797. Rebellion gathering. Armed levies in Ulster and insurrection planned in Dublin. The Government compelled to strike. Want of a regular

250   *Ireland.*   [CHAP.

military force. Ulster disarmed in part. Many barbarities committed, but a rising prevented. The Directory of the conspirators in Dublin arrested. Arrest and death of Lord Edward Fitzgerald. The rising forced to a head. Conduct of Lord Clare. Atrocities in parts of the South. Outbreak of the Rebellion of 1798. Civil war in Wicklow and Wexford. Gallantry displayed on both sides. The rising put down. Deeds of blood and cruelty. Lord Cornwallis made Viceroy. State of Ireland in 1798—9. The Parliament of Grattan. The descent of Humbert. Death of Wolfe Tone. Preparations for the Union. The policy of Pitt. The Union at last carried and by what means. Reflections.

THE Settlement of 1782, we have said, made Ireland approximate to an independent state; her Parliament was, in theory, all but Sovereign in foreign, commercial, and domestic affairs. The King of England, indeed, was necessarily King of Ireland; the British Executive Government had an authority, analogous to a ministerial veto[1], on laws enacted by the Irish Parliament. But by the letter of the new Constitution, at least, Protestant Ireland, through her Legislature, was nearly supreme, almost absolute within the domain appertaining to it. The King of Great Britain and Ireland could declare war; the British Parliament might enthusiastically support this policy; but the Irish Parliament had, conceivably, a power to thwart it, to refuse supplies and troops to maintain it, to pass resolutions protesting against it. So too, there was nothing to prevent the Irish Parliament from prohibiting British imports by hostile tariffs, from encouraging Irish exports by extravagant bounties, nay even from encroaching on the monopolies of English foreign trade by arrangements of its own. Above all, the Constitution of 1782 gave to the Irish Parliament logically a right to have an Irish Executive dependent on it, to select, to appoint, and to dismiss its ministers, nay to make it impossible for a Viceroy to hold office against its will, though he had been nominated by the Crown, and though he possessed the confi-

[1] See on this point, Ball, *Legislative Systems*, 136 and note 278—6.

dence, in every respect, of the British Government. It should be added that the ministerial veto on enactments passed by the Irish Parliament was, as we have remarked, of scarcely any avail; in the words of one of the ablest Irishmen of his day, it was "a restraint that created a theoretic dependence, but left a practical independence[1]"; and abstractedly, we repeat, Ireland was now connected with Great Britain by the tie of the Crown only.

It is scarcely necessary to point out how a relation like this—anomalous, irrational, and by means of which two states, nearly coequal in theory, were brought together and called a single state—was full of elements of trouble and grave danger. The Irish Constitution of 1782, however, was widely different in fact from what it was on paper; its essential vices were in a great measure checked by influences which prolonged its existence, and possibly might have made it endure. Protestant Ireland, we have seen, was in the main loyal, and devoted to the connexion with England; it therefore usually followed the lead of the British Parliament and the British Government; and even under the new arrangements it acquiesced, as a rule, in what was done at Westminster, recalcitrant as it had been of late. The Irish Presbyterians, indeed, had for many years shown signs of disaffection, soon to become perilous, and Catholic Ireland, as yet an inert mass, was obviously a force that might prove formidable; but the Irish Protestants, as a people, remained disposed to bow to the will of the mother country, throughout the whole range of affairs of state, unless attacks were made on their own interests. The Irish Parliament, again, supreme in Ireland, was, we have seen, largely an instrument of English power; it represented the rule of the Castle and of a narrow oligarchy, attached necessarily to

[1] Speech of Speaker Foster in the Irish House of Commons, Feb. 17, 1800. For the reason that the ministerial veto was so inoperative see Ball, *ante*.

British rule; it was powerfully swayed by gross corruption; and though it sometimes showed a will of its own, and, as always, was liable to sudden fits of change, it continued generally to follow in the wake of the British Parliament, and to obey the dictates of the British Ministry. More important too, perhaps, than anything else, the Irish Parliament never claimed a right to create an Executive subject to it; under the Constitution of 1782, as under the state of things that existed before, it accepted the Viceroy and the Ministers appointed, in England, by the Crown; and this single circumstance had a most potent effect in keeping it in the line of British politics, and in maintaining the connexion between the two countries. The centrifugal forces, in a word, were extremely strong under the Settlement of 1782; but they were largely controlled by centripetal forces, which prevented its flying, almost at once, to pieces[1].

The tendency of the British and Irish Parliaments, nay of England and Ireland, to come into conflict under the conditions we have briefly described, would evidently be strongest in times of trouble and war, and in these instances would be most dangerous. It manifested itself, however, even in the years of peace and of general tranquillity in both islands which preceded the outbreak of the Revolution in France, and the world-wide upheaval and strife that followed. On three occasions, from 1782 to 1789, the relations between the two Legislatures were more or less strained, and signs of dissension became apparent which might have developed very grave results. The new Irish Constitution had hardly been made when it was strenuously urged in the Irish Parliament that the—

---

[1] The checks, which enabled the Irish Parliament of 1782 to work, in some degree, in harmony with the British Parliament and British Executive, could not exist in the case of any Irish Parliament at the present day; and no paper constitution could create them. Every one acquainted with Irish affairs knows that the centrifugal forces would master the centripetal.

"Simple Repeal" of the Declaratory Act, in which the English
Parliament had asserted a right to bind Ireland by laws passed
at Westminster, could not completely annul the claim. Flood,
who had been lately eclipsed by Grattan, and had begun to
detest his successful rival, eagerly took up a cry which, it must
be added, was not without valid legal sanction. The British
Parliament eluded a possible quarrel by passing an Act solemnly renouncing the right; but, at this very moment,
Portland and other English statesmen were secretly con-
demning the recent settlement, and were at least thinking of
expedients by which the supremacy of England over Ireland
might be restored. A somewhat graver occasion of dispute
arose only three years afterwards. The second Pitt, by this
time in power, with the economic instinct which was his best
gift, wished to extend the trade between England and Ireland,
still, as we have seen, in part restricted; he sought, in return,
to induce Ireland to make a contribution to Imperial Defence;
and he probably entertained a design of securing for the
British Parliament and the British Government a regulating
power over Irish foreign commerce, an object which Fox, also,
had certainly at heart. The Irish Parliament in 1785 assented
to the propositions of the English minister; but these aroused
such a tempest of wrath in England—the idea of an increase
of free trade with Ireland was odious to English commercial
jealousy—that Pitt was compelled to modify his first project;
and the propositions subsequently laid before the Irish Parliament not only pressed hardly on Irish commerce, but trenched
on the legislative independence which had been the great gain
of the Revolution of 1782. Grattan denounced the whole
scheme in one of the most brilliant and powerful of his
impassioned speeches; it was so ill received that the measure
was dropped. The last difference was the most serious of all;
but for an accident it might have had untoward results. In
1788, when George III became insane, the British Lords and

Commons, as is well known, practically elected a Regent by a stretch of power; but this was resented by the Irish Parliament as an interference with its Constitutional rights; and Grattan persuaded the Irish Houses to disregard what was being done at Westminster, and to invite the Prince of Wales[1], by an address of its own, to become "Regent of Ireland." The recovery of the King brought the dispute to a close, and no mischief was actually done; but it had become evident that, owing to the divergence in the conduct of the British and the Irish Parliaments, the Head of the State in Great Britain and Ireland might be the same person with very different rights, or even, conceivably, different persons.

The Irish Parliament, however,—it has been given the name of Grattan, its chief founder on its new basis—seemed to be more endangered at this period by its weakness and its shameful abuses, than by its relations with the British Parliament. It had not been forgotten that it had resisted Protestant Irish opinion for a long time in the movement of 1779-82; and Flood, backed by the force of the Volunteers, still a most formidable power in the state, made a great effort to reform it in 1783. The British Parliament of the eighteenth century was by no means free from the grossest defects; but it was very different from the ill-ordered Assembly which held its sittings in College Green, not far from the centre of the Irish capital. The Irish Parliament contained some independent men, especially of the class of the great resident gentry; it possessed a really patriotic party led by an illustrious chief, Grattan; it abounded in able and brilliant lawyers; its debates reveal considerable powers of thought and of eloquence. But, taken as a whole, it was a corrupt assembly, badly constituted, and subject to evil influence; nor did it represent in any real

[1] Excellent authorities have long ago maintained that the conduct of the Irish Parliament, on this occasion, was more wise and constitutional than that of the British Houses.

sense even the dominant caste of Protestant Ireland. Its House of Lords had a large array of Bishops, mere mouthpieces of the Government of the day; its lay Peers were for the most part composed of ennobled descendants of the old plebeian settlers, and of men elevated to their present rank by the worst kind of patronage. Such a body was not an aristocracy worthy of the name; the Irish House of Commons was, in many respects, even worse. Its constitution had not been changed by the Revolution of 1782; it remained, as regards the mass of its members, an assembly of nominees of the Government, and of the great ruling oligarchy of the "Irish interest." Of its 300 seats, not 100 were open, that is, subject to the Electorate's will; more than 200 had become the property of the Crown, and of leading nobles and commoners, the absolute owners of the numerous petty boroughs, who were thus supreme in the Lower House in Ireland. The Irish House of Commons, too, had been long crowded with pensioners and placemen of many kinds; it contained, it has been said, more than 100 of these; and Grattan compared these mere tools of the Castle to "animals of prey in the guise of senators, disgracing the seats which once belonged to the people." And the Irish House of Commons, we must bear in mind, was not only wholly composed of the Protestant caste, but was elected by the Protestant caste only, and its electorate was exceedingly small. Catholic Ireland was no more represented in it, than a Red Indian tribe is in the American Senate.

The movement, however, of Flood for reform completely collapsed and came to nothing. The Volunteers, indeed, held an Assembly in Dublin; an eccentric Prelate, the Bishop of Derry, spoke at this Convention, as it was called, in the most reckless language. But Charlemont had wisely placed himself at their head; the Delegates were, for the most part, moderate men; and no attempt was made to overcome the Parliament

by a display, as was feared, of military force. The Reform
Bill of Flood would have made a real change in the electorate
and the representation of Protestant Ireland; but, in con-
sonance with his well-known views, it kept the Irish Catholics
still excluded from the state; it denied them the smallest
share of political power; it could have only been a makeshift
for a time. It was twice summarily rejected by the Irish
Parliament; and Grattan, though a reformer, even then, on
principle, gave it, it should be observed, but a lukewarm
support, perhaps because he was fiercely opposed to Flood,
whom he had lately denounced in a ruthless philippic. There
was in fact no pressure from without at the time to compel the
Irish Parliament to reform itself; the very idea was odious to
the English Government; and the present season was by no
means opportune. From 1782 to 1789 the material progress
of Ireland was very marked; an organic change in her constitution seemed out of place and reason. Her prosperity, no
doubt, was comparative only, and was interrupted by one or
two bad years; whole counties were still in a most backward
state, especially parts of Munster and Connaught; and there
was a fresh outbreak of Whiteboy outrages and many other
signs of agrarian disorder. But the correspondence of all the
Viceroys in office, and numberless speeches in the Irish
Parliament, prove that Ireland made a real advance in wealth
and resources at this period, and that, too, tried by every
possible test. Her finances were in a singularly flourishing
state; they even bore the strain of the evil times that followed.
Her agriculture developed apace; huge areas of pasture
became tillage; and if this was largely an artificial change,
the result was an immediate increase of opulence. Her linen
manufacture, too, made immense progress; the chief seat of
this industry, Ulster, became the most stirring and perhaps the
richest of the Irish provinces, notwithstanding the troubles of
a not distant past; and other manufactures grew up in Leinster

and Munster. Nor were the causes of this improvement difficult to ascertain; the expansion of trade, to a great extent set free, the relaxation of the barbarous Penal Code, which brought land into commerce again, nay the hopes inspired by the Revolution of 1782, quickened enterprise and increased wealth; even the legislation of the Irish Parliament, which favoured bounties, corn laws and protective duties, had tendencies in the same direction, at least for a time.

The prospect for Ireland, therefore, from 1782 to 1789, was not without promise in the future, anomalous as was her political system. But, apart from her relations with England, the dominant state, we can now see that her institutions must have been greatly changed, if her Constitution was to have a chance of permanence. Her Parliament, the corrupt conclave of an exclusive caste, divided from the people in race and faith, should have been thrown open to Protestant and Catholic alike; the petty boroughs should have been swept away; the electorate should have been composed of all classes, without regard to religious distinctions. Catholic Ireland should have been received within the Pale of the State, not treated as a subject community; Catholics should have been admitted to all offices of trust, and placed on the same level of rights as Protestants. If the Established Church, too, was to be left standing, the iniquity of the tithe should have been removed, especially as the impost oppressed the Presbyterian no less than the Catholic, and was felt by both to be a cruel grievance. But even Grattan, the chief of the Irish Liberals, did not in these years advocate such large reforms, though they were in accord with his political sympathies. He contented himself at this time with denouncing the abuses of the Irish Parliament, and with proposing a change in the system of tithe; he did not, earnestly at least, as yet urge the questions of Parliamentary Reform and Catholic rights. He doubtless felt that it would be hopeless to attempt to bring forward projects of this kind; and he seems to have thought that Ireland was in need of political rest after the events of 1782. Unquestionably, however, Parliamentary Reform and Catholic Emancipation, as it had begun to be called, were objects next to this great man's heart; his ideal was an Ireland really made a nation by the union of her races and creeds under an equal law and represented in a free and popular Parliament; but an Ireland, too, in which the Protestant classes would retain the ascendency inseparable from the ownership of the great mass of the land of the country, and from a superiority in civilisation and wealth.

The reforms, indeed, that Ireland required were simply impossible at this period. Pitt was in the plenitude of his power in England; but as a constitutional statesman he did not interfere with the state of things established in 1782, except indirectly, and at grave crises. He gave little attention to Irish affairs at this time; his knowledge of them, indeed, was always imperfect, a defect unhappily common to many who have filled his place; and he had nothing of his great father's insight into men and things beyond his experience. As an economist he recommended a commutation of the Irish tithe, but he made no attempt to settle a question already provoking intense discontent. Whatever may have been the case as to England, he trifled with Parliamentary Reform in Ireland; and as to Catholic Emancipation[1], he professed himself opposed to it in the early years of his ministry. In this state of things the men in power at the Castle and the oligarchy who ruled the Irish Parliament were given a free hand to do as they pleased; and they rejected every project of reform, a commutation of the tithe, a plan to remove the worst abuses in the Irish Parliament, any change in the existing Parliamentary system, even the slightest extension of

[1] See a remarkable letter of Pitt cited by Mr Lecky, *History of England in the Eighteenth Century*, VI. 375.

Catholic liberty. They entrenched themselves, in a word, behind institutions, as narrow and iniquitous as those of Venice, but without the grand Venetian traditions; as things went on reasonably well in Ireland they governed without a thought of the morrow. The master-spirit of this selfish Junta was John Fitzgibbon, a lawyer of humble origin, but a man of remarkable parts and great force of character, a most commanding figure in Irish politics in the later years of the eighteenth century. Fitzgibbon had meditated deeply on Irish History; he believed that the liberalism of his own time had not effaced the animosities of the past in Ireland, or even made a great change in the profound distinctions of race and faith which divided her people; he thought the ideal of Grattan midsummer madness; and he declared that Ireland could never become a nation in the true sense of the word. For these reasons he had convinced himself that Protestant ascendency must be maintained in Ireland; that Catholic subjection must continue; that if Protestant Ireland was to exist, it must depend for support on England; that the best way to accomplish this was to leave things in their present state; and he therefore strenuously opposed the policy of reforming the Irish Parliament, and of making further concessions to Catholic Ireland. His views unquestionably contained much truth, and some of his predictions have been unhappily fulfilled; but history may ask if his own course of conduct did not largely contribute to these results.

The French Revolution came like a tempest to disturb a season of comparative peace in Ireland, and to shake to its foundations the ill-ordered structure of her constitution and social life. Its influence was first seen in Presbyterian Ulster, where many causes concurred to give it no ordinary force. The National Assembly had swept away the old order of things in France, had put an end to exclusive privilege, had founded institutions on a democratic basis; all this aroused the sympathies of the Presbyterian Irish, who had long been kept down by unjust laws and by the rule of an aristocratic caste, who had scarcely a voice in the Irish Parliament, and who disliked a system of government which shut them out from its sphere. The Church, too, in France had fallen and the tithe with it; French republican ideas were abroad; and a community, chiefly composed of farmers and traders, which could not endure Prelacy, had long denounced tithe, and had a traditional distaste for monarchy, especially when upheld by a narrow dominant class, was deeply stirred by these great and sudden changes. A movement in favour of a thorough reform of the Irish Parliament, of a large extension of the electoral franchise, and perhaps against the Established Church and tithe, spread from Belfast, now a growing seat of trade, over many towns of the Northern Province and even in large parts of the rural districts; and it drew into it all that was most daring and enthusiastic in Presbyterian Ireland. Several leaders of the movement, which in a few months acquired considerable strength and volume, were able and energetic men; its chief director was Theobald Wolfe Tone, a young lawyer of no common powers and a very remarkable man of action, who even at this time had revolutionary ends in view, and probably was at heart a rebel. Tone saw clearly that even to attain the objects his colleagues had set before them, still more to compass what he aimed at himself, it would be necessary to obtain general and powerful popular support; and for this he looked to the mass of Catholic Ireland, still almost passive, but beginning to stir in some of its parts with quickening life, and subject to many grievances and wrongs. He founded in 1791 the Society of United Irishmen, the original centre of which was in Ulster; its professed aim was to combine a demand for Parliamentary reform with the concession of Catholic emancipation in the widest sense; it hoped in this way to enlist Catholic Ireland in its cause.

The French Revolution had meanwhile been making its influence felt in Catholic Ireland. The few Catholic nobles and gentlemen of high degree,—descendants, for the most part, of the old Englishry—who had preserved the wrecks of their estates, were alarmed at its anarchic tendencies; their sympathies were with the perishing French Monarchy; and this was the feeling of the higher Catholic clergy. But the Catholic mercantile class, which had been growing up in Ireland, and had gradually acquired wealth and power, saw in the inauguration of the new era in France and in the establishment of a political system based on the assertion of the Rights of Man and of religious and civil equality in the extreme sense, the prospect of abolishing the whole Penal Code and of raising Catholic Ireland out of its present condition; the very concessions which had been obtained made it the more determined to seek a less imperfect liberty. A Catholic Committee to sustain the Catholic cause had existed in Dublin since 1759; its aristocratic leaders left it at this juncture; but their places were filled by men of a very different type; and these co-operated with the United Irishmen. The appointment of Wolfe Tone to be the secretary of the Catholic Committee marked the alliance of that body and the Society in Belfast; the two began thenceforward to act in concert. The French Revolution at the same time had gradually affected the subject masses of the Irish Catholics, still little better than serfs. They heard that in the great land, whither their fathers had gone for three generations to fight its battles, a dominant and oppressive Church had been overthrown; that an aristocracy, lording it over the children of the soil, had fallen; that tithe had been abolished and the exactions of landlords; and, in the liberation of the peasantry of France, they felt dimly a hope of liberation for themselves. A movement, dull, feeble, and aimless as yet, stirred these inert multitudes in a few counties; but it showed itself, not in a cry for political changes, but in a widespread disinclination to pay tithe, and even rent, and in occasional risings against the landed gentry. Emissaries from Wolfe Tone and his colleagues quickened the impulse; the Whiteboy system had prepared the way; there was a considerable outburst of agrarian disorder and crime.

The two movements, distinct as yet, but already tending to run into each other, went on rapidly through 1792. The United Irishmen established a violent Press in Ulster; volunteers were enrolled in the name of National Guards; the Society organised itself in many parts of the North; and numerous societies were affiliated to it, in Dublin, and other towns of the South. From these centres the new doctrines were disseminated far and wide through the country; and exactly as had happened in France, where the ruin of the Seigneurs had illustrated the Rights of Man, the revolt of the peasantry against their superiors became more and more general. The state of lawless disturbance on the increase in Ireland, and especially the inclination of two forces, Presbyterianism and Catholicism, hitherto fiercely opposed, to form a coalition, ominous and strange, perplexed and alarmed the British Ministry, the more so that many Protestants of the Anglican Church had joined the ranks of the United Irishmen. After many hesitations and long delays, Pitt, completely reversing his late policy, resolved to make the Irish Catholics large concessions; in this he probably was inspired by Burke, the lifelong friend of Catholic Ireland, who always had strong Catholic sympathies, and who, in the existing state of Europe, sought to combat French Jacobinism with the powerful forces through which Catholicism appeals to man; and Pitt, doubtless, too, was alive to the facts, that war with France was already at hand, and that England would have Catholic Powers as allies. In 1792 the Irish Parliament had passed an Act, which removed, but only to a small extent, the disabilities still affecting the Irish Catholics; Pitt, a few weeks before war was proclaimed, insisted that a much larger measure should be brought forward, against the protest of the Irish Government, and especially of Fitzgibbon, who had been made Chancellor, and for some time was supreme at the Castle. The proposed scheme though with large and somewhat galling exceptions admitted the Irish Catholic to many offices of trust; and it thus secured him, really for the first time, a share of political rights in the State. But its most striking and greatest feature was this: it gave the Catholic the electoral franchise, while it did not permit him to have a seat in Parliament.

The measure was introduced into the Irish Parliament under conditions that illustrate, very clearly, the nature of the Constitution of 1782. According to true Parliamentary usage, Grattan and his adherents should have been placed in office, and should have had the honour and the responsibility of a great reform carrying out their policy, at least in part; this would have been the case, as a matter of course, at Westminster. But the conduct of the Bill was left to the men in power at the Castle, notoriously its professed opponents; the majority in their hands were bidden to support it, and it was thus deprived of all that would give it grace and significance. It passed, however, easily through both the Irish Houses— if not without a bitter speech of Fitzgibbon—for the Government was all powerful in both; and not only Grattan and his followers, but the independent party of the leading and resident Irish gentry, assailed as they already were as landlords, were still in favour of concessions to the Irish Catholics, as they had been from 1771 to 1782. But the essential vices and defects of the measure were exposed, with great ability, by two or three of these very men; in truth it was an ill conceived and mischievous scheme, too characteristic of the inexperience of Irish affairs, often exhibited by Pitt and his colleagues. It proposed to enfranchise the Catholic multitude, that is to flood the constituencies, at a critical moment, with masses of servile and ignorant peasants; and yet it kept out of Parliament the Catholic gentry, the very class which it ought to have brought in. It is not easy to understand the reason of such a plan, certain in time to be fraught with great evil; but not improbably Pitt and the English Ministers thought—as actually was the case for many years—that the Irish Catholic voters would continue to be mere passive instruments of their superiors, and that the Bill therefore would not have much effect, and would be a large reform in appearance mainly. The measure was accompanied by other measures which reduced the number of placemen and pensioners in the Irish House of Commons, and faintly presaged further reforms in Parliament; and steps were taken to form a militia force in Ireland, and to disband the Volunteers in Ulster, who had proclaimed themselves a National Guard.

The United Irish and agrarian movements appear to have become less active, for some months, after the Relief Act, as it was called, of 1793. Their organisations, indeed, were no doubt extended, and communications had begun to be opened with France, now engaged in a desperate strife with Europe; but they were not so potent as they had been, at least on the surface. This was probably due, in part, to the still uncertain state of the war; in part to the repressive measures of the Irish Parliament, and to its attitude of loyalty to the British Government; but in part, also, to the recent concessions, which detached some Catholic leaders from their Protestant allies. A Catholic Convention, which had been called together, was dissolved when the late Act was passed; it is very remarkable that the failure to carry a measure of Parliamentary Reform, in the Session of 1794, though it blasted the hopes of the United Irishmen, did not cause an outburst of widespread disorder. For a moment, indeed, it seemed not impossible that the elements of trouble in Ireland might be set at rest. In the first days of 1795, Lord Fitzwilliam, a member of the great Whig Secession, was sent to Ireland, as Lord Lieutenant; and, beyond question, he had permission to give the countenance of the Government to further concessions to demands made by the Irish Catholics, who, very properly, were not satisfied with the imperfect measure of 1793, and claimed to be placed on a complete equality of political and civil rights with the Protestants. All Catholic Ireland concurred in this demand, especially the Peerage, the gentry, and the superior clergy, Conservative, to a man, in their instincts; and had it been complied with, it might have happened that Irish History would have opened a brighter page, and have not had to record the tragic events that followed. Fitzwilliam entered, as was his Constitutional course, into negotiations with Grattan and his friends, who, however, refused to take office; and he repeatedly urged on the English Cabinet the pressing need of Catholic Emancipation in the fullest sense. He was, however, somewhat hasty and indiscreet; he infuriated the Junta in power at the Castle, by dismissing one of their most prominent men, and by threatening to dismiss others; and he was perhaps rather too pronounced in his official language. He was at a moment's notice removed from his post, with an angry ministerial reproof, though the Cabinet had at least acquiesced in his conduct, and it was announced that concessions to the Irish Catholics were not to be made, nay, that a complete change in Irish policy was to take place. It is impossible for us to enlarge on this subject[1]; but it is almost certain that Fitzwilliam was made a victim of intrigues begun at the Castle, and calculated to tell with effect in England, and also of the bigotry of George III, who through representations made by Fitzgibbon —his "leprous distilment" seems to have reached the ear of the King—had set his conscience against the Catholic claims.

---

[1] By many degrees the best account of this most important episode in Irish history will be found in Mr Lecky's *History of England in the Eighteenth Century*, Vol. VII. chap. 26, pp. 32, 97.

Fitzwilliam's departure from Ireland was a day of mourning; farewell was bidden him in the voice of a disappointed people; "a cloud," it has been said, "has ever since hung on the land." It is impossible to assert that a frank compliance with the demands of the Catholics, at this juncture, would have prevented the horrors of 1798; all that is certain is that an opportunity was lost, and that thenceforward events took a most unhappy course. Lord Camden was made Fitzwilliam's successor; his mission was to restore the old system of Protestant Ascendency in a changed era, and to keep Catholic Ireland down, when the United Irishmen were appealing to it, when it was already gravely disturbed, and when the French Republic, triumphant over a world of foes, was proclaiming the Evangel of the Rights of Man. The Junta at the Castle was given a new lease of power; Fitzgibbon was raised to the historic peerage of Clare; efforts were made to arouse religious animosities in the Irish Parliament, and even in different parts of the country. This bad policy—Pitt probably was not aware of it—was severely condemned by leading men in not a few counties; their able protests remain, and do them honour.

The conduct of the Government now gave an enormous impulse to the United Irish movement, and to the agrarian disorder of Catholic Ireland; the success of the arms of France, no doubt, cooperated in the same direction. The United Irish leaders, seeing there was no hope of accomplishing their ends by Constitutional means, began, as Tone had done from the first, to think that revolution was their only chance; they gradually turned into dark and desperate courses. Their organisation was made military; their societies were prepared for a call to the field; supplies of arms were eagerly sought; the districts in which they possessed influence were placed under the command of officers; and attempts were made secretly to enrol and drill levies capable of an armed rising. The emissaries sent to France became more numerous; the principal of these was Lord Edward Fitzgerald, a scion of the great Geraldine name; and the heads of the French Republic were invited to strike England through Ireland, and to set the Irish people free. At the same time, true to their policy from the first, the United Irishmen made renewed efforts to drag Catholic Ireland into their wake; the confiscation of the land was held out as a bribe to a credulous peasantry; Irishmen were to have their own when they were released from the bonds of landlords and the collectors of tithe. A movement, now distinctly rebellious, was thus linked with a movement springing from the land; thousands of Catholics fell into the United Irish ranks; agrarian outbreaks, in many places, assumed the aspect of a predial war; and the tendency of Irish agrarian trouble to resist the power of the State, and to become revolutionary, grew very manifest. As yet, however, the United Irishmen, except in Ulster, were hardly organised; and the Catholic peasantry were still a chaotic mass, tossed hither and thither, without real leaders.

A movement, meanwhile, of a very different kind, directly opposed to that of the United Irishmen, but indirectly giving it powerful aid, had been acquiring considerable strength in Ulster, and even extending beyond its limits. In the Northern Province, the Celtic Irishry, all Catholic, and the Protestant descendants of the old settlers, were, in many districts, closely intermixed; perennial feuds had existed between them. This state of disorder had greatly increased, as lawlessness had spread through parts of Ulster; and from 1791 to 1795 the Protestant Peep-of-Day Boys, as they were called, and the Catholic Defenders came into repeated conflict. The first-named body, largely composed of members of the Established Church in the lower ranks of life, disliked the Presbyterian and United Irish movement, which Catholic Ireland was invited to join; they formed the Orange Society, as it has ever since been called; and they began to proclaim a kind of

Holy War against the Catholic population in parts of Ulster. The ranks of the Orangemen rapidly increased; their organisation became powerful, and spread even to the Southern Provinces; undoubtedly it obtained the support of a considerable number of the Ulster gentry, and possibly even of the Irish Government. Irregular attacks, often savagely avenged, were made, from time to time, on the Catholics of the North; and hundreds of peasant families were driven from their homes, and sent in poverty and despair to find refuge in counties of the South. This crusade, which quickened the religious animosities of the past, thwarted the policy of the United Irish leaders, who sought to combine all Irishmen in support of their cause; but they perceived how they might turn it to account; and they acted with no little skill and promptitude. They spread abroad the report, multiplied by a thousand tongues, that the dreaded Protestant Saxons of Ulster had banded themselves together to effect the destruction of Celtic and Catholic Ireland; that what was being already done was a presage only of atrocities worse than the Cromwellian Conquest; and that the only hope for the Irish Catholic was to join heart and hand the patriotic League, which offered him liberty, and would secure him safety. These rumours had extraordinary effect on an ignorant and down-trodden peasantry; after the Orange outrages, immense numbers of the Catholics of the South, as well as the North, took the oath of the United Irishmen, and enrolled themselves on the lists of their musters, many, without knowing it, thus embarking in a rebellious cause.

It is certain, however, that at this juncture, the Irish Catholics were not prepared to attempt to rise against the State in force. Wolfe Tone landed at Havre in the first months of 1796—one of other emissaries but their born leader; and his capacity and earnestness made a real impression on the Directory, then in the seat of power in Paris. He advocated a formidable descent on Ireland, with the arguments of an enthusiastic rebel; it is to his credit that he made scarcely a stipulation for himself, and that he tried to obtain pledges that, in the event of success, his country was not to be made a dependency of France. A large fleet, carrying 15,000 troops, under the command of the illustrious Hoche, set sail from Brest, in December, upon the enterprise; it is remarkable that it did not make for Dublin, or a port of Ulster as Tone had advised; it sought to effect a landing on the extreme verge of Munster, perhaps because an attempt of the kind had proved successful more than a century before. The French navy, however, was in a wretched state; Hoche, in a frigate, never reached the Irish coast, and the principal part of the invading fleet, after making Bantry Bay in safety, was driven out to sea by a furious tempest. It has been thought, however, that Grouchy, the second in command, might have landed with a not inconsiderable force; if so Munster, might have been overrun, and become for a time a French province[1]; on this occasion, as on the day of Waterloo, Grouchy perhaps did England really good service. The failure of the expedition has been ascribed to chance; History more justly points out that it is not easy to invade an island, cut off from the Continent by a dangerous and most stormy sea, especially with an inferior naval force. Yet the most striking feature of the descent was this: the Irish Catholics, assumed by Tone and his colleagues to be burning to rise in arms, remained quiescent, and even showed signs of loyalty; and some of the most Catholic towns of Munster—their governing bodies were, however, Protestant—declared, with apparent enthusiasm, for the existing Government. Too much is not to be made of this: the Celts of Connaught did not spare the survivors of the Armada wrecked on their shores, though their hearts were probably in the Armada's cause; but the fact remains, and it is very significant.

[1] Traditions of the incapacity of Grouchy still exist at Bantry.

The failure at Bantry did not change the purpose of the United Irish leaders; but it made them cautious, and they resolved, if possible, not to attempt a rising before the French had made a successful landing. Ulster, nevertheless, and other parts of Ireland, were in a state of hardly suppressed rebellion, sustained by a savage war of classes, throughout nearly the whole of 1797. A United Irish Directory had been formed in Belfast, enforcing its mandates far and wide; an insurrectionary army was held in the leash, drilled, and to a certain extent, disciplined; it may have numbered, on paper, 100,000 men. Meanwhile, regular and sometimes successful efforts were made to seduce the troops in the province, and the militia, largely Catholics, from their allegiance; the arm of justice was often paralysed by the intimidation of juries and hideous outrages; in short a kind of anarchic government acquired despotic power by means of a system of terror. At the same time the feud of the Orangemen and Defenders grew more desperate; an ever-increasing stream of Catholics was swept into the United Irish ranks; fresh crowds of fugitives were driven southwards, fleeing, they spread abroad, from the Protestant wrath to come. Another United Irish Directory had its seat in Dublin; some of its leaders were able men; but their chief trust was placed in Lord Edward Fitzgerald, who was to command the armed levies of the South, and whose great name seemed a tower of strength. These levies, it was said, numbered 200,000 men—an estimate, beyond doubt, excessive; but tens of thousands of the Catholic peasantry had by this time become United Irishmen, and many of them had been rudely armed and disciplined. The plan of the conspirators was to seize the Castle of Dublin, as in 1641, to occupy the capital, and to make the men in power prisoners; and then to rise generally throughout the country, when the invasion of the French had been made certain. In the interval of time remaining, fresh efforts were made to exasperate and extend the

VIII.]   *The Rebellion of* 1798.   271

agrarian war; maps of the old confiscated lands were prepared; old prophecies that the Saxon was to be expelled from Ireland were noised abroad, sometimes by the lower orders of priests; the peasantry were told that their alien masters were doomed. In this way the rebellious and the agrarian movements became thoroughly united in some districts; plantations were cut down and smithies blazed for the manufacture of a formidable weapon, the pike; and the organisation of the Whiteboy system, with its central and local secret societies, was set on foot to promote the United Irish cause, and to oppress, terrorise, and despoil its opponents. This combination, however, does not appear to have been complete in more than a few counties; and it did not exist, it has been said, in Connaught.

This state of things in Ireland was perilous in the extreme; affairs in Europe, and even in England, increased the peril. Notwithstanding the failure of 1796, a great French fleet had assembled at Brest, and a Dutch fleet was at anchor near the Texel, in order to renew a descent on Ireland—Tone had indefatigably pressed on the enterprise;—France had already nearly mastered the Continent; the very naval power of Great Britain had been shaken, especially by symptoms of disaffection in the fleet. The Irish Government was perfectly justified in resolving to crush out rebellion in time; Clare, its masterspirit, deserves credit for a resolution and daring worthy of Strafford. But it was most unfortunate that it had not the support of a regular and well organised military force; the army in Ireland was only a few thousand men; the militia had become deeply tainted; the men at the Castle had largely to rely on the yeomanry, a numerous volunteer levy, raised to a great extent by the local gentry, and mostly Protestants burning with Orange passions. Under these circumstances, it was inevitable, perhaps, that, when an effort was made to put down a rising, horrible excesses should take place; unhappily these were widespread and revolting. Ulster was selected as the first point of attack; the leaders of the conspiracy were arrested; the incendiary Press was scattered to the winds; a general process of seizing and collecting arms was enforced in the Province without scruple or mercy. Houses were burned down wholesale to compel the surrender of weapons; bands of yeomen harried the Catholic districts; confessions were extorted by atrocious methods; wherever an attempt at resistance was made, it was repressed by wild and relentless cruelties. In a word a kind of savage guerilla warfare, not unlike that of the Desmond conflict, and aggravated by a furious strife of race and creed, raged for a time in many parts of Ulster; and hundreds of captives were hurried off, and put on board the fleet, an event ominously connected with the Mutiny at the Nore. The head of the rebellion was broken by these means; it should be added that, ruthless as they were, these deeds had been sanctioned by the Irish Parliament, which, indignant and alarmed at a state of affairs in which the Protestant caste seemed marked out for destruction, had given the freest scope to severities of every kind, by passing laws of draconic harshness. The Government, after a pause of a few weeks, turned against the conspiracy in the capital; it must be borne in mind that though a French invasion had been stopped by the great fight of Camperdown, the warrior of Italy was at this very moment on the French coasts, planning a descent on England. Spies and informers had kept Camden, Clare, and the Council apprised of all that was going on; the rebel Directory were made prisoners; and the arrest and subsequent death of Lord Edward Fitzgerald deprived the leaders of the intended rising of a head in whom they placed extraordinary trust, though there was little to recommend him except a name, still a spell of power among the peasantry of the South[1].

[1] Of the influence of the Geraldine name on the Irish peasantry, Davis has finely and truly written:—

If frightful excesses had already occurred, the Irish Government, up to this point of time, recollecting the situation, can be hardly blamed. Thenceforward, however, it must be gravely censured, if some excuse can be made for its conduct. The brain of the conspiracy, had, so to speak been smitten; but the paralysed members still stirred with life; all prospects of a rising had not disappeared. Fitzgibbon knew that the plan of the rebel leaders was not to move until the French had landed; he seems, like Claverhouse, to have deliberately resolved to force insurrection into premature being, and to stifle it in blood before it could obtain aid from abroad. By his counsels more than by those of any other personage, the system of terror which had succeeded in the North, was carried out with infinitely more recklessness and severity in parts of the southern provinces. The yeomanry were let loose like banditti; villages were burned and sacked to get at hidden arms; the Catholic peasantry were hunted down and plundered; torture was inflicted on hundreds of ill-fated prisoners. This evil policy, which, be it observed, was denounced by Abercromby, the commander-in-chief of the regular army, and a true soldier, had the result expected from it. It became impossible to await the coming of the French; the people in several counties were driven into revolt; and the sanguinary rebellion of 1798 broke out on the 23rd of May in that year.

The rising was confined to a part of Leinster; it was generally feeble and ill-combined; it became formidable in a

"True Geraldines! brave Geraldines! as torrents mould the Earth,
You channelled deep old Ireland's heart by constancy and worth;
When Ginkle leaguered Limerick, the Irish soldiers gazed,
To see, if in the setting sun dead Desmond's banner blazed!
And still it is the peasant's hope upon the Cuirreach's mere,
They live who'll see ten thousand men, with good Lord Edward here!
So let them dream till brighter days, when, not by Edward's shade,
But by a leader true as he, their lines shall be arrayed!"

The Spirit of the Nation, p. 101.

nook of the province only. An attempt to attack Dublin from without, connected with an insurrection within, was easily quelled by the armed force on the spot, and by the energy of the Protestant citizens; and though barbarous deeds of blood were done, the rebels in Kildare, Carlow, and Meath were quickly subdued. The rising, however, was universal and fierce in the two beautiful counties of Wicklow and Wexford, the fairest part of the south-eastern tract of Ireland. In this prosperous region, the strife between the Orangemen and Defenders had raged for some months; and the efforts of the Government to bring rebellion to a head had been marked with peculiar cruelties. The conflict from the first was a savage war of religion; it was also to some extent a struggle of race; but, in this instance, the double lines of distinction in Ireland did not coincide; the rebels were for the most part, of Anglo-Norman or English descent; it was a war of armed Protestants, backed by a military force, waged with a Catholic peasantry, half maddened by wrong. For nearly a month the issue of the contest was very doubtful; it assumed a terrible and hideous aspect; it is impossible to adjust the balance of evil deeds done on either side,—the loyalists especially disgraced themselves by outrages on women to an appalling extent. The horrors of the scenes that were witnessed are relieved by the proofs of devoted courage that were shown; the Protestants fought with the reckless pride characteristic of a dominant race; the Catholics exhibited heroic daring, at Vinegar Hill, Oulart, and New Ross; the fowling-piece and the long pike had great effect in brave and resolute hands: and one of the rebel leaders—these were often priests—displayed a capacity worthy of a born general. After many efforts the rising was at last quenched in ashes and blood; but the rebels had occupied the town of Wexford for a time; and had the march of the Catholics on Arklow proved successful, the capital would have been in the gravest danger.

VIII.] *The Rebellion of* 1798. 275

The rebellion scarcely made a sign in Connaught; it appeared in Munster in only a few weak gatherings. Ulster, where the conspiracy had been most deeply laid, did not stir during the war in the South-East; the causes of this deserve passing notice. The preparations for a rising had been already prevented; the Presbyterians waited the advent of the French; they resented too, a quarrel between France and the United States. But the most effective cause of their inaction was this: the struggle in Wicklow and Wexford was one of religions; and the United Irishmen of Ulster stood aloof from a purely Protestant and Catholic conflict, which ran counter to their hopes and sympathies. The rebellion of 1798 was almost wholly fought out by Irishmen; it had nearly ceased when troops poured in from England; it called out high Irish qualities, if it was full of horrors. By this time Camden had been replaced by Cornwallis, a capable and humane soldier; but a kind of guerilla struggle lingered for a few months among the valleys and hills of Wicklow, the fastness of the Celtic mountaineers of old. A short period like a White Terror followed, marked by the passions of a dominant race let loose against one alike subject and despised; and many disgraceful deeds were certainly done. These atrocities however were rather the work of officials of the Castle, of the yeomanry and their chiefs, and of Protestant bigots of the middle and lower classes, than of the landed gentry, of any degree; hundreds of these, even in Ulster, condemned what was going on; and Cornwallis was in error when he involved all the loyalists of Ireland in a common censure. Nevertheless the state of Ireland was lamentable after the close of 1798; it left a legacy of blighted hopes and most evil memories. It was not only that fair parts of the country had been ravaged by a barbarous strife; the material was as nothing to the moral ruin. The influences that had, for many years, seemed to lessen the differences of blood and faith, and even to have healed many wounds of the past, had disappeared in an inhuman struggle; the old distinctions had come out, deeply marked as ever; the conflict, if not wholly, had been in the main a war of race, and above all of religion. The visions of the United Irishmen had sunk in a sea of blood; the ideal of Grattan had proved impossible; the aspirations of a new era had been as idle as the French dreams of 1789. The ruling orders of Ireland had been made revengeful; the classes beneath them had beheld the prospect of enlarged liberties suddenly withdrawn; the lines of demarcation between the owners and occupiers of the soil, and between Catholic and Protestant had been greatly widened. This change for the worse, which put the whole country back, was very marked in the Irish Parliament; it had become a mere court to register what the Castle and Clare ordered; the independent party in it had dwindled almost to nothing; and Grattan and his followers, indignant at recent events, unable to check the course of the Government, and saddened at the failure of the hopes of 1782, had seceded from it in anger and despair. Long before this time they had made a last fruitless effort in the cause of Catholic emancipation and Parliamentary Reform.

Before the rebellion had finally collapsed, a French squadron, and a few hundred men, had landed near Killala, on the coast of Mayo. Napoleon had taken the main fleet of France to the East, where it perished in the great fight of the Nile; he had no taste for rebellion, Irish or other; the French Directory sent only an insignificant force to the shores of Ireland. Its leader Humbert, however, was a brilliant soldier; he routed a body of militia, three-fold in numbers, in a combat known as the "Race of Castlebar"; he gave Cornwallis much to do before he was compelled to surrender. Another petty French descent was remarkable only for the capture of Wolfe Tone, after a sharp engagement; the unfortunate chief of the

United Irish movement—he had served in the expedition to Bantry, and had witnessed the disaster of Camperdown—was doomed to the ignominous death of a felon, though he held the commission of a French general; he only averted his fate by suicide. Tone was infinitely the first of the rebel leaders; he had capacity, resource, true faith in his cause, and patriotism, distempered but sincere; his figure will live in Irish History. After a few severe examples had been made, the conspirators, who had fallen into the hands of the Irish Government, were amnestied, under not unfair conditions; their lives were spared, but they had to leave the country. They were, none of them, men of marked powers: but some won honour in foreign lands; two or three gallantly followed Napoleon's eagles; more than one made a name for himself in America. Much in their conduct is to be sternly condemned; yet, at this distance of time, it deserves a kind of sympathy. They had at first only Constitutional reforms in view; they were drawn into rebellion and its evil courses, in part by the revolutionary ideas of France, but in part by the misdeeds of the Irish government. And if they were guilty of the unhappy attempt of connecting rebellion with an agrarian rising, and of hounding on an ignorant peasantry against their superiors, we must bear in mind that Ireland had genuine wrongs at this time: that they had a lofty, if a mistaken ideal; that they staked their lives on the cause they upheld; that they did not appeal to the base passion of greed only; that they were not subsidised by incendiaries of blood; that, when all was lost, they did not turn against each other, in Ireland at least, and sully the name of Irishmen[1].

The rebellion of 1798 had only just ended, when Pitt began to lay grounds for the Union. The contest had been tardily put down; reinforcements from England had come in late;

[1] For a favourable view of the United Irish leaders, see the fine ballad, "Who fears to speak of Ninety-Eight." *The Spirit of the Nation*, p. 41.

but we may summarily reject the wicked myths—evil phantoms rising from a field of carnage—that Pitt fomented a rising in arms, and let Irish factions tear each other to pieces, in order to promote a measure he had at heart. The Union of Great Britain and Ireland had not only been projected, we have said, by many able thinkers; it had been in the minds of several English statesmen, ever since the Revolution of 1782. Apart, however, from faults, on which we shall say a word hereafter, Pitt, it is evident from his letters and speeches, did not thoroughly comprehend the whole reasons that made a Union a necessity of State at this time, or perceive the consequences that might flow from it. He saw, as the Regency Question had made manifest, that the two Legislatures might dangerously clash; he saw, too, the danger of this at a period of war, though, in England's struggle with Revolutionary France, the Irish Parliament had given him most cordial support. He saw, also, that probably the best means to secure the Established Church in Ireland, to keep the land in Protestant hands, in a word to maintain what he called "the Protestant Settlement," was to make Ireland one with Great Britain; nor was he blind to the possible evils of the existing state of Catholic Ireland. But, though he was not insensible to them, he did not completely grasp the truths that, after the horrors of 1798, the only hope for Ireland, torn as she had been by a barbarous strife of race and faith, was to bring her under the control of an Imperial Parliament; and that the only wise policy for a British Minister, was, with the aid of a strong and just government, to place Catholic and Protestant, Saxon and Celt on an equal level of civil and religious rights. This justification of the Union he did not fully realise, at least he did not act boldly as if he did; and we may smile at his notions that the introduction of Irish members into the United Parliament might largely increase the power of the Crown, and that a Union would cause Irish faction quickly to cease. Pitt, in fact, as we have before remarked, was ignorant of the true state of Ireland, like most British statesmen[1]; and in the case of Ireland as in that of France in 1792-3, he had not the genius to perceive what was beyond his immediate ken.

It was the wish of Pitt to combine the Union with the emancipation of the Irish Catholics, and with measures to provide funds for the support of the Catholic Irish priesthood, and for the commutation of the tithes of the Established Church; he had seen, we have said, the bad effects of this impost. This policy was in the right direction; but it was not original, as has been alleged; the Irish Parliament would have conceded the Catholic claims in 1795; the payment of the priests was an old idea, and had been advocated by Irish writers and statesmen; the commutation of the tithe was a favourite plan of Grattan. Pitt, however, did not persist in the project, which he had hoped to make an essential part of the Union; he yielded to the counsels of Clare, greatly trusted by him in Irish affairs, and consented to deprive his measure of its best features; he knew, too, at this time, that George III was obstinately opposed to the demands of the Catholics. This was the first of his grave mistakes on the subject: it is the more to be blamed because Cornwallis, able to gauge Irish opinion on the spot, always insisted that the Union could not succeed, if Catholic Emancipation was not made, so to speak, its gift. Means were taken, towards the close of 1798, to ascertain the judgment of Irishmen on the question; a few of the great borough-mongering Peers agreed to support the scheme, should it serve their interests; a number of members

---

[1] We have seen what Swift thought on this subject. Burke wrote thus:—"The fashion relative to Ireland is the wish that they should hear of it, and its concerns, as little as possible." Grattan expressed himself in these words:—"Ireland is a subject the Cabinet considers with a lazy contumely, and picks up here and there, by accident or design, interested or erroneous intelligence." This may be read with profit at this hour.

of the Irish Houses were ready to obey the Minister on the usual terms; some of the independent landed gentry, alarmed at the events of 1798, beheld, in a Union, safety for themselves; the leading men of Catholic Ireland, much as they had resented Fitzwilliam's recall, were not unwilling to consider the subject. But an immense majority of the Irish Protestants, the trading classes of Dublin, almost to a man, and nine tenths, at least, of the Irish Bar, were indignant at the very thought of a Union, and expressed their sentiments in emphatic language: this is the more remarkable because the country was held down by a British armed force, and the views of the British Ministry was perfectly well known. In these circumstances, Robert Stewart, Lord Castlereagh, the Chief Secretary of Cornwallis, announced, somewhat vaguely, the policy of Pitt, in the Irish House of Commons, in a speech on the address, made in January 1799; but an amendment was rejected by one vote only; and as this was plainly equivalent to a defeat, the measure was permitted to drop for a time[1].

Though the Government had been baffled in the Irish Lower House, it obtained a large majority in the Irish House of Lords, where the influence of Clare was easily supreme. The British Parliament had, about the same time, passed Resolutions in favour of the Union, by an overwhelming superiority of votes; and Pitt insisted that the measure should be carried out in Ireland. But it was far from easy to give his purpose effect; and means were adopted, the exact nature of which has been matter of controversy ever since, but of which the general character is not doubtful. The Irish Parliament had long been swayed by corrupt influence; this had probably increased since 1782; it had been openly exercised on the Regency Question; and it was resolved, in Castlereagh's cynical phrase, to "buy up the fee-simple of Irish corruption,"

[1] In a debate on the report to the Address the Government was defeated by 5 votes.

by an accelerated purchase made once for all, and to secure a majority for a Union in the Irish Houses, by largely extending the processes which had long been in use. Direct bribery was not employed; but promises of peerages were lavishly scattered; places were created and places unscrupulously filled, in order to obtain support for the scheme; officials were threatened with dismissal if they did not vote for the Government; appeals were persistently made to the hopes and the fears of the members in both parts of the Irish Parliament. Simultaneously pledges were given that immense sums were to be paid to the patrons and the proprietors of the numerous boroughs to be disfranchised; and one of the reforms effected in 1793, by which placemen in the House of Commons were compelled to vacate their seats, was twisted into a method to secure a majority. By these expedients, regarded by Cornwallis with disgust, but employed by his Chief Secretary with unflinching boldness, the Irish Parliament was packed to vote for a Union; but it is only just to add that, from the first, many of its members—and the number certainly tended to increase—conscientiously approved of Pitt's policy. Recourse, too, was had to other means, to influence Irish opinion outside the Parliament in behalf of the contemplated measure. Able pamphlets were published, and a Press subsidised; Cornwallis went on progress through different counties, to canvass, so to speak, for the Union; and many favourable addresses were obtained, though these were of a questionable kind, and the adverse petitions were much more numerous. The Irish Government, however, chiefly directed its efforts to enlist Catholic Ireland on its side; and incidents occurred, even yet obscure, that form an unhappy passage in Irish History. Pitt had informed Cornwallis that the Union was to be a "Protestant Union," in the phrase of the time; he told the Lord Lieutenant, very plainly, that Catholic Emancipation was to be no part of the measure. But his own speeches in the British

House of Commons implied that he approved of the Catholic claims, and that they might be conceded when the Union had become law; he certainly encouraged Cornwallis, and gave him power to bid openly for Catholic support; he perhaps authorised Cornwallis to assure the Irish Catholic leaders that their cause was his own. That upright but not very astute nobleman, always the earnest champion of the Irish Catholics, placed his own interpretation on Pitt's hints and words: he had many conferences with the Heads of Catholic Ireland, and entreated them to use their influence to promote the Union; he unquestionably held out hopes, if he did not make promises; he left them under the impression that their Emancipation was certain and at hand. It should be added that, before this time, Cornwallis had been negotiating with the Irish Catholic Bishops, with reference to a provision for the priesthood; Pitt seems to have been not aware of this; but the fact is, not the less, of extreme significance. The broad result was that the Catholic leaders generally threw in their lot with the Union, and drew the Catholic masses with them; Catholic Ireland, in the main, declared for the measure; and this, Pitt and Cornwallis agreed, was of supreme importance. A small minority, however, of the Irish Catholics, with more insight, and perhaps with more ambitious views, protested vehemently against the proposed scheme; among these was Daniel O'Connell, a young lawyer, just beginning his career.

The devices employed to bring about the Union made their effects apparent in the Irish Parliament, when it assembled again in January 1800. An amendment to the Address, by which it was sought to stop the progress of the measure, was rejected; the Question was introduced, a few days afterwards, by a message from the Viceroy sending to both Houses the Resolutions voted by the British Parliament, and recommending the policy sanctioned by it. The debates on the subject, arising in different ways, were impassioned, and took up much time; but they are marked by ability of a very high order. Castlereagh advocated the scheme, with calm power and thoroughness; Clare, in a speech of real insight and force, insisted, that in a Union lay the only hope of Property, of Law, and of the Established Church, in Ireland. A fine array of eloquence was marshalled on the other side; the Bar engaged its most brilliant ornaments, Saurin, Plunket, Bushe, and other eminent worthies; the Speaker Foster rose to the height of a great argument, in a most weighty and thoughtful harangue. But Grattan towered above all his fellows —he had lately returned to the House of Commons—in language of singular beauty and pathos, accompanied by solemn and prophetic warnings, he advised the Parliament not to destroy itself, and to preserve its existence for the Irish "nation." All opposition, however, proved vain; the Government retained the majority it had procured; Resolutions, passed by the Irish Parliament, in favour of a Union, were translated into Articles and Bills; and the measure of Pitt received the sanction of both the Irish and the British Parliaments. It deserves notice that a proposal to refer the decision of the question to the Irish electorate was angrily resented by Pitt and Castlereagh; the voice even of Protestant Ireland, though that of a minority of the Irish people, and of a minority in the main loyal, was not allowed to pronounce on this matter[1]. It is certain however, that, in its later stages at least, the measure did not provoke widespread discontent; there was no passionate outburst of opinion against it. Dublin and the Irish Bar, indeed, remained bitterly hostile; but there was little murmuring in the country districts; the mass of Catholic Ireland did not stir; its leaders looked forward with anxious hope; the trading classes were induced to expect that the Union would bring them large benefits; Presbyterian

[1] The Catholic Irish multitude, however, it must be borne in mind, had possessed the suffrage since 1793.

Ireland seems to have thought that its favourite linen manufacture would make great progress. The attitude of the majority of the people was one of apathy; it was felt that a measure, backed by the British Parliament and the British army, could not be withstood; but unquestionably a minority, growing in strength, inclined very decidedly towards a Union.

The Union was accomplished by evil means; nor was it a well conceived measure, even within the narrow limits traced out by Pitt. The Irish and British Legislatures were merely combined, and emerged in a single Imperial Parliament; Ireland retained the Viceroy, a separate Government, a separate Administration, separate Courts of Justice, even separate Exchequers for a considerable time. The shadow of an independent State was suffered to exist; as Foster truly predicted, an occasion was offered to demands to give the shadow substance; the consequences have not proved to be fortunate. The worst feature, however, of the Union was this: what should have been its most vital part was not found in it; Catholic Emancipation, a provision for the priests, even the commutation of the tithe were left out; Catholic Ireland was still deprived of legitimate rights. The remaining portions of the scheme were of less importance, and do not deserve peculiar attention. The maintenance of the Established Church was made a solemn and fundamental law; with what results time was to show in its fulness; the settlement of the Land was left, of course, as it was; but undoubtedly the hope of preserving this had weight with numbers of the landed gentry, alarmed at the threats, uttered in 1798, to undo the confiscations of the past. The fiscal arrangements were harsh to Ireland; she was to contribute two seventeenths to the Imperial expenditure, a proportion certainly in excess; her trade was somewhat further enlarged, and ultimately was to be completely free; but the commercial benefits, which, Castlereagh declared, would follow the Union, have not been realised. The Irish Peers lost their seats in the Irish House of Lords; a small body of the order have ever since been chosen to represent them in the Imperial Parliament; the 300 members of the Irish House of Commons were reduced to 100 in the Imperial House, a number that ought to have been adequate to make the will of Ireland sufficiently felt. For the rest, while much that the Union should have contained was unhappily not comprised in it, much that was discreditable, in its incidents, was faithfully carried out; the borough-mongering nobles and commoners were gorged with the spoil that had been promised; and the pledges of corruption were duly fulfilled.

Pitt was a large minded and enlightened statesman; he certainly desired, when the Union was secure, to carry out the measures of relief for the Irish Catholics which, from the outset, he had had in view. He probably reckoned on his prodigious influence; but he had unhappily kept the king in the dark, though fully aware of the king's sentiments; a ministerial cabal was formed against him; and George III, on a preposterous plea, pressed with the obstinacy of a distempered mind, peremptorily refused to listen to the Catholic claims. The subsequent conduct of Pitt in this matter has indisputably thrown a shadow on his name. He resigned his office, when he had persuaded himself that he could not carry out his Irish Catholic policy; he is entitled to every credit attaching to the act. But in a very short time he let his master know that he would not urge the question again; he supported a violent Anti-Catholic Ministry; he returned to office, but took no steps to vindicate the demands of Catholic Ireland. All this has exposed his memory to grave suspicion; and History can hardly withhold its censure. It is idle to say that he told Cornwallis that the Union was to be a Protestant one only: he held out hopes himself to the Irish Catholics; he invited Cornwallis to do the same; he carried the Union, to some extent at least, by obtaining Irish Catholic support, secured only by what were deemed promises, that Catholic relief would certainly follow. In these circumstances, it was not enough to have simply abandoned the helm; he ought to have insisted on the king's adopting his measures, and had he done so, he must have attained his object; and his subsequent attitude has a look of insincerity if not worse. We fear it must be said that, in his wish to accomplish the Union, he did not scruple to allow the Irish Catholics to entertain hopes which, he well knew, might not be fulfilled; that he all but pledged himself to them, through his Lord Lieutenant, though he felt he might not be able to redeem the pledge; and that he thought his conscience absolved by a resignation, which he took care should not last long, without even trying to give effect to a policy, to which he stood committed as a man and a minister. The best excuses perhaps to be made for him are that, in his ignorance of Ireland and her real state, he did not understand all that was involved in the course he took, and that, in the death struggle of 1804–5, he believed it was his duty to become the Head of the State, without regard to consistency, or too fine a sense of honour. A most unfortunate fact, nevertheless, remained: by one of those accidents so frequent in Irish History, Catholic Ireland was again deceived; what was done had only too much in common with Strafford's "Graces," and the broken Treaty of Limerick.

Under the Constitution of 1782 Ireland unquestionably made social and material progress; the ancient divisions of blood and creed, which for centuries have kept her races apart, and her feuds of class had, to some extent, disappeared. In these circumstances it was not impossible, though, in our judgment, it was not probable, that Grattan's ideal might have been realised, that Ireland might have become "a nation," with a free Parliament and a powerful landed gentry, the respected superiors of a contented peasantry. But the French

Revolution scattered these hopes to the winds; its destructive influence was as fatal, perhaps, in Ireland as in any part of Europe; it blighted the fair promise of the close of the eighteenth century. We must add, too, that having regard to the relations it created between Great Britain and Ireland, the Constitution of 1782 was not likely to endure; it was hardly compatible with the security of the British Empire; it was an anachronism distrusted by British statesmen. Be this as it may, the French Revolution, searching Irish institutions to the very core, proved how ill-ordered and dangerous they were; society in Ireland was seen to be deeply diseased, and divided by distinctions only hidden for a time; and errors of policy and faults of the British and Irish Governments prevented reforms which might, conceivably, have averted the disastrous events that followed. Rebellion, however, began to lift its head; a revolutionary movement to combine Irishmen in a league against England, the common enemy, and to stir up anarchical strife, was crossed and baffled by another movement, characteristic of the hatreds of the past; and the end was a horrible war of race and religion. For much that was done in 1798, Clare and the men at the Castle are to be severely blamed; but their position, we must recollect, was difficult in the extreme; and if they forced civil war to come to a head, they certainly prevented a worse catastrophe. As affairs stood when the rebellion had ended, a Union had become a necessity of State, in the interest of Ireland and of Great Britain alike; but Pitt managed the settlement badly; and the Union was an ill-designed measure, carried by sinister means through the Irish Parliament, and accompanied by an act of wrong to Catholic Ireland, of which the results are felt to this hour. Still Pitt must not be too harshly judged; in the existing state of the world he was bound to accomplish a Union at almost any risk and cost.

Ireland entered into a Union with England under unhappy

conditions, and at an inauspicious time. The Catholic question was one of pressing importance, and if unsettled, certain to cause trouble; the country required other reforms, the necessity of which had begun to be seen by some of the best men in the Irish Parliament. Ireland was in want of a strong but progressive government; but she had been united with Great Britain at the very time when the conflict with France was soon to become one of life and death; when all hopes of changes in the State seemed gone; when reactionary ideas had immense force; when unbending Toryism was supreme, nay absolute. And the reforms she needed were, in some instances, in direct conflict with British prejudice, in others were little understood by British statesmen; and Ireland was to be ruled by a Parliament that knew her not, and by politicians well meaning, indeed, but often ill-informed and without sympathy; it being doubtful, too, at least, if in the peculiar state of her representation, she would possess sufficient influence of her own. The prosperity of Ireland, too, had been largely destroyed; the land had been devastated by civil war; the dregs of rebellion lingered; animosities of race and faith had been fearfully revived; above all, perhaps, the island, as had always been the case, was ages behind England in civilisation and wealth. These circumstances alone made it no easy task to govern Ireland well in an Imperial Parliament, and by ministers dependent on it. If the Union was a necessity of the time, if, on the whole, it was to effect great good, it was to be seen that it was not an unmixed blessing, and that it was to be accompanied, at least, with some real evils.

CHAPTER IX.

FROM THE UNION TO CATHOLIC EMANCIPATION.

The effect on Ireland of the renewal of the war with France in 1803. Emmett's rebellion. Measures of repression. Spread of Orangeism. The Catholic Irish Question in the Imperial Parliament. Failure of the Catholic leaders. Rise of O'Connell. His character and political aims. His efforts at first of little avail. The Question of the Veto. The Catholic Question in the Liverpool Government. Its position near the end of the war. Growing attachment of Ulster to the British connection and the Union, and the causes. Material progress of Ireland up to 1815. The Amalgamation of the Irish with the Imperial Exchequer. Irish Finance. Sudden and continuous decline of Ireland after the war. Irish landed relations. Their evils and dangers. Policy of the British Government. Sir Arthur Wellesley and Peel. Creation of the Irish Constabulary force. O'Connell forms the Catholic Association. Its enormous influence in Ireland. The proposed compromise of 1825. Its failure. The Clare Election. Triumph of O'Connell. Catholic Emancipation. Reflections.

THE Union was accomplished a few months only before the brief truce concluded with France at Amiens. The renewal of the great war, in the spring of 1803, was a disaster for the whole civilised world; like other passages of the French Revolution it was attended with evil results for Ireland. Some of the United Irish leaders, who, after the late amnesty, had made their way into France, began to conspire anew against the British Government; and they sought the assistance of the

First Consul, now bent on an invasion of England, to further, if possible, another Irish rising. They were, however, unable to agree in a common design; the fatal discords of Irishmen kept them apart; and Napoleon, who throughout his whole career detested rebellious, and even popular movements, regarded them, we have seen, with distrust and contempt[1]. He treated them as he treated Italians and Poles who sought to make him a champion of a "national cause" and appealed to him in the name of "national liberty." He flattered them with fair words and promises; made some officers of an "Irish Legion," partly formed of the emigrants of 1798, and partly, perhaps, of veterans of the old Irish Brigade; he enrolled this force in the ranks of the "Army of England"; he kept it as near the Irish coasts as possible; and though, unlike Hoche and the French Directory, he never had Irish independence in view, or thought of making Ireland a principal point of attack, a "diversion," in this direction, he believed worth trying, and in one of his many projects for a descent on England a secondary descent on Ireland has a place. Napoleon, in a word, made Ireland a mere pawn in his game; and when Trafalgar had put an end to all hope of striking England at the heart, the "Irish Legion" followed the fortunes of the Grand Army, a small fraction of the gigantic military power of France. The conspiracy, however, which had been formed again, and the presence of an Irish armed force on the French seaboard, unhappily led to another attempt at Irish rebellion, which, though contemptible in its results, might have been more disastrous than has been commonly supposed. Robert Emmett, a young enthusiast of 1798, had interviews with the United Irishmen in France, and, it has been said, with the First Consul; he resolved to embark on the desperate enterprise of assailing, once more, British power in Ireland. His plan was the old one of seizing the Castle, and of summoning

---

[1] See Chapter I. note, ante, p. 20.

the populace of Dublin to arms; but he had the assistance of an able man, in after years a distinguished soldier of France, and he was promised considerable support from the adjoining counties. His plot, however, was probably disclosed; and "Emmett's rebellion" ended in a mere street brawl, unfortunately disgraced by the murder of an eminent Irish judge. The ill-fated youth paid ere long the penalty of his crime; his memory in Ireland is not forgotten; but though not without daring, and even resource, he was only an inferior Lord Edward Fitzgerald.

This petty outbreak caused alarm in England and Ireland, which seems excessive at this distance of time; severe measures of repression followed, prolonged unhappily for many years, and too common an expedient of Irish government. Insur--rection Acts, the enforcement of martial law, and repeated suspensions of the Habeas Corpus Act, became regular methods of British rule in Ireland, with little interruption, until the end of the war, and even during the succeeding period. These severities were no doubt a legacy bequeathed by the defunct Irish Parliament, which had never hesitated to put disorder down, and had been extravagantly merciless in the crisis of 1798; nor should we forget that Irish rebellion would have been a terrible danger to the State from 1803 to 1805, when the Grand Army was encamped round Boulogne, nay, until after Waterloo and the fall of Napoleon. But repression was much too indiscriminately applied, and was made to extend to a series of social ills for which different remedies should have been found; and though it is impossible to assert that, had the state of things before the Union continued to exist, legislation and administration would have been better or more wise, still we see in this system a bad sign of the hard and oppressive Toryism of the day, and in some degree, perhaps, of the want of intelligence and of sympathy of British statesmen in Irish affairs. Another pernicious result of the war and of the spirit prevailing in Irish government was a great increase and extension of what we may describe as Orangeism, and all that is implied in the name. The Orange societies, we have seen, had been long established; they had unquestionably weakened the United Irish movement; they had done good service, though in an evil way, in forcing rebellion in Ireland to a head, and in subduing it in the open field. They had also been supported by the Irish Government as far back, perhaps, as 1795; and here again British rulers had succeeded to a state of things they found in existence. But Orangeism was directly encouraged after the Union for many years in Ireland; it was deemed a check on Irish disaffection and crime; it furnished the army with thousands of recruits, and especially with a body of brave and loyal officers; it had two of the Royal Family on its lists, it was powerfully sustained by opinion in England, and it made rapid and widely reaching progress. The Orange Associations spread far and near; they drew into their ranks immense numbers of Irish Protestants of the lower orders—the worst specimens of the Ascendency that bore their name; and they had adherents in some of the Irish landed gentry, distrustful, since recent events, of Catholic Ireland. This organisation of domineering sectarian faction, backed by the State, but lawless and no part of it, had a most mischievous effect in making more wide and broad the old distinctions of blood revived in Ireland, and in exasperating passions of class; it was Protestant oppression in its most odious aspect; it quickened all that was most dangerous and bad in Catholic Ireland. Undoubtedly, when its evils had become manifest, it was not favoured by the few real statesmen in power in Ireland soon after the Union; but its disastrous work was not easily undone; and, in another way, it had an injurious tendency. The great majority of the Irish gentry have never been Orangemen in any sense, or can be said to have had Orange sympathies; yet they were largely subjected to this reproach when Orangeism was condemned in high places; and the results for them have not been fortunate.

The Catholic Question was however the main incident in the affairs of Ireland, that in which the gravest issues were involved at this period, and for years afterwards. Pitt returned to office in 1804; the Irish Catholic leaders, for the most part men of high degree, had remained quiescent during the rule of Addington; they now confidently believed their opportunity had come. A deputation from their body waited on the Minister; they relied on what they conceived were the pledges on the strength of which they had given the Union support; they dealt, it has been alleged, with emphasis on two papers written by Castlereagh and Cornwallis, and placed in their hands. But Pitt threw them over, whatever the excuse; he declared that the time was not expedient; he put them off with faint words of compromise. They then turned in their strait to Fox; a vehement and able debate followed, remarkable for the appearance, for the first time, of Grattan in the Imperial Parliament—his speech was a magnificent display; but Pitt voted against any measure of relief, though he recognised, he said, the Catholic claims "in principle." When Fox and Lord Grenville came into office, Fox candidly informed the Catholic leaders that Catholic emancipation was not possible; the obstinate bigotry of George III was, in truth, approved by nearly his whole family; indeed, as is well known, this Ministry fell in an attempt to obtain a concession for English Catholic officers, which had been extended by the great measure of 1793 to their Irish fellows. The Government of "all the Talents" was well disposed to Ireland; but it accomplished little, save to mitigate, in part, the system of repression for years in force; and it should be added that, when it resigned, it had coercive measures in view, owing to the apprehension of French influence, and of the effects of Napoleon's conquests on disaffected Ireland. These measures were adopted by their Tory successors and, to a certain extent, received the sanction of Grattan, an enemy of the French Revolution in all its phases; it may be said too, here, that he had attached himself to the small party of Whigs who sought to continue the war; his speech against Napoleon in 1815 remains one of his most brilliant efforts. Meanwhile the Irish Catholic Question had begun to lose ground in the Imperial Parliament, and Irish Catholic hopes were painfully deferred. At the general election of 1807 the subject was made a battle cry of party, and British opinion, become intensely Protestant, through the influence of the narrow Toryism of the time and of the evangelical school of teaching, pronounced decisively against the Irish Catholic claims. A national sentiment also concurred; Catholic France was at the feet of Napoleon; the Pope was Napoleon's submissive instrument; was this the time to listen to Catholic Ireland, the friend of England's declared foes?

The Irish Catholic leaders, we have seen, were nearly all nobles and great gentlemen; one only, indeed, represented the middle and trading class prominent at the Catholic Committee of 1792-93. Their somewhat feeble efforts had conspicuously failed; they were now to give place to a very different personage, the Liberator, as he has been justly called, of Catholic Ireland. O'Connell, by this time, though still kept down by one of the exceptions in the Act of 1793, which prevented him attaining the rank of King's Counsel, had risen to eminence at the Bar of Ireland; he was soon to become its most striking figure, less on account of mere learning, or even eloquence—great as were the effects of his rude strength of speech—as for his unparalleled skill in the conduct of causes. He had, we have seen, when almost a youth, made an energetic protest against the Union; he doubtless believed, with other able men, that the cause of the Irish Catholic would, not improbably, be thrown back in the Imperial Parliament; he clearly perceived that Catholic Ireland would necessarily acquire, in the course of events, enormous power in an Irish Parliament. Nor is it possible to deny that he retained these views throughout his long and chequered career, and that he was sincere as a champion of Repeal, if he certainly put the question more than once aside, and even dealt with it as a mere party move. At this juncture, however, the Catholic claims engrossed the attention of the Irish Catholics; and O'Connell devoted his commanding powers to their cause. He obtained a place on the Catholic Committee; gradually forced aside by his capacity and will its aristocratic and inefficient leaders; and became, as Chairman, its master spirit in 1810, when in his thirty-sixth year. His antecedents, his training, his remarkable gifts made him singularly fitted to direct the cause of Catholic Ireland to a triumphant issue. He had been versed in the arts of the smuggler from early boyhood; he was perfectly skilled in the wiles of the law; though a Celt of the Celts, and richly endowed with the gaiety, the fancy, the quick mind of the Celt, his intelligence was massive, his sagacity profound; unlike most Celts he had hard common sense, the power of seeing things as they really are, the spirit of compromise and of waiting on events; he was the very man to vindicate, with success, claims urged on behalf of a still wronged people, certain to be opposed by the party dominant in the State, and by powerful interests backed by Government and ultimately tending to agitation and trouble. It was, however, the distinctive mark of O'Connell's genius that he saw how in the existing condition of Catholic Ireland, and especially of the Irish Catholic priesthood—forces utterly disregarded since 1798—it was possible to combine a vast array of power, which might compel a settlement of the Catholic Question, and this too without violence, disorder and crime, by the mere organisation of a great popular movement. For the rest, O'Connell had strong Conservative sympathies; he hated the French Revolution and all its works; he condemned the United Irish, and the late agrarian risings; he had the instinct of the rights of property in the highest degree; and he had thus much in common with parts of Protestant Ireland, and especially with the Irish landed gentry, of whom he attracted numbers to his side, though it was his fate ultimately to injure the whole order.

O'Connell breathed a new life into the almost dying movement, in behalf of the Catholic claims, from the first moment. He made vehement appeals to the Catholic masses, in homely, coarse, often scurrilous language, required, he insisted, to rouse them up; he endeavoured to extend the Catholic Committee in Dublin, by affiliated Committees, throughout the country. His influence, however, was but little felt for a time; it was chiefly manifested, indeed, in the masterly craft with which he turned aside the arm of the law, directed against him by the Irish Government—especially in his evasion of a celebrated Act prohibiting assemblies of a representative kind, and aimed at the Catholic Convention of 1792-3,—and in his powerful speeches at the Bar, in defence of the Catholic Press, to which he had given a great impulse. The Catholic Question languished for some years; its prospects were gravely imperilled by dissensions, which divided the Catholic community in Great Britain and Ireland. So far back as 1799, in the negotiations before the Union, the Heads of the Catholic Church in Ireland had consented that the appointment of the Irish Bishops should be subject to a veto on the part of the Crown; the policy of the Holy See had, for many years, been in this direction, as was notably seen in the famous Concordat between the Church and the State in France; and in 1808, and again in 1814, two high personages supposed to express the sentiments of Pius VII, the Pope, unequivocally declared for the veto in Ireland. The Catholics of England and Scotland almost to a man, and a large majority of Irish Catholics of the higher orders, supported a measure, which they deemed a security for order and peace in the State; but O'Connell, and the whole Catholic Irish priesthood, denounced it as Erastianism of the very worst kind, and insisted that the Church—it received nothing from a State which had been for ages its deadly enemy—should retain the freedom which, in a qualified sense, it possessed, even under the Penal Code[1]. These differences of opinion almost caused a schism; the advocates of the Catholic Cause seemed to be in the position of a house divided against itself. Grattan—he supported the veto—brought forward the Catholic claims in 1809 and 1810; but as usual Parliament pronounced against him, though his eloquence never rose to a more imposing height. The Question, however, made some progress, especially as the fortunes of the war turned; it was treated by the Liverpool Ministry as an open question—a proof that its importance was not understood; but Canning and Castlereagh were in its favour. It obtained a majority in the House of Commons in 1813, the veto being part of the proposed scheme; but the Bill was destroyed in Committee, and was ultimately let drop.

The results, therefore, of our rule in Ireland, during the fifteen years that followed the Union, had been, if we speak generally, these. A system of severe repression had been established, and, for the most part, affected Catholic Ireland; there had been a large growth of Orangeism favoured by the State, and stirring the passions of the Irish Protestants; divisions of race and religion had probably widened; and Catholic Emancipation had been long postponed, nay, at the present moment, seemed all but hopeless. We must seek for the causes of this state of things, mainly in the feelings engendered in 1798, in the measures then adopted by the Irish Parliament, in the apprehensions produced by the war, and in the reactionary Tory spirit of the time; but something,

[1] Burke, it is evident from many passages in his writings, would have opposed the veto in Ireland.

too, must, certainly, be ascribed to narrow-minded bigotry in high places, to prejudice and ignorance in the Imperial Parliament, and to the want of insight of many of the statesmen in power. Signs of a change for the better were, however, visible; the Catholic Question would have made progress, but for disunion in the Catholic Body as a whole; in some respects distinct and hopeful improvements in Irish affairs had become manifest. The extension of trade, soon to become free, had greatly increased the wealth of Ulster; her linen manufacture made an immense advance; many tracts of the province were enriched; Belfast became a large port and a noble seat of commerce. The very district of Ireland which had been the centre of the rebellious movement of 1793-8, became, in its Teutonic and Protestant parts,—and these were in all respects dominant—attached by degrees to British rule and the Union; and this sentiment, ever since growing stronger, was promoted by a wise act of policy, the significance of which should have been more clearly perceived. The Irish Presbyterian Ministry had, for many years, received a small endowment from the State; this was considerably augmented after the Union, and so distributed that it enlisted the interests of the clergy on the side of the Government; and the Presbyterian Church, in Ulster, a most potent influence, has ever since been devotedly loyal, and a firm ally of the British connection, some proof at least what the result would have been had the Catholic Irish Church been treated in the same way, as was contemplated in 1799 and 1800. It should be added that, while the war continued, the wealth of Ireland generally was certainly increased. This comparative prosperity was, no doubt, to a great extent, fictitious; it largely depended on mere passing causes; the parade made of it by politicians, at the time, was another instance of the delusive optimism respecting Ireland, too often seen in opinion; and the whole social structure of Ireland, as was soon to appear, was resting on dangerous foundations, that were becoming worse. Still the influence of enlarged trade told; and as long as the high war prices lasted, Ireland made real material progress.

A short time after the close of the war a change in the financial system of Ireland was made on which it is necessary to say a word. Ireland, it was soon found, could not afford to pay the two-seventeenths of the expenditure, which, we have seen, had been the share arranged at the Union—the amount was certainly too large—; and the Debt of Ireland had, accordingly, increased much more quickly than that of Great Britain. It had been settled when the Union took place that when the Debts of the two countries and their contributions stood in the same ratio, they might be thrown, so to speak, into one; this event happened in 1816-17; the two Debts became a single National Debt; and the separate Irish Exchequer ceased to exist, being merged in the Imperial Exchequer. The Debt of Ireland before the Union was, proportionately, very much less than that of Great Britain; by the amalgamation of the two Debts, the two islands were made liable, apparently, to a common burden; and this has been denounced as a gross wrong, not only by clamorous Irish faction, but by more than one capable and well-informed thinker. It must be borne in mind, however, that, for more than thirty years after the consolidation of the twofold Debt, the taxation of Ireland was much lower than that of either England or Scotland; the burden, therefore, was not, in fact, common; and if a grievance existed in this matter, it was not nearly so great as has been often alleged. Soon after the middle of the present century the taxation of Ireland was enormously increased by the very Minister who has been held up to the mass of Irishmen as their best friend,—the notable champion of their rights and liberties; and it seems probable—this at least is the better opinion—that it has been, ever since, excessive, compared to that of Great Britain. On the other hand, the contributions to Irish demands and needs, made lavishly by the Imperial exchequer, often in the nature of free grants, and amounting to an immense sum, must be considered on the other side; and it is idle to argue that this is not to be taken into account. We cannot examine the problem further; it has been the subject of prolonged enquiries, one actually being held at this moment; all that can be said is that if we recollect the numberless, complex, and uncertain elements, which necessarily enter into the question, it will be difficult in the extreme ever to adjust the balance.

The close of the war was followed by a period of distress, felt severely in Ireland for a considerable time, accompanied by grave social evils, and culminating in famine in parts of the country. The contraction of the currency produced suffering in a community where there was little credit, where, as at all times, the middle class was weak, and where the mass of the people was a rent-paying peasantry. But the chief immediate cause of distress was the sudden collapse of prices, an inevitable incident of the peace, which affected in a great variety of ways the different classes connected with the soil, and disorganised relations, never well-ordered, and becoming, for some time, more and more vicious. The main structure of the landed system of Ireland continued to be what it had long been; except in a part of Ulster the owners and occupiers of the soil were parted by distinctions of blood and faith; even in Presbyterian Ulster there was a separation of this kind; absenteeism still, to a great extent, prevailed; middleman tenures, though fast diminishing, were still numerous; and the great body of the peasantry were poor and servile, especially in parts of Munster, and throughout Connaught. But a whole series of events had, for many years, concurred to increase the population in a remarkable degree, and to create an immense change in landed relations, of which the evil effects became but too apparent. The long war produced a demand for corn and meat, threw millions of acres into tillage, and covered them with a teeming peasantry living from hand to mouth. The corn laws of the Irish Parliament cooperated in the same direction; and this was an effect, too, of the Relief Act of 1793, which by giving the franchise to the Catholic masses encouraged their superiors to multiply them on the soil, in the position as it was called of "forty shilling freeholders," but really of dependent serfs. By these means the population, it is believed, more than doubled in less than forty years; and by the end of the war it had begun to press heavily on the resources of the land, if not yet so fearfully redundant as it was to become.

The economic consequences of this abnormal growth were that rents rose extravagantly in a short space of time, that the wages of labour immensely diminished, and that a huge mass of penury was thrown upon the land eking existence out on a most precarious root. The social consequences were also well marked; middleman tenures began to disappear quickly; but the landed gentry lived at a more expensive rate, and many became more harsh and strict in their dealings with the peasantry than their fathers had been. Things, however, went on tolerably well, so long as the high war prices lasted; Ireland certainly became, by degrees, more wealthy; what was rotten in her social condition hardly attracted notice. But when her resources were immensely reduced by the fall in value of nearly all her products, the evils of the increase of her population were most acutely felt; the misery of her backward districts became infinitely worse; hundreds of thousands of souls were brought to the verge of starvation; from 1818 to 1822, especially in the last named year, parts of some counties were afflicted by famine. Yet these were not the only, or perhaps the most grave results: rents suddenly fell with the fall of prices; a collapse of the wages of labour followed;

society from top to bottom became out of joint and disordered. Evictions took place in portentous numbers; thousands of the occupiers of the soil were driven from their homes, like the humble peasants of England in the sixteenth century; and widespread discontent filled whole parts of the country. One circumstance of extreme importance made this process of dispossession most harsh and iniquitous. It is a necessary incident of the Irish small farm system—the same fact has been seen in other lands—that the occupier makes the improvements on his farm; in fact creates what may be called its plant; this had become almost a universal custom with the extension of tillage and population; and in this way the tenant class in Ireland had acquired a kind of concurrent right in their holdings. It is perfectly true that, in the great mass of instances, the Irish landed gentry had respected this right—it curiously corresponded in some respects to the archaic joint ownership of Celtic tenure, that of the comparatively "free tenants"—; and in Ulster it had become a recognised form of property[1]. But too many exceptions to the usage were made; and as evictions multiplied in this period of distress, the rights of the Irish occupier were not seldom destroyed by extravagant, thoughtless, and needy landlords, especially of the middleman order. The evil consequences became at once manifest: the Whiteboy system arrayed a law of its own, to which the tenant appealed for aid against the law of the land he had always thought his foe; secret societies enforced their mandates by assassination and outrages of many kinds; and the divisions in society in Ireland opened wide again.

This season of distress was a kind of prelude to one far

[1] The Ulster custom of Tenant Right has been ascribed to the Celtic tenure of the "free tenants." This seems doubtful, for the custom prevailed most strongly in the colonised country. Still Ulster was colonised at a later period than the other provinces.

more terrible that was to come. The conduct of the people of England and of the men who ruled Ireland, at this crisis, must be rapidly glanced at. British charity flowed into the famine-stricken districts; Parliament held enquiries, and voted a large sum for relief. But no attempt was made to understand or lessen the deep-seated social ills of the country; they were, indeed, aggravated by bad laws and by bad statesmanship. A Poor Law should have been enacted to compel property to guard against an excessive population, ever in want, and to bear its already weighty burden; the middleman tenures should have been abolished, or made perpetual in some instances; above all, eviction should have been discouraged, and the rights of the occupier in the soil should have been made secure. Nothing, however, in these directions was done; Ireland had never been subject to the English Poor Law, and this, perhaps on account of its grave abuses, was not extended to her at this time; no changes were made in the middleman system, great and evident as were its numerous mischiefs; the process of wholesale eviction was not checked; the rights of the tenant were permitted to be wrongly confiscated in many thousand cases. Unhappily, on the contrary, the law of ejectment was made more expeditious and cheap than before, so that facilities for eviction were recklessly given; and in supposed respect for the rights of property, the rights of the tenant were sacrificed to the English law of tenure, imposed on Ireland—like other institutions of the kind—at no time in accord with Irish ideas, and absolutely unjust, in the landed relations, which had been growing up for some years in Ireland. Nor was this all; it was not perceived that Whiteboyism and agrarian trouble were symptoms of evil in the frame of society, and a kind of rude defence against social wrongs; the whole force of the law and of repressive measures, designed to deal with rebellious movements, was directed against "a system of wild justice,"—the phrase is

O'Connell's—which commanded sympathy; and the result was to quicken the angry discontent felt widely through the Irish community. England had, certainly, to complain at this time of the "Six Acts," and of other examples of bad government; but the case of Ireland was by many degrees worse.

During the first twenty years that followed the Union, Ireland was ruled almost wholly by English statesmen, nearly all men of an inferior order. "The English interest," in a word, became again dominant; "the Irish interest" was held of little account; and this is the more remarkable because Ireland had many public men of conspicuous parts. The change was very apparent in the Irish Bar, placed under English Chancellors for years; it may be said generally that, throughout this period, little regard was given to Irish opinion. To the mediocrities from England there were two exceptions, Sir Arthur Wellesley,—Irish by birth indeed, but English in blood, in faith, in ideas,—was Chief Secretary for Ireland for some months; and Peel from 1812 to 1818. Of Wellesley at the Castle little need be said; he was true to the narrow Toryism of the day; gave proof as always of sound common sense; and showed a strong aversion to the corrupt jobbing of administration in Irish affairs, an evil heritage of the past for which Englishmen are chiefly to blame. Peel, however, made a real mark in Ireland; his Irish career was notable for several reasons. He was bitterly denounced as "Orange Peel," by O'Connell, and his sympathies were on the side of Protestant Ireland; but he fully perceived the evils of the whole Orange system, its fiercely sectarian and factious temper, dangerous to public order, and even to the State; he kept it under, and gave it no countenance. But Peel's most remarkable work in Ireland—a social reform of the first importance—was the creation of the great Constabulary force, followed ultimately by the institution of paid magistrates, which has long formed the general police of the country. A measure of this kind was greatly needed; the old local Irish Constabulary was feeble and worthless; the military power in Ireland had performed, hitherto, many of the duties of a police with mischievous results; and if ordinary justice was well administered by the landed gentry of high degree, a large section of the magistracy was ignorant and corrupt, and represented Protestant Ascendency too faithfully on the Bench. The reform of Peel, fully developed in time, has contributed powerfully to preserve public peace and order throughout Ireland; to make the administration of justice more pure and impartial; to lessen one of the worst of Irish ills—the bad result of a lamentable past—the spirit of lawlessness, and of want of self-restraint, pervading unhappily many classes of men. Yet Peel was wanting in much, as a ruler in Ireland: he did nothing to mitigate the social mischiefs which grew out of Irish landed relations; he was the author, it is believed, of the cheap code of ejectment; he carried out the severest repression in protecting what he unwisely regarded as the rights of landlords. He was, also, an able opponent of the Catholic claims; in fact, he was a good specimen of a great middle class Englishman, conservative, prejudiced, slow to be moved, unable to grasp ideas that were foreign to him. He changed, indeed, his views as to Ireland more than once afterwards; but the change unfortunately was very late.

The policy adopted for Ireland, in these years of distress, once more illustrated the ignorance of British statesmen[1] as to the conditions of social life in Ireland; and showed very clearly how difficult it was to govern, with success, a country linked to Great Britain, but centuries behind it in general progress. An incident happened in 1821, not without interest to students

---

[1] This was often noticed by O'Connell, like so many of his predecessors.

of Irish History; George IV made an entry, in state, into
Dublin, the first King of England, since Richard II, who had
set foot in Ireland, except as an enemy. He was one of the
worst of British Sovereigns; and yet his presence was greeted
with tumultuous acclaim, a significant proof of what might
have been the effect of Kingship, on the spot, on Celtic
nature, always attached to persons rather than to institutions and
laws. During the period between 1813 and 1820, Grattan had
continued to advocate the Catholic claims, but under circumstances in many respects adverse. The Veto still divided
the whole Catholic Body; and Grattan was repudiated, as a
champion of their cause, by O'Connell, the priesthood, and
the mass of Catholic Ireland. Yet the high souled patriot
clung, as he said, "with desperate fidelity," to right and
justice; and though he never obtained a majority in behalf of
his demand, he lived to see that his adversaries were evidently
losing ground. He passed away quietly in 1820, a great
orator, a real statesman, a lover of his country, in the best
sense of the word; it deserves notice, too, that, in his later
years, he seems to have approved of the Union he had so
fiercely denounced. His successor was Plunket, greatly his
inferior in every way as a political figure, but a Parliamentary
speaker of the very first order, whose cogent logic and sedate
eloquence were more in harmony with a British audience than
the declamation and fiery passion of Grattan, injured as these
sometimes were, by a bad mannerism. By this time the
Catholic Question was gradually making way in British
opinion; it was ably sustained by the united Whig party,
which was slowly regaining its place in the State. Nevertheless, though Plunket, in 1821, succeeded in carrying a Bill
through the House of Commons, in favour of the Catholic
claims, this was thrown out by the House of Lords; and as
provisions for the veto had been attached to it, the measure
was condemned by O'Connell and his adherents.

If the Catholic Question had, by this time, distinctly made an advance in England, in Ireland it seemed as if it had gone back. O'Connell, indeed, had never lost heart; he continued to address meetings and to give effect to "agitation," a word he had made his own; but the "Veto" had greatly weakened his efforts; and not to speak of numbers of Liberal Protestants, the Catholic nobles and gentry held aloof from him. With his singular fertility of resource, however, he formed, at last, a plan of operations, so to speak, which ere long combined all Catholic Ireland into an overwhelming popular movement, and made Catholic Emancipation a necessity of the time. With a few followers, for the most part young men of the gown, he created in 1823 the Catholic Association, a League organised on a very different model from the Conventions and the Committees of the past. O'Connell had always looked to the Catholic priesthood; he found in them most able and eager allies in furthering the great combination he had in view. A complete change had passed over this order of men, since the days when they were only able to do their office in secrecy and stealth under the Penal Code; and when, trained as they usually had been under the old Church of France, they had acquired habits of slavish respect for authority. The Irish Parliament had given them the College of Maynooth; as Wolfe Tone had predicted, their education at this place had inspired them with strong Irish sympathies; they were chiefly drawn from the ranks of the higher peasantry; and they had no liking for British rule in Ireland, or for the rights of Irish Protestant landlords. They were, in fact, animated by the spirit of the old Confederates of 1643; and their Church, besides, had become a real power in the State, spreading its fine edifices far and wide, very different from the miserable chapels of a century before. O'Connell had soon drawn the priesthood to him; but the problem was how to make their influence tell decisively on the Catholic masses, and to attract these in full strength towards the cause. To attain this object the priests were engaged to appeal to their flocks in every parish, to make Catholic Emancipation an article of faith, to unite all Catholics in the demand in the name of religion. But O'Connell felt that this was not enough: a social movement was to sustain the political; and general and earnest efforts were to be made to redress or to mitigate the wrongs of the Catholic peasantry. For this purpose a fund was to be raised by subscriptions, however small, from every part of Ireland; and the Catholic Association, backed by a popular Press, and working, through its societies, in every county, was to leave nothing undone to expose acts of injustice, to defeat the process of ejectment in the Courts of Law, to protect, by all means in its power, the Catholic occupier of the soil.

The movement, inaugurated in this way, went on with extraordinary force and speed. O'Connell proved a tower of strength in himself; his energy, his daring, his masterly skill in combining arrangements, in thwarting the attempts of officials eager to bring him within the meshes of the law, and in winning the hearts of thousands by his stirring appeals, had effects that quickly became manifest. Yet the priesthood played, perhaps, a more striking part; their immense spiritual authority was everywhere employed to extend what was preached as a kind of crusade; and the Catholic Association had, in a few months, active centres in every part of Ireland drawing into their midst the humbler Catholics to a man. All Catholic Ireland felt the impulse; the aristocratic classes, lukewarm before, felt inspired by a great Tribune with sudden confidence; the universal support the movement obtained was seen in the vast sum of the "Catholic Rent," the penny contributions of distressed millions. Not the least patent of the influences that gained the people was, as O'Connell had foreseen, the successful efforts made to defend the peasantry from acts of wrong: bad landlords were baffled by ingenious lawyers, or denounced by village orators and in county newspapers; Orangeism on the Bench was unmasked and condemned; and in this way evictions were very largely checked, and instances of oppression made less common. The most significant feature of the whole movement was this: the passions of great bodies of men had been aroused; but O'Connell and the priesthood held them in the leash; Catholic Ireland obeyed its leader's command, "shed not a drop of blood, it will only help the enemy[1]"; and at his bidding agrarian disorder and crime, before rampant, almost disappeared. Prosecutions of O'Connell proved idle as the wind; an Act specially passed to put the Association down was eluded as usual, and made impotent. Canning said, with truth, that within two years, an "Imperium in Imperio" had been formed in Ireland, more powerful than the State, and more generally obeyed. Yet, at this conjuncture, when it seemed probable, that he could secure emancipation almost on his own terms, O'Connell gave a signal proof of the spirit of compromise, which was one of his distinctive qualities. A Bill, drawn it is believed by his hand, and conceding most of the Catholic claims, passed the House of Commons in 1825; but it was accompanied by what were known as its "wings," proposals to make a provision for the Irish Catholic clergy, and for disfranchising the peasant masses—the "forty shilling freeholders" before referred to—for their power, it was perceived, might become dangerous. O'Connell assented to these measures, though, hitherto, he had been opposed to them;

---

[1] "The red right hand of God's avenging justice," said O'Connell in one of his harangues to the peasantry, "hangs over the land of the murderer." Compare this with Parnell's cynical phrase, "crime is unnecessary"; and compare the attitude of the Catholic Association, with the Reign of Terror promoted by the Land and the National Leagues of late years.

but the whole scheme was rejected by the House of Lords, one of the most unfortunate decisions that was ever made.

The fate of these measures, which, had they passed, might have changed the character of subsequent Irish History, only urged O'Connell to redoubled efforts. With much adroitness he appealed to the English Dissenters, announcing that he was fighting their cause—the Repeal of the Test Act was at hand; he sought aid from the Irish emigrants, already numerous, in the United States; he made a profound impression on Catholic France, some of whose leading men openly expressed their sympathy. Meanwhile the agitation at home became more formidable and irresistible week after week; and by the close of 1827 the Association had not only become the dominant force in Irish affairs, but was enabled successfully to defy the Government. The ascendency of O'Connell was, in fact, complete; many circumstances had concurred to extend his influence and to urge the Catholic Question forward. He had called, not in vain, on the Liberal Irish Protestants, the sons of the adherents of Grattan in the Irish Parliament; they had zealously advocated the Catholic claims; with their assistance he had wrested several seats from the Ascendency party at the General Election of 1826. Lord Wellesley, too, a real and far-seeing statesman, had been Viceroy since 1821; he not only favoured the Catholic cause, but pronounced for more than one of the social reforms which Peel and others had deemed impossible; and he had set his face steadily throughout the country against Orangeism and its violent partisans, who kicked fiercely, but to no purpose, against the pricks, by public meetings, wild clamour, and even riots.

The occasion ere long came which suddenly brought to a head a crisis evidently for some time impending. Mr Vesey Fitzgerald accepted office in the Wellington Administration in 1828; he was obliged to seek re-election for the County of

Clare. He was an amiable, enlightened, and able man; his father had been an ally of Grattan's; Catholic Emancipation had no more loyal friend. But the time had come for a trial of strength between the Association and the forces opposed to it; O'Connell, though with reluctance, resolved to stand against Fitzgerald for the representation of Clare, though as a Catholic he could not enter Parliament. The contest that followed is not yet forgotten; it marked a turn in the course of Irish history. The landed gentry of the county took the side of Fitzgerald to a man; they canvassed for him with assiduous zeal, for they resented, not unreasonably, what they thought the intrusion of a stranger backed by a dictatorial League; they called upon their submissive dependents for their votes; they never doubted but that, as had been their wont, these vassals would flock to the poll for their candidate. But a moral change had passed over the Irish peasant; the word of the Association had gone forth; the "Liberator's" influence swept opposition away; the priests of Clare proclaimed from a hundred altars that the struggle was one for the faith of God; the forty shilling freeholders broke away, in one mass, from their lords; and O'Connell was returned in an easy triumph.

A Revolution in Ireland seemed now at hand; the Catholic Association ruled five-sixths of the island; it was clearly perceived that the great body of the peasantry would not obey their superiors, and was eager to follow the example set by Clare. Opinion in Ireland, too, there can be little doubt, had even among the chief part of the Protestants inclined for some time towards the Catholic claims; an immense meeting of the landed gentry had declared for them; their opponents for the most part were Orangemen and their partisans. The representatives of Ireland, indeed, did not fully reflect this sentiment in the Imperial Parliament; but though in numbers they were quite sufficient, they were largely composed of Tory nominees, and of men from Ulster of extreme Protestant views; the Liberal party, if very able, was relatively small. (Peel and Wellington however saw that the time had come when Catholic Emancipation could no longer be deferred; after a show of opposition on the part of the King, Parliament gave its assent in 1829 to a measure of relief which ought to have been an essential part of the Union a generation before, and which—though probably, in any case, it could not have been very long delayed—was actually obtained by an agitation which had convulsed Ireland, and had made too evident the weakness of British rule. The galling disabilities of the Irish Catholics, left existing under the Act of 1793, were finally removed by this concession; and Catholic Ireland was, for the first time, admitted fully within the pale of the State, and, with scarcely an exception, was placed on a level of political rights with Protestant Ireland. The full policy which Pitt had contemplated was not, however, carried out; no provision was made for the Irish Catholic clergy; above all there was no commutation of the tithe. The boon of Emancipation, too, was grudgingly given; Peel and Wellington yielded with bad grace; O'Connell was not permitted to take the seat he had won; he was not even raised to the rank of King's Counsel, to which he had been made eligible by the late measure. And if, as is most probable, it had become necessary to disfranchise the forty-shilling freeholders, and to deprive masses of the peasants of votes unwisely given them many years before, this was an unfortunate accompaniment of a remedial policy; it bore too much the look of angry revenge.

Catholic Emancipation was a measure of justice; it was certainly attended with good results. A Revolution in Ireland was perhaps stayed by it; it may have made Irish agitation less violent and dangerous than it would have been otherwise; it contributed to some important reforms. But it was a measure of justice far too long delayed; and evil consequences have flowed from it, not only for Ireland, but for the whole Empire. Time was soon to show how unfortunate it was that it was not accompanied by an endowment for the Irish Catholic priesthood, and that the Anglican Church in Ireland was allowed to retain the wrongful and oppressive claim to an uncommuted tithe. But worse and more permanent ills followed: Catholic Emancipation, extorted as it was, added to the discord of race and faith in Ireland; the agitation through which O'Connell triumphed deprived property of its legitimate influence, broke up the structure of Irish society, made ruins, but put nothing in their place. It increased the aversion to British rule and law, inherited by the peasantry through ages of wrongs; it made them dangerously conscious of their power. It also enthroned faction in the Imperial Parliament, to which statesmen have often most unwisely yielded; it has tended to make the Irish representation a reproach and a byeword. Above all it gave immense authority in the State to a mass of ignorant and extreme opinion, not tempered by middle class ideas, swayed by sacerdotal or worse influence, and often extravagant and unjust; and this has repeatedly had disastrous effects, not only in purely Irish affairs, but on the course of the national policy.

There is much in the conduct of affairs in Ireland, from 1800 to 1829, which impartial history regrets and condemns. The Irish Catholic leaders were wronged; Protestant Ascendency secured a new lease of power; encouragement to Orangeism was unwisely given; severe measures of repression were continued too long, and administered in a reckless fashion; the necessity of social reforms was not perceived, especially in the sphere of landed relations; a bad landed system was made worse by bad laws; the Catholic Question was put back for years; Catholic Emancipation was too late, was ungracefully conceded, and under the worst conditions. The train of evils that followed has been made manifest; in this whole course of policy we see proof of prejudice and narrow-mindedness in the Imperial Parliament, and of ignorance and want of sympathy in British statesmen. Yet the circumstances of the period must be taken into account; it was an age of war, reaction, and hard Tory ideas; if Ireland had cause of complaint, England had cause also; the time was unpropitious to test the Union and its effects. Nor is there any reason to suppose that Grattan's Parliament would have governed Ireland better, or even nearly as well: from 1782 to 1789, when the opportunity really offered, it set its face against every reform in Ireland; its measures from 1795 to 1799, especially during the rebellion of 1798, were atrocious, and marked by the rage of a dominant caste. It is a most significant fact—it cannot be got over—that, from 1800 to 1829, there was no movement in Ireland against the Union, nothing more than a few weak protests; Grattan accepted the Union, and so did the whole Whig party, its vehement adversaries in 1799-1800; this is almost a conclusive proof that Ireland was more contented after the Union than she had been before. On the other hand, notwithstanding a season of terrible distress, Ireland certainly made material progress in the thirty years that followed the Union; above all, Protestant Ulster became devotedly loyal, having previously been on the verge of rebellion; the forces of Irish disaffection were extremely weakened; and it must be fairly added that the mind of England had, however slowly, begun to turn towards Ireland. Looking at the subject from an Imperial point of view, the Union may have saved these islands from conquest; a single Parliament and a centralised Government were required to conduct the war with Napoleon; after this experience England can hardly doubt that she must keep Ireland in her own hands.

The long reign of Toryism, and of reaction in the State, was about to pass away in 1829. England, strong, masterful, ruled by ideas in many respects inapplicable to Irish affairs, was entering on a path of great general reform; she could only attain her ends through Parliamentary government, and the ascendency of the party of progress. Ireland was weak, divided, infinitely behind Great Britain; her whole social system was deeply diseased, especially in what related to the land; her population was becoming alarmingly dense; if some of her grievances were fully perceived, others were less intelligible to English statesmen. And her Catholic millions, serfs for ages, untrained to freedom and self-government, had been suddenly invested with power, which was practically in the hands of a great demagogue, and of a priesthood which carried out his commands. In these circumstances, was it not probable that many Irish reforms would be ill conceived, would be delayed and injured by the strife and the spirit of party? Was it not probable that Ireland might become the battle ground of contending English factions, and, in the result, might gravely suffer? Was it not probable that what was most peccant in the structure of her society would not be understood, or would be understood when it was too late, and that immense evils might be the consequence, even though much had been done for her by a well-meaning and enlightened policy? And might not the enfranchisement of Catholic Ireland, as affairs stood, lead to extravagances and mischiefs of many kinds, injurious to Great Britain and Ireland alike, and attended with numerous and dangerous ills? Time was to give an answer, at least in part, to questions even yet not finally answered.

CHAPTER X.

FROM 1829 TO 1868.

State of England in 1832. The Irish Reform Act. O'Connell declares for Repeal of the Union. Failure of the movement. The Question in the House of Commons. Great speech of Peel. The war against Irish Tithe. A measure of commutation passed after a long delay. The Irish Anglican Church. Partial reform. National education in Ireland. Vices of the system. The Irish Administration of the Melbourne Government. O'Connell abandons Repeal. His influence in the Government. Drummond. His authority in Irish affairs. Extension of the Constabulary force. Orangeism discountenanced. Bureaucratic rule of the Castle. The Irish Poor Law. The Irish Municipal Reform Act. The second administration of Peel. O'Connell and Repeal. The Monster Meetings. Trial of O'Connell. His release. The Young Ireland Party. Put down by O'Connell and the priesthood. Significance of this. The increased Maynooth grant. The Queen's Colleges. The Devon Commission. The Report. The Famine, 1845, 1846, 1847. Conduct and policy of Peel and Russell Governments. World-wide Charity. The rising of 1848. Smith O'Brien. John Finton Lalor. The Irish Exodus. Immense results. Visit of the Queen in 1849. The Encumbered Estates Acts. Their mischievous effects. Condition of Ireland after the Famine. Optimism. Superficial prosperity. Dangerous symptoms. State of Irish Letters. Art and Science. The Fenian rising of 1867. Reflections. Conclusion.

THE agitation for Reform in 1831–32 shook society in England to its depths; revolution, perhaps, was only averted by the good sense of the aristocracy, and of a well ordered people, trained for centuries in self-government. The time, both before and after 1832, was unpropitious to Irish affairs; the attention of British statesmen was chiefly directed to the condition of England, and of our foreign relations. The Irish Reform Act added a few members to the Irish representation in the House of Commons; but it placed the franchise on rather a high level; and, after the extinction of the forty-shilling freeholds, it was supposed that the Catholic masses would lose much of their power. The first part of Lord Grey's Ministry was chiefly remarkable, as respects Ireland, for a strenuous but unsuccessful effort made by O'Connell to arouse popular feeling against what he called "the accursed Union." He may have clung to the faith of his youth, and thought the measure a disastrous event; but personal motives certainly concurred; he had resented the petty affronts of 1829; he had supported the administration at the crisis of Reform with great ability and important results; yet he found himself excluded from office in the State, nay the Emancipation Act made a dead letter, as regards the demands of Catholic Ireland. His agitation for Repeal, however, completely failed, though he had drawn into the House of Commons a train of followers, nominees of his own and of the Catholic priesthood, a number that was soon to increase; it was notable chiefly for his characteristic baffling of the law, and his savage quarrels with Mr Stanley, the Chief Secretary. He brought the subject before the House of Commons in 1834; but he gained the vote of only a single English member; the occasion was most worthy of notice for the conclusive proof afforded in the debate that the wealth of Ireland, faulty as was the state of her social life, had been steadily on the increase. The speech of Peel was perhaps the ablest defence of the Union ever made in the Imperial Parliament; and O'Connell—the fact is of great significance—let the question drop for a series of years.

At this period, indeed, the mind of Catholic Ireland had

been concentrated on a very different matter; a wild movement attended by a frightful outbreak of crime had been sweeping over large parts of the country. As we have seen, the Anglican Church had retained its tithe; the commutation, advocated by Pitt and Grattan half a century before, had not been carried out; a feeble attempt in that direction, recently made, had practically had hardly any results. As the population of Ireland increased and the land became more and more divided into little tillage holdings, the grievance of the impost was more acutely felt; it was in fact a gross wrong, which the Catholic occupier of the soil, made aware of his power by the events of late years, could not be expected patiently to endure. The collection of the tithe, too, had for some time been made more onerous, in not a few instances, by Protestant clergymen of extreme views; and Orange faction had given them sinister support. O'Connell pronounced against tithe, with no uncertain voice; the Catholic priesthood, angry perhaps that the State had made no provision for them, came again enthusiastically to his aid; the power of the Catholic Association, though nominally suppressed, was arrayed to some extent on behalf of the new cause. It should be observed however that, on this occasion, O'Connell and his satellites were not able to keep the forces of disorder down, as had been the case from 1823 to 1829; indeed O'Connell made scarcely an attempt of the kind. The Catholic peasantry took the matter into their own hands; the payment of tithes was resisted in many counties; the efforts of the law and of a strong government proved utterly unable to enforce payment. The Tithe War, as it was not improperly called, raged with little intermission for several years; and in two or three places bloody encounters occurred between the Constabulary and the half-armed levies they met. But these were not the worst symptoms; the crusade against Tithe was backed by the Whiteboy system, at times quiescent, but never defunct; and the machinery of that organisation of crime was put in force to uphold the movement. Secret societies, spreading far and wide, sent forth their mandates; assassinations and deeds of outrage rapidly multiplied; and the arm of the law was paralysed, in whole districts, by intimidation and the refusal of juries to convict. In 1833, there were 9000 cases of crimes of this type; political agitation had again been sustained by agrarian trouble.

A measure of repression, the most severe perhaps of any enacted in Irish affairs, was passed to put down this frightful state of things; it was opposed by O'Connell with great power and skill, and, indeed, proved the forerunner of events that led to the fall of the Grey Cabinet; but it was completely successful in its immediate object; the reign of criminal anarchy soon came to an end. The wrong of the Tithe, however, was at last recognised, unhappily owing to the effects of a social conflict; and measures were adopted to redress a grievance, which ought not to have lasted down to the nineteenth century. Incidents followed that showed, only too plainly, how a reform for Ireland, in itself well designed, might be delayed for years, in the existing state of politics, and be made into a pretext for the mere strife of faction. The question of the tithe was mixed with the question of appropriating to the use of the State part of the excessive revenue of the Established Church in Ireland; this caused the resignation of Mr Stanley in 1834; and a Bill proposed by Peel, in his first short Ministry, for the simple Commutation of the Irish Tithe, was defeated by the Whig opposition of the day, because the principle of appropriation was not found in it. When this party move had driven Peel from office, the two questions were again combined by the Government of Lord Melbourne in 1836; but the policy of appropriation was rejected by the House of Lords; and ultimately the Melbourne Ministry gave it up. A measure for the Commutation of the tithe alone, the famous "Appropriation Clause" being left out, was passed by Parliament in 1838; and justice in this matter was done to Ireland, but justice deferred too long, and after disastrous events. The reform effected, nevertheless, was excellent and wise; the tithe was commuted into a rent charge, a quarter less in amount than the total impost; the owners of land, and not its occupants, were rendered liable to the payment of the substituted charge. By these means the Irish Catholic peasantry were relieved from a most odious tribute to an alien Church; complaints on this subject were never heard again; the Irish Established Church, in fact, obtained a new lease of existence.

The position, however, of that Church had attracted attention, long before this time, especially among English Liberal statesmen. Superficially it had undergone considerable change, since we have seen what it was in the eighteenth century. It had been graced by some very able Divines, if by no prelate who can be named with Berkeley; it had been almost completely freed from the moral scandals which had been its reproach; its ministers, as a class, were good and amiable men, in many cases worthy country gentlemen. Its discipline, too, had been greatly improved; it had felt, through all its parts, the beneficent influence of the religious opinion of the nineteenth century, requiring, as it did, a high standard of clerical duty. But its essential nature had remained the same; it was still the institution of a conquering race planted in the midst of a conquered people, a spiritual, but a hostile, watchtower; it possessed great revenues to little purpose; it was "a lodge in a garden of cucumbers," that bore no fruit; it had not much authority over its own flocks; it was an object of hatred to the Catholic priesthood, and of the fierce detestation of the Catholic peasant as long as it continued to exact tithe. Through the effects, besides, of the Evangelical English movement, it had become somewhat rudely proselytising of late; and yet as a Church it had not fulfilled its mission; it was no living image of its Divine Master; its high places were filled with sons of the great landed gentry, who looked to the Castle rather than to Heaven; and its revenues had been misapplied and wasted. No wonder then that, in 1831–2, it became the object of persistent attack; but the Liberal opinion of that day never contemplated Disestablishment in any sense; it aimed only at a reform of the Church; as it was, indeed, this so-called sacrilege was the origin of the great Oxford Tractarian movement. The Irish Establishment was deprived of ten sees, and its revenues were redistributed, to some extent, in order to make it more efficient, by a measure which passed, with little difficulty, in 1833, the principle of appropriation not being pressed; and this, and the far greater measure, commuting the tithe, were the only changes attempted for a long series of years. The maintenance of the Anglican Church in Ireland had, indeed, we have seen, been made a part of the Union; but though the compact was respected for more than half a century, the end of the institution came at last, as had been foreseen by most thoughtful minds. To describe the process is not within our limits; Disestablishment, we shall only remark, was not accompanied, as it ought to have been, by the provision for the Irish Catholic priesthood, which Pitt, Grattan, and many of their best successors in England and Ireland had always had in view.

Another important measure of reform for Ireland was carried into effect by Lord Grey's Government (1830–34). The "English Schools" of the Tudor period, made appendages of the Established Church, had disappeared into the night of the past; the Charter Schools, worthy of the Penal Code, maintained an existence only in name. Peel had appointed a Commission, in 1812, to consider Irish Education of the primary kind; but its labours had, virtually, had no results; and Irish Primary Education, as to the work of the State, had fallen into the hands of a Society, not without merit, but

Protestant in its complexion, and disposed to make proselytes. Catholic Ireland justly resented this: and, meanwhile, the children of the dense Catholic masses grew up, to a great extent, in ignorance, though, be it said to their parents' honour, petty or "hedge" schools had been set up at their expense in many places, and had thousands of scholars. Mr Stanley established in Ireland, in 1831-4, the system of Primary Education long known as National; it was founded on principles in accord with the rather shallow Liberal ideas of the day. The children of the humbler classes were to be instructed in schools of the State; for secular education they were to be taught together; they were to receive religious education apart, from pastors of their respective communions. This system, largely modified indeed, has been in existence for more than sixty years; Parliament has lavished enormous free grants upon it; and unquestionably it has had a large measure of success, for the children of a people that sat in darkness have had their eyes opened to the light of knowledge. But the instruction afforded has not been very good; except in parts of Ulster it is not popular; the principle on which it rests was never accepted by the clergy of the Irish Anglican Church; it is secretly disliked by the Catholic priesthood; it is not in harmony with the convictions of five-sixths of the Irish community. It is, in fact, a principle which degrades spiritual things, and makes them secondary, so to speak, to temporal; it sacrifices the Divine to the human; it shocks the religious, if you will, the superstitious conscience. After years of contention and angry bickering, the system actually in force at present, is this: the principle of "united secular education, and separate religious education" has been tacitly given up in most places; and of the thousands of National Schools in Ireland, the great majority are of a sectarian character, that is, the scholars are all Catholics or all Protestants. But the system is still pervaded by the original principle:—the schools are sectarian with a conscience clause, as it is called; the Bible cannot be read in a Protestant school; in a Catholic school there can be no Catholic emblem. The immense majority of the Irish people will never approve of this state of things at heart, though it has found favour in the sight of Presbyterian Ireland[1].

O'Connell's attitude to the Ministry of Lord Grey had been repeatedly one of fierce hostility; and this had contributed, with other causes, to retard the march of reforms in Ireland. The situation had changed when Lord Melbourne came into office (1835); his Government was weak in England and Scotland; but O'Connell's following, known as his "Tail," had grown into very large proportions; and the Minister sought the great Irishman's support. A compact angrily denounced at the time, but hardly to be condemned by History, was made between the Whigs and O'Connell; its terms were of most marked significance. The Government placed the lion's share of Irish patronage in O'Connell's hands, and undertook to further Irish reforms; O'Connell in turn gave them the numerous votes at his command, and formally abandoned the demand for Repeal, a circumstance that must be borne in mind in considering his conduct as respects the Union. The period that followed was, on the whole, one of just and enlightened rule in Ireland, and of legislation on the side of progress, if this was somewhat feeble, and not marked by peculiar insight. O'Connell did not abuse his trust; the appointments he practically made were nearly always good, especially his appointments to places at the Bar; he gave proof of discernment, fair play, and a sincere regard for the maintenance of the just

---

[1] Burke, the deepest of political thinkers, especially on Irish affairs, has over and over again insisted that education in Ireland should be, above all things, religious. He would have condemned the principle of the National system. Ireland, as a whole, would wish Primary Education to be what is called Denominational.

rights of property, in the great but difficult position which he held. It may be said of him that Protestant Ireland had little reason to complain of his acts, and that Catholic Emancipation was made, for the first time, a reality by him in Irish affairs; this was certainly one of the best episodes in his career. In this policy he was loyally upheld by Lord Mulgrave, the Lord Lieutenant, and by the Chief Secretary, Lord Morpeth; and he had the assistance of Catholic law officers of great powers, who did much to make Irish administration equal and just, without regard to distinctions of race and faith.

The Under-Secretary Drummond, too, played a conspicuous part at the Castle, in these years, though his influence on events, great as it certainly was, has been somewhat unduly magnified, and its effects have not been in all respects beneficent. Drummond was a Scotchman of fine parts and of an iron will, in his views rather a hard doctrinaire, but able and gifted with the faculty of command. His conception of the true policy for Ireland was, to make the supremacy of a just administration universally felt; to hold the balance even between contending factions and sects; to do right to Protestant and Catholic alike; and, in order to further these great objects, to extend and strengthen the power of the central government. Much that he accomplished deserves high praise, if his conduct was not always right or judicious. His authority was soon felt by the men in power; and in conjunction with them he laboured, with success, to give Catholic Emancipation real effect, to make the Irish Catholic feel that the State was his friend, to keep Protestant ascendency, and its excesses, under. He struck a blow at Orangeism, its adherents, and its evil works, which may be said to have been almost fatal; the organisation and influence of that bad system, of lawless association, have never since been so strong. Yet Drummond, unquestionably, was too disposed to identify the great body of the Irish landed gentry with Protestant ascendency in a bad sense; his frequent lectures to them were not wise; he was not just to the order, as a whole, especially to its more prominent members. The principal achievement, however, of this remarkable man was to make a large increase in the Constabulary force established by Peel many years before, and to extend the arrangements for paid magistrates; and he set the system, in part, on a new footing, by throwing the appointments largely open to Catholics. By these means Ireland was virtually placed under the control of a highly organised police, possessing immense authority and administrative powers; and this development of Peel's policy has had, but to greater extent, the effects it produced from the first. The Constabulary force and the paid magistrates have done wonders in maintaining order, and in keeping lawlessness of all kinds down; the system has gained the confidence of all classes; it is not too much to say that it has held up to Irishmen the example of a high standard of well performed duty, the value of which has been very great. Yet disadvantages are to be set against this: the system, as, indeed, was Drummond's object, has enormously increased the power of the Castle; but, in combination with other causes, it has greatly diminished the influence of the Irish landed gentry, and this has been, on the whole, unfortunate. It has tended to strengthen in Ireland "the English interest," and to make the Central Government, more and more, what it has always been, a bureaucratic *régime*.

The Melbourne Government deserves the credit of settling the great Question of the Tithe in Ireland (1838). Its leaders however, like almost all the English statesmen of that generation, did not attempt to apply a remedy to the grave evils of Irish landed relations; they were certainly not fully alive to them. These relations had, in some respects, improved; but in others they were growing distinctly worse; we shall briefly examine the subject afterwards, when the attention of Parliament was directed to it, unhappily at an untoward season. The Melbourne Administration however, possibly because the new English Poor Law was coming into effect, did really see what was the worst feature, perhaps, in the structure of social life in Ireland, the presence of a huge population on the soil, and did try to make a change for the better. A late Report had disclosed the appalling fact that two millions and a half of beings in Ireland were sunk in the lowest depths of wretchedness; and society was injured in all its parts, owing to the destructive burden of this vast mass of penury. All the evils we have noticed before, rents forced up, wages beaten down, millions squatted on the land in little patches, and the potato made the only staff of life, had been increasing to a marked extent; there had been no actual dearth since 1822, but this state of things was fast becoming dangerous. The Melbourne Government gave Ireland (1838), what should have been given a century before, a Poor Law framed on the English model; and this measure, asserting as it did the principle that Property is bound to support Poverty, and above all, to provide against its excess, has ultimately had very good results. But it was introduced, as it were, at the eleventh hour; its immediate effects could not be great; and it utterly failed, as we shall see, to deal with the calamity of a few years afterwards, which involved Ireland in a great catastrophe. The last important measure of the Melbourne Ministry was a well-designed but imperfect reform of Municipal Government throughout Ireland (1840). The great majority of the Irish Corporate Bodies were the rulers of the small Parliamentary boroughs, originally set up by James I, and of boroughs of a similar class; they had become centres of Protestant ascendency of the worst kind; and they were very properly swept away. But Municipal Government was not placed on a popular basis in the great towns of Ireland, largely owing to the opposition of the Tories of the time; and a reform in this respect has to be yet accomplished. It is scarcely necessary, however, to remark that municipal life in Ireland can never be as powerful and free as it is in Great Britain; the differences between the two countries make this impossible.

The policy and the measures of the Melbourne Government had certainly accomplished much good in Ireland, if their shortcomings have been long ago apparent. The Union was very decidedly strengthened; Catholic Emancipation was effectually carried out; especially all orders and classes of men were made to feel they were under an equal law, a result for Irishmen of supreme importance. The Ministry, however, weak in Great Britain from the first, became year after year weaker; it ultimately sank into mere impotence. The causes of this were threefold: the people of England and Scotland were eager for reforms, which the Government did not try to undertake, and resented the time devoted to Irish affairs; the country was rallying around Peel, the great leader of an Opposition of formidable power; and the conduct of O'Connell, and of the men in his train, had, in Parliament and elsewhere, given extreme offence. The representation of Ireland, indeed, had, by this time, become much degraded; the "Tail" of O'Connell was composed of very inferior men, mere instruments of his will, without station or wealth, and thrust into the House of Commons by himself and the Irish priesthood; O'Connell had, over and over again, shocked Englishmen by his abusive language; and all this had caused very general disgust.

The Melbourne Ministry was swept away in 1841; but "the Irish difficulty," to use his own words, confronted Peel almost from the outset, though he was at the head of a very strong Government. The Whig Opposition, Catholic Ireland, and O'Connell loudly pronounced against him; and he was greatly hampered by Orange partisans, and by the supporters of Protestant ascendency throughout Ireland, who persisted in seeing their champion in him. He had really no sympathy with men of this type; but he was not quite free from the associations of the past; and some appointments he made were supposed to indicate that he was returning to the exclusive and sectarian Irish Tory policy, which had prevailed before 1829. O'Connell instantly seized the occasion; declared that "justice to Ireland" had become impossible; and, for the second time, made an effort to combine a great popular movement against the Union.

Whether this crusade was a mere party move, or whether the Irish leader had faith in it, and believed that he could achieve Repeal, is, perhaps, impossible to determine; but the circumstances point to the first conclusion. O'Connell once more brought into play the forces which had proved irresistible in 1824-28: he called on the priesthood to rally around him; he appealed to the Catholic millions to join the cause; he adjured all Irishmen to remember the days of the Volunteers, and to strike for the free Parliament of 1782. The powerful, well-contrived, and far-spreading machinery of the Catholic Association was again employed; the Catholic Rent was again collected; and the agitation against the Union, with hundreds of priests at its head, was made, to a certain extent, a religious cry, and was maintained throughout the country by numerous bodies of men affiliated to the great central League of Repeal. The movement, organised and directed in this way, assumed in 1843 gigantic proportions; Catholic and Celtic Ireland flocked around O'Connell, and especially around its sacerdotal leaders; "monster meetings," as they were fitly called, attended by hundreds of thousands of peasants, were assembled, in different places, in the southern provinces; and O'Connell addressed them in impassioned language, not seldom of all but a treasonable kind. Yet this agitation had nothing like the strength of that which had caused the Catholic claims to prevail; and it was resisted by forces which made it hopeless. Very different from what happened from 1813 to 1828,

England and Scotland condemned it to a man; it was discountenanced by more than one Irish Catholic bishop, and by a certain number of the Irish Catholic clergy. But above all—and this was the most marked distinction—the property of Ireland and her intelligence were almost wholly arrayed against it; Liberal Protestants of the school of Grattan agreed, in this matter, with extreme Orangemen, and with the great body of the Catholic gentry; in fact the best and most vigorous elements in Irish social life were thoroughly combined to support the Union. The real lesson of the movement of 1843 was, in truth, this, that Irish Nationality, a vain phantom that never existed in any true sense, was, in the eyes of the Irish Catholic Celts and their leaders, what it had been in those of Rinuccini and his priests, and that Catholic ascendency was not to be endured by the Ireland of loyalty, substance, and thought.

It may be affirmed with certainty that an armed rising was never within O'Connell's mind; but the Government took only due precautions, in subjecting the use of arms to close restrictions, and in sending an additional military force to Ireland. Peel confronted the movement with calm steadfastness; declared that he preferred civil war to Repeal; and when a great monster meeting had approached Dublin, caused O'Connell and several of his lieutenants to be placed under arrest. The trial that followed was, in some respects, unfortunate; the foremost man of Catholic Ireland was arraigned before a Court of Protestant judges, one, notoriously, an extreme partizan; Catholic jurors were excluded from the jury list, through a mistake not discovered to this day; and the proceedings wore a look of real injustice. But the wrong that was done was redressed by the House of Lords, adverse in politics as it was to the accused; the omission in the jury list was sternly condemned; O'Connell and his associates were at once set free. The movement against the Union, nevertheless, had been completely stayed; the whole agitation speedily collapsed; O'Connell practically abandoned Repeal once more, covering a timid and even an ignominious retreat by a pretence in favour of a Federal scheme of Irish Government, which a few politicians had seemed to approve. It is more than doubtful, we repeat, if, at this time, he felt the hatred of the Union he professed; still more so that he believed its abolition possible; and it is certain that, imposing as were the arrays of his masses of Catholic Celts, they had not the cause of Repeal at heart, and saw in it a means only to effect other ends. One remarkable episode of the movement deserves the attention of the student of Irish History. O'Connell obtained the enthusiastic support of a small knot of very able men, who represented the ideas of the nobler spirits of the United Irishmen of another day; one, Davis, was gifted with real genius; others, especially Duffy—he still survives, in honoured old age—had great parts; all advocated Repeal in the firm belief that it would make Ireland a nation, and do good to the different races and faiths. Yet the "Young Ireland" party, as it was called, was summarily put down by O'Connell and the priests, the moment it ventured to cross his will; in a few weeks it was simply effaced. This was another example of the divisions which have wrecked so repeatedly an Irish cause; but the fate of Young Ireland was of deeper import; it proved what the conceptions were of "Nationality" and political freedom, in the mind of Catholic and sacerdotal Ireland.

The Repeal movement, easily stopped as it was, unquestionably made a deep impression on Peel. Circumspect and cautious, he received new ideas slowly, but he could act boldly on them when once convinced; he turned his mind to a remedial Irish policy. Very possibly, if he had had the power, he would have tried to effect what Pitt and Grattan had wished, and have made a provision for the Irish Catholic priesthood; still the attempt would have destroyed his Ministry. But he largely increased the revenue of the College of Maynooth, in the hope, probably, that this would raise the status and position of the Irish priests, and attract into their ranks sons of the Catholic gentry; the measure was in the right direction; but the immense majority of this order of men is still drawn from the class of the superior peasantry, and has the feelings of the Catholic occupier of the soil. Another important measure of Peel was an effort to improve and extend the education of the higher middle class in Ireland, which had remained in a deplorably low condition. He established the "Queen's Colleges," as they have been called; but these institutions embodied the faulty principle of the Primary or National system referred to before; they were condemned as "godless" by the Irish Catholic Bishops; and though they have been, in some degree, successful, and have flourished in Presbyterian Ireland, Catholic Ireland has no sympathy with them. Since Peel's time, a kind of University, on the French model, has been set up in Ireland, with fruitful results; but the education provided for the upper middle class of the Irish Catholics is still bad and imperfect. The University of Dublin indeed, to her great credit, has long ago thrown open her degrees and honours of every kind to the Irish Catholic; this liberality began as far back as 1793; it has been steadily, and ever since, continued. But the University of Dublin remains a Protestant place of learning; its teaching and spirit are distinctly Protestant; a Catholic atmosphere, so to speak, does not breathe in it. Catholic Ireland, as Burke and Newman have written, has a just claim to a Catholic University of its own.

It is scarcely necessary to say that, by this time, Peel had broken completely with the system of Protestant ascendency in Irish affairs, with which, indeed, he never had heartfelt sympathy. He soon dissociated himself still further from the past; he took an important step in his reforming Irish policy, which, but for subsequent events, might have had immense results. As Chief Secretary, we have seen, he had disregarded the rights of the tenant in Irish landed relations; he had, perhaps, sanctioned the code of speedy ejectment; he had steadily enforced the demands of landlords. But he was the first economic statesman of his day; his mind had, by degrees, opened to the evils and dangers of the landed system of Ireland; he resolved, if possible, to devise a remedy. He appointed the well-known Devon Commission to report on the condition of the Irish land, on its modes of tenure and occupation, and the social results; and certainly, had he long remained Minister, he would have made very considerable changes in it. The essential features of the Irish landed system, since we glanced at what they were thirty years before, were still, to a great extent, unaltered; there were the same divisions between the owner and the occupier of the soil; if absenteeism had, perhaps, increased, absentee estates were being better managed; middleman tenures had continued to grow less, but they still wrought harm in great tracts of the country; the large body of the peasantry was still in a most backward state. For the rest the landed gentry had markedly improved, in manners, habits of life, and reverence for law; in these respects they were different even from their fathers; but the events of 1824–29 had broken down their power and alienated their dependents from them; as the value of their estates rose, and the system of large farming became developed, the tendency to exaction became stronger in them; their relations with the peasantry grew, by degrees, less friendly. Yet these bad characteristics of the landed system of Ireland were as nothing compared to its worst vices. The enormous increase of the population, before referred to, had, we have seen, forced up rent to an excessive rate, had covered the land with dense swarms of misery, had reduced wages to the very lowest point, had, in a word, as was truly said, "based society in Ireland on the potato"; and all this had made Irish landed relations disorganised in the highest degree, and perilous to all classes, and even to the State. Meanwhile the concurrent rights in their holdings, which the peasantry had acquired by what they had done on them, had continued to increase to an enormous extent; and as the competition for the soil became more intense, by the multiplication of beings on it, large sums were paid for the "good will" of farms, which really conferred a proprietary right in them. The moral claims to the land, created by these means, were, we repeat, protected in the great mass of cases; indeed they never could have grown up otherwise; and the wild complaints made, in this respect, against the Irish landed gentry, have been grossly exaggerated, or are absolutely false. The claims, however, which in fact approached a joint ownership over millions of acres, continued, as before, to be not law-worthy: they had never been recognised by the State; and, in consequence, they were too often destroyed by eviction and other unjust proceedings. The result was that agrarian disorder and the Whiteboy system had never ceased; Lord Wellesley had described this state of things, a few years before, as "a complete system of legislation, with the most prompt, vigorous and severe executive power, armed for all purposes of savage punishment"; and, in 1844, more than 1000 agrarian crimes had disgraced Ireland. In Ulster landed relations were in a better condition; but, even in Ulster, what was known by the name of the Tenant Right had been sometimes invaded.

The Report of the Devon Commission was composed by landlords, but, if somewhat timid, it was of great value, especially in showing how the landed system of Ireland grew out of the conquests and confiscations of the past. The evidence appended is of extreme importance; it illustrated amply and with perfect clearness the numberless social and economic ills which had been the results of Irish land tenure, especially in the fifty years previously, and the dangers of a redundant population crowded on the soil. The recommendations of the Commission were, however, faulty, and too characteristic of British ignorance of Irish affairs; they did not aim at giving the sanction of law to the joint ownership of the Irish tenant[1], which ought to have been their main object; they described it in the spirit of the Tudor lawyers, who sneered at the landed usages of the Celt, as an excrescence on the true rights of property, and this caused grave discontent in Ulster. The Commission, nevertheless, proposed measures for compensating tenants for improvements added to their farms; a Bill to this effect was introduced afterwards; but it perished in the wreck of Peel's Ministry. The Irish Land Question, as it has ever since been called, remained nearly untouched for a long series of years; feeble attempts to deal with it failed in different ways; English statesmen held to the belief that it would settle itself without legislation of a searching kind. Repeated and earnest efforts, however, have been made to settle it in quite recent times; but the subject falls outside the period of this work; a word or two only can be said on it. An endeavour to secure the joint ownership of the Irish tenant was made in 1870; the measure was based on sound principles; but it did not completely solve the problem. Another experiment was tried in 1881, a surrender to a rebellious movement fastening, as in 1798, on agrarian trouble, and loathsome for many base deeds of wickedness; the joint ownership of the tenant received the fullest protection; but this was accomplished by so bad a process that the Irish landed system has been almost torn to pieces. The Irish

---

[1] Burke, with his superior insight, saw even a century ago that the Irish tenant was morally a joint-owner of the land, and indicated, too, the true principles by which his joint-ownership should be vindicated by law, namely, turning him into a copyholder at a just rent.

tenant has now large proprietary rights in the land; his mode of tenure, once perhaps the worst in Europe, has been made liberal in the highest degree; but the Irish landlord has been grossly wronged; and the relations between the two classes have been so adjusted that a notion is abroad that the whole landed system of Ireland must be turned upside down, by a general expropriation of Irish landlords and the conversion of tenants into owners in their stead, as if Irish confiscations had not already pointed their moral.

In Ireland, however, as too often has been the case in India, Nature ere long suddenly interposed to show, by an awful example, what terrible ills may overtake a community, seated in the land in overflowing multitudes, and depending for existence on a supply of perishable food. In the autumn of 1845 the potato failed, to a considerable extent, in most parts of Ireland; and the results, though less tragic than they were to become, were, even from the first moment, dreadful. No premonitory signs of the visitation had appeared; it fell on the land like the ravage of war and pestilence. The millions of wretchedness, vegetating on patches of the soil, were torn from their homes in destitute masses, driven to and fro in search of the means of life; and even the classes next above were reduced to extreme want. This was especially the condition of things in the great Celtic districts west of the Shannon, and in three or four of the counties of Munster, in which poverty had for ages prevailed; and though famine was largely averted in these, the enormously dense population cruelly suffered. In the better parts of Ireland there was less actual want; but even in these there was great distress; loud murmurs of discontent were heard, and society became more or less disorganised. These evils, however, were but the prelude to the appalling catastrophe which quickly followed. In 1846 the potato all but wholly perished; the crop of cereals too was lamentably short; and dearth, which became devouring famine in too many places, spread over nine-tenths certainly of the afflicted country. The recently made Poor Law, as may be supposed, was utterly unable to meet the strain of starving millions crying out for relief; the efforts made by the Government, gigantic as they were, but not well conceived in some respects, proved to a certain extent fruitless; and though the destitute population was for the most part saved, many thousands of lives were unhappily lost. In nearly all the poverty-stricken districts, wherever the land had been densely occupied, wherever the means of communication were few, and especially along the distant coasts of the sea, the famine had a fearfully large tale of victims; it was a famine of the middle ages in the nineteenth century. The more prosperous counties witnessed no scenes like these; but still they suffered severely; and almost everywhere disease and fever followed in the train of indigence. Meantime as the calamity developed itself, society in some districts simply went to rack; and hundreds of thousands of peasants fled from a land which seemed smitten as it were by a plague of Egypt.

The attempts made by the State to cope with this crisis were extraordinary, and successful in the main; but, as we have said, they were not without mistakes; they strikingly showed how difficult it was for a Government, ruled by English ideas, to deal with the disaster which had befallen Ireland. O'Connell by this time was approaching his end; the great agitator, baffled and sick at heart, had almost left the political scene; but when it had become evident that famine was threatening Ireland, with other thoughtful men, he adjured the Ministry not to permit the export of grain from Ireland until the population had been secured a sufficient amount of food. But the principle of *laissez faire* then prevailed in our Councils; a proposal of the kind was rejected, as an illegitimate interference with trade; and, indeed, there were solid objections to it, though it would probably have been tried by a Parliament of this day. Peel, however, with a true statesman's instinct, did not allow the relief of Irish distress to depend wholly on the so-called laws of supply and demand; he caused large supplies of corn and flour to be secretly introduced into the most impoverished districts; he set a system of Public Works on foot; and by these means the suffering of 1845 was, to a very considerable extent, lessened. He had left the helm when the trial of 1846 came; Lord John Russell and his colleagues had to confront a calamity infinitely worse and more general. They were able, humane, and enlightened men; they were firmly resolved that the starving multitudes of Ireland should be, if possible, fed; with this object in view they freely lavished, with the approval of Parliament, the wealth of the Treasury. Nor can it be doubted that they achieved great results; hundreds of thousands of lives were beyond question saved; the fell hand of famine was removed from many districts; the land passed through an ordeal of fire, scathed indeed cruelly, but still spared. The Government, however, were too much swayed by economic doctrines, which probably would have had sufficiently good results in Great Britain, but which, in some measure, were wrongly applied to Ireland. They did not follow the example of Peel; they left to the resources of ordinary trade the supply of food to the poor and remote parts of Ireland; this would have done well enough in a commercial country, but was unfortunate in one where there was comparatively little traffic; and, in consequence, many unhappy beings perished. The Government, too, refused to expend any money on reproductive Public Works, for this would check, they imagined, private enterprise, a notion, in the existing state of things, most false; and yet they squandered enormous sums, at the rate, indeed, of five millions a year, on useless works, nearly all to this day unfinished. They made the conditions of relief, moreover, stringent in the extreme; the peasant was compelled to give up all but the smallest plot of land before he could obtain aid from the State; and if this principle was certainly sound, it was carried out with unbending harshness, and it provoked far-spreading terror and discontent. And while the Government were giving effect to a policy, of which the necessary result was to force multitudes of beings from their little homes, they did nothing to make provision for the immense emigration which quickly followed; this, too, was abandoned to trade and its energies. The consequences were lamentable in the highest degree; hundreds of fugitives from the famine met untimely deaths in the bad and half-seaworthy vessels of that day, and never saw a new home across the Atlantic[1].

Notwithstanding, however, errors like these the Government, we repeat, did prevent famine, except in a few isolated and remote spots; it indisputably deserves the high praise of history. Its conduct contrasts most honourably with that of the Irish Parliament and Executive in 1740-1, when a disastrous famine had swept over the land[2]; these were then in their worst and lowest state; and they appear to have done scarcely anything to mitigate distress. And whatever may have been the shortcomings of the State, the heart of the English people went out to Ireland; its charity was most profuse and noble; it showed in many ways the most kindly sympathy. This impulse, indeed, was world-wide and general; contributions for the starving Irish millions flowed in from the United States, from all lands on the Continent, and even from the Ottoman Empire; the sorrows of Ireland had made mankind her kin. Nor were numberless and magnificent instances of

---

[1] A noble-minded philanthropist, the present Sir Stephen De Vere, braved the horrors of more than one of these passages in order to direct the attention of the Government to these evils. Another, Mr Vere Foster, followed his example.

[2] Very interesting details respecting this famine will be found in Berkeley's *Letters*.

good works wanting on the part of Irishmen of the upper classes, and especially of the great landed gentry. Too many evictions indeed took place; too many peasants were expelled from their dwellings, in circumstances that must be called deplorable; but the Government, it must be remembered, had set the example of this by making the surrender of land a condition of relief; and it encouraged evictions by different means, for the belief was universal that the petty occupiers of the soil must, by some process or other, be removed from it. But rents and arrears of rents were very largely remitted; estates were deeply mortgaged to procure funds to make provision for humble dependents; great works of enclosure were completed, at the expense of landlords, in order to create supplies of wages; hundreds of families of the higher orders were zealous in deeds of good. The facts should be noticed, for the conduct of the Irish gentry in the Famine of 1845-7, as it has been named, has been repeatedly denounced by lying demagogues, for the unscrupulous purposes of mere faction.

The events of 1846-7 aroused fierce passions in Ireland, which culminated at last in a petty show of rebellion. This movement was altogether different in character and aim from the great Repeal movement. O'Connell had by this time gone—he had sunk broken-hearted into the grave, a light disappearing in gloomy eclipse; and the more violent spirits of the young Ireland party, indignant at what they denounced as the wicked Irish policy of the British Government, lifted up their heads again, and began to think of a rising. An attempt was made to stir up the country; an incendiary Press was set up in the capital; appeals were made to the people to take up arms and to die in the field, not in a ditch, of starvation. The French Revolution of 1848 gave an impulse to an agitation of no essential force; a deputation from Ireland was received by Lamartine; and the condition of affairs in Dublin, and in a few other districts, appeared menacing in the spring of that year. The Catholic priesthood, however, condemned the movement, and kept the Catholic masses aloof; its leaders, in fact, were for the most part Protestants; it had more in common with the United Irish movement of 1793-8 than with those of which O'Connell was the head. The "chiefs of the men of 1848," as they were called, were easily put down by the arm of the law; some were prosecuted and sent into exile abroad; and a miserable exhibition of puny armed force, directed by Smith O'Brien, a landed gentleman of considerable parts, but a vain enthusiast, was suppressed by a small party of police. The rising was treated in England with contempt and ridicule; but it might have been more grave than it actually was had not Smith O'Brien, greatly to his honour, refused to appeal to agrarian passions and to proclaim a war to the knife against landlords, as his less scrupulous partisans advised. The failure, however, of 1848 left a legacy, so to speak, which deserves notice. John Finton Lalor, one of the minor leaders, an obscure but a capable man, saw the power of the ideas of 1793-8; he adopted the doctrines of the extreme United Irishmen; he placed on record sentiments of no slight significance. "The cry of Irish nationality," he wrote in substance, "and the cry against the Union, are of little use; they have no real hold on the minds of the people; what the peasantry want is the land for themselves; this cry must be combined with the others; the British Government can be only attacked successfully through an attack on the Irish landed gentry." This republication of the United Irish faith attracted no attention at the time; but it has indicated the unquestionable truth that, although nearly a century has elapsed, it has been impossible to create in Ireland a general and persistent movement against the Union that has continued in force for any length of time; and it has marked out, as it were, the lines of the agitation of late years in Ireland, revolutionary and agrarian at once, and characterised by a savage war against rent and landlords.

The emigration from Ireland, meanwhile, had continued; it was being developed into that great exodus of the Irish race which has so powerfully affected subsequent events. The Queen visited Ireland in 1849; notwithstanding the famine and the late rising she received an enthusiastic greeting, an incident that conveys its own lesson; that the visit has not been often repeated and prolonged has been one of the few mistakes of a most glorious reign. Society in Ireland was now gradually settling down; the occasion seemed a fitting one to make a great experiment in the adjustment of Irish landed relations. Little had hitherto been done for the occupier of the soil; but the events of the last few years, it was thought, would make the subject of his tenure of slight importance; and the Government turned their eyes towards the Irish landed gentry. That order of men, from many causes, of which mere extravagance was certainly the least, had had their estates heavily charged with debt; the law made the transfer of these difficult; and they had suffered terribly through the effects of the famine. At the same time they had lost most of their political power since 1828, and the events that followed; they had become divided more and more from their tenants; they had been deprived of much local influence, through the growing bureaucratic rule of the Castle; and they had, as a class, provoked opinion in England, which forgot that the evictions it condemned had been encouraged by the State and made a part of its policy. They were, in a word, weak, isolated, and unpopular; it was resolved to expropriate by a summary process as many of the body as it was supposed could not fully discharge the duties of property. An Act of Parliament of the most drastic kind was passed to effect the sale of Irish Encumbered Estates, and a tribunal was set up to carry out its objects. The proceedings that followed had too much resemblance to the shameful confiscations of the seventeenth century. Estates were flung into the market wholesale, until land became a mere drug; hundreds of old and worthy families were involved in ruin; the rights of thousands of creditors were ruthlessly destroyed. This state of things went on for some years; and ultimately nearly a sixth part of the land of Ireland has been transferred under the Encumbered Estates Acts. Confiscation, however, is seldom a good thing; this policy of wrong has proved a complete failure. Its authors hoped that a large number of Englishmen and Scotchmen possessing wealth would become owners of the Irish land to a considerable extent; and that these would improve the condition of the occupiers of the soil, and develope the resources of a backward country. The result has been almost wholly the reverse: English and Scotch capital has only reached the land of Ireland in the mischievous form of great absentee mortgages; the purchasers under the Encumbered Estates Acts have been nearly all poor and hard-fisted Irishmen, for the most part of an inferior class; and these have proved landlords of a very bad type, successors of the nearly extinct middleman, and gravely responsible for all that has been worst in Irish landed relations for many years. The Encumbered Estates Acts, too, it is scarcely necessary to say, have struck a blow at the Irish landed gentry from the effects of which they have never recovered; and the consequences have been, in many ways, unfortunate.

The Census of 1851 disclosed the fact that the population of Ireland had been reduced by the huge number of two millions of souls. This diminution has steadily gone on; a new Irish people, in truth, has been created by emigration, in the United States. History will have to say, in the future, whether this change has ultimately made for good or for evil; but unquestionably it had most beneficial effects on the material condition of Ireland for many years. A dense mass of wretchedness, which preyed on the land, injured all its relations, and opposed an almost insuperable bar to social progress, was removed by the events of 1845-7; the immediate good that followed was not doubtful. Districts filled by millions who could not till them, were laid open to improved husbandry; the wages of labour rapidly increased; the competition for the soil, for a time, lessened; rent ceased to be unnaturally forced up. A long period ensued, in which Ireland made a certain and steady advance in wealth, and put on a look of even marked prosperity. The middleman tenures almost disappeared; thousands of acres were occupied by English and Scotch farmers, who spent large sums in improvements of many kinds; the results, for many years, were full of brilliant promise. The mud hovel and the potato patch vanished gradually from large and increasing areas; the face of the landscape wore a better aspect; the Ireland of half-starving multitudes was seen no more. A number of causes concurred to multiply the resources of the country in different ways; the prices of agricultural produce were high; the railway system opened new markets and made them easy of access; immense sums were lent by the State on favourable terms for great works of drainage; the Irish linen manufacture made decisive strides. The material good effected was striking and great; the country seemed transformed in many places as regards its husbandry and the breeds of its animals; some of the towns, especially Belfast, grew immensely in population and wealth; above all the condition of nine-tenths certainly of the peasantry was extraordinarily improved. The misery and rags of the past seldom offended the eye; the potato ceased to be the only chief staple of food.

This material progress, too, seemed to many observers accompanied by a real moral progress. The Ireland of 1852-65 appeared in a state of comparative content; scarcely a ripple disturbed the surface of things; the great body of the people uttered no murmurs. The memories of the late troubled era were deemed forgotten; not a sound against the Union was heard; political agitation was voted a thing of the past. A movement in favour of Tenant Right, indeed, made a faint stir in 1852-3; but it passed away and had no results, an attempt to improve Irish landed relations, in accord with the proposals of the Devon Commission, foiled by a not creditable intrigue in Parliament, collapsed, and yet no general complaints were made. Even agrarian disorder immensely diminished; a few agrarian crimes were provoked, now and then, by harsh evictions and acts of the kind; but it sank to an ebb never known before; it seemed extinguished by the prosperity of the time. The land, as a whole, was almost at rest; the relations between the owners and the occupiers of the soil were thought to have very greatly improved, for rents were well paid, and there was little social trouble; the old divisions between them seemed much less; even laws, framed on English ideas and disregarding the moral rights of the Irish tenant, provoked no opposition worthy of the name. Meanwhile the forces that had crossed British rule in Ireland, and had shaken society but a short time before, had, apparently, lost their hold on the people; they were, at least, quiescent and scarcely thought of. The heads of the Irish Catholic Church, recollecting the events of 1848, forbade their clergy to take part in politics, and set their faces against all movements of the kind. The representation of Catholic Ireland had sunk into a weak and querulous faction, occasionally trying to make itself felt by throwing its weight into the scales of party, but usually dragged in the wake of Liberal Ministries. Ireland seemed peaceable, submissive, reconciled to England; the period was like that of the reign of Ormond between the Restoration and the Revolution of 1688.

In these circumstances many believed that the "Pacata

Hibernia" of Tudor writers had emerged over the horizon at last; a large majority of British statesmen thought the "Irish difficulty" had been set at rest. Yet Ireland was tranquil on the surface only; elements of disorder and peril were gathering by degrees, which were to explode the shallow optimism of the hour. The growth of Irish prosperity was beyond dispute; but it mainly depended on a mere accident, the flourishing state of agriculture and almost excessive prices. The social structure of Ireland had been radically changed, with consequences, in many respects, excellent; but the system of small farms, and all that this implies, remained much more general than was commonly supposed; it deserves notice that the large English and Scotch occupiers who had "planted" whole districts seldom fared well; many left the country, like the colonists of old, or sank into the mass of the Irishry. Meanwhile landed relations had not become essentially better in some of their features, in spite of apparent signs to the contrary; in others they grew worse by degrees. The bureaucratic rule of the Castle successfully enforced obedience to law; but it had continued to weaken the landed gentry, and this was attended with many evils. That order of men, we have said, in the last century resembled the old seigneurs of France; they had developed into an aristocracy attached to their country, and kindly in nature, many as were their faults: they were now being assimilated again to the French seigneurs, living among dependents, but without influence, and ruled by the officials of a Central Government. They had thus privileges without powers or duties, a thoroughly false position for a dominant class, which gradually lessened the deference felt for them, and estranged them more and more from the people; and, at the same time, the purchasers of lands under the Encumbered Estates Acts proved, we have seen, generally harsh landlords, and this cast discredit on the body of landlords as a whole. Things went on well enough while the tenant-farmer throve; but discontent began slowly to seethe; and signs of it occasionally appeared in agrarian crimes, though as yet too few to attract much notice. Simultaneously rents rose, as the riches of the country increased; and, in addition, the rights which the tenant had gained through improvement and the sale of "goodwill," rights equivalent often to real joint-ownership, had been augmented to an extraordinary extent. Yet these rights were still kept outside the pale of the law; and thus if much positive wrong was not frequently done, law and fact continued to be in conflict throughout the sphere of Irish landed relations.

All this sank deep into the minds of the peasantry; if they acquiesced, they had the memory of the Celt; they had acquired a rapidly increasing sense of their power, as education had made way among them; and though they did not combine in any agrarian movement, for an opportunity did not occur, their apparent content was not real. A young generation too of priests was arising, which looked to agitation and its hopes again; these secretly fanned a flame beneath its ashes; and the complete failure of reform as regards the land, in Parliament, caused sullen passions to burn beneath the surface. The discontent, however, beginning to gather, had its principal source and origin outside Ireland. The millions of emigrants since 1846 had formed a new Ireland in the far West; they had never forgiven the British Government for extruding them, as they thought, from their homes, nor yet the evictions of a terrible time; and they had become a formidable power in the United States, incensed against England and Irish landlords. The exiles and their descendants were in close contact with the Irish peasantry in numberless ways; their communications became every year more frequent; and the feelings they treasured passed by degrees, to some extent, into the hearts of the people which remained seated on the soil of Ireland, and especially of the Catholic masses. Hundreds of Irish Americans preached to their kinsfolk hatred of England and of the Irish landed gentry; rebellious and socialistic ideas, as regards the land especially, were widely diffused. These influences were almost dormant for years; their existence was not suspected by British statesmen; they did not even become strongly manifest in the petty rising which marks the close of this period. But they had attracted the notice of keen-eyed observers as early as 1864-65; and unquestionably they supplied potent elements to the revolutionary and anarchic agrarian outbreak of 1879-80 and 1886-7.

We may glance back at this point of time at the intellectual growth and progress of Ireland since the later years of the eighteenth century. The Established Church, we have said, has produced some great divines; we may refer to Magee, O'Brien, Fitzgerald, Salmon; the Catholic Irish Church, too, has had illustrious names, Doyle, Murray, Russell, and several others. The Irish Bench and Bar has shown a noble succession of advocates and lawyers of the first order; real orators, from Curran to Plunket, Sheil and Whiteside; great jurists, Saurin, Perrin, Lefroy; and O'Connell, easily supreme in the field of politics. In Literature and Philosophy there have been no "lights of the world" compared to Swift, to Berkeley, to Burke, but in either sphere we find writers of rare gifts and excellence. Sterne may fitly be called the Irish Rousseau; Moore is the first of Irish lyrical poets, filled in the highest degree with the Celtic genius; Davis approaches him, and had a stronger intellect; Archer Butler, McCullagh, Brinkley, Ball, Butt, held high places in the domain of thought. In History, we possess Lecky, at this time the first historian of the English tongue, whose works on Ireland should be prized by his countrymen; Mahan, the best living authority on naval warfare, is believed to be of Irish descent. Science has also placed many great Irishmen on her roll; the mind of Ireland during this period has been especially rich in fiction. Of these writers, beside the author of *Jane Eyre*, Maria Edgeworth is by far the greatest; inferior to Jane Austen in delicacy of touch, she has more breadth and knowledge of mankind; but her distinctive merit—and its value is immense—is that she has drawn incomparable sketches of the life and manners of Irish society in its higher grades. The distinction in letters referred to before, between Protestant and Catholic Ireland, has continued down to the present time; it reflects the still existing divisions of race and faith; we see this very clearly in Miss Edgeworth's novels, happiest in their description of the upper class in Ireland, and in those of Banim and Carleton, which bring before us the feelings and thoughts of the Irish peasant. The mind of Catholic Ireland still turns as before to a great extent to the past, and in this province it has done great things; O'Donovan, O'Curry, Sullivan, and many others, have explored Irish antiquities with extraordinary research. Ireland has had few remarkable painters and architects; but she has given the world more than one renowned sculptor; and in the histrionic, the handmaid of the dramatic art, Miss O'Neill was the most perfect Juliet of her day. Yet, in spite of this fine record of the works of the intellect, the state of education in Ireland is still backward. The University of Dublin, indeed, has long ago blotted out the obsolete reproach of the "Silent Sister"; she has among her sons writers of high merit. But the standard of education in Ireland, we repeat, is to this day low, compared with that of England or Scotland.

The elements of trouble which had been gathering beneath the surface in Ireland for a long time, came at last to a head in an abortive outbreak. Societies, called by the old Celtic name of Fenian, had been formed in the United States by degrees; they were composed of Irish emigrants and their sons; they had endeavoured to propagate in Ireland with a definite aim and with organised means the rebellious doctrines referred to. The end of the American Civil War, through which Irish soldiers were sent adrift with no occupation, in many thousands, gave a great impulse to these conspiracies; and a movement was set on foot which had as its object an armed rising in Ireland and a confiscation of the land. The Confederates in the United States combined in large numbers; considerable sums of money were raised; the plans of the leaders were to make a descent on Ireland with the officers and staff of a military force, to call on the peasantry to assist them in the field, and to divide the estates of the gentry among the "Fenian army." Agents were despatched to Ireland to effect their projects; some thousands perhaps of the youth of the towns, and of reckless, landless, and broken men were enrolled in the musters of the Fenian levies; and dexterous attempts were made to debauch British regiments and secretly to procure supplies. The movement, however, proved a sorry failure, almost as impotent as that of 1848. The Irish priesthood denounced Fenianism as wicked anarchy; the occupiers of the soil, ready enough to join in a cry for reduced rents and improved tenures, feared a revolution which might have deprived them of their farms; self-interest kept them aloof from it. A few Irish-American soldiers landed in Ireland in the first months of 1867; but they found no force, except on paper, to command; they were either arrested or allowed to escape; and three or four petty bands, which made an attempt to rise, were dissipated by the Constabulary without the loss of blood. Two or three of the leaders were tried and punished; but the whole affair was over in a very short time, if trouble was still latent beneath the surface of things. Some outrages, however, took place in England, the expiring efforts of Fenianism in great towns; and these, like flashes of lightning in a serene sky, turned the minds of Englishmen to the state of Ireland, which, they had believed, had been for years at peace. Mr Gladstone took up the subject with characteristic energy; he came into power after the General Election of 1868; and he entered on the path of reform for Ireland, which he has ever since followed wherever it has led.

The ensuing period was one of immense change in Ireland, political, social and economic; it is not comprised in this brief narrative. History will have to pronounce hereafter on the nature and tendencies of the policy since adopted or proposed in Irish affairs.

It remains for us, however, to say a few words on the general condition of Ireland since the Union. The hopes of Pitt have not been fully realised; Ireland is not wholly one in heart with Great Britain; she has not made the material progress which Pitt expected. The old divisions in her social structure continue; Catholic and Protestant Ireland remain apart, separated by profound distinctions of race and faith. If Protestant Ireland is loyal to the State and the Union, and so is the Irish Catholic upper class, a large part of Catholic Ireland is not; it is not bound to England in genuine sympathy. Ireland is still infinitely behind Great Britain in all that constitutes civilised life; she is still the weak and distorted member of the Three Kingdoms. And it would be vain to deny that legislation and administration for Ireland have been, sometimes, ill conceived; that more than one measure passed by the Imperial Parliament had done real, nay, great mischief, and that the system pursued at the Castle has been, in some respects, mistaken; above all, it must be admitted, that several Irish reforms, of supreme importance, have been deferred, and, especially, have been often too late. Irish interests have been repeatedly postponed to give place to English and Scotch questions; Ireland has been made the stalking-horse of British party; and the great majority of British statesmen have found it very difficult to understand Ireland, to minister to her wants, to comprehend her ideas. If the occupiers of the Irish soil have obtained immense advantages, the Irish landed gentry have been unjustly treated and reduced to a state of social impotence; the representation of Ireland is very bad; public opinion, in Ireland, is feeble, unsound, unhealthy. Yet, notwithstanding these undoubted drawbacks, the Union, and the system of government that has been a part of it, have been attended by immense and far overbalancing good. Most of the grievances of the Ireland of the past have been removed; the few that remain will soon disappear; Ireland has made an extraordinary advance in wealth; however it may be ascribed to the events of 1846-7, the condition of the mass of the population shows an improvement, which, sixty years ago, would have been thought impossible. Nor has real moral and social progress been wanting; the rebellious Ulster of 1793 is, in its Teutonic parts, devoted to England; all Protestant Ireland, the Catholic gentry, an overwhelming majority of the professional and commercial classes, in a word, the wealth, the education and the thought of Ireland, with rare exceptions, befriend the Union, and are deeply attached to the British connection; the demand for "Repeal," or, for the same thing, "Home Rule," as the events of many years have proved, has no real hold on the Irish masses; even the peasant occupiers of the Irish soil, after the enormous benefits that have been lavished on them, appear disposed to rest and be thankful, spite of the appeals of lay and sacerdotal demagogues. But the most decisive proof of the good which the Union has done, is that through the many troubles of well-nigh a century, it has succeeded in making the law administered and obeyed in Ireland in a way never known before; that it has kept Protestant ascendency down, and made Catholic subjection a thing of the past; that it has maintained a salutary restraint on warring Irish factions; that if it has not effaced the ills of distinctions of race and faith, it has checked the worst animosities which grew out from them. In these important respects the contrast presented by the Ireland of

1790-95, and the Ireland of 1890-95 must strike every well-informed enquirer.

In considering this subject we must recollect, besides, what the condition of Ireland was before Pitt's great measure. Undoubtedly the Union had defects in itself, and was accomplished by means that must be deplored, and also at an unpropitious time; undoubtedly it has been, in some degree, a failure. But those who cry it down because it has not transformed the Ireland of 1800 into a social paradise, and made the desert blossom like a rose, appear to forget, if they ever knew, that the Ireland of that day was a wreck of civil war, to a great extent in a half-barbarous state, above all bleeding from the wounds of a horrible conflict of race and faith, which had effaced civilisation ere it was grown up, and had aroused the worst hatreds and strife of the past. These facts must be taken into account; they reasonably explain why, in some respects, the Union has not effected all that was hoped from it. Circumstance, too, has told against the Union over and over again; it has been denounced as the cause of ills which in no sense can be ascribed to it. To refer only to two instances, the Tory reaction against the French Revolution, and the disputes of the Catholics about the veto retarded Emancipation much more than the Union or anything pertaining to it; and the Irish Land Question would probably have been settled long ago but for the accident of the fall of Peel's Government, and, in some degree, the events of the Famine.

It would be an invidious, nay, an impossible task to attempt to adjust the balance of right and wrong between England and Ireland through long centuries. But England owes a large debt to Ireland, without reference to considerations like these. We have alluded to some of the great men of Catholic Ireland, who won renown for her in foreign lands; unhappily, but for no faults of their own, they were for the most part resolute, if most honourable foes of England. But Catholic Ireland has, for some time past, seen better days; hundreds of her sons have risen to eminence in our Imperial state; thousands have fought and conquered in the battles of England. "Where were the aliens at Waterloo?" was the just retort of an Irish orator to a vulgar sneer; in War, in Letters, in all the arts of Peace, the aliens have shed glory on the British name. Nor should Englishmen forget the great deeds of Protestant Ireland; Burke remains the first of our political thinkers; Eyre Coote, Canning, the two Lawrences, and Dufferin stand high among the founders or governors of our Indian Empire; Arthur Wellesley, one of the "English in Ireland," was born an Irishman; Wolseley and Roberts, the great living soldiers of the British army, are Irishmen, in no doubtful sense. Yet we should set aside distinction of race in looking back at all that Ireland has done for England; and it should be added that, probably, the Celtic Irish genius has been a much more powerful, if a subtle element, in giving beauty and grace to the English intellect, and even in fashioning its best works, than is suspected by the great mass of Englishmen. For these, not to speak of many other reasons, England is bound generously to discharge a debt which Ireland has a just right to demand.

In following the course of Irish History, until we reached the close of the seventeenth century, we have pointed out how much that was most unfortunate may be ascribed to circumstances, and to what we call accident. The same remark applies to Irish History down to this day; how different might its course have been, had William III, following the traditions of the House of Nassau, secured religious liberty to the Irish Catholic, and been true to his word after the fall of Limerick; had Pitt, before the Union, been as firm of purpose as he had been on other occasions; had Catholic emancipation been accomplished in 1825, not in 1829! These considerations, we repeat, do not excuse acts of injustice or a policy of folly or wrong; but they should diminish the bitterness of evil memories; they should lead us to judge events with a calm and sane mind; while they give a mournful interest to Irish History, they should teach the lesson of charity and good will. Whatever may be the policy pursued towards Ireland, time must elapse before the deep wounds of the past can be completely healed, before the old and bad distinctions can be smoothed away; before there can be a real Union of Hearts with England, not the false shibboleth of the thoughtless partisan, but the genuine reconciliation of two still divided peoples. But, while the historical student looking back on the past cannot hope this consummation to be close at hand, he may show how it can be brought more near; above all he may indicate the true moral to be drawn from an impartial survey of the sad but most instructive tale of the affairs of Ireland.

APPENDIX.

LIST OF AUTHORITIES ON THE PERIODS OF THE HISTORY OF IRELAND COMPRISED IN THIS VOLUME.

I.

For the period before the Anglo-Norman Conquest.

THE Annals of the Four Masters. [The narrative goes down to the seventeenth century.] *O'Curry's Manners and Customs of the Ancient Irish. O'Curry's Lectures on the Manuscript materials of Irish History. The Senchus Mor and the Book of Aicill, with the Prefaces. Maine's Early History of Institutions,* a most admirable work. Early Christian Architecture, by Miss Stokes. Petrie's Tara. Petrie's Round Towers of Ireland. Keane's Towers and Temples of Ancient Ireland. Brenan's Ecclesiastical History of Ireland. [The narrative goes down to 1829.] Keatinge's History of Ireland. *The story of Burnt Nial translated by Dasent.* Joyce's History of Ireland. [The narrative goes down to the seventeenth century.] Moore's History of Ireland. [The narrative goes down to 1646.] *Irish History and Irish Character,* by Goldwin Smith, a singularly brilliant and able, but not always just, essay. The Story of the Irish Nation, by the Hon. Emily Lawless, a sketch of Ireland from the earliest to the present time. McGee's Popular History of Ireland. [The narrative goes down to 1829.]

II.

For the period between the Anglo-Norman Conquest and the Irish Administration of Sir Edward Poynings.

The Irish Statutes from 1310 to 1495 [most of these have not been published, and are known only by their titles. The Irish

Magna Charta will be found in the Appendix to Leland's History, Vol. I.] The *Statute of Kilkenny edited by James Hardiman.* This is the best existing account of Ireland in the feudal age. The Notes are of special value. *Documents relating to Ireland in the Public Record Office* to the end of the Reign of Henry VII: edited by H. S. Sweetman. *The Works of Giraldus Cambrensis,* especially the Topographia Hibernica, and the Expugnatio Hibernica. *The Discoverie of Sir John Davies,* extremely valuable, but full of the spirit of a Tudor and an English lawyer. *Spenser's View of the State of Ireland.* Ware's Annals. Gilbert's Viceroys. Finglas's Breviate. *Harris' Hibernica.* Campion's History of Ireland. *Leland's History of Ireland.* This is, on the whole, the best modern authority for this period. The work contains most of the important references. [The narrative goes down to the Treaty of Limerick.] Plowden's History of Ireland from the Reign of Henry II. [The narrative goes down to the Union.] Froude's English in Ireland. This must be called a bad book. [The narrative goes down to the Union.] Froude's History of England, Vol. II., Chapter 8. Mant's History of the Irish Church. *Hallam's Constitutional History,* Vol. III., Chapter on Ireland. [The narrative goes down to the Reign of George III.] *Ball's Irish Legislative Systems,* a very valuable treatise. [It goes down to the Union.] *The O'Conors of Connaught,* by the O'Conor Don, very valuable and interesting.

III.

For the period between the Administration of Sir Edward Poynings and the death of Henry VIII.

The Irish Statutes, 1495 to 1543. [For the results and working of the celebrated Act known as Poynings' Law, reference should be made to the Irish Parliamentary Debates, and especially to Flood's Speeches, to Hallam's Constitutional History, Vol. III., on Ireland, and to Ball's Irish Legislative Systems.] *State Papers relating to the Reign of Henry VIII,* in the Public Record Office, edited by Hans Claude Hamilton. *The Carew Papers* edited by J. S. Brewer and William Bullen. [The series extends from 1515 to 1624 and is of the greatest value and importance.] *Holingshead's Chronicles of Ireland.* Cox's History of Ireland. [Leland has collected numerous authorities in this part of his History, Vol. II., Book III., Chapters 5, 6, 7, which may be referred to. The works of Ware and Harris, *ante*, and Archbishop Ussher on the Reformation should be studied.] Froude's History of England, Vol. II., Chapter 8, *ante*, and Vol. IV., Chapter 14, and the authorities cited. *Ball's Reformed Church in Ireland*, an excellent review of the institutions of the Irish Anglican Church. [The narrative goes down to the period of Disestablishment.] *The Earls of Kildare*, by the Marquis of Kildare, very interesting and well informed. [The work goes down to the close of the eighteenth century.] *Richey's Lectures on Irish History*, the First and Second Series.

IV.

For the period between the death of Henry VIII and the end of the reign of Elizabeth.

The Irish Statutes, 1556—1586. *State Papers* relating to the reigns of Edward VI, Mary and Elizabeth, edited by Hamilton, *ante*. *The Carew Papers* as *ante*, *Davies and Spencer*, *ante*, are of special value for this period. [Authorities collected in Leland's History, Vol. II., Book III., Chapter 8; Book IV., Chapters 1, 2, 3, 4, 5. The principal of these are Camden, Stanihurst, Hooker, Ware, Fynes Morison, Cox. The Sydney Papers. The life of Sir John Perrott and his Letters. Sullivan's History of the Irish Catholics. Carte's Introduction to the Life of Ormond. Leland's narrative may also be read with profit throughout his whole work.] Froude's History of England, Vol. V., Chapter 28; Vol. VIII. (2 of the Reign of Elizabeth), Chapters 7, 11; Vol. X. (4 of the Reign of Elizabeth), Chapter 24; Vol. XI. (5 of the Reign of Elizabeth), Chapter 27. The authorities collected by Mr Froude are very numerous; his research is admirable, the brilliancy of his style is well known. But he is very inaccurate, and his animus against the Irish Celtic race has repeatedly distorted his judgment. *Lecky's History of England in the Eighteenth Century*, Vol. II., Chapter 6, pp. 92 *seqq*. This great work is by many degrees the best account of Ireland from the beginning of the Reign of Elizabeth to the Union. The pages here referred to are only preliminary to the narrative, which does not fully open until its proper date. The numerous authorities are contained in the Notes. The Irish chapters have been published as a separate work. *The Calendar of the Ancient Records of Dublin*, by John T. Gilbert, published by the authority of the Municipal Council. This important work at present extends from the earliest times to the end of the seventeenth century, and will be continued. The second series of Richey's Lectures, *ante*, and the O'Conors of Connaught, by the O'Conor Don, *ante*, are very valuable for the whole Tudor period.

V.

For the period between the end of the reign of Elizabeth and the Restoration.

The Irish Statutes, 1612—1639. *Ireland, State Papers relating to*, of the reign of James I, edited by C. U. Russell, D.D., and John P. Prendergast. *The Irish State Trials* contained in Cobbett and Howell's Collection, A.D. 1163—1820, and in the New Series, 1820—1848. The trial of Connor Lord Maguire in 1645 is worth reading. *An Historical Account of the Plantation of Ulster*, 1608—1620, by the Rev. George Hill. This book is written in an anti-English spirit, but is very learned and full of information. The authorities collected are numerous and valuable. The work contains Pynnar's Survey, made soon after the Plantation. *History of Land Tenure in Ireland*, by Dr Sigerson, able and useful. The *Carew Papers*, *ante*. The series ends in 1624. *Carte's Life of Ormond*, most important. *Strafford's Letters*. *Strafford's Trial*, Rushworth. Bernard's Life of Ussher. Lord Castlehaven's Memoirs. Borlase's History of the Rebellion. *Warner's History of the Rebellion and Civil War in Ireland*, very valuable as regards the alleged Massacre in 1641. *Curry's Historical Account of the Civil War in Ireland*, very valuable for the same reason, and unjustly condemned by Hallam. Clarendon's History of the Rebellion (the Irish chapters). These are chiefly remarkable as showing the dislike and contempt felt towards Ireland and the Irish by the Stuarts and the Royalist party in England. *Lord Clanricarde's Memoirs*, very valuable. *The Letters of Cromwell*, edited by T. Carlyle (the Irish letters). Mr Carlyle's views as to Ireland and the Irish people require no comment. *Leland's History*, Book IV.,

Appendix. 359

Chapters 6, 7, 8; Book V., Chapters 1, 2, 3, 4, 5, 6, 7; Book VI., Chapters 1, 2, and the authorities collected. This is, on the whole, a fair and judicious narrative. *Lecky's History* as *ante*, Vol. II., Chapter 6, pp. 100—174. The evidence as to the alleged massacre of 1641 is very ably summed up and judged. *Gardiner's* History of England from the Accession of James I to the Outbreak of the Civil War (the Irish chapters). *Gardiner's History of the Great Civil War* (the Irish chapters), see especially Vol. I., Chapters 6, 11; Vol. II., Chapters 27, 37, 44. *Gardiner's History of the Commonwealth and Protectorate*, Vol. I. (the Irish chapters), see especially Chapters 4, 5, 6. The authorities in these learned and judicious histories are numerous. *The Cromwellian Settlement of Ireland*, by John P. Prendergast, written in an anti-English spirit, but extremely learned, and rich in original and useful information. *The Life of Sir William Petty*, by Lord Edmond Fitzmaurice, very instructive and interesting. *The Introduction to "The Patriot Parliament"* of Thomas Davis, by Sir C. G. Duffy. The Irish Ballads of Davis and Duffy, to be found in a volume called the "Spirit of the Nation," are admirable, and should be studied. Beside the above references, passages will be found in Burke's Irish writings relating to the confiscations of the period of James I, Charles I, and Cromwell, and to the alleged Massacre of 1641, which are marked by his keen insight and deep political wisdom. They deserve attention and careful thought. *Reid's History of the Irish Presbyterians.*

VI.

For the period between the Restoration and the Capitulation of Limerick.

The Irish Statutes, 1660—1692. The principal Acts passed by King James's Irish Parliament, of 1689, will be found in Davis's Patriot Parliament, *ante*. *The Irish State Trials.* That of Archbishop Plunket is the most important for this period. The charge of Chief Justice Keating is valuable, as showing the character of Irish agrarian disorder in 1689-91. The Manuscripts of the Marquis of Ormonde. The Historical Manuscripts Commission. *Carte's Life of Ormond*, *ante*. *Sir William Petty's Political Anatomy of Ireland*, very valuable. *Lord Clarendon's Letters* when Lord Lieutenant. King's State of the Protestants of Ireland. *Walker's Diary of the Siege of Derry. Mémoires Inédits de Dumont de Bostaquet*, very interesting. Story's Impartial History of the War in Ireland and the Continuation. Macariæ Excidium. *The Abbé MacGeoghegan's History of Ireland*. Mémoires de Berwick. *Leland's History*, Book VI. and the authorities. The work, as said before, ends at the Treaty of Limerick. *Macaulay's History of England* (the Irish chapters), Vol. IV., Chapter 12; Vol. V., Chapters 14—16; Vol. VI., Chapter 17, and the authorities. It would be superfluous to refer to the learning and the splendour of Macaulay's narrative. But there are some errors in his Irish chapters, especially in his point of view, and his account of King James's Irish Parliament is very deceptive. *Lecky's History of England, ante,* Vol. II., Chapter 6, pp. 174—196. The refutation of Macaulay is admirable. *The Patriot Parliament*, by Thomas Davis, *ante*, very valuable. *Lord Wolseley's Life of Marlborough*, Vol. II., Chapters 62—67. This is by far the best account of Marlborough's Campaign in Ireland.

VII.

For the period of the Penal Laws in Ireland, and up to the Revolution of 1782.

The Irish Statutes, 1692—1782-3. [See also the English Declaratory Act of 6 George I, Chapter 5, repealed in 1782, and the Renunciation Act of 23 George III, Chapter 28.] *The Irish State Trials.* [The only one of importance is that relating to the proceedings in Annesley and Sherlock, 1719, which involved the question of the Appellate Jurisdiction of the Irish House of Lords.] *The Irish Parliamentary Debates.* Parts of these have been reported towards the close of this period. O'Conor's History of the Irish Catholics. Curry's State of the Irish Catholics. Vincent Scully on the Penal Laws. Howard's Popery Cases. *Burke's Tracts on the Popery Laws*, a mere sketch, but very valuable. *O'Callaghan's History of the Irish Brigade. The Last Colonel of the Irish Brigade.* This is a short biography of Count O'Connell, an uncle of Daniel O'Connell. Interesting details about this distinguished soldier will be found in General Thiébault's Memoirs.

Appendix. 361

Primate Butler's Letters. Archbishop Synge's Letters. Swift's Tracts on Ireland. Berkeley's Tracts on Ireland. Burke's writings on Ireland. [All valuable in the very highest degree.] *Molyneux' Case of Ireland. Monk Mason's Authority and Constitution of the Irish Parliament. Hutchinson's Commercial Restraints.* Very valuable. *Caldwell's Restraints on the Trade of Ireland.* Lord Mountmore's History of the Irish Parliament. Campbell's Philosophical Survey of the South of Ireland. *Arthur Young's Tour in Ireland*, 1776—1778, most instructive, interesting and important. *Sir George Lewis on Irish Disturbances.* Philosophic and excellent. [The narrative goes down to 1836.] *Flood's Life and Speeches. Grattan's Life and Speeches. Hardy's Life of Charlemont.* Barrington's Rise and Fall of the Irish Nation. O'Leary's Tracts. *L'Irlande, Sociale, Politique, et Religieuse, by Gustave de Beaumont.* [Very able and full of admirable research and thought, but ruled by the ideas of a French doctrinaire, and not just to the Irish landed gentry.] *O'Flanagan's Lives of the Irish Chancellors.* A learned and interesting work. [The narrative goes down to the Chancellorship of Lord Plunket.] *Lecky's History, ante,* (the Irish chapters), Vol. II., Chapter 7; Vol. IV., Chapters 16, 17. For the general reader nothing more is required. The authorities are collected : the refutation of Mr Froude is excellent. *Froude's Two Chiefs of Dunboy* is a brilliant romance, that illustrates from the point of view of the author the political and social life of this period, or rather of the first part of it, remarkably well. *Ireland from the Siege of Limerick to the present time,* by John Mitchell. Written in the spirit of an Irish rebel of 1848, but containing some valuable information. [The narrative goes down to 1851.] *Two Centuries of Irish History,* 1691—1870. Edited by James Bryce, M.P., written in the spirit of Radical English Home Rule, but a very valuable *résumé* of events, well worth reading.

VIII.

For the period from the Revolution of 1782 to the Union.

The Irish Statutes, 1782—1800. The Act of Union, in the Irish Parliament, is 39, 40 George III, Chapter 67. *The Irish State Trials.* These are very numerous for this period. That of

Theobald Wolfe Tone possesses the most historical interest. *The Irish Parliamentary Debates*. These are well reported from 1781 to 1797; there is then a hiatus until the Debates on the Union. These are very remarkable. See especially the speeches of Castlereagh and Clare, of Grattan, Foster, Saurin, and Plunket. *The Lives and Speeches of Flood and Grattan, ante. The Speeches of Curran*, wonderful specimens of advocacy. *Burke's Correspondence*. Letters on Ireland down to his death, very important and valuable. The Auckland Correspondence. *The Life of Theobald Wolfe Tone. The Memoirs of Theobald Wolfe Tone.* [The Diary is very valuable and interesting.] *The Cornwallis Correspondence*, most important and instructive, but not just to the real Irish gentry. *The Castlereagh Correspondence*, also most important, especially on the subject of the Union. The Colchester Papers and Diary. Buckingham's Courts and Cabinets of George III. *Maddon's United Irishmen*, full of research and of valuable information. *Memoirs of Miles Byrne*, very interesting. *Holt's Memoirs of the Rebellion*. Musgrave's Rebellions in Ireland, written in the evil Orange spirit. Maxwell's History of the Rebellion. *Gordon's History of the Rebellion of* 1798. By far the fairest and best account. Hay's History of the Rebellion in Wexford. *Stanhope's Life of Pitt. Pitt's Speeches*. That on the Union should be studied, and so should the Debates, on this subject, in the British Parliament. Pitt, by Lord Rosebery. *Pitt, by Goldwin Smith*, in Three English Statesmen. *Brougham's* Statesmen of the Reign of George III. *Moore's* Life of Lord Edward Fitzgerald. *McNevin's* Pieces of Irish History. *Plowden's History of Ireland* after the Union. [The narrative goes down to 1810, and expresses the views of a loyal, but disappointed Irish Catholic.] *Massey's History of England* (the Irish chapters), Vol. II., Chapters 24—26; Vol. IV., Chapter 38, written from the point of view of an English Whig. Newenham's State of Ireland. Killen's Continuation of Reid's History of the Irish Presbyterians. *Ingram's History of the Irish Union*. A piece of elaborate paradox, to prove that the Union was not, in any sense, carried by corruption. *Lecky's History* as *ante* (the Irish chapters), Vol. VI., Chapters 24, 25; Vols. VII. and VIII. The extra volumes are, perhaps, the most important and valuable parts of this great work. The correspondence between the

Ministry in England and the Irish Government, and the confidential reports sent to the Castle, from all parts of Ireland, during the troubled years, from 1792 to 1800, have been collected from original sources, and are most instructive and interesting. All available authorities are collected with the most praiseworthy industry.

IX.

For the period between the Union and Catholic Emancipation.

The Statutes of the United Parliament (Ireland), 1801—1829. *The Irish State Trials.* These are also numerous for this period. The most remarkable is that of Robert Emmett. Several of these trials illustrate the extraordinary powers of O'Connell at the Bar. *The Parliamentary Debates* (Ireland). See especially the speeches on Irish affairs of Pitt, Fox, Grattan, Canning, Castlereagh, Lord Wellesley, the Duke of Wellington, Peel, Plunket. *The Cornwallis Correspondence, ante. The Castlereagh Correspondence, ante. The Colchester Papers and Diary, ante. The Supplementary Despatches* of Arthur, Duke of Wellington. The papers on Ireland in 1807-8, and again in 1828-30, are of special value. *Sir Robert Peel*, 1788—1827. From his private correspondence. Edited by Charles Stuart Parker. This work contains all the correspondence of Peel on Ireland when Chief Secretary. *Reports of Parliamentary Committees* on Irish Incomes, Expenditure and Taxation, 1815—1864. *Evidence on the state of Ireland taken before Parliamentary Committees in* 1825. Extremely important and instructive. *Baron Fletcher's Charge* to the Grand Jury of Wexford in 1814. A remarkable deliverance on the state of Ireland severely condemned by Peel. *Stanhope's Pitt, ante.* Plowden's History, *ante. Lewis on Irish Disturbances, ante. An Account of Ireland, by Edward Wakefield.* A work of great research and value, and an admirable exposition of the social and economic condition of Ireland in 1812. The Life of Canning, by Stapleton. *Memoirs and Correspondence* of Richard Marquis Wellesley, by Pearce. The Life of Plunket, by D. R. Plunket. *O'Connell's Life and Speeches, by John O'Connell. Life of O'Connell, by Miss Cusack.* Life of O'Connell (Statesmen Series), by J. A. Hamilton. Ireland and the Irish, by Daniel O'Connell. A book quite unworthy of O'Connell. *Wyse's History* of the *Catholic Association*. *Peel and O'Connell*, by Shaw Lefevre. Written from the English Radical point of view, but well informed and able. *Life and Times of Lord Cloncurry, including his personal recollections.* Very interesting. *Ireland, Past and Present*, by J. W. Croker. Ireland since the Union, by J. H. McCarthy. *Peel, by Goldwin Smith* in the Encyclopedia Britannica. Very able, but too eulogistic. *Lecky's Leaders of Public Opinion in Ireland.* Rather immature in thought, but very able and eloquent. The series comprises Swift, Flood, Grattan and O'Connell. The sketch of O'Connell is perhaps the best.

X.

For the period between 1829 *and* 1868.

The Statutes of the United Parliament (Ireland). *The Irish State Trials.* The regular series goes down to 1848, and is being continued. Much the most important of these trials is that of O'Connell in 1843-44. The trials of Smith O'Brien and the other participators in the movement of 1848 are not without interest. The trials of some of the Fenian prisoners of 1867-8 have been separately published. The *Parliamentary Debates* (Ireland). See especially the speeches of the Duke of Wellington and of Lord Grey, Brougham, Lyndhurst, Melbourne, and Lansdowne in the House of Lords, and of Peel, Lord Palmerston, Lord John Russell, Disraeli, O'Connell, Smith O'Brien, Sheil, Cobden, Bright and Mr Gladstone in the House of Commons. *The Supplementary Despatches of the Duke of Wellington, ante.* Many of the papers on Ireland during this period are important. *The Report of Sir George Nicholls on the Irish Poor Law.* Very important. *The Report of the Devon Commission and the Evidence.* Of the greatest possible value on the subject of the Irish Land. [The Parliamentary Reports of Committees and Commissions on Irish affairs during this period are extremely numerous; the reader can only be referred to them.] *Selections from the Speeches and Despatches of Earl Russell* (Ireland). *Recollections and Suggestions of Earl Russell. Cloncurry's Personal Recollections, ante.* These are very valuable for part of this period. *The Life of Thomas Drummond*, by McLennan. Memoir of Earl Spencer (Lord Althorp), by Le

Marchant. The Life of Lord Melbourne. The Memoir of Lord Hatherton. *Report of the Parliamentary Committee of the Loyal National Repeal Association.* (Well worth reading.) *Essays on Repeal of the Union.* Awarded prizes by the Loyal National Repeal Association. *The Nation Newspaper*, 1842—1848. Most interesting, as showing the views of the Young Ireland party. *The Spirit of the Nation.* A collection of Irish Ballads, some very beautiful, written in the same sense. *The Irish Crisis* (Edinburgh Review, Vol. 87, 1848), written by Sir Charles Trevelyan. An able and fair account of the Famine of 1845-6, written from the point of view of an English Whig. *A History of the Great Irish Famine of* 1847, by the Rev. John O'Rourke, P.P. Written from the point of view of an Irish Catholic priest. *The Irish Landlord since the Revolution*, by the Rev. Patrick Lavelle. Illustrating the animosity felt against some Irish landlords since the Famine. *Irish Emigration and the Tenure of Irish Land*, by Lord Dufferin. Well worth reading. *Policy of England towards Ireland*, by Charles Greville. *Journals, Conversations and Essays relating to Ireland*, by Nassau Senior. The views of a moderate Whig, between 1850 and 1860. *Young Ireland*, by Charles Gavan Duffy. Very valuable and interesting. *New Ireland*, by A. M. Sullivan. *The Life of Lord Palmerston*, by Sir H. L. Bulwer. Contains some passages referring to Ireland that may be read with advantage. *The Irish Land*, by Isaac Butt. *Ireland in* 1868, by Gerald Fitzgibbon. *Fifty Years of Concessions to Ireland*, by Barry O'Brien. *Irish Wrongs and English Remedies*, by Barry O'Brien. These works are written in a bitter and unjust anti-English spirit, but may be read with profit. Walpole's History of England. Molesworth's History of England, 1830—1870. *The Reign of Queen Victoria*, by Sir Rowland Blennerhassett. The parts of this work that relate to Ireland are interesting and valuable.

INDEX.

Abercromby, General, 313
Aghrim, Battle of, 191
Agricola, 2
Allen, Bog of, 41, 113
Allen, Papal Envoy, 101, 103
American War, The, 234
Anglican Church in Ireland, The, 104, 116, 117, 130, 132, 136, 214, 215, 226, 318, 320, 321, 353
Anjou, Henry of, Henry II, 23, 29, 31
Annals of the Four Masters, 16
Annals, Irish, 15
Ascendency, Protestant, in Ireland, 130, 168, 173, 174, 206, 224, 305, 313, 324, 353
Aston, Sir Arthur, 150
Athlone, 152, 161
Athunree, Battle of, 34
Attainder, Great Act of, in 1689, 184

Baker, at Derry, 181
Ball, a distinguished Irishman, 347
Baltinglass, Lord, 102
Banim, Irish Novelist, 347
Bantry, Landing at, 269
Bedell, Archbishop, 214
Belfast, 218, 260
Bellahoe, Battle of, 78
Bellingham, Sir Edward, Deputy, 86, 87
Benburb, Battle of, 145
Berkeley, Bishop, 172, 217, 221, 226, 231, 243
Berkeley, Lord, of Stratton, Viceroy, 173

Berwick, bastard of James II, 186
Bingham, President of Connaught, 111
Black Friday, 33
Black Rent, 55
Blount, Charles, Lord Mountjoy, 112, 114, 123
Boleyn, Anne, 70
Bonaghts and Cosherings, 48
Bonaparte, 161
Borlase, John, Lord Justice, 137
Boulter, Archbishop, 214
Boyne, Battle of, 187
Breakspeare, Nicholas, Pope Adrian, 25, 48, 76
Brehon Laws, 14, 50, 51
Brehon Lawyers, 14, 50, 53, 123
Brian, King of Ireland, 21
Brigade, The Irish, 207, 290
Brinkley, a distinguished Irishman, 347
Browne, Archbishop, 76
Browne, Bishop, 214
Browne, General, 207
Bruce, Edward, 34
Buckinghamshire, Lord, Viceroy, 237
Burgh, Hussey, 237
Burke, Edmund, 129, 236, 239, 244, 353
Bushe, 283
Butler, Archer, a distinguished Irishman, 347
Butlers, The, 35, 38, 40, 43, 44, 57, 69, 71, 78
Butt, a distinguished Irishman, 347

Index. 367

Cæsar, 19, 20
Caldwell, Sir James, 244
Camden, Lord, Viceroy, 266, 272, 275
Canning, 297, 353
Carew, Sir Peter, 98
Carleton, 348
Carlisle, Lord, Viceroy, 238
Carolan, 18
Cashel, Synod of, 29
Castlereagh, 281, 283, 293, 297
Cathal of the Red Hand, 34
Catherine, Queen, 70
Catholic Association, 307, 308, 311; Church in Ireland, 131, 215, 226; Committee, 261, 296; Convention, 265; Emancipation, 279, 284, 297, 312, 353; Question, 293, 294, 295, 296, 298, 306
Catholicism set up in Ireland, 87
Cecil, 93
Ceile, The, 10, 47, 126
Celtic, The ancient, Irish Church, 6, 7, 12, 48, 49, 74, 75
Celtic Irish genius, The, 353
Celtic Land, The, 45
Celts, *passim*
Charlemont, Lord, 236, 243, 255
Charles I, 134, 137, 142, 143
Charles the Great, 32
Charles II, 148, 152, 157, 164, 165, 166
Charles V, 70, 77
Church in England, The, 68
Church of the Pale, 48, 49, 74, 75, 91, 105, 116
Clanricarde, Earl of, 80, 142
Clans, The Irish, 1
Clarendon, 156, 165
Clarendon, Viceroy, 176
Clonmel, Siege of, 151
Clontarf, Battle of, 21
Cnocktue, Battle of, 64
Cogan, Miles de, 28
Commissioners, Irish, of Henry VIII, 80
Confederation of Catholics in Ireland, 141, 143
Conn of the Hundred Battles, 3

Constabulary, The Irish, 304, 326
Coote, Eyre, 353
Cornwallis, Viceroy, 275, 276, 277, 282, 293
Corporate Reform in Ireland, 326
Coyne and Livery, 10, 43
Cromer, Archbishop, 76
Cromwell, Henry, 157
Cromwell, Oliver, 148, 149, 150, 151, 153, 154, 156, 158, 247
Cromwell, Thomas, 74, 76
Crosses, The Ancient Irish, 18
Curran, Irish orator, 347
Curry, Irish Historian, 244

Daer Stock Tenants, 10, 126
Danes in Ireland, 20
D'Aquila, Don Juan, 113
Davis, Thomas, 330, 347
Debt of Ireland, 299
De Burgh, work of, on Irish Dominicans, 244
De Burghs, The, 33, 35, 64, 79
Declaration of Legislative Independence of Ireland, 240
De Courcies, The, 46
Dermod, King of Leinster, 26, 27, 28
Derry, 128, 179, 180, 181, 182; Bishop of, 255
Desmond, Gerald, The Last Earl of, 97, 101, 104
Desmond, The Geraldines of, 43, 44, 45, 54, 57, 63, 64, 73
Desmond, Sir John of, 99
Devereux, Walter, Earl of Essex, 98
Devon Commission, The, 332, 333
Dowdal, Primate, 85
Doyle, a distinguished Irishman, 349
Drogheda, Synod of, 25; massacre at, 150
Drummond, Thomas, 324, 325
Dublin, 28, 30, 41, 71, 149, 172, 185, 187, 188, 218
Dufferin, Lord, 353
Duffy, C. G., 330
Dundalk, rout of, 34; town of, 41, 185

Dungannon, The Volunteer Meeting at, 239; The Baron of, 91

Edgeworth, Maria, great Irish Novelist, 348
Edward I, 36
Edward III, 37
Edward VI, 84, 86
Election, The Clare, 310
Elizabeth, Queen, 89, 99, 112, 115
Emmett, Robert, 290
Encumbered Estates Acts, 341, 342, 345
England, *passim*
Englishry, The, *passim*
Enniskillen, 179, 182
Eric, The, 14, 50
Essex, The Earl of, 112, 175
Established Church, The, *see* Anglican Church in Ireland
Eva, Daughter of Dermod, 28
Eyre, Jane, Charlotte Brontë, the author of, 348

Famine in Ireland in 1740-1, 338, note; in 1822, 301; in 1845-6, 336, 337, 338, 339
Felim the Lawgiver, 3
Fenian Outbreak, The, 348, 349
Feredach the Just, 3
Firbolgs, The, 1
Fitzgerald, Irish Divine of eminence, 347
Fitzgerald, Edward, Lord, 267, 290, 291
Fitzgerald, Maurice, 26
Fitzgerald, Vesey, 310, 311
Fitzgibbon, John, Earl of Clare, 259, 265, 266, 272, 273, 276, 279, 280, 283
Fitzmaurice, James, 99, 100, 101
Fitzstephen, Robert, 26, 27
Fitzwilliam, Sir William, Deputy, 108
Fitzwilliam, Lord, Viceroy, 265, 266
Flood, Henry, 232, 239, 243, 255
Fomorians, The, 1
Foster, The Irish Speaker, 283

Fox, Charles, 239, 293
Fuidhir Tenants, 10, 48

Galway, 46, 152
Gavelkind, Irish, 9, 11, 51, 124, 125
Gaveston, Viceroy, 37
George II, 230
George III, 229, 231, 253
George IV, 306
Geraldines, The, 35, 38, 40, 44, 70, 71, 100, 101, 102, 273, note
Ginkle, General, 190, 191, 193
Glamorgan, Lord, dealings of, with Charles I and the Irish Confederates, 144
Goldsmith, Oliver, 244
Graces, The, 134, 135, 137
Grattan, Henry, 212, 224, 237, 239, 240, 241, 243, 248, 253, 257, 276, 283, 293, 297, 306, 311
Grenville, Lord, 293
Grey Administration, 317, 319, 321
Grey, Lord de Wilton, 103
Grey, Lord Leonard, 72, 73, 78
Gros, Raymond Le, 28
Grouchy, General, at Bantry, 269

Harcourt, Lord, Viceroy, 233, 234
Hasculf, 28
Heber, son of Milesius, 2
Henrietta Maria, Queen of Charles I, 147
Henry III, 36
Henry VII, 54, 57
Henry VIII, 65, 67, 68, 73, 76, 78, 81
Heremon, son of Milesius, 2
Hoche, General, 269
Houghers, The, 228
Humbert, General, 276
Hutcheson, Francis, 244
Hutchinson, Hely, 233, 244
Hy-Niall, The, 4, 5, 6, 41, 77, 95

Inchiquin, Lord, 141, 147, 151, 177

Index. 369

Injured Lady, Swift's History of, 220
Interest, The English and Irish, in Ireland, 38, 62, 81, 132, 167, 211, 225, 325
Invasions, Danish, of Ireland, 20
Ir, son of Milesius, 2
Ireland, *passim*
Irish, The, an Aryan Community, 2
Irishry, The, *passim*

James I. 31, 32
James II, 174, 175, 178, 185
John, King, 31, 32
Jones, Michael, 147

Kildare, Gerald, Eighth Earl, the Great, 57, 58, 63, 64, 65; Gerald, the Ninth Earl, 65, 66, 69, 70, 73; Thomas, Silken, the Tenth Earl, 70, 71, 72; Gerald, the Eleventh Earl, 73, 88, 94, 102
Kildare, The House of, Heads of the Geraldines, 42
Kilkenny, Confederation of Catholics at, 141; Siege of, by Cromwell, 150; Statute of, 39, 60
King, Archbishop, 214
Kingston, Lord, 179
Kinsale, Siege and Battle of, 114, 190
Kirke, at Derry, 182

Lacy, General, 207
Lalor, John Finton, 340
Land, The Anglo-Norman, 43
Land and Landed System of Ireland, 10, 11, 12, 125, 203, 217, 227, 300, 302, 332, 333, 334
Lauzun, General, 190
Lawrences, the two, 353
Laws, Early, of Ireland, *see* Brehon Laws and Brehon Lawyers
Lecky, eminent Irish Historian, 347
Lefroy, Irish jurist, 347
Leinster, The Duke of, 236
Leix, 45, 86, 87, 88, 112

M. I.

Leland, Irish Historian, 244
Letters, The Drapier, by Swift, 219, 220
Limerick, Siege of, 189, 190; Treaty of, 193, 194, 202
Lionel, Duke of Clarence, 37
Londonderry, *see* Derry
Lord of Ireland, original title of King of England in Ireland, 76
Louis XIV, 180
Lucas, Charles, 230
Ludlow, 157
Lundy, 180
McCullagh, distinguished Irishman, 347
MacGeoghegan, 244
McGilpatrick, 80
MacMurrough, Art, 34
Magee. eminent Irish Divine, Archbishop, 347
Maguire, General, 207
Mahan, eminent writer on naval warfare, 347
Malone, Anthony, 217, 222, 226
Marlborough, 190
Maryborough, 88
Massacre, alleged, of 1641, 138
Maynooth Castle, 72; College, 307, 331
Melbourne Ministry, The, 313, 325, 327
Milesian Settlement, The, 2
Molesworth, Lord, 244
Molyneux, William, 218
Monarchy, The Irish, 8
Monk, 157
Monroe, General, 145
Montesquieu, 247
Moore, 17, 347
Morpeth, Lord, Chief Secretary, 324
Mountjoy, Lord, Viceroy, 114, 123
Mulgrave, Lord, Viceroy, 324
Murray, eminent Irish Divine, Archbishop, 347

Napoleon, 20, 274, 290, 291, 294
National Education in Ireland, 321, 322, 323

24

Niall of the Nine Hostages, 4
Northumberland, Earl of, 84
Nugent, Field Marshal, 207

Oakboys, The, 228
O'Brien, Chief of Thomond, 79; eminent Irish Divine, 347; Smith, 340
O'Byrne, Tribe of, 98
O'Carroll, Irish chief, 69
O'Connell, Daniel, 282, 294, 295, 296, 304, 306, 308, 310, 311, 313, 317, 318, 319, 323, 327, 328, 329, 330, 338, 339, 340
O'Connor, Chief of Offaley, 69
O'Connor, The tribe of Offaley, 86, 89, 112
O'Connor, Brian, Chief of tribe, 73, 77, 86, 88, 89
O'Connor, Mary, wife of Brian, half sister of Surrey's fair Geraldine, 73
O'Conor, Aedh, 34
O'Conor, Charles, eminent Irish antiquary, 244
O'Conor Don, the, his work on the O'Conors of Connaught, 8
O'Conor, Roderick, last Monarch of Celtic Ireland, 22, 26, 27, 29
O'Conor Turlogh, "King with opposition," 22
Octennial Bill, The Irish, 232
O'Donnell, Chief and tribe of, 92, 93, 94, 109, 110, 111, 113
O'Donnell, Chief, made Earl of Tyrconnell, 123
O'Donovan, eminent Irish writer, 348
Offaley, now the King's County, 45, 65, 84, 87, 88, 112, 206
O'Moore, Chief and tribe of, 86
O'Moore, Roger, 137
O'Neill, Chief and tribe of, 4, 57, 63, 109
O'Neill, Conn, Earl of Tyrone, 77, 78, 79, 91
O'Neill, Donald, 34
O'Neill, Hugh, Earl of Tyrone, 108, 109, 110, 111, 112, 113, 114, 123, 126
O'Neill, Hugh, defends Clonmel and Limerick, 151, 152
O'Neill, Owen Roe, 140, 145, 146, 147, 148
O'Neill, Phelim, 138
O'Neill, Shane, 92, 93, 94, 95, 96
O'Neill, Miss, famous Irish actress, 348
Orangeism and Orange societies, 268, 292, 297, 309, 311, 324
Organisation of ancient Irish society, 10, 11, 12
Ormond, Lords and Earls of, 44, 45, 54, 63, 99, 103
Ormond, Earl of and Duke, Viceroy, 144, 146, 147, 148, 151, 152, 165, 170, 172
O'Ruarc, Chief, 26
O'Sullivan, eminent Irish writer, 348
O'Toole, Tribe of, 98

Pale, The Irish, 30, 32, 37, 40, 41, 42, 47, 50, 53, 55, 91, 98, 115
Parliament, The English and British, 55, 137, 201, 211, 237, 241; The Imperial or United, 293, 313, 314; The Long, 137, 139, 184; The Irish, 41, 53, 60, 79, 90, 97, 107, 132, 166, 200, 212, 224, 225, 231, 233, 234, 239, 254, 255, 262, 263, 279; Irish, of 1689, 183
Parsons, William, Lord Justice, 137
Patrick, Saint, 4
Peace of 1646, 145
Peel, 304, 305, 312, 314, 321, 327, 329, 330, 331, 337
Pelham, stern soldier in Desmond War, 103
Penal Code, The Irish, 203, 204, 205, 207, 209
Perrin, Irish Jurist, 377
Perrott, Sir John, Deputy, 100, 106, 108

Index. 371

Petty, Dr, 155, 175, 247
Philipstown, 88
Pitt, the first, 229
Pitt, the second, 253, 258, 266, 277, 278, 279, 280, 281, 283, 285, 286, 293, 353
Plantation of Ulster, The, 127, 128
Plunket, Irish orator and statesman, 283, 306
Plunkett, Oliver, 173
Poetry, Ancient Irish, 16
Pole, Reginald, 88
Poor Law for Ireland, 327
Popes connected with Irish affairs, 25, 48, 63, 77, 88, 97, 101, 276
Portland, Duke of, 239, 240
Poynings, Sir Edward, Deputy, 58, 60, 61
Poynings' Law, 61, 97, 135, 167, 185, 213, 238, 239, 240, 241
Presbyterian, The, Church in Ireland, 298
Presbyterians, Irish, 212
Presidents in Ireland, 97
Preston, General, 140, 146

Queen Victoria, visit to Ireland in 1849, 341
Queen's Colleges, 331
Querist, The, by Berkeley, 221

Rebellion of 1798, 274, 275, 276
Reform Bill of Flood, 256
Reform of 1832, Irish, 317
Reformation in Ireland, 74, 84, 85, 90
Regency Question in 1789, 256
Relaxation of the Penal Code, 242, 243
Renunciation Act, The, 253
Repeal of the Union movement, 317, 328, 329
Restrictions on Irish commerce, 172, 211
Revolution, The French, effects of, on Ireland, 259, 261
Revolution of 1782, 242, 247
Richard II, 37
Richelieu, 161

Rinuccini, Papal Nuncio, 145, 146, 147, 148
Rising of 1641, 138
Roberts, Lord, 353
Round Towers, The Irish, 18
Russell, eminent Irish Divine, 347
Russell, Lord John, 337

Saer Stock Tenants, The, 10, 126
St Leger, Deputy, Sir Anthony, 80, 84
St Ruth, General, 191, 192
Salisbury, John of, 25
Salmon, eminent Irish Divine, 347
Sanders, Papal Envoy, 101, 103
Sarsfield, General Patrick, 186, 189, 191, 192
Saurin, Irish Jurist, 283, 347
Schomberg, 185, 186, 187, 191
Schools, The Charter, 223; The National, 322
Septs, The Irish, 11
Settlement, Acts of, 168, 174, 183
Settlement of 1782, The, 250
Sheil, Irish orator, 347
Short View of Ireland, by Swift, 220
Sidney, Sir Henry, Deputy, 92, 97, 100
Sidney, Lord, Viceroy, 201, 232
Simple Repeal, 253
Skeffington, Deputy, 69, 72
Smerwick, Massacre at, 103
Smith, Adam, 247
Somerset, Protector, 84
Stanley, Mr, Chief Secretary, 317
Steelboys, The, 228
Sterne, Laurence, 347
Stone, Archbishop, 214, 226
Strafford, Viceroy, 135, 136, 137
Strongbow, 27, 30
Stuart, Mary, 93, 100
Subjection, Catholic, 139, 161, 169, 174, 224, 353
Sullivan, eminent Irish antiquary, 348
Supremacy, Oath of, 90, 131
Surrey, Lord Deputy, 66, 67, 68
Sussex, Thomas Radcliff, Lord, Viceroy, 88, 92

Index.

Swift, 172, 214, 217, 219, 243
Synge, Archbishop, 214

Tanist Succession, 9, 51, 124, 125
Tenant Right, Irish, 344
Tilly, General, 161
Tirlogh, Lenagh, 96, 109
Tithe in Ireland, 215, 257, 318, 325
Tone, Theobald Wolfe, 260, 261, 268, 277
Townshend, George, Lord, Viceroy, 232
Tribes, The Irish, 11, 12
Trinity College, The University of Dublin, 117, 171, 245, 331
Tuatha-na-Danaans, 2
Tudor, Mary, 87
Tyrconnell, Earl of, *see* O'Donnell
Tyrconnell, Richard Talbot, Commander in Chief and Deputy in Ireland, 176, 177, 183, 192

Undertakers, The, in Ireland, 106, 127, 225
Union, Cromwell precursor of, 157, 229, 277, 278, 279, 280, 281, 284, 289, 314, 327
Union of Hearts with England, a real, 354

United Irishmen, The, 260, 261, 262, 266, 267, 270, 275

Veto, The, 294, 306, 307
Viceroys of Ireland, *passim*, and *see* under names set forth
Victoria, *see* Queen Victoria
Volunteers, The Irish, 237, 239, 255

Walker, at siege of Derry, 181
Warner, value of his history, 244
Waterford, 27, 28, 151
Waterloo, Battle of, 291
Wellesley, Sir Arthur, 304, 353
Wellesley, Lord, Viceroy, 310
Wellington, Duke of, 312
Wexford, 26, 28; massacre at, 150
Whiteboy Movement, The Irish, 228, 229, 302, 318, 338
Whiteside, Irish orator, 347
William III, 178, 180, 186, 188, 189, 201, 353
Wings, The, 309
Wolseley, Lord, 183, 353
Wolsey, Cardinal, 66, 69, 70

Yellow Ford, Battle of, 111
York, Duke of, 165
Young, Arthur, 224, 228
Young Ireland Party, 330

www.ingramcontent.com/pod-product-compliance
Lightning Source LLC
Chambersburg PA
CBHW030401230426
43664CB00007BB/700